ALSO BY TRISTRAM HUNT

Building Jerusalem

MARX'S GENERAL

MARX'S GENERAL

THE REVOLUTIONARY LIFE OF
FRIEDRICH ENGELS

TRISTRAM HUNT

METROPOLITAN BOOKS

Henry Holt and Company ▪ New York

Metropolitan Books
Henry Holt and Company, LLC
Publishers since 1866
175 Fifth Avenue
New York, New York 10010
www.henryholt.com

Metropolitan Books® and ▥® are registered trademarks of
Henry Holt and Company, LLC.

Library of Congress Cataloging-in-Publication Data

Hunt, Tristram, 1974–
    Marx's general : the revolutionary life of Friedrich Engels /
Tristram Hunt.—1st ed.
        p. cm.
    Includes bibliographical references and index.
    ISBN-13: 978-0-8050-8025-4
    ISBN-10: 0-8050-8025-2
    1. Engels, Friedrich, 1820–1895.   I. Title.
    HX274.7.E53H896 2009
    335.4092—dc22
    [B]   2009003845

Henry Holt books are available for special promotions and
premiums. For details contact: Director, Special Markets.

First Edition 2009

Designed by Kelly S. Too

Printed in the United States of America

1   3   5   7   9   10   8   6   4   2

To D.W.H.H.

CONTENTS

ILLUSTRATIONS

MARX'S GENERAL

PREFACE

On 30 June 1869, Friedrich Engels, a Manchester mill owner, gave up his job in the family business after nearly twenty years. Ready to greet him on his return to his small cottage in the Chorlton suburbs were his lover Lizzy Burns and houseguest Eleanor Marx, daughter of his old friend Karl. "I was with Engels when he reached the end of his forced labour and I saw what he must have gone through all those years," Eleanor later wrote of Engels's final day at work. "I shall never forget the triumph with which he exclaimed 'for the last time!' as he put on his boots in the morning to go to his office. A few hours later we were standing at the gate waiting for him. We saw him coming over the little field opposite the house where he lived. He was swinging his stick in the air and singing, his face beaming. Then we set the table for a celebration and drank champagne and were happy."[1]

Friedrich Engels was a textile magnate and foxhunter, a member of the Manchester Royal Exchange, and president of the city's Schiller Institute. He was a raffish, high-living, heavy-drinking devotee of the good things in life: lobster salad, Château Margaux, Pilsener beer, and expensive women. But Engels also for forty years funded Karl Marx, looked after his children, soothed his furies, and provided one half of history's most celebrated ideological partnership as coauthor of *The Communist*

Manifesto and cofounder of what would come to be known as Marxism. Over the course of the twentieth century, from Chairman Mao's China to the Stasi state of the GDR, from the anti-imperial struggle in Africa to the Soviet Union itself, various manifestations of this compelling philosophy would cast their shadow over a full third of the human race. And as often as not, the leaders of the socialist world would look first to Engels rather than Marx to explain their policies, justify their excesses, and shore up their regimes. Interpreted and misinterpreted, quoted and misquoted, Friedrich Engels—the frock-coated Victorian cotton lord— became one of the central architects of global communism.

Today, a journey to Engels begins at Moscow's Paveletsky rail station. From this shabbily romantic tsarist-era terminal, the rusting sleeper train heaves off at midnight for the Volga plains hundreds of miles southeast of the capital. A grinding, stop-start fourteen-hour journey, alleviated only by a gurgling samovar in the guard's carriage, eventually lands you in the city of Saratov with its wide, tree-lined streets and attractive air of lost grandeur.

Bolted onto this prosperous provincial center is a crumbling six-lane highway that bridges the mighty Volga and connects Saratov to its unloved sister city, Engels. Lacking any of Saratov's sophistication, Engels is a seedy, forgotten site dominated by railway loading docks and the rusting detritus of light industry. At its civic center squats Engels Square, a bleak parade ground encircled by housing projects, a shabby strip mall dotted with sports bars, casinos, and DVD stores, and a roundabout clogged with Ladas, Sputniks, and the odd Ford. Here, in all its enervating grime, is the postcommunist Russia of hypercapitalism and bootleg Americana. And amid this free market dystopia stands a statue of Friedrich Engels himself. Fifteen feet high, atop a marble plinth and with a well-tended municipal flower bed at his feet, he looks resplendent in his trench coat, clutching a curling copy of *The Communist Manifesto*.

Across the former USSR and Eastern bloc, the statues of Marx (together with those of Lenin, Stalin, and Beria) have come down. Decapitated and mutilated, their remains are gathered together in monument graveyards for the ironic edification of Cold War cultural tourists. Inexplicably, Engels has been given leave to remain, still holding sway over his eponymous town. As a quick conversation with local residents and early-evening promenaders in Engels Square reveals, his presence here is the product neither of affection nor of admiration. Certainly, there is little hostility toward the cofounder of communism but rather a nonchalant indifference and weary apathy. Like the myriad plinths laden with nineteenth-century generals and long-forgotten social reformers that litter the squares of Western European capitals, Engels has become an unknown and unremarkable part of the civic wallpaper.

In his birthplace, in the Rhineland town of Wuppertal (now a commuter suburb for the nearby finance and fashion city of Düsseldorf), a similar disinterest is evident. There is a Friedrich Engels Strasse and a Friedrich Engels Allee but little sense of a town overly eager to commemorate its most celebrated son. The site of Engels's *Geburtshaus*, destroyed by a Royal Air Force bombing raid in 1943, remains barren and all that marks the place of his arrival into the world is a dirty granite monument modestly noting his role as the "cofounder of scientific socialism." Covered in holly and ivy, it is edged into the shadowy corner of a run-down park, overlooked by aging portable toilets and a vandalized phone booth.

In modern Russia and Germany, let alone in Spain, England, or America, Engels has slipped the bonds of history. Where once his name was on the lips of millions—as Marx's fellow combatant, as the author of *Socialism: Utopian and Scientific* (the bible of global communism), as the theoretician of dialectical materialism, as the name regularly grafted onto city streets and squares by revolutionary insurgents and left-wing councils, as the man whose visionary, bearded features appeared on the currency and in textbooks and, alongside Marx, Lenin, and Stalin, stared down from vast flags and Soviet Realist billboards onto May Day parades—it is now barely registered in either East or West. In 1972, an official GDR biography could claim that "nowadays there is hardly a corner of this earth of ours where Engels's name has not been heard of, where the significance of his work is unknown."[2] Today, he is so innocuous his statue isn't even pulled down.

The same cannot be said of his colleague Karl Marx. Two decades on from the fall of the Berlin Wall and Francis Fukuyama's hubristic declaration of "the end of history," Marx's reputation is enjoying a remarkable renaissance. In recent years, he has been transformed from the ogre responsible for the killing fields of Cambodia and labor camps of Siberia to modern capitalism's most perceptive analyst. "Marx's Stock Resurges on a 150-Year Tip" was how the *New York Times* marked the 150th anniversary of the publication of *The Communist Manifesto*—a text that, more than any other, "recognized the unstoppable wealth-creating power of capitalism, predicted it would conquer the world, and warned that this inevitable globalization of national economies and cultures would have divisive and painful consequences."[3] As Western governments, businesses, and banks faced an economic hurricane of free market fundamentalism at the turn of the twenty-first century—financial meltdowns in Mexico and Asia, the industrialization of China and India, the decimation of the middle class in Russia and Argentina, mass migration, and a worldwide "crisis of capitalism" in 2007–09—the Cassandra-like voice of Marx started to echo down the decades. The post-1989 neoliberal capitalist consensus, Fukuyama's endpoint of mankind's ideological evolution all set to be built on the historical wreck of communism, seemed to falter. And there was Marx waiting in the wings. "He's back," screamed the *Times* in the autumn of 2008 as stock markets plunged, banks were nationalized, and President Nicolas Sarkozy of France was photographed leafing through *Das Kapital* (sales of which surged to the top of the German best-seller lists). Even Pope Benedict XVI was moved to praise Marx's "great analytical skill."[4] The British economist Meghnad Desai, in a work that formed part of an increasingly effusive literature on Marx, had already labeled the phenomenon "Marx's revenge."[5]

For it was now a truth universally acknowledged that Marx was the first to chart the uncompromising, unrelenting, compulsively destructive nature of capitalism. "It has pitilessly torn asunder the motley feudal ties that bound man to his 'natural superiors,' and has left remaining no other nexus between man and man than naked self-interests, than callous 'cash-payment,'" as *The Communist Manifesto* puts it. "It has drowned the most heavenly ecstacies of religious fervour, of chivalrous enthusiasm, of philistine sentimentalism, in the icy water of egotistical calculation."[6] It was Marx who revealed how capitalism would crush languages, cultures, traditions, even nations in its wake. "In one word, it creates a world after its own image," he wrote long before globalization became a byword for Americanization. In his best-selling 2005 biography, *Karl Marx, ou l'esprit du monde*, the French politician-cum-banker Jacques Attali located Marx as the first great theorist of globalization. Even the *Economist*, the great weekly promulgator of neoliberal dogma, had to give him credit for "envisioning the awesome productive power of capitalism." As the magazine conceded in a 2002 article entitled "Marx after Communism," "he saw that capitalism would spur innovation to a hitherto-unimagined degree. He was right that giant corporations would come to dominate the world's industries."[7] At the same time, Attali's book, together with Francis Wheen's popular biography of Marx (*Karl Marx*, 1999), helped cast the man in a sympathetic light as a struggling journalist, endearing rapscallion, and loving father.[8] Since the 1960s and Louis Althusser's "discovery" of the "epistemological break" between the young and mature Marx—between the Marx of the *Economic and Philosophical Manuscripts* concerned with alienation and morality and the later, materialist Marx—we had already come to know of Karl Marx's early philosophical humanism. Now we were offered the biographical complement of a rounded, engaging, and strikingly contemporary individual.

Where does Friedrich Engels fit within this generous new alignment? In the absence of a similar slew of biographies and perhaps as part of a conscious post-1989 forgetting, Engels has been excised from popular memory.[9] Or, more worrisomely, in certain ideological circles he has been landed with responsibility for the terrible excesses of twentieth-century Marxism-Leninism. For as Marx's stock has risen, so Engels's has fallen. Increasingly, the trend has been to separate off an ethical, humanist Karl Marx from a mechanical, scientist Engels and blame the latter for sanctifying the state crimes of communist Russia, China, and Southeast Asia. Even in the mid-1970s, E. P. Thompson was noting the urge to turn "old Engels into a whipping boy, and to impugn to him any sin that one chooses to impugn to subsequent Marxisms. . . . I cannot accept the pleadings which always find Marx and Lenin innocent and leave Engels alone in the dock."[10] Similarly, Richard N. Hunt commented on how "it has lately become fashionable in some quarters to treat Engels as the dustbin of Classical Marxism, a convenient receptacle into which can be swept any unsightly oddments of the system, and who can thus also bear the blame for whatever subsequently went awry."[11] Thus, the attractive Marx of the Paris notebooks is compared and contrasted unfavorably with the dour Engels of *Anti-Dühring*. The Marxist scholar Norman Levine, for instance, has been in no doubt that "Engelism [*sic*] led directly to the dialectical materialism of the Stalin era. . . . By asserting that a fixed path of development existed in history, by asserting that pre-determined historical development was moving towards socialism, Engelism made Soviet Russia appear as the fulfilment of history. . . . During the Stalin era, what the world understood as Marxism was really Engelism."[12] Suddenly, Engels is left holding the bag of twentieth-century ideological extremism while Marx is rebranded as the acceptable, postpolitical seer of global capitalism.

Of course it is true that we largely know about and are interested in Friedrich Engels because of his collaboration with Marx, a partnership in which the devoted Engels was always careful to cast himself as second fiddle. "Marx was a genius; we others were at best talented. Without him the theory would not be by far what it is today. It therefore rightly bears his name," he announced conclusively after his friend's death.[13] It is equally true that much of the official ideology of Marxism-Leninism in the twentieth century sought its validity, however spurious, in elements of Engels's later codification of Marxism. But just as it is now possible, as the post-1989 polemical dust settles and the socialism of Marx and Engels is no longer automatically obscured by the long, Leninist shadow of the Soviet Union, to take a renewed look at Marx, so we can also begin to approach Engels afresh. "Communism defiled and despoiled the radical heritage," Tony Judt has written of the "dictatorial deviation" that marked its perverted implementation during the twentieth century. "If today we face a world in which there is no grand narrative of social progress, no politically plausible project of social justice, it is in large measure because Lenin and his heirs poisoned the well."[14] But as that historical tide at last begins to ebb, it is now possible and valuable to return to the lives and works of "the old Londoners." For they offer not just an insightful critique of global capitalism but new perspectives on the nature of modernity and progress, religion and ideology, colonialism and "liberal interventionism," global financial crises, urban theory, feminism, even Darwinism and reproductive ethics.

To all of which Engels contributed profoundly. Managing a mid-Victorian Manchester cotton business, dealing daily with the economic chain of world trade, which stretched from the plantations of the American South to the Lancashire mills to the British Raj, it was *his* experience of the workings of global capitalism that made its way into the pages of Marx's *Das Kapital* just as it was *his* experience of factory life, slum living, armed insurrection, and street-by-street politicking that informed the development of communist doctrine. And, again, it was Friedrich Engels who was far more adventurous when it came to exploring the ramifications of his and Marx's thinking in terms of family structure, scientific method, military theory, and colonial liberation. As Marx immersed himself ever deeper in economic theory, Engels ranged freely on questions of politics, the environment, and democracy with unexpectedly modern applicability. If Marx's voice is being heard again today, then it is also time we stripped away Engels's modesty and allowed for his richly iconoclastic ideas to be explored apart from the memory of Marx.

What makes Engels a fascinating source of biographical inquiry is the personal background to this philosophical prowess, the rich contradiction and limitless sacrifice that marked his long life. It was a life, moreover, set against the great revolutionary epoch of the nineteenth century: Engels was with the Chartists in Manchester, on the German barricades in 1848–49, urging on the Paris Communards in 1871, and witness to the uncomfortable birth of the British Labor movement in 1890s London. He was a man who believed in praxis, in living his theory of revolutionary communism as practice. Yet the frustration of his life was that he so rarely got the chance, since from his earliest meetings with Marx he decided to relinquish his own ambitions for the sake of his friend's genius and the greater good of the communist cause. Over twenty long years, in the prime of his life, he endured a self-loathing existence as a Manchester millocrat in order to allow Marx the resources and freedom to complete *Das Kapital*. The notion of individual sacrifice, so central to communist self-definition, was there at the movement's birth.

Engels's extraordinary deference to Marx often made for a life of painful contradiction. Of course a dynamic of contradiction—the inter-penetration of opposites, the negation of the negation—stands at the heart of Marxist theory. Right from his initial conversion to commu-nism, Engels, the well-born scion of Prussian merchants, lived that ten-sion in a transparently personal way. And so this biography is also the memoir of a foxhunting man: a womanizing, champagne-drinking capitalist who helped to found an ideology that was contrary to his class interests and would, over the decades, transform into a dull puritanical faith utterly at odds with the character of its creators. Engels himself would never admit any contradiction between his gentleman's lifestyle and his egalitarian ideals—but his critics did then and certainly do now.

Indeed, introspection was not a vice familiar to Engels. Instead, he regarded his life's work as an uncomplicated act of service to the philo-sophical ideals and political project of Karl Marx. Whether it was street-level party activism, providing the primary material for *Das Kapital*, churning out propaganda, pursuing ideological enemies, or extending Marxian thought into unconquered territory, Engels was a model of military discipline. "At every difficulty that we who work in the vineyard of our master, the people, come across, we go to Engels," wrote Eleanor Marx in 1890. "And never do we appeal to him in vain." Always think-ing strategically, frequently challenging his superiors, an intellectual as much as a soldier, Engels was "The General." A nickname given to him by Eleanor in light of his military journalism, it instantly caught on as it so obviously embodied a deeper truth about the man—not simply his immaculate personal grooming and straight-backed demeanor but the overarching sense of control, the inspirational leadership, and cool pro-fessionalism that typified his role within the Marxian project. No man made a greater contribution to its nineteenth-century successes.

But a general is only as good as his army, and many Marxist historians would certainly disparage the biography of a single man at the expense of a broader history of the masses. Yet this would be to succumb to a particularly restrictive interpretation of Marxism and neglect the attractively nondoctrinaire thinking of Engels himself. He not only had an abiding interest in biography (especially the lives of British army generals) but was adamant that "men make their own history . . . in that each person follows his own consciously desired end, and it is precisely the result of these many wills operating in different directions and of their manifold effects upon the world outside that constitutes history." For Engels history was always, in part, a question of individual desires. "The will is determined by passion or deliberation. But the levers which immediately determine passion or deliberation are of very different kinds." They may be external factors or ideologies, personal hatreds or even individual whims. The question was: "What driving forces in turn stand behind these motives? What are the historical causes which transform themselves into these motives in the minds of the actors?"[15] It is the ambition of this biography to unpick those passions and desires, personal hatreds and individual whims—as well as the driving forces and historical causes—of a man who made his own history and who continues to shape ours.

1

SIEGFRIED IN ZION

"Rejoice with me, dearly beloved Karl, that the good Lord has heard our prayer and last Tuesday evening, the 28th, at 9 pm presented us with a babe, a healthy well-shapen boy. We thank and praise Him from the fullness of our hearts for this child, and for the merciful assistance and care for mother and child during confinement." In late November 1820, after his wife's difficult labor, the Rhineland businessman Friedrich Engels was delighted to announce to his brother-in-law Karl Snethlage the birth of his first son and namesake. Instantly anxious for the child's spiritual state, Engels also wrote of his hopes that the Lord "grants us the wisdom to bring it up well and in fear of Him, and to give it the best teaching through our example!" This prayer would go spectacularly unanswered.[1]

The infant Friedrich was ushered into a family and a culture that offered no inkling of his revolutionary future. There was no broken home, no lost father, no lonely childhood, no school bullying. Instead, there were loving parents, indulgent grandparents, plentiful siblings, steady prosperity, and a sense of structured familial purpose. "Probably no son born in such a family ever struck so entirely different a path from it. Friedrich must have been considered by his family as the 'ugly duckling,'" mused Eleanor Marx in 1890, when the wounds of the Engels clan were still raw. "Perhaps they still do not understand that the 'duckling' was in reality a 'swan.'"[2]

Engels's upbringing in the Rhineland town of Barmen took place within a safe, cloistered neighborhood that resembled something of a family compound. Across the road from his home stood the detached four-story late-Baroque house his own father was born in (now the threadbare *Engels-Haus* museum); nearby he could see the showy mansions of his uncles Johann Caspar III and August and, dotted among them, the steaming, stinking yarn bleacheries that had funded them. Factories, workers' tenements, and merchant houses mingled together in what resembled an early industrial model village. For Friedrich Engels was delivered straight into the furnace of the nineteenth century. The historic transformations he would make his life's work—urbanization, industrialization, social class, and technology—were there at his birth. "The factory and cottages of the esteemed family of Caspar Engels, together with the bleacheries, almost form a small semicircular city," confirmed an 1816 report on the state of Barmen's housing.[3] Leading down to the Wupper River, this damp, marshy district was officially called the "Red Brook"; in the early 1900s, it was still widely known as "Engels's Brook."

While the Engels line can be traced back to Rhineland farms of the late sixteenth century, the family's prosperity begins with the arrival of Johann Caspar I (1715–87), Engels's great-grandfather, in the Wupper Valley in the latter half of the eighteenth century. Exchanging agriculture for industry, Caspar was drawn to the lime-free waters of the Wupper River—one of the tributaries of the Rhine—and the riches it promised from linen yarn bleaching. With just twenty-five thalers in his pocket and a pannier on his back (as family legend had it), he chose to settle in the tiny town of Barmen, which clings to the steep slopes lining the Wupper. An assiduous entrepreneur, he built up a highly successful yarn business, complete with a bleachery, and then a workshop for a pioneering form of mechanical lace production. When he handed over the company to his sons, it was one of Barmen's largest enterprises.

Yet the commercial ethos of Caspar Engels und Söhne stood for more than just the cash nexus. In an era when gradations between workers and masters were subtler than full-throttle industrialization would later allow, the Engelses fused paternalism with profits and were widely renowned for the benevolence of their employment and refusal to use child labor. Down the generations, the Engelses provided homes, gardens, and even schools for family employees, and a granary cooperative was set up during food shortages. As a result, Engels spent his early years mixing easily with ribbon makers, joiners, and craftsmen, an experience that fostered in him a class-free ease that would serve him well in the Salford slums and communist clubs of Paris.

Johann Caspar's sons had continued in the family firm, expanding operations to include the production of silk ribbons. By the time of his death in 1787, the family's combination of commercial success and high-minded philanthropy had secured them a preeminent social position within Wuppertal society: Engels's grandfather, Johann Caspar II, was appointed a municipal councilor in 1808 and became one of the founders of Barmen's United Protestant Church.[4] But when the business was passed on to the third generation—Engels's father and uncles—the family unity shattered. After repeated fallings out, in 1837 the three brothers drew lots to decide who would inherit the firm. Friedrich Engels senior lost and started up a new business, going into partnership with two Dutch brothers, Godfrey and Peter Ermen. There, he rapidly revealed his greater entrepreneurial gifts and his new company, Ermen & Engels, diversified from linen bleaching into cotton spinning, setting up a series of sewing thread factories in Manchester and then in Barmen and nearby Engelskirchen in 1841.

This then was the world of the merchant-manufacturer elite (the so-called *Fabrikanten*) within which Engels grew up, a world circumscribed by industry and commerce, civic duty and family loyalty. Of course, wealthy families like the Engelses—who lived, as one observer put it, in "spacious and sumptuous houses, often faced with fronts of cut stone and in the best architectural styles"—were protected from the more nefarious effects of industrialization. But they could not avoid them altogether, for following the steps of Johann Caspar along the Wupper had trudged tens of thousands of workers equally determined to share in the riches of industry.

Barmen's population grew from 16,000 in 1810 to over 40,000 in 1840. In Barmen and Elberfeld combined, the population topped 70,000 in 1840—roughly the same size as 1840s Newcastle or Hull. The valley's workforce consisted of 1,100 dyers, 2,000 spinners, 12,500 weavers in a variety of materials, and 16,000 ribbon weavers and trimmings makers. The vast majority did their work in modest homes and small workshops, but a new generation of sizable bleaching grounds and cotton mills was also starting up, and by the 1830s there were nearly two hundred factories operating along the valley. "It is a long, straggling town, skirting both sides of the river Wupper," a visitor noted in the 1840s. "Some parts are well-built, and are nicely paved; but the greater part of the town is composed of extremely irregular and very narrow streets. . . . The river itself is a disgusting object, being an open receptacle for all sewers, disguising the various tinctures contributed from the dyeing establishments in one murky impenetrable hue, that makes the stranger shudder on beholding."[5]

What might once have been compared with the kind of pleasant rural-industrial mix seen in the mill towns of the Pennines or Derbyshire's Derwent Valley—high valleys topped with green fields and forests, bottomed out by clear, fast-running streams providing the initial water power for mills and workshops—soon came to resemble a polluted, overcrowded "German Manchester." "The purple waves of the narrow river flow sometimes swiftly, sometimes sluggishly between smoky factory buildings and yarn-strewn bleaching-yards," was how Engels would come to describe his birthplace. "Its bright red colour, however, is due not to some bloody battle . . . but simply and solely to the numerous dye-works using Turkey red." From his earliest days, amid the acrid stench of workshops and bleaching yards, Engels was exposed to this witches' brew of industrialization: the eye-watering, nose-bleeding pollution blanketed the intense poverty and ostentatious wealth. As an impressionable young boy, he soaked it all up.[6]

Beyond the industry, visitors to the Wupper Valley noticed something else: "Both Barmen and Elberfeld are places where strong religious feelings prevail. The churches are large and well attended, and each place has its own bible, missionary, and tract societies."[7] Contemporary sketches reveal a forest of church steeples jostling for space in the skyline of factory chimneys. For Engels, the Wupper Valley was nothing less than the "Zion of the obscurantists." The spirit that dominated Barmen and Elberfeld was an aggressive form of Pietism, a movement within the German Lutheran (Protestant) Church that had first emerged in the late seventeenth century and stressed "a more intense, committed and practical form of Christian observance."[8] As the movement developed and diversified it often distanced itself from the formal structures and theology of the Lutheran Church and, along the Wupper Valley, allied itself with a Calvinist ethic that emphasized sin, personal salvation, and a renunciation of the world. The result was a religion of introspection that saw God's hand at work in all the mysteries of life, as the letters that passed between Engels's parents clearly testify. In 1835, as Engels's mother, Elise, tended her dying father, her husband proffered to her the comfort of faith in God's omnipotent mercy. "I am happy and thank God that you are coping with the illness of your beloved father in such a composed way," he wrote from the family home. "We all have good reason to thank the Lord for His guidance so far. . . . He [Elise's father] has enjoyed a generally happy life full of strength and health and now the good Lord seems to want to take the old man to him gently and without any pain. What can mortal man wish for more?" God's will could also be bathetically revealed in the most trivial occurrences. "Things don't look good for your potatoes, my dear Elise," Engels senior ominously warned his wife while she was on holiday in Ostende. "They looked so fine but now have also been infected by this disease that is spreading everywhere. . . . It has never been seen before in this form and is now appearing in almost every country like a plague." The lesson was clear: "It is almost as if God wanted to show humanity in this godless age how dependent we are on Him and how much our fate rests in His hands."[9]

In true Protestant fashion, the Wupper pietists subscribed to the idea of a priesthood of all believers finding salvation through unmediated individual prayer and the difficult task of scriptural exegesis. The churches fulfilled a useful religious function, but it was through brotherhood and sermonizing, rather than celebration of the Eucharist, that they delivered their mission. Much of the psychological severity of

Friedrich Engels senior can be traced to this deeply personal, often over-
weening faith. And, at least to begin with, his eldest son shared it. Engels
was baptized at the Elberfeld Reformed Evangelical parish church, which
was "well known as an exemplary Reformed church, soundly Calvinist
in its doctrine, well versed in Scripture, and reverent in worship."[10] In
1837, Engels marked his confirmation with a suitably evangelical poem:

> Lord Jesus Christ, God's only son,
> O step down from Thy heavenly throne
> And save my soul for me.
> Come down in all thy blessedness,
> Light of Thy Father's holiness,
> Grant that I may choose Thee.[11]

The curious reverse side of Pietism was a ruthless engagement with
the material realities of the world drawn from the Calvinist notion of
predestination: at the dawn of time, God marked out the saved and the
damned, and while no one could be certain of his or her status as chosen
or condemned, one of the surest signs of election was worldly success. In
true Max Weber style, the Protestant ethic and the spirit of capitalism
were hard at work among the churches and factories of the Wupper Valley. Industriousness and prosperity were signs of grace, and the most
ardent pietists were among the most successful merchants—including
Johann Caspar II, whose sense of prudence and sobriety dictated both
his religious and his business ethos. "We have to look to our own advantage even in spiritual matters," he told his son Friedrich Engels senior in
1813. "I think as a merchant in these matters too and seek the best price,
as no person with whom I might like to waste an hour on trivial things
can give me back a single minute of it."[12]

If all time was God's time and wasting a minute was a sin, then life
was certainly not meant for enjoyment and socializing. And, indeed, the
Barmen *Fabrikanten* displayed a Puritan-like morality that valued as-
ceticism, studiousness, individual uprightness, and personal reserve. As
Engels's first biographer, Gustav Mayer, recorded, in the early nineteenth
century the evangelical parishes in Elberfeld-Barmen petitioned the

government against the erection of a local theater, claiming that the allure of the stage could not coexist with industriousness in the Wupper
Valley. For the pietists, "pleasure" was one of the heathen blasphemies.[13]
The poet Ferdinand Freiligrath condemned Elberfeld as "a cursed nest,
prosaic, small-townish, somber; and reviled," and the adult Engels always recalled with a shudder its dour public culture.[14] "Why, for us, the
philistine Wuppertalers, Düsseldorf was always a little Paris, where
the pious gentlemen of Barmen and Elberfeld kept their mistresses, went
to the theatre, and had a right royal time," he told the German social
democrat Theodor Cuno, before adding sourly, "But the sky always looks
grey where one's own reactionary family lives."[15] Such Puritan public
morals were the product of a close alignment between political power
and church authority. Elberfeld's powerful church elders, who governed
the congregations, also held sway over the municipal institutions, with
their influence running through both the spiritual and the secular realms.

And the church's power was only growing. In the wake of an agrarian crisis and economic downturn during the 1830s, the pietist message
became more doctrinaire, mystical, even chiliastic. A revivalist movement took hold in the Wupper Valley, led by a charismatic preacher, Dr.
Frederick William Krummacher. "He thrashes about in the pulpit, bends
over all sides, bangs his fist on the edge, stamps like a cavalry horse and
shouts so that the windows resound and the people in the street trem-
ble," recorded the young Engels. "Then the congregation begins to sob;
first the young girls weep, then the old women join in with a heartrending soprano and the cacophony is completed by the wailing of the
enfeebled drunken pietists. . . . Through all this uproar Krummacher's
powerful voice rings out pronouncing before the whole congregation innumerable sentences of damnation, or describing diabolical scenes."[16]

The Engelses were not such hot Protestants as that. Indeed, put off by
this godly fervor, many leading Barmen families began to retreat from
church activity during the 1840s to focus instead on hearth and home.
Just as the evangelical revival in England led the way for the Victorian
celebration of patriarchy and domesticity (think here of the sentimental
poetry of William Cowper, the garden aesthetic of John Claudius Lou-
don, or the novels of Hannah More), so in the picturesque merchant

homes of Barmen there was a renewed cultural stress on the value of a tight-knit household. This vehement championing of the family unit expressed itself in an almost suburban ethic, a high-bourgeois desire to draw the curtains tight, seal off the corrupting outside world, and seek spiritual renewal in the simple pleasures of domestic ritual—reading, embroidery, pianoforte performances, Christmas celebrations, and birthday parties. "It is really nice and homely to have a piano!" Engels's father put it with almost Pooterish delight.[17] In the coming years, this parlor culture would be summed up in the cutting term *Biedermeier*, which combined the adjective *bieder*, a condescending designation of plainness, with the common surname *Meier* to describe the middle-class visual style, literature, and values of the period.[18]

Despite the later sneers, this was a safe and caring if not always joyful environment for Engels, his three brothers, and his four sisters to grow up in. Best of all, their parents adored each other. "You may not believe it but I was thinking about you all day and I could not find contentment in anything in the house," Engels senior wrote to Elise, then visiting her parents in Hamm, before signing off with "a few tender words for you. . . . Look, I suddenly feel like someone head over heels in love again. In all seriousness I can feel a spot of longing under my waistcoat (the one with the mother of pearl buttons, you know it). I don't think I will be able to last the four weeks." Indeed, his correspondence from the early 1820s is replete with the most passionate protestations of love for his wife: "Truthfully, dearest Elise, my heart yearns for us to be reunited, because I now feel a constant need to share everything with you."[19] Engels's mother, descended from a family of an intellectual rather than a commercial bent (the van Haars boasted headmasters and philologists in their ancestry), owned a far more generous, humorous, even subversive nature than her husband. One Christmas she went so far as to give Engels a book of poetry by Goethe, a writer generally dismissed in Barmen circles as "a godless man" but for Engels "the greatest of Germans."[20] Meanwhile, Elise's own father, the pastor Gerhard van Haar, introduced the adolescent Engels to the legends of classical mythology, a subject that found fertile ground in his grandson's energetic imagination. "O you dear Grandfather, who always treat us so kindly," Engels began one poetic thank you note,

> Always helping us when our work isn't going so smoothly,
> While you were here, you told me many a beautiful story
> Of Cercyon and Theseus, and Argus the hundred-eyed monster,
> The Minotaur, Ariadne, and Aegeus drowned in the ocean,
> The Golden Fleece, the Argonauts and Jason defiant.[21]

Within this comfortable setting, Engels's father is traditionally portrayed as an unhappy, rigidly religious, money-hungry philistine, thanks in no small part to his son's later, bitter characterizations. Philistine, it should be added, was a favored term of abuse that Engels had co-opted from Goethe: "A Philistine is an empty gut filled with fear who hopes that God will take pity on him." But a reading of Engels senior's letters to Elise reveals a very different side to the man: commercial-minded, yes, patriotic, and God-fearing, but also a loving son, doting father, and uxorious husband who shared numerous business decisions with his wife and frequently sought her advice. For all his puritanical reputation, he was also a keen musician who could play the piano, cello, and bassoon and enjoyed few things more than a family concert. Nevertheless, it was his mother to whom Engels remained close long after his acrimonious split from his father. "Were it not for my mother, who has a rare fund of humanity . . . and whom I really love," Engels wrote some years later, "it would not occur to me for a moment to make even the most paltry concession to my bigoted and despotic old man."[22] If his childhood occasionally seemed to gasp for air under the weight of commerce and piety, there was also a warm foundation of music, laughter, and love.

"Friedrich had a pretty average report last week. As you know, he has become more polite, outwardly, but in spite of the severe chastisements he received earlier, not even the fear of punishment seems to teach him unconditional obedience," Engels senior wrote censoriously to Elise in

August 1835 while she was back in Hamm caring for her father. "Thus today I was again distressed to find in his desk a dirty book which he had borrowed from the lending library, a story about knights in the 13th century. The careless way he leaves such books about in his desk is remarkable. May God watch over his disposition, I am often fearful for this otherwise excellent boy."[23]

Much to his father's chagrin, from an early age Friedrich chafed against the pietist strictures of Barmen life. His initial tutoring was in the local *Stadtschule*, where intellectual ambition was generally not encouraged. At age fourteen, he was transferred to the municipal *Gymnasium* in Elberfeld, where he lodged with a Lutheran schoolmaster. Purportedly one of the finest schools in Prussia, the more liberal *Gymnasium* certainly fostered Engels's gift for languages and, under the tutelage of a Dr. Clausen ("the only one who can arouse a feeling for poetry among the pupils, a feeling which would otherwise be bound to perish miserably among the philistines of Wuppertal"), nurtured his growing interest in the myths and romance of ancient Germania. As his final school report put it, "Engels showed commendable interest in the history of German national literature and the reading of the German classics."[24]

Indeed, a romanticized patriotism was to be one of the earliest intellectual influences on the young Engels. In later decades, he would often come to be unfairly decried as a dull, mechanistic Marxist—with Marxism itself frequently described as a reductionist offshoot of Enlightenment thought—but the first seedlings of Engels's philosophical development are to be found in some of the most idealized writings in the Western cultural canon. Part of the response to the political excesses of the French Revolution and the universalist rationalism of the Enlightenment was a flourishing of romanticism. From the late 1700s, particularities of language, culture, tradition, and custom confidently reasserted themselves across European intellectual life. In Scotland, the movement was led by the Celtic mythmaker James Macpherson and then by Walter Scott, author of the Waverley novels. In France, Chateaubriand's *Le Génie du Christianisme* venerated the much-decried Catholic Church while Joseph de Maistre excoriated the Enlightenment for its shallow understanding of human nature. And in England, the poetry of Wordsworth, Blake, and Coleridge dwelled on the unique attributes of a national tradition, with "The Rime of the Ancyent Marinere" a conscious affront to any cosmopolitan notion of common culture, language, and reason. "In England, in Germany, in Spain, old native traditions, even superstitions, acquired a new force, a new respectability," as Hugh Trevor-Roper put it. "The old, customary organs of society, the old established beliefs, which had seemed so contemptible to the rationalists of the *Encyclopaedia*, now acquired a new dignity."[25]

And nowhere more so than in Germany. As an aesthetic, cultural, and political movement stretching over many decades and assuming simultaneously complementary and contradictory forms, romanticism remains difficult to codify. However, if the Enlightenment was committed to a uniform and predictable human nature, romanticism stressed the opposite—the irrational, emotional, imaginative, and restless desire among its adherents to escape the narrow, prosaic present.[26] Intellectually, German romanticism traced its roots back to the work of the Sturm und Drang dramatists or Goethe's remarkable novel of passionate self-immersion, *The Sorrows of Young Werther* (1774). By contrast, writers Johann Gottfried von Herder and J. G. Hamann chose a more consciously nationalist response, reacting to enlightened French civility by stressing the centrality of earthy German language to the construction of culture. In his "Treatise on the Origins of Language," Herder described language as a lyre with a tone all its own and each national tongue as the peculiar product of a specific people, or *Volk* ("the invisible, hidden medium that links minds through ideas, hearts through inclinations and impulses, the senses through impressions and forms, civil society through laws and institutions"). As such, a people's essence was traceable through a nation's primitive folktales, songs, and literature; a peculiarly democratic notion of culture that helped to spur a growing interest in the German national, notably medieval past. Strasbourg's high Gothic cathedral, the pre-Reformation Catholic Church, hoary fairytales, and the art of Dürer all became unique totems of Germany's communal greatness. As Madame de Staël put it in her best-selling history, *De l'Allemagne*, because the Teutonic people had never been conquered by the Romans and had passed straight from barbarism to medieval Christianity, "their imagination disports itself in old towers and battlements, among knights, sorceresses, and spectres; and mysteries of a thoughtful and solitary nature form the principal charm of their poetry."[27]

Friedrich Schiller aestheticized this romantic impulse, suggesting that the collapse of organic medieval society could be reversed only by a broad ethic of beauty and creativity. This was the call that Friedrich and August Wilhelm Schlegel answered in 1798 as they launched the golden age of German romanticism with their Jena-based journal, *Athenaeum*. Through its pages, the romantic artist, poet, wanderer, or mystic appeared center stage. Caspar David Friedrich's moody paintings of heroic subjects confronting vast forests and pounding waterfalls, E. T. A. Hoffmann's elusive, transcendent scores; and Schiller's poetry of freedom, rebellion, and betrayal caught this introspective spirit in which individual experience was all.

But while Schiller and the Schlegel brothers stressed the calling of the artist to rebind the social ties, their contemporaries the poet Novalis and the philosopher Johann Gottlieb Fichte sought to revive the proto-nationalist ideas of Herder. His patriotic notion of the *Volk* proved particularly prescient in the aftermath of 1806 when Prussia succumbed to Napoleon at the battle of Jena.[28] Despite the generally enlightened nature of subsequent imperial French rule—with its civil code allowing for greater freedom of speech, constitutional liberty, and Jewish rights than the Hohenzollern monarchy had permitted in Prussia—foreign occupation is rarely a popular condition and the years of French governance served only to intensify an aggrieved sense of Germanic identity. Fichte nursed this sentiment with a provocative series of lectures, "Homilies to the German Nation," delivered at the Berlin Academy in 1807–08 in which he elevated Herder's idea of nationhood to new emotional heights. Only through identification with the *Volk*, he announced to a Berlin audience laboring under French rule, could individuals realize their full freedom, while the nation itself was a beautiful, organic entity with a soul and a purpose.

The result was a renewed outpouring of interest in the vernacular

German past as embodied by the country's most famous philologists, the brothers Jacob and Wilhelm Grimm. Having already published a journal entitled *Altdeutsche Wälder (Old German Forests)*, which provided an archaeology of German customs, laws, and language, in 1815 they issued a new appeal: "A society has been founded that is intended to spread throughout all of Germany and has as its goal to save and collect all the existing songs and tales that can be found among the common German peasantry." It was a work of "imaginative state-building," and despite the fact that many of the fairy and folktales the Grimms collated into their best-selling *Kinder- und Hausmärchen* came from middle-class ladies of French Huguenot origin, they had successfully added another inventive layer to the national German tradition.[29]

Behind the poetry, folktales, operas, and novels rumbled the hard-edged politics of romanticism. When peace finally came to Europe in 1815, following Napoleon's defeat at the battle of Waterloo and the ensuing diplomatic carve-up at the Congress of Vienna, the Rhineland was annexed by Prussia. The freethinking, industrial, urban world of the Rhine now fell subject to the Hohenzollern monarchy of Berlin and its dry Junker ethos that set the merits of hierarchy and authority far above any vernacular spirit of broader German culture. Yet across Prussia—as well as within the other principalities, kingdoms, and free cities that would later constitute Germany—romantic, progressive patriots raised on the poetry of Novalis and the nationalism of Fichte were mobilizing in support of a more unitary, more liberal German nation. Inspired by the legends and language of invented tradition, radicals now wanted to cleanse the memory of French occupation and Enlightenment hubris with a reinvigoration of national sentiment.

Beginning in Jena in 1815, student *Burschenschaften* (fraternities or clubs) campaigned for constitutional reform based on the idea of a Germanic *patria*. They decked themselves out in the black, red, and gold colors of the Lützow volunteers (a patriotic free corps made up of armed students and intellectuals who supposedly heroically fought the French at the 1813 battle of Leipzig) and swore loyalty to the fatherland—rather than to the indecisive Prussian king, Friedrich Wilhelm III, who was then retreating from his earlier plans for constitutional reform. Part

of this patriotic cult found expression in the 150 gymnastics clubs and
100,000-member choral societies that sang ballads across Prussia and
organized festivals in praise of the fatherland. The choral society movement's high point arrived in October 1817 when students from all over
Germany gathered at Wartburg Castle (where Martin Luther had translated the New Testament into German) to celebrate the 300th anniversary of the Reformation and the fourth anniversary of the battle of
Leipzig. Through a radical political culture built around a strong set of
patriotic symbols, the Prussian war against Napoleon was being woven
into a broader narrative of emerging German nationhood.[30]

All of which was deeply troubling to the kings and first ministers of
Austria and the German Confederation, who fervently believed in dynasties, not nations, monarchies, not democracies. They responded with
the Karlsbad Decrees of November 1819, which closed down the student
societies, ended any talk of a written constitution, put the universities
under police surveillance, and quashed press freedoms. Masterminded
by the Austrian chief minister, Count Klemens von Metternich, whose
fearmongering exercised a remarkable sway over the Prussian authorities, an accomplished campaign on behalf of the royal authorities attempted in the 1820s to snuff out any hint of romantic radicalism.

How much of this romanticism made its way to Barmen, that inward-
looking Zion of the obscurantists? Here, remember, Goethe was just "a
godless man." Yet encouraged by Dr. Clausen and his own reading of
dirty medieval romances, young Friedrich Engels was enlivened by
this revival of German nationalism. In 1836 he penned a small poem
altogether less godly than his confirmation ode, eulogizing the deeds
of such romantic heroes as "The Archer William Tell," "The Warrior-
Knight Bouillon," and Siegfried, the dragon-slaying hero of the medieval *Song of the Nibelungs*. He wrote articles championing the democratic
tradition of the German *Volksbüchner* and the work of the Brothers
Grimm. "These old popular books with their old-fashioned tone, their
misprints and their poor woodcuts have for me an extraordinary, poetic
charm," he announced airily. "They transport me from our artificial

modern 'conditions, confusions and fine distinctions' into a world which is much closer to nature."[31] There were more poems venerating the life of the German national icon and father of printing, Johannes Gutenberg, and even pantheistic accounts of the divine glory of the German countryside ("gaze over the vine-fragrant valley of the Rhine, the distant blue mountains merging with the horizon, the green fields and vineyards flooded with golden sunlight").[32] Throughout his long life, Engels never abandoned this youthful cultural patriotism. Even when he was championing the international solidarity of the proletariat and banned on pain of execution from his homeland, Engels retained an unexpected emotional empathy for the world of Siegfried and the heroic destiny he represented.

But it was never a sympathy shared by his father. Despite Engels's wish to stay on in school to study and glowing reports from his headmaster, in 1837 he was summarily withdrawn from the *Gymnasium* and ushered into the family business. Already concerned about his son's literary foibles and questionable piety, Engels senior had no qualms about removing him from the dubious intellectual circles surrounding Dr. Clausen. Friedrich's hopes of studying law at university, perhaps entering the civil service, even becoming a poet—all hinted at in his final report from headmaster J. C. L. Hantschke, who spoke of how Engels was "induced to choose [business] as his outward profession in life instead of the studies he had earlier intended"—were not to be.[33] Instead, for an arduous twelve months, he was inducted into the dull mysteries of linen and cotton, spinning and weaving, bleaching and dyeing. In the summer of 1838 father and son embarked on a business trip around England to arrange silk sales in Manchester and *grège* (raw silk) purchases in London and to look over the Ermen & Engels concerns. They returned via the northern German city of Bremen, where Friedrich was set to embark on the next stage of his commercial apprenticeship, a crash course in international capitalism.

The coastal air of Bremen, a free town and Hanseatic trading city, proved altogether more congenial to Engels than the low Barmen mists. Of course, it too was a place of piety ("their hearts have been scrubbed with the teachings of Johann Calvin," complained a resident of his fellow citizens) but as one of Germany's largest ports it was also a center of intellectual as well as commercial exchange. Apprenticed to the Saxon consul and linen exporter Heinrich Leupold, Engels worked as a clerk in the trading house and lodged with a friendly clergyman, Georg Gottfried Trevinarus. After the suffocating Biedermeier gentility of Barmen, the more relaxed Trevinarus household seemed almost riotous. "We put a ring in a cup of flour and then played the well-known game of trying to get it out with your mouth," he wrote to one of his sisters about a Sunday afternoon pastime. "We all had a turn—the Pastor's wife, the girls, the painter and I too, while the Pastor sat in the corner on the sofa and watched the fun through a cloud of cigar smoke. The Pastor's wife couldn't stop laughing as she tried to get it out and covered herself with flour over and over. . . . Afterwards we threw flour in each other's faces. I blackened my face with cork, at which they all laughed, and when I started to laugh, that made them laugh all the more and all the louder."[34]

This was just one of a series of letters to his favorite sibling, his younger sister Marie, or "goose." They reveal a part of Engels's character that remained constant through the years: a roguish, gossipy, sometimes malicious sense of humor (which would meet its counterpart in Karl Marx's) and an uncomplicated appetite for life. His correspondence is littered with nicknames, terrible puns, jottings, even musical chords, together with bragging accounts of doomed romances, alcoholic endurance, and practical jokes. Unlike the cyclically despondent Marx, Engels rarely suffered from low spirits. Physically and intellectually, Engels was a Victorian man of action rather than of emotional reflection. Whether it was learning a new language, devouring a library, or pursuing his Teutonic urge for hiking, Engels needed to be on the move, channeling his restless energies into seeking out the best of any situation. As the Victorian radical George Julian Harney noted, "There was nothing of the 'stuck-up' or 'standoffish' about him. . . . He was himself laughter-loving, and his laughter was contagious. A joy inspirer, he made all around him share his happy mood."[35]

Engels's work in Bremen mainly involved handling international correspondence: there were packages to Havana, letters to Baltimore, hams to the West Indies, and a consignment of Domingo coffee beans from Haiti ("which has a light tinge of green, but is usually grey and in which for every ten good beans, there are four bad ones, six stones and a half ounce of dirt").[36] Through this clerking apprenticeship, he came to know the ins and outs of the export business, currency deals, and import duties—a detailed knowledge of capitalist mechanics that would, in years to come, prove exceedingly useful. But for a wistful young romantic like Engels, it was numbing stuff. And, as his father no doubt warned, idle hands made easy work for the devil. "We now have a complete stock of beer in the office; under the table, behind the stove, behind the cupboard, everywhere are beer bottles," he boasted to Marie. "Up to now it was always very annoying to have to dash straight to the desk from a meal, when you are so dreadfully lazy, and to remedy this we have fixed up two very fine hammocks in the packing-house loft and there we swing after we have eaten, smoking a cigar, and sometimes having a little doze."[37]

In addition to the relaxed working environment, Engels took advantage of Bremen's more liberal society. He signed up for dancing lessons, combed the city's bookshops (and helped to import some more politically risqué texts), went horseback riding, traveled widely, and swam across the Weser sometimes four times a day. He also became a keen fencer. Quick to take offense and even quicker to defend the honor of friends, family, or political ideals, Engels liked his swordplay. "I have had two duels here in the last four weeks," he glowingly announced in one letter. "The first fellow has retracted the insulting words of 'stupid' which he said to me after I gave him a box on the ear. . . . I fought with the second fellow yesterday and gave him a real beauty above the brow, running right down from the top, a really first-class prime."[38]

Tempering his pugnacity, he also attended chamber concerts, attempted a few of his own musical compositions, and joined the Academy of Singing—as much for the chance of meeting young women as for exercising his baritone. For Engels was a suavely attractive, if not ruggedly good-looking, fellow: nearly six feet tall with "clear, bright eyes," sleek dark hair, and a very smooth complexion. Encountering him in the 1840s, the German communist Friedrich Lessner described Engels as "tall and slim, his movements . . . quick and vigorous, his manner of speaking brief and decisive, his carriage erect, giving a soldierly touch."[39] Accompanying his good looks came a shade of vanity. Engels's friends recalled his being especially "particular about his appearance; he was always trim and scrupulously clean."[40]

In future years, his youthful appearance would bring him numerous female admirers but in Bremen he tried to mitigate his boyishness with a determined facial hair strategy. "Last Sunday we had a moustache evening [at the town-hall cellars]. For I had sent out a circular to all moustache-capable young men that it was finally time to horrify all philistines, and that could not be done better than by wearing moustaches." Ever the poet, Engels composed a suitable toast for the heavy drinking that accompanied the evening:

> Philistines shirk the burden of bristle
> By shaving their faces as clean as a whistle.
> We are not philistines, so we
> Can let our mustachios flourish free.
> Long life to every Christian
> Who bears his moustaches like a man.
> And may all philistines be damned
> For having moustaches banished and banned.[41]

This masculine flamboyance constituted more than just fun and games. Joining a choral society and sporting a moustache (of which Engels was inordinately proud just as, in later years, he would be of his beard) were something of a political statement in the watchful, authoritarian era that followed the Karlsbad Decrees. The result of the crackdown on freedom of expression in newspapers and political associations was a remarkable politicization of everyday life across Germany, with clothes, insignia, music, and even facial hair deployed as signs of republican patriotism—the Bavarian authorities even outlawed moustaches on security grounds. Engels embraced this culture of subversion. In addition to growing his moustache and participating in choral outings, he had Pastor Trevinarus's wife embroider a purse for him in the black, red, and gold tricolor of the Lützow volunteers and he developed an ostentatious admiration for the great *German* composer Beethoven. "What a symphony it was last night!" he wrote to Marie after attending an evening concert of the C Minor (Fifth) and *Eroica* symphonies. "You never heard anything like it in your whole life. . . . What a tremendous, youthful, jubilant celebration of freedom by the trombone in the third and fourth movement!"[42]

Engels's political education—his journey from romanticism toward socialism—also began in Bremen, with his discovery of "the Berlin party of Young Germany." Early-nineteenth-century Europe spawned an eclectic range of "young" movements, from Giuseppe Mazzini's *Giovane Italia* to Lord John Manner's Young England cabal of aristocratic Tories to the Young Ireland republican circle, each of them championing a revival of patriotic sentiment based around a romanticized idea of nationhood. *Das Junge Deutschland* was far less of an identifiable political project and more a loosely aligned, "realist" literary grouping centered on the dissident and radical-liberal poet Ludwig Börne. Their unwritten manifesto demanded that the romantic Age of Art give way to the Age of Action, and Börne, a fierce opponent of Metternich's authoritarianism, was scathing toward the craven political quietism that had been adopted by Goethe and other high-minded priests of romanticism. "Heaven has given you a tongue of fire, but have you ever defended justice?" he demanded of the Sage of Weimar, whose career he ridiculed for its courtierlike servility toward princes and patrons.[43]

Börne's cause was cultural and intellectual freedom under a system of modern, liberal governance and he was highly dismissive of the nostalgic forests-and-ruins conservatism of traditional romanticism. Exiled in Paris, having run afoul of Metternich's censors, he moved steadily toward republican politics while aiming sarcastic barbs at the Prussian occupation of the Rhineland. Joining Börne in the Young Germany firmament was the poet Heinrich Heine, the novelist Heinrich Laube, and the journalist Karl Gutzkow. Gutzkow's notoriety came from his 1835 novel, *Wally the Skeptic*, which combined a racy narrative of sexual liberation with religious blasphemy and cultural emancipation. The lengthy

ramblings of Wally, the "new woman" heroine—with her liberal sentiments on marriage, domesticity, and the meaning of the Bible—managed
to encompass just about every known anathema to Biedermeier society.
Metternich was not slow to act on such a dangerous affront to public
morals and political stability, and in 1835 he had the Diet of the German
Confederation condemn the entire oeuvre of Heine, Gutzkow, and Laube.

Engels identified enthusiastically with Young Germany's rejection of
romanticized medievalism. Although he continued to be drawn to the
heroic myths of the past on a literary level, Engels was convinced that
Germany's political future could not entail a retreat back to the feudal
nostalgia of the Middle Ages. Instead, he expressed sympathy for a program of radical, progressive patriotism that looked enticingly possible in
the early years of the reign of Friedrich Wilhelm III. This was a call not
for democracy but for the liberation of Germany from the parochialism
of feudal principalities and their absolutist rulers. Above all, as Engels
wrote, what Young Germany wanted was "participation by the people in
the administration of the state, that is, constitutional matters; further,
emancipation of the Jews, abolition of all religious compulsion, of all
hereditary aristocracy, etc. Who can have anything against that?"[44]

Spurring Engels along this political journey was the poetry of "the
genius, the prophet," Percy Bysshe Shelley (whom he read together with
Byron and Coleridge).[45] No doubt the office-bound Engels was excited
by the heroics of Shelley's rebellious, priapic lifestyle: the breach with his
reactionary father, the doomed love affairs, and the devil-may-care romantic bravado. But he was also attracted by Shelley's political passion.
Not yet for Engels the "recognizably pre-Marxist" writings of *An Address to the People on the Death of the Princess Charlotte* (1817), which, in
contrasting public reaction to a royal death with the case of three recently executed laborers, directly connected political oppression to economic exploitation.[46] Rather, at this stage of his thinking, Engels was
drawn to the republican, antireligious, socially liberal creed that Shelley
explored in *Queen Mab* (1812):

> Nature rejects the monarch, not the man;
> The subject, not the citizen; for kings

And subjects, mutual foes, forever play
A losing game into each other's hands,
Whose stakes are vice and misery.

No doubt he also enjoyed Shelley's thoughts on the mercantile calling:

Commerce! beneath whose poison-breathing shade
No solitary virtue dares to spring,
But poverty and wealth with equal hand
Scatter their withering curses, and unfold
The doors of premature and violent death.

Here was an idea of personal liberation tailor-made for Engels, the radical romantic doomed to a life of commerce. Yet Shelley's celebration of political freedom in his "Ode to Liberty" also touched a chord with Engels, who responded with an 1840 poem, "An Evening" (and an epigraph from Shelley, "Tomorrow comes!").

I, too, am one of Freedom's minstrel band.
'Twas to the boughs of Börne's great oak-tree
I soared, when in the vales the despot's hand
Tightened the strangling chains round Germany.
Yes, I am one of those plucky birds that make
Their course through Freedom's bright aethereal sea.

Shelley's philhellenic epic *Hellas* similarly appealed to Engels's growing nationalism. Indeed, the cause of Greek independence was a popular one in the Rhineland as dozens of local associations sprung up to assist in the 1820s struggle against the Ottomans, with the conflict used as something of a proxy for enthusiasts of Germany's own quest for national autonomy.[47] Engels himself had earlier penned a piece of narrative fiction, "A Pirate Tale," that whimsically recounted a young man's struggle against the Turks and his "fight for the freedom of the Hellenes, . . . men who still have a taste for freedom."[48] On multiple levels, the life and work of Shelley served as a source of inspiration for Engels and, stuck in

Bremen during a dull summer in 1840, he even made plans to publish his own translations of "The Sensitive Plant." Later, he would boast to Eleanor Marx that at the time "we all knew Shelley by heart."[49]

Less loftily, events in France were also sharpening Engels's political position. He did not yet regard 1789 as the epoch-making event he would later see it as; at this stage, he was more enamored of the bourgeois revolution of July 1830, which had seen the ejection of King Charles X and his replacement with the constitutional monarch Louis-Philippe. For Young Germany, this had been the supreme example of "freedom" in action. "Each item was a sunbeam wrapped in printed paper, and together they kindled my soul into a wild glow," recalled Heine of receiving the news. "Bold, ardent hopes spring up, like trees with golden fruit."[50] Along the industrial settlements of the Rhineland, Paris's successful deployment of popular will against an aloof monarch was widely celebrated in a series of anti-Prussian riots. Once reviled for its occupation of the Rhineland but now again admired for its national aspiration for liberty, France and its July days stood for the overthrow of antiquated authoritarianism in the name of progress, freedom, and patriotism. Compared with the revolutionary communism of his coming years, Engels's support for this bourgeois constitutionalism—with its commitment to the rule of law, the balance of power, the freedom of the press—was fairly mild stuff. But at the time it was exhilarating enough. "I must become a Young German or rather, I am one already, body and soul," he wrote in 1839. "I cannot sleep at night, all because of the ideas of the century. When I am at the post-office and look at the Prussian coat of arms, I am seized with the spirit of freedom. Every time I look at a newspaper I hunt for advances of freedom."[51]

In his spare time, when he wasn't socializing, partaking in the Trevinarus family fun and games, or working in the counting house, Engels began to pursue the hunt for freedom in his writing. Historically, Engels's style has been deemed inferior to Marx's: commentators are given to contrast the leaden, clinical prose of Engels with Marx's glittering, chiasmus-ridden wit. This is unfair. For Engels was, in fact, an elegant author in both his private and his public writings right up until his work took a more doggedly scientific turn in the 1880s. That said, the case for the defense does not begin promisingly:

> Sons of the desert, proud and free,
> Walk on to greet us, face to face;
> But pride is vanished utterly,
> And freedom lost without a trace.
> They jump at money's beck and call
> (As once that lad from dune to dune
> Bounded for joy). They're silent, all,
> Save one who sings a dirge-like tune.

"The Bedouin"—Engels's first published work—was an Orientalist poem eulogizing the noble savagery of the Bedouin people undone by their contact with Western civilization. Where once they walked "proud and free," now they slavishly performed for pennies in Parisian theaters. Even for an eighteen-year-old the poem was a clumsy effort. Still, it showed that under the dull routine of his commercial correspondence, Engels retained his romantic, Shelley-like ambitions. The work was, in fact, something of a tribute to Wuppertal's most celebrated poet-clerk, Ferdinand Freiligrath, who combined his job in the Barmen firm of Eynern & Söhne with a flourishing literary career. From the provincial banality of the Rhineland ("this blasted nest," as he put it), Freiligrath conjured up a dreamland of exoticized tribes and sun-drenched land-scapes peopled by beautiful Negro princesses. Engels, the bored clerk, was enchanted and in numerous verses he shamelessly ripped off Freiligrath's tropes of Moorish princes, proud savagery, and corrupt civilizations.

Yet he could not shake his youthful literary passion for the German mythical past and, in April 1839, he penned an unfinished epic play based on the life of the folk hero Siegfried. It is full of demands for ac-tion and an end to reflection, of battles entered and dragons slain. Most intriguing is the stress Engels lays on the psychological struggle between Siegfried and his father, Sieghard: while the former wants to run free

("Give me a charger and a sword / That I may fare to some far land / As I so often have implored"), the king thinks "it's time he learned to be his age" ("Instead of studying state affairs, / he's after wrestling bouts with bears"). After a war of words, the father finally lets go and Siegfried is free to follow his own path in life ("I want to be like the mountain stream / Clearing my route all on my own"). It doesn't require too much insight to realize that, in the words of Gustav Mayer, this unfinished play represents "the virtual embodiment of the battle that may have taken place in the Engels family in relation to Friedrich's choice of vocation."[52]

More successful than his poetry was Engels's journalistic prose. "The Bedouin" had been published in the Bremen paper *Bremisches Conversationsblatt*, and Engels—like any other good hack—had immediately complained about the editor ruining his copy ("the fellow went and changed the last verse and so created the most hopeless confusion").[53] So he moved on to write for Karl Gutzkow's paper, *Telegraph für Deutschland*, and began to make his name as a precocious cultural critic from the Young Germany stable. Or rather, he began to make the name of his chosen, suitably medieval-sounding pseudonym, "Friedrich Oswald," which was an early indication of the tensions that would come to mark Engels's career. He wanted his opinions and criticisms to be heard, but at the same time he was keen to avoid the stress and anguish that would inevitably come from any open break with his family. To ensure his financial security and avoid embarrassing his parents, Engels as "Oswald" started out on his double life.

The *Telegraph*'s style was the feuilleton: inhibited by Prussian censorship from publishing detailed political commentaries, the progressive papers embedded their criticism in literary and cultural pieces, even travelogues. The writer became an intellectual flâneur interspersing social and political points among reflections on regional culture and cuisine, memory and myth. Landscapes, boat journeys, and poetry provided Engels with just the romantic cover he needed to expound his liberal, nationalist sensibilities. Thus a travelogue on Xanten, "Siegfried's Native Town," allowed Engels to mount a critique of conservatism in the name of freedom and youth. As our correspondent enters the town, the sound of High Mass filters from the cathedral. For the emotional "Oswald" the sentiments are almost too much to bear. "You, too, son of the nineteenth century, let your heart be conquered by them—these sounds have enthralled stronger and wilder men than you!" He gives himself up to the myth of Siegfried, drawing from it a modern message: the need for energy, action, and heroic contempt in the face of the petty, deadening bureaucracy of the Prussian state and its newly ascended monarch, the religio-conservative Friedrich Wilhelm IV. "Siegfried is the representative of German youth. All of us, who still carry in our breast a heart unfettered by the restraints of life, know what that means."[54]

Engels's most substantive writing for the *Telegraph* was markedly less high-flown and more rooted in the travails of his home region. During the 1830s, the Rhineland textile industry was finding it increasingly difficult to compete with its English counterparts. The old-fashioned outwork practices of the Barmen artisans—with textile goods produced by hand in home workshops—were proving no match for the efficient, mechanized manufactories of Lancashire. Even within Germany, with its free-trade *Zollverein* (Prussia-led Customs Union), the situation was bleak as the Rhenish advantage in textile goods fell away to competition from Saxony and Silesia. French demand for silk weaving and ribbon took up some of the slack, but it was a volatile, fashion-driven market subject to sharp drops in demand. These economic changes brought a steady worsening of conditions among Barmen workers and the gradual disintegration of the paternalist corporate structures that the Engels family had traditionally prided itself on. Guilds were disbanded, incomes squeezed, working conditions undermined, and the old social economy of apprenticeships, wage differentials linked to skill levels, and properly paid male labor came under sustained assault. In their place sprung up a stark new divide between worker and manufacturer that for those on the edges of the textile economy—handspinners, hosiers, and weavers—meant a rapid diminishment of income and position.

This new economic reality was reflected in the growing use of the terms *pauperism* and *proletariat* by journalists and social commentators in referring to the kind of rootless, propertyless, casual urban workers who lacked regular employment and security—the thousands of unemployed and underemployed knife grinders, shoemakers, tailors, journeymen, and textile laborers who crowded into the towns and cities of the Rhineland. In cities such as Cologne, between 20 and 30 percent of the population was on poor relief. The German social theorist Robert von Mohl described the modern factory worker—unlikely ever to be apprenticed, to become a master, to inherit property, or to acquire a skill—as akin to a "serf, chained like Ixion to his wheel." The political reformer Theodor von Schon used *proletariat* as a synonym for "people without home or property."[55]

"Friedrich Oswald," however, did something rather different. In a style he would in the coming years define as his own, Engels went among the people to produce an extraordinarily mature piece of social and cultural reportage. No lofty social theories about the nature of pauperism and the meaning of the proletariat for this son of a factory owner. Instead his "Letters from Wuppertal"—published in the *Telegraph* in 1839—offered an unrivaled authenticity, an eyewitness experience of the depressed, drunken, demoralized region. When Engels contrasted the reality of Barmen life with his romanticized ideal of the fatherland—the imagined nation of Herder, Fichte, and the Brothers Grimm, peopled by a lusty, patriotic *Volk*—the disappointment was tangible. "There is no trace here of the wholesome, vigorous life of the people that exists almost everywhere in Germany. True, at first glance it seems otherwise, for every evening you can hear merry fellows strolling through the streets singing their songs, but they are the most vulgar, obscene songs that ever came from drunken mouths; one never hears any of the folksongs which are so familiar throughout Germany and of which we have every right to be proud."[56]

Written by a nineteen-year-old industrial heir, the "Letters" provided a magnificently brutal critique of the human costs of capitalism. Engels points to the red-dyed Wupper, the "smoky factory buildings and yarn-strewn bleaching yards"; he traces the plight of the weavers bent over their looms and the factory workers "in low rooms where people breathe in more coal fumes and dust than oxygen"; he laments the exploitation of children and the grinding poverty of those he would later term the lumpenproletariat ("totally demoralized people, with no fixed abode or definite employment, who crawl out of their refuges, haystacks, stables, etc., at dawn, if they have not spent the night on a dungheap or on a staircase"); and he charts the rampant alcoholism among the leather workers, three out of five of whom die from excess schnapps consumption. Decades on, this memory of industrializing Barmen continued to haunt him. "I can still well remember how, at the end of the 1820s, the low cost of schnapps suddenly overtook the industrial area of the Lower Rhine and the Mark," Engels wrote in an 1876 essay on the social effects of cheap alcohol. "In the Berg country particularly, and most notably in Elberfeld-Barmen, the mass of the working population fell victim to drink. From nine in the evening, in great crowds and arm in arm, taking up the whole width of the street, the 'soused men' tottered their way, bawling discordantly, from one inn to the other and finally back home."[57]

The prose in the "Letters" was biting, but did the high-living and studiously intellectual Engels, the moustachioed fencer and feuilleton author, feel any personal empathy for these Wuppertal unfortunates? Official communist biographies are unequivocal that Engels's politics "rested on a profound and genuine feeling of responsibility vis-à-vis the lot of the working people. Their sufferings grieved Engels, who was anything but a prosaic, cold, matter-of-fact person."[58] Certainly, any reader of Engels's work takes away a clear picture of injustice and its causes, but whether the author was emotionally affected or merely ideologically motivated by such misery remains unclear. At this stage, all that can be said is that his strength of feeling for the Barmen underclass was probably as much the product of a rebellious antagonism toward his father's generation as a considered sentiment for the workers' plight.

Whatever his motivation, Engels's criticisms cascaded down the *Telegraph* columns, as if carefully noted and steadily accumulated since childhood. The miserly vulgarity of the Wuppertal employers was reflected in the town's design, with "dull streets, devoid of all character," badly built churches, and half-completed civic monuments. To the now sophisticated eye of the Bremen-based Engels, the town's so-called educated elite were nothing more than philistines. There was precious little talk of Young Germany along the Wupper valley, only endless gossip about horses, dogs, and servants. "The life these people lead is terrible, yet they are so satisfied with it; in the daytime they immerse themselves in their accounts with a passion and interest that is hard to believe; in the evening at an appointed hour they turn up at social gatherings where they play cards, talk politics and smoke, and then leave for home at the stroke of nine." And the worst of it? "Fathers zealously bring up their sons along these lines, sons who show every promise of following in their fathers' footsteps." It was already apparent that that was not a fate Engels was willing to chance.

Despite the critique of working conditions and the human price of industrialization, Engels's target in the "Letters" was not capitalism per se. He had as yet no real understanding of the workings of private property, the division of labor, or the nature of surplus labor value. The true focus of his ire was the religious pietism of his childhood. Here was a conscious, studied rejection of the guiding ethic behind his family's lineage by a young man disgusted at the social costs of religious dogma. Learning, reason, and progress were all stunted by the deadening, sanctimonious grip of Krummacher and his congregations. And the factory workers were embracing the pietist fervor in the same way they consumed their schnapps: as a mystical route out of their all-enveloping misery. Meanwhile those manufacturers who most ostentatiously advertised their godliness were well known as the most exploitative of employers whose personal sense of election seemed to absolve them of respectable human conduct. To Engels, the Wuppertal was sinking beneath a tide of moral and spiritual hypocrisy: "This whole region is submerged in a sea of pietism and philistinism, from which rise no beautiful, flower-covered islands."[59]

"Ha, ha, ha! Do you know who wrote the article in the *Telegraph*? The author is the writer of these lines, but I advise you not to say anything about it, I could get into a hell of a lot of trouble." Engels's "Letters from Wuppertal" sparked a highly gratifying public storm along the Wupper valley. The detailed personalized criticism of Krummacher together with the linkage of pietism and poverty was strong stuff, and though delighted by the controversy, "Friedrich Oswald" was not quite ready to be exposed as one of Barmen's leading sons. Instead, he was content to enjoy a knowing chuckle with Wuppertal friends from the safety of Bremen.[60] His correspondents were his old classmates Friedrich and Wilhelm Graeber, sons of an Orthodox priest and themselves training for the priesthood. Through a typically candid series of letters that Engels wrote to them between 1839 and 1841, we are offered an insight into the most important intellectual shift of Engels's Bremen years: his loss of faith.

It is a cliché of nineteenth-century intellectual historiography that the road to socialism was paved by secularism. From Robert Owen to Beatrice Webb to Annie Besant, the disavowal of Christianity was a familiar rite of passage for those whose spiritual journey would culminate with the new religion of humanity. But its obviousness does not invalidate its truth. "Well, I have never been a pietist. I have been a mystic for a while, but those are *tempi passati*. I am now an honest, and in comparison with others very liberal, super-naturalist" was how Engels described his religious temperament to the Graebers in April 1839. He had long been dissatisfied with the narrow spiritualism offered by Wuppertal pietism, but he remained at age nineteen a long way from rejecting the central tenets of Christianity. Amid the intellectual liberalism of Bremen life, however, Engels felt he now wanted more from his church than predestination and damnation. He was increasingly troubled by the notion of original sin and hoped somehow to unite his Christian inheritance with the progressive, rationalist thinking he had absorbed from Young Germany. "I want to tell you quite plainly that I have now reached a point where I can only regard as divine a teaching which can stand the test of reason," he informed Friedrich Graeber, before pointing out the numerous contradictions within the Bible, querying God's divine mercy, and taking special delight in exposing a series of astronomical howlers in a recent Krummacher sermon.[61]

In the summer of 1839, he thought he might have found an acceptable compromise to his spiritual crisis in the teachings of Friedrich Schleiermacher, whose redemptive theology, with its stress on an intuitive religion of the heart compatible with the modern demands of reason, seemed a very different canon from the hellfire and damnation of "our valley of hypocrites." For Engels, Schleiermacher seemed to "teach the word of Christ in the sense of 'Young Germany.'" But even that paled after Engels came across *the* theological bombshell of early-nineteenth-century Europe. David Friedrich Strauss's *Life of Jesus Critically Examined* had appeared in 1835–36 and to many young men proved a revelation. "The spell that this book exercised over one was indescribable," was how the liberal philosopher Rudolf Haym put it. "I never read any book with so much pleasure and thoroughness. . . . It was as though scales fell from my eyes and a great light was shed on my path."[62]

Strauss directly questioned the literal truth of the Bible: he regarded the Gospels not as infallible holy scripture but rather as the historically and culturally contingent product of its time. It was preferable, he said, to approach the Gospels as Jewish myths or imaginative representations expressive of a specific stage of human development—and, consequently, not applicable to the current age. In turn, the figure of Christ was best understood as an expression of the idea of "humanity." The effect of *The Life of Jesus* was to open the Bible to a more rigorous process of intellectual and scriptural inquiry, and Engels rushed to be in the vanguard. "I am very busy at present with philosophy and critical theology. When you get to be eighteen years of age and become acquainted with Strauss . . . then you must either read everything without thinking or begin to doubt your Wuppertal faith," he priggishly informed the Graebers. Over the next few months, Engels returned again and again to biblical contradictions, the impact of new geological findings on Christian time lines, and the question of original sin. But, as he recounted in a letter to Frederich Graeber, shedding a lifetime's indoctrination was not an easy or comfortable process:

> I pray daily, indeed nearly the whole day, for truth, I have done so ever since I began to have doubts, but I still cannot return to your faith. . . . My eyes fill with tears as I write this. . . . To be sure, you lie comfortably in your faith as in a warm bed, and you know nothing of the fight we have to put up when we human beings have to decide whether God is God or not. You do not know the weight of the burden one feels with the

first doubt, the burden of the old belief, when one must decide for or against, whether to go on carrying it or shake it off.[63]

By October 1839, the doubts had passed. There was no autumnal "Dover Beach" melancholy for Engels—once the decision was made, he embraced his new spiritual status with relish. "I am now a Straussian," he told Wilhelm Graeber matter-of-factly. "I, a poor, miserable poet, have crept under the wing of the genius David Friedrich Strauss. . . . *Adios* faith! It is as full of holes as a sponge."[64] Engels was, as he later put it, "utterly and wholly lost" from the standpoint of orthodox Christianity. And, true to form, he now supported his newly adopted stance with total conviction, teasing Frederich Graeber as the "great hunter of Straussians."[65]

Behind the banter, Engels seemed relieved that his spiritual journey had come to a conclusion. Having lost one faith, he moved swiftly to assume another: the psychological vacuum left by the demise of his Christian convictions was filled by an equally compelling ideology. For Strauss had proved just a stepping stone: "I am on the point of becoming a Hegelian. Whether I shall become one I don't, of course, know yet, but Strauss has lit up lights on Hegel for me which makes the thing quite plausible to me."[66] The purpose of Strauss's biblical criticisms had never been to show that Christianity was false; rather, he had hoped to show that the doctrine was no longer adequate for the new age of science and learning. Strauss's ambition was to take his readers to the next stage of spiritual development after Christianity, Hegelian philosophy.[67] "Now I'll study Hegel over a glass of punch" was how Engels wisely approached the work of nineteenth-century Europe's most abstruse, arcane, and brilliant philosophers. But it would prove worth the struggle: the writings of Hegel eventually shunted Engels along the path toward socialism. In the coming decades, Marx's reinterpretation of Hegel's dialectics would loom large over communist ideology, but at this stage of Engels's self-tutelage it was Hegel's pure philosophy that was of greatest interest.

At the core of the Hegelian system was an interpretation of history that consisted of the realization or unfolding of "Mind," or "Spirit" (the notoriously untranslatable *Geist*). Spirit, or self-conscious reason, was perpetually in motion and constituted the only true reality in the world; its unfolding was the chronicle of human history. Engels was instantly attracted to the new sense of a rational, ordered development of the past as laid out in Hegel's *Philosophy of History*, a transcription of his lectures at the University of Berlin in 1822–23. "What distinguished Hegel's mode of thinking from that of all other philosophers was the exceptional historical sense underlying it," as he later put it.[68]

Propelling the history of Spirit was the concrete actualization of the Idea of freedom in human affairs, and the achievement of that freedom was Spirit's absolute and final goal. In its essence the passage of history consisted of the organic growth of freedom and reason in civilization in a teleological manner, culminating in the fulfillment of the Spirit. "The history of the world is none other than the progress of the consciousness of freedom," in Hegel's words. At every stage, history was advancing in that direction even when it seemed most wayward and hopeless. For beneath the chaos and anarchy of human affairs the sly cunning of reason remained steadily at work.

Since true freedom could be the product only of reason and rationality—as embodied in language, culture, and the "spirit of a people"—humans could be free only once they had the capacity of judgment. A rational self-consciousness of collective freedom first dawns with the emergence of the Greek city-state, according to Hegel, and soon undergoes an alienating hardening in the oppressive legalism of the Roman Empire. Christianity then joins this story of all-encompassing progress—it, too, fits within the framework of rational development. It is through the faculty of reason, which man shares with God, that man comes to self-consciousness and is reconciled with God. But, as Greece gives way to Rome, Christianity in turn dialectically prepares its own replacement: by proclaiming the reconciliation of finite and infinite, of man and God, "in Christ," the medieval faith lays the foundations of a higher self-consciousness of free community in which personal autonomy will be synthesized with public institutions. This comes about in the modern superseding of religious belief and practice by philosophic knowledge and humane culture: universities and schools, even concert halls and parliaments, are to subsume the work of the Church.

In that sense the latent rationality of Christianity comes to permeate the everyday experience of the modern world—its values are now variously incarnated in the family, civil society, and the state. What Engels particularly embraced in all of this was an idea of modern pantheism (or, rather, pandeism), a merging of divinity with progressing humanity, a happy dialectical synthesis that freed him from the fixed oppositions of the pietist ethos of devout longing and estrangement. "Through Strauss I have now entered on the straight road to Hegelianism. . . . The Hegelian idea of God has already become mine, and thus I am joining the ranks of the 'modern pantheists,'" Engels wrote in one of his final letters to the soon-to-be-discarded Graebers.[69]

After the doubts and confusions of the previous few months, Engels embraced his new Hegelian faith with characteristic enthusiasm. In a classic feuilleton for Gutzkow's *Telegraph* entitled "Landscapes" (1840), Engels compared the refreshing spray and glistening sun enjoyed on a voyage across the North Sea to "the first time the divine Idea of the last of the philosophers [Hegel], this most colossal creation of the thought of the nineteenth century, dawned upon me. I experienced the same blissful thrill, it was like a breath of fresh sea air blowing down upon me from the purest sky." Engels had found temporary solace in a new, animating, naturalistic God. As Gareth Stedman Jones puts it, Hegel offered "a secure resting place to replace the awesome contours of his Wuppertal faith."[70]

Those other elements of Engels's intellectual makeup didn't simply fade away. Alongside the Hegelianism, there was still the passion for German romanticism, the allure of Young Germany's liberal constitutionalism, and the republican impulses of Shelley and July 1830. These strands came together in one of his last Bremen articles. A review of the German dramatist and novelist Karl Immermann's *Memorabilien* provided Engels with the occasion for a cri de coeur that wove together the "new philosophy" with his favorite trope of Siegfried-like heroism: "He who is afraid of the dense wood in which stands the palace of the

Idea, he who does not hack through it with the sword and wake the king's sleeping daughter with a kiss, is not worthy of her and her kingdom; he may go and become a country pastor, merchant, assessor, or whatever he likes, take a wife and beget children in all piety and respectability, but the century will not recognize him as its son."[71]

By early 1841, Engels had concluded that his own recognition as one of the century's sons was far from assured if he remained desk-bound in Bremen. "There is nothing to do but fence, eat, drink, sleep and drudge, *voilà tout*," he wrote to Marie. He returned to Barmen, but his lofty, romantic soul found the parental home and office work in the family firm even more tedious. So in September 1841 he agreed to the Prussian state's demand that he fulfill his military duties and he "volunteered" for one year's service with the Royal Prussian Guards Artillery, Twelfth Company. Berlin, the Prussian capital, would offer this bourgeois son of a provincial textile merchant just the stage he needed in support of the Idea. Here, at last, he could reveal himself as a latter-day Siegfried in the service of the modern age.

2

THE DRAGON'S SEED

"Ask anybody in Berlin today on what field the battle for dominion over German public opinion is being fought," Engels wrote in 1841, "and if he has any idea of the power of the mind over the world he will reply that this battlefield is the University, in particular Lecture-hall No. 6, where Schelling is giving his lectures in the philosophy of revelation."[1] Even for such a bullish philosopher as Friedrich Wilhelm Joseph von Schelling, it must have been a daunting class to teach. It was, said another observer, "an extraordinary audience, . . . select, numerous and diverse." Present in the lecture hall were some of the most gifted minds of the nineteenth century. Earnestly taking notes at the front was the autodidact Engels, happy at this point to describe himself simply as "young and self-taught in philosophy." Alongside him perched Jacob Burckhardt, the nascent art historian and Renaissance scholar; Michael Bakunin, the future anarchist (who dismissed the lectures as "interesting but rather insignificant"); and the philosopher Søren Kierkegaard, who thought Schelling talked "quite insufferable nonsense" and, worse, committed the cardinal academic crime of ending his lectures past the hour: "That isn't tolerated in Berlin, and there was scraping and hissing."[2]

Engels, however, was mesmerized by the gray-haired, blue-eyed Schelling and his relentless critique of Engels's hero, Hegel. In a battle royal, week by week Schelling attempted to unpick Hegel's philosophy by insisting on the direct power of the divine in history. It was revelation versus reason. "Two old friends of younger days, room mates at the Tübingen theological seminary, are after forty years meeting each other again face to face as opponents; one of them ten years dead but more alive than ever in his pupils; the other, as the latter say, intellectually dead for three decades, but now suddenly claiming for himself the full power and authority of life." And Engels had no doubts as to where his sympathies lay: he was in the lecture hall, he said, to "shield the great man's grave from abuse."[3]

Though his official remit in Berlin was military training in support of the Prussian monarchy, Engels spent his time garnering the ideological tools to undermine it. As often as possible, he left behind the parade ground for the university campus to immerse himself in theorems that would prove far more deadly than a six-pounder cannon. And he did so in deeply hostile terrain.

The Berlin that Engels encountered in 1841 was fast turning into a civic monument to the Hohenzollern dynasty. Its residents, numbering some 400,000 by the mid-1840s, had witnessed much over the previous half century: the flight of their king, Friedrich Wilhelm III, and Emperor Napoleon's 1806 victory march through the Brandenburg Gate; liberation by the Russians in 1813 and, with it, a steady churn of reform, romanticism, and then reaction. The last of these had triumphed in the 1820s and 1830s as Friedrich Wilhelm marked the restoration of royal authority with a neoclassical building boom. Under architect Karl Friedrich Schinkel, the modern Berlin of bombastic public spaces and royal grandeur was carved out. His Doric Schauspielhaus (now the Konzerthaus Berlin), his ornately sculptured Schlossbrücke, the imperial Roman Neue Wache guardhouse along Unter den Linden, and, his masterpiece, the Pantheon-inspired Altes Museum, all expressed the newly resurgent Berlin of the court, the army, and the aristocracy of the East Prussian plains. In later years, Engels remembered how utterly ghastly it all was, "with its scarcely formed bourgeoisie, its loud-mouthed petit-bourgeoisie, so unenterprising and fawning, its still completely unorganized workers, its masses of bureaucrats and hangers-on of nobility and court, its whole character as mere 'residence.'"[4]

But, as would so often be the case with this endlessly divided city, there was another Berlin. Close by the parade grounds of his Kupfergraben barracks lay a bustling public sphere of cafés, alehouses, and wine cellars.[5] By the mid-1830s, Berlin boasted over one hundred cafés in the city center alone, providing official and unofficial newspapers, debating forums, and drinking dens. A thriving *Konditorei* culture of political and literary discourse sprang up around the Gendarmenmarkt district, with each café attracting its own clientele: the Kranzler, on the corner of Friedrichstrasse and the Linden, was known as the "Walhalla of Berlin Guard lieutenants" for its officer regulars and swanky interior; the Courtin, near the bourse, catered to the bankers and businessmen; and Stehely's, across the road from Schinkel's Schauspielhaus, was home to artists, actors, and the "literary elements."[6]

The nearby Friedrich-Wilhelms-Universität—renamed in 1949 the Humboldt-Universität after its founder, Wilhelm von Humboldt—also provided much of the café crowd. Charged by Friedrich Wilhelm III during the more liberal period of his reign in the early 1800s with crafting an educational system for an enlightened citizenry, Humboldt and education minister Baron von Altenstein brought together in Berlin an extraordinary constellation of talents. Engels's onetime favorite theologian, Friedrich Schleiermacher, was appointed a professor, the reactionary Karl von Savigny taught law, Georg Niebuhr lectured in history, while in 1818 Hegel succeeded Fichte as chair of philosophy. With Hegel on the faculty, the university naturally became a leading center of Hegelian thought—so much so that the poet Heinrich Heine, a regular at Stehely's, expressed his relief in 1823 at leaving a city of "thick sand and thin tea" inhabited by a population of know-it-alls "who have long comprehended everything under the sun . . . through Hegelian logic."[7]

Not everyone regarded this profusion of Hegelian logic with such weary detachment—especially not the new king, Friedrich Wilhelm IV (who had succeeded his father in 1840), and his chief minister, Johann Albert Friedrich Eichhorn. After a brief flirtation with a free press and liberal reform, the Hohenzollern distrust of political pluralism reasserted itself. Friedrich Wilhelm "commenced with a show of liberality," Engels recounted, "then passed over to feudalism; and ended in establishing the government of the police-spy."[8] And so in 1841, as part of a broader clampdown on left-wing thinking, the minister recalled the graying sixty-six-year-old Schelling to Berlin "to root out the dragon-seed of Hegelianism" in the very university where it had first been sown. This was the philosophical tussle Engels was so enjoying from his ringside seat in lecture hall No. 6.

Why was Hegelianism so feared by the Prussian authorities? It certainly hadn't unnerved von Humboldt and Friedrich Wilhelm III, who had consistently appointed known Hegelians to influential professorships and state posts. "The Hegelian system," Engels later remarked of this period, "was even raised, as it were, to the rank of a royal Prussian philosophy of State" while "Hegelian views, consciously or unconsciously, most extensively penetrated the most diversified sciences and leavened even popular literature and the daily press." But that official endorsement was now set to be withdrawn.[9]

The answer to this divergence lies in two, often contradictory readings of Hegel. The first is conservative. If history is the process that oversees the triumphant march of reason toward freedom, then each consecutive era is necessarily more progressive, more rational, and freer than the preceding one and every component of that era—its art, music, religion, literature, forms of governance—represents a higher stage of reason than the last. This is most especially the case when it comes to the state, which Hegel took to mean an organic body encompassing elements of both government and civil society.

For Hegel, the state was the means by which the individual will was reconciled with the grander imperatives of universal reason, through obedience to the law: "In duty the individual finds his liberation . . . from mere natural impulse. . . . In duty the individual acquires his substantive freedom."[10] True freedom came when man's subjective sensibilities were aligned with the progressive development of Spirit, as it manifests itself through the medium of the state. In the Hegelian template, the modern state represented "the realization of freedom, an end in itself, 'the divine idea as it exists on earth' and the reality which alone gives value to the individual life."[11] In theory, the modern state embodied progress, reason, and the Idea of freedom. Each individual had to submit to it to gain the elixir of self-knowing freedom.

There seemed a brief moment, in the aftermath of the 1806 Jena defeat, when the Prussian state signified that Hegelian ideal of rational freedom as set out in *The Philosophy of Right*. For this was the era of liberal reform that had been forced upon Friedrich Wilhelm III by his military humiliation in 1806 and then implemented by his progressive-minded ministers Baron Karl vom Stein and Prince Karl August von Hardenberg. Hereditary service was abolished, Jews were emancipated, economic controls freed up, and gentle moves made in the direction of democratic representation. As part of this liberalization project, Hegel was brought from the University of Heidelberg to the newly founded Berlin University (where he held the chair of philosophy until his death in 1831) to give the movement his intellectual imprimatur. "Hegel in turn hailed the reformed Prussian state as an example of a state that had attained world-historical stature by making the political actualization of Reason its inner purpose and essence," according to Hegel biographer John Edward Toews.[12] And there is no doubt that Hegel's philosophical elevation of the state granted a rich spiritual dignity to the bureaucratic apparatus of Friedrich Wilhelm III.

His advocacy of the state as a living entity, possessing in its laws and political structures a defined purpose based upon reason and freedom dramatically elevated its purpose. The state was not just a necessary evil to protect private property, defend the realm, and manage the rule of law. Instead, it now had a far loftier purpose, representing as it did the realization of absolute reason. And while the finer phenomenology of Hegelian philosophy might have been lost on some of the Berlin court, its members quickly realized the political opportunities this reverence for authority presented. "Hegel's writings provided an exalted legitimation for the Prussian bureaucracy, whose expanding power within the executive during the reform era demanded justification," according to the historian Christopher Clark. "The state was no longer just the site of sovereignty and power, it was the engine that makes history, or even the embodiment of history itself."[13] No wonder Friedrich Wilhelm and vom Stein were happy to pack the university lecture halls with orthodox, or "right," Hegelians.

Hegel's radical protégés, meanwhile, offered a more progressive interpretation of their master's work. Facing the actual Prussian state—with its growing authoritarianism, religious restrictions, and diminishing possibility of constitutional reform—many of Hegel's disciples could not accept that their mentor (who had once planted a liberty tree in honor of the French Revolution) really believed this state of affairs to constitute the pinnacle of reason. Indeed, history seemed to be moving in a decidedly unprogressive direction when in 1840, as Engels put it, "orthodox sanctimony and absolutist feudal reaction ascended the throne" with the succession of Friedrich Wilhelm IV.[14] If not quite a subscriber to the divine right of kings, Friedrich Wilhelm IV certainly held an exalted idea of Christian monarchy, with the sovereign linked to the people by a mystical, sacred bond that no parliament or constitution could sully. Friedrich Wilhelm IV's watch was to be no epoch of progress—instead, a sturdy commitment to tradition, continuity, and hierarchy. And it was increasingly apparent that the new left Hegelianism being discussed on the Prussian campuses was at odds with such conservative dogma.

When it came to Hegel, the danger was in the dialectic. "Whoever placed the emphasis on the *Hegelian system* could be fairly conservative in both spheres; whoever regarded the *dialectical method* as the main thing could belong to the most extreme opposition, both in religion and politics," was how Engels later described the difference. "Dialectical progression" was how the march of history happened: each age and its ruling idea were negated and subsumed by the following epoch. "Position, opposition, composition," as a young Karl Marx explained. "Or to speak Greek we have the thesis, antithesis and synthesis. For those who do not know the Hegelian language, we shall give the ritual formula: affirmation, negation, negation of the negation."[15] Thus, the realization of Spirit in history involved a perpetual critique of every established political system and its prevailing form of consciousness—each successively undermined by this tension within itself—until rationality and freedom prevailed. "Therein lay the true significance and the revolutionary character of Hegelian philosophy," as Engels put it. "All successive historical states are only transitory stages in the endless course of development of human society from the lower to the higher. . . . Against it [the dialectic] nothing is final, absolute, sacred."[16]

This interpretation offered an extraordinarily powerful ideological solvent. For Hegel's more radical readership, there now existed no immutable, eternal truths: every civilization had its own realities, philosophies, and religion, all liable to be negated and subsumed. What was more, this was as true for Hegel's own thinking as for any previous philosophy. The publicly funded Berlin professor had made the crucial mistake of thinking that the reformist-era Prussian state—of Stein, Hardenberg, and Humboldt—might have been the culmination of reason in history. But, in fact, it was just another transitory stage now set to be negated. For those skeptical students sitting through Schelling's lectures, Hegel's philosophical method provided not a justification of the Prussian status quo but tools for a progressive critique of the Hohenzollern state. To these "left," or "young," Hegelians, Hegel's philosophy became a spur to action, his writings an empowering demand for liberal reform.

As was often the case with early socialism, it was religion that generated the sharpest attacks. Just as Hegel had regarded the Prussian state as the final fulfillment of reason, so his Lutheran faith had led him to endorse a narrow conception of Protestant Christianity dominant in the 1820s as the summum bonum of spiritual life. Once again it appeared that history had conveniently managed to culminate precisely in the cultural and religious practices of Hegel's own era. And, so with religion just as with politics, the Young Hegelians criticized Hegel for not appreciating his own historicism, for not understanding that what he considered the realization of freedom was simply another step toward the Idea. How, they asked, was modern European Christianity different from Roman paganism or the Hindu faith of ancient India? Was not each simply a product of its times? In an anonymous critique of Schelling's lectures published in Leipzig in 1842 under the title "Schelling and Revelation," Engels announced that the Young Hegelians would "no longer regard Christianity" as off-limits for critical investigation. "All the basic principles of Christianity, and even of what has hitherto been called religion itself, have fallen before the inexorable criticism of reason."[17]

The groundwork for this religious critique had been laid by David Strauss's reinterpretation of the Gospels as myth. Bruno Bauer, a theologian and philosopher who had studied under Hegel, took the critique a stage further with a detailed analysis of Christianity as a cultural construct. Known as "a very decided man who, under a cold exterior, burns with an inner fire," Bauer thought the dialectic could progress only through a process of violent intellectual assault. Each age's verities needed to be ripped down in the face of reason. And such a process of rational assault led Bauer to conclude that in the modern era Christianity was an obstacle to the development of self-conscious freedom. The worship of an exterior God, the submission to creed and dogma, alienated man from his true essence. There could be no chance of human self-consciousness or realization of freedom as long as the ritual demands of mystical subservience remained in place. Summoning the dialectic, Bauer declared that such alienation was hindering the onward march of history and had to be transcended.

Behind this lofty metaphysics lurked a direct political challenge to the Christian principles that legitimized the Hohenzollern monarchy and its right to govern. Once regarded as the very bulwark of the state, Hegelian philosophy was now being deployed to undermine Prussia's religio-political foundations. Unsurprisingly, Friedrich Wilhelm IV was appalled and, in March 1842, he had the subversive Bruno Bauer dismissed from his post at the University of Bonn. But it would take more than that to temper the Young Hegelian advance. The next salvo was launched by Ludwig Feuerbach's *Essence of Christianity* (1841), which finally expunged the last conservative remnants of Hegelianism. As Engels recalled, "With one blow it pulverized the contradiction, by plainly placing materialism on the throne again. . . . Nothing exists outside nature and man, and the higher beings our religious fantasies have created are only the fantastic reflection of our own essence. The spell was broken; the 'system' was exploded. . . . One must have experienced the liberating effect of this book for oneself to get an idea of it. Enthusiasm was universal: we were all Feuerbachians for a moment."[18]

Feuerbach, too, was a former pupil of Hegel's and just as keen as Bauer to apply the dialectical method to Christianity. Expanding upon Bauer's notion of alienation, he argued that the advance of religion must be understood as the progressive separation of man from his human, sensuous self. In the Christian Godhead man had created a deity in his own image and likeness. Yet so replete with perfection was this objectified God that man started to abase himself before its spiritual authority. Consequently, the original power relationship was reversed: "Man—this is the secret of religion—projects his essence into objectivity and then makes himself an object of this projected image of himself that is thus converted into a subject." And the more fervently man worshiped this exterior God, the more internally impoverished he became. It was a zero-sum relationship: for the Deity to prosper, man had to be degraded. "Religion by its very essence drains man and nature of substance, and transfers this substance to the phantom of an other-worldly God, who in turn then graciously permits man and nature to receive some of his superfluity," as Engels put it. "Lacking awareness and at the same time faith, man can have no substance, he is bound to despair of truth, reason and nature." In his 1844 *Contribution to the Critique of Hegel's Philosophy of Right*, Karl Marx would put it more succinctly: "Religion is the sigh of the oppressed creature, the heart of a heartless world, and the soul of soulless conditions. It is the opium of the people."[19]

True to the critical ethos of the Young Hegelians, Feuerbach then turned his fire on his former tutor, Hegel himself. What, Feuerbach wanted to know, was the substantive difference between the theology of Christianity and the philosophy (or "rational mysticism") of Hegel? Were they not both metaphysical belief systems involving self-alienation—in order to elevate God in one case and the even more intangible *Geist* in the other? "Speculative theology [i.e., Hegelianism] distinguishes itself from ordinary theology by the fact that it transfers the divine essence into this world. That is, speculative theology envisions, determines, and realizes in this world the divine essence transported by ordinary theology out of fear and ignorance into another world."[20] Philosophy was nothing more than religion brought into the realm of thought.

In terms of separating man from the realities of his existence, Feuerbach suggested, there was little to choose between Hegelian philosophy and the Christian religion. Feuerbach advocated an end to both. In place of God or the Idea, he wanted Man: anthropology not theology. "Whoever fails to give up the Hegelian philosophy, fails to give up theology. The Hegelian doctrine, that nature or reality is *posited* by the Idea, is merely the *rational* expression of the theological doctrine that nature is created by God."[21] And both needed to be shed for man to regain his true essence, his "species-being." The idealistic Hegel had made the mistake of deriving being from thought rather than thought from being and, as such, had turned reality on its head. What Feuerbach urged was not idealism but materialism: in place of the metaphysical theorizing of Hegel and the ethereal march of Spirit, a concentration on the lived reality of Man's natural, corporeal, "immediate" existence.

This was heady stuff for a young artillery officer supposed to be learning his way around a smooth-bore six-pounder and seven-pound howitzer. Yet the allure of parade ground drilling and projectile arithmetic had quickly paled for Engels. Allowed as a volunteer with a generous private income to live in private lodgings rather than barracks, he spent his days in lecture halls, reading rooms, as well as the beer cellars of demimonde Berlin. There was only one element of military life he truly relished. "My uniform, incidentally, is very fine," he wrote to his sister Marie soon after his arrival in Berlin. "Blue with a black collar adorned with two broad yellow stripes, and black, yellow-striped facings together with red piping round the coat tails. Furthermore, the red shoulder-straps are edged with white. I assure you the effect is most impressive and I'm worthy to be put on show." Engels liked nothing more than wowing polite society with his glittering attire. "Because of this the other day I shamefully embarrassed Ruckert, the poet, who is here at present. I sat down right in front of him as he was giving a poetry reading and the poor fellow was so dazzled by my shining buttons that he quite lost the thread of what he was saying. . . . I shall soon be promoted to bombardier, which is a sort of non-commissioned officer, and I shall get gold braid to wear on my facings."[22]

He also acquired a dog, a handsome spaniel playfully named Namenloser, or Nameless, which he took to his favorite Rhineland restaurant to fill up on pork and sauerkraut. "He had a great talent for boozing and if I go to a restaurant in the evening, he always sits near me and has his share, or makes himself at home at everybody else's table." Too skittish to be trained properly, the dog had managed to learn only one trick. "When I say 'Namenloser, . . . there's an aristocrat!' he goes wild with rage and growls hideously at the person I show him." In 1840s Berlin this could have been a rather regular occurrence.[23]

In addition to evening excursions with his growling spaniel, Engels would pass his time thrashing out matters philosophical with the Young Hegelians over a glass of the capital's industrial-strength white beer. "We would meet at Steheley's and, in the evenings, at this or that Bavarian ale-house in Friedrichsstadt or, if we were in funds, at a wineshop in the Postrasse."[24] At various times the inner circle included Bruno Bauer and his brother Edgar, the philosopher of "ego" Max Stirner, the historian and Buddhist scholar Karl Köppen, political science lecturer Karl Nauwerck, journalist Eduard Meyen, renegade University of Halle lecturer Arnold Ruge, and others. Their iconoclastic ethos extended seamlessly from the philosophical realm to their public personae. Known as "Die Freien"—or "beer literati," as Bauer termed them—this band of aggressive, arrogant intellectuals ostentatiously discarded modern morality, religion, and bourgeois propriety.[25] In his memoirs, the protocommunist and apprentice typesetter Stephan Born recalled the world of "Bruno Bauer, Max Stirner and the circle of noisy characters that surrounded them, who had called attention to themselves through their open dealings with emancipated women." Edgar Bauer's penchant for pornography was especially disturbing to the straitlaced young Born. "Already just upon entering his room, I was shocked by the obscene lithographs he had hung on the wall; and the conversation he began with me as he read the proofs [of his novella] was no less repulsive in character."[26]

Engels, always liberal-minded in matters of sex and morality, embraced the lifestyle of "The Free" with alacrity. If his father had hoped that Engels might shed his youthful radicalism in Berlin's rigid court society, he could not have been more disappointed. Instead, Engels now dropped the prevaricating idealism of Young Germany (just as he had earlier discarded the religiosity of the Graeber brothers) and gave his heart and head to Bauer, Stirner, Köppen, and the rest.[27] The attraction of the circle was no doubt enhanced by the terrible shock such counter-culture camaraderie would have given his respectable parents. So enamored was Engels of his new band of friends that he sketched a picture of The Free at one of their debauched drinking sessions. There are fallen chairs, half-empty wine bottles, an enraged Edgar Bauer smashing a table, a cool Max Stirner smoking, a grumpy (or sozzled) Köppen sitting at the table, and a pugnacious Bruno Bauer marching toward Arnold Ruge with his fists raised. Floating in the sky above the tussle are a squirrel, symbolizing the Prussian minister Eichhorn (in a play on the German *Eichhörnchen* for "squirrel"), and a guillotine, which is either an acknowledgment of Bruno Bauer as the "Robespierre of theology" or a signature reference to Engels himself.

The Insolently Threatened Yet Miraculously Rescued Bible; or, The Triumph of Faith was a mock-epic poem Engels coauthored with Edgar Bauer. Written in protest at Bruno Bauer's dismissal from Bonn, it took the form of a *Paradise Lost*–style meditation on the struggle between Satan and God for the souls of the Young Hegelians (who are all destined for hell). A heavy-handed mix of theology and philosophy, it reads now as little more than a cleverly done student skit. Still, the description of Bruno Bauer has about it something of the catchiness of Gilbert and Sullivan's "I Am the Very Model of a Modern Major-General."[28]

> I've studied matters Phenomenological,
> Theological also, to my distress,

Aesthetical too, Metaphysical, Logical,
Not entirely without success.

Similarly, Hegel's cameo appearance is wittily done:

To Science I've devoted every hour,
And I've taught Atheism with all my power.
Self-consciousness upon the Throne I seated,
And thought that God had thereby been defeated.

Behind the farce, some more revealing elements are discernable—not least, Engels's depiction of himself. "Friedrich Oswald," the aspirant Siegfried and author of high-flown feuilletons, had metamorphosed amid the Berlin beer cellars into an altogether more fiery figure, nothing less than a French revolutionary readying his guillotine:

Right on the very left, that tall and long-legged stepper
Is Oswald, coat of grey and trousers shade of pepper;
Pepper inside as well, Oswald the Montagnard;
A radical is he, dyed in the wool, and hard.
Day in, day out, he plays upon the guillotine a
Single solitary tune and that's a cavatina,
The same old devil-song; he bellows the refrain:
Formez vos bataillons! Aux armes, citoyens!

Close behind him appears a figure whom, in the coming years, Oswald—and Engels—were to come to know rather well:

Who runs up next with wild impetuosity?
A swarthy chap of Trier, a marked monstrosity.
He neither hops nor skips, but moves in leaps and bounds,
Raving aloud. As if to seize and then pull down
To Earth the spacious tent of Heaven up on high,
He opens wide his arms and reaches for the sky.

He shakes his wicked fist, raves with a frantic air,
As if ten thousand devils had him by the hair.[29]

What is there left to say of Karl Marx, the "swarthy chap of Trier"? "He is a phenomenon who made a most deep impression," was how Moses Hess described him. "Be prepared to meet the greatest, perhaps the only real philosopher living now. When he will appear in public he will draw the eyes of all Germany upon him. . . . He combines deepest philosophical seriousness with cutting wit. Can you imagine Rousseau, Voltaire, Holbach, Lessing, Heine and Hegel combined—not thrown together— in one person? If you can, you have Dr. Marx." Gustav Mevissen, a Cologne businessman, depicted an equally mesmerizing figure: "a powerful man of 24 whose thick black hair sprung from his cheeks, arms, nose and ears. He was domineering, impetuous, passionate, full of boundless self-confidence, but at the same time deeply earnest and learned, a restless dialectician who with his restless Jewish penetration pushed every proposition of Young Hegelian doctrine to its final conclusion."[30]

Marx was born two years before Engels, into a similarly bourgeois household along the banks of another tributary of the Rhine (the Mosel rather than the Wupper), but the atmosphere in his family was significantly different from the tight Pietism of the Engelses. In this southwestern region of the Rhineland, the post-1806 Napoleonic occupation had fostered a notably more liberal outlook among the middling sort. Marx's father, Heinrich, an attorney and small-scale vineyard owner, was imbued with the ideals of the French Enlightenment and precisely the kind of Rhineland liberalism that Ludwig Börne and others of the Young Germany school had sought to disseminate. He knew his Voltaire and Rousseau by heart, his heroes were Newton and Leibnitz, and he was active in Trier's Casino Club, where like-minded progressives spent their evenings mulling over the political and cultural controversies of the day.

However, Heinrich was really Hirschel (or Heschel), having changed his name, abjured his Jewish faith, and been baptized into the Lutheran Church in 1817. The Prussian annexation of the Rhineland from the French in 1815 had deprived the Jews of Trier of their Napoleonic freedoms, subjecting them to a range of sanctions that forbade them to hold public office or practice law. Rather than become "breadless," Heinrich converted. In doing so, he abandoned a rabbinical lineage that stretched back to the early 1700s and included several rabbis of Trier. Heinrich—the Enlightenment acolyte of Newton and father of nine hungry children—did not seem overly upset about jettisoning his Judaic ancestry. His wife, Henriette, found the rupture more difficult: she spoke Yiddish and kept certain Jewish customs alive in the household long after she and the children had been baptized.

Despite Heinrich's politic conversion, his broad outlook could not have been more different from the evangelical conservatism of Friedrich Engels senior. He was also a more obviously affectionate father. His lengthy letters to the adolescent Karl are heartfelt, indulgent, and full of earnest paternal trepidation. His often febrile, anxious tone was aggravated by Henriette, who turned a myopic love of family into a habit of congenital worrying. Nonetheless, Marx's childhood, like Engels's, was all in all a happy one, spent making mud pies with his sisters and getting into scrapes at school. But by the time Karl entered the University of Bonn at the age of seventeen, he had begun to distance himself from his family. Indeed, Marx's subsequent, steely separation from his parents and siblings was far more systematic than Engels's tortured efforts at detachment.

Instead, he directed his emotional energies toward another family altogether, the von Westphalens. Baron Ludwig von Westphalen was a Protestant in a predominantly Catholic Trier, a liberal-minded career civil servant within the Prussian government. Despite his aristocratic ancestry he became friends with the bourgeois Heinrich Marx and enjoyed taking Marx's gifted son Karl on long country hikes during which he would recite great chunks of Shakespeare and Homer. Karl however was more interested in Ludwig's daughter, the beautiful Jenny von Westphalen. And to everyone's surprise, Jenny—the sophisticated daughter of a Prussian aristocrat and "the most beautiful girl in Trier"—fell in love with the lively wit and dashing bravado of the hairy Jewish boy. In 1836, she broke with her officer fiancé and promised herself to the man she would come to call her "wild black boar," her "wicked knave"—and, the tag that finally stuck, her "Moor" (or "Mohr"), with its implications of levantine mystery and hirsute oriental otherness. While Marx's own family expressed horror at his increasingly reckless activities, Jenny only reveled in his troublemaking, student radicalism, and fiendish impetuosity. They married in 1843. "Their love survived all the trials of a life of constant struggle," in the words of Stephan Born. "I have rarely known such a happy marriage, in which happiness and sorrow (mostly the latter) were shared and all pain was overcome in the assurance of complete, reciprocal belonging."[31]

The young Marx was certainly wild. He was indulged and scolded in equal measure by his parents, and when he was given the freedom of campus life in 1835 the results were predictably transgressive. At Bonn, he skipped Law Faculty lectures to assume the presidency of the Trier Tavern Club, which involved raucous drinking sessions, nights in police cells, and even a duel with a Prussian officer that he was lucky to escape with only a cut above the left eye. "Is duelling then so closely interwoven with philosophy?" vainly inquired Heinrich. "Do not let this inclination, and if not inclination, this craze, take root. You could in the end deprive yourself and your parents of the finest hopes that life offers."

Engels's swordmanship was far more reliable—as was his constitution. While Engels was rarely under the weather, Marx seemed constantly at the very edge of his intellectual and physical capacities. "Nine lecture courses seem to me rather a lot and I would not like you to do more than your body and mind can bear," Heinrich warned him as he started university. "A sickly scholar is the most unfortunate being on earth. Therefore, do not study more than your health can bear." Marx took no notice as he embarked on his lifelong habit of smoking, reading, and working long into the night. Combining this workload with prodigious drinking bouts proved nearly lethal. After one "almighty binge" many years later, the oxlike Engels emerged punctually for work the next morning clearheaded while Marx was knocked out for two weeks.

After a wasted year at Bonn, Marx departed for Berlin to complete his legal studies. Heinrich dispatched him with a warning of the intellectual perils awaiting him in the heartland of Hegelianism, where "the new immoralists twist their words until they themselves do not hear them." Naturally discarding such advice, Marx abandoned his legal training for philosophy just as swiftly as Engels would flee the parade ground for the lecture hall. His conversion to Hegelianism was not long in coming. Like any good member of Die Freien, he celebrated it in the beer cellars of Französische Strasse with the Young Hegelian circle. Together with Arnold Ruge and Bruno Bauer, he formed the heavy-drinking, heavy-philosophizing Doktorklub, based in Hippel's *Weinstube*.

At home in Trier, Heinrich was mortified. "Alas, your conduct has consisted merely in disorder, meandering in all the fields of knowledge, musty traditions by sombre lamplight; degeneration in a learned dressing gown with uncombed hair has replaced degeneration with a beer glass," he wrote to his son. "Your intercourse with the world is limited to your sordid room, where perhaps lie abandoned in the classical disorder the love letters of a Jenny and the tear-stained counsels of your father." But the fire had been lit and Marx now had even less time for the petty concerns of his parents—despite continuing to extract money from them as he scaled the philosophical uplands of Hegelianism. Despairing to his final days at the way his son's life was unfolding, Heinrich died of tuberculosis in 1838. Karl Marx failed to attend the funeral—and then, with characteristically lachrymose self-indulgence, spent the rest of life carrying a portrait of Heinrich with him.

Freed from his father, Karl abandoned his law degree the following year and began a Ph.D. on what appeared a dry-as-dust topic—"The Difference between the Democritean and Epicurean Philosophy"—but was, in fact, a comparative critique of contemporary German philosophy in the aftermath of Hegel in light of a similarly transformative period in Greek thought. Its conclusion embraced the Young Hegelian project of philosophical critique in the name of ever-widening human self-consciousness. Under the beady eyes of Eichhorn, Schelling, and the "Right Hegelian" university administration, the thesis had little chance of passing in Berlin. Thankfully, the University of Jena was altogether more pliable and in 1841 Karl Marx emerged with a doctorate dedicated to Baron von Westphalen.

The question then was what to do next. Family funds were running low after his father's death, while plans for academic work with Bruno

Bauer at the University of Bonn were quashed by Bauer's dismissal in 1842. The solution was journalism. Marx started channeling his philosophical analysis into more concrete political directions with a series of articles on censorship (which were instantly censored), property rights, economic distress, and the Prussian administration. Slowly, Marx was turning his revolutionary intellect from philosophical reflection to social realities. He wrote initially for Arnold Ruge's *Deutsche Jahrbücher*, then joined the Cologne-based *Rheinische Zeitung*. By October 1842, his energy, political skills, and obvious writing talent had secured him the editor's chair.

Under his stewardship, the paper's circulation doubled, and it gained a national reputation for provocative, close-to-the-wind reporting. "It was immediately clear that he had the qualities which are essential in all great journalists: a determination to speak truth to power, and absolute fearlessness even when writing about people whose friendship or support he might need."[32] There is much in this assessment by Francis Wheen of Marx's editorial courage. Which is not to say that Marx did not suffer from the common usual journalistic weakness of keeping the proprietors happy. And in this case the funders of the *Rheinische Zeitung*—as it said on the masthead, "For Politics, Commerce, and Industry"— were a Cologne-based mercantile elite committed to protecting the liberal advances of the Napoleonic years from Prussian absolutism. For commercial if not necessarily political reasons, they wanted to retain religious toleration, freedom of speech, and constitutional liberty and to work toward national German unification. Marx was happy to do their bidding even if it meant ditching some old friends.

To these staid Rhineland liberals, the notorious Berlin antics of Die Freien—the atheism, loose lifestyles, political extremism, and drunken rows—risked torpedoing their gently reformist agenda. Realizing his association with them was jeopardizing his career prospects, the former president of the Trier Tavern Club and drunken stalwart of the Doctors' Club now sternly informed his readers, "Rowdiness and blackguardism must be loudly and resolutely repudiated in a period which demands serious, manly and sober-minded persons for the achievement of its lofty aims." He was even blunter in a letter to Ruge complaining how irresponsible Young Hegelian contributors were raising the censor's hackles and the threat of closure. "[Eduard] Meyen & Co. sent us heaps of scrawls pregnant with world revolutions and empty of thought, written in a slovenly style and flavoured with some atheism and communism (which these gentlemen have never studied). . . . I declared that I considered the smuggling of communist and socialist ideas into casual theatre reviews was unsuitable, indeed, immoral, and a very different and more fundamental treatment of communism was required if it was going to be discussed at all."

Given this bad blood, it was little surprise that one of the most influential friendships in Western political thought got off to a thoroughly unpromising start. When, as Engels recounted, he dropped into the *Rheinische Zeitung* offices in November 1842, "I ran into Marx there and that was the occasion of our first, distinctly chilly meeting. Marx had taken a stand against the Bauers, i.e. he had said he was opposed not only to the *Rheinische Zeitung* becoming predominantly a vehicle for theological propaganda, atheism, etc., rather than for political discussion and action, but also to Edgar Bauer's hot air brand of communism. . . . Since I corresponded with the Bauers, I was regarded as their ally, whereas they caused me to view Marx with suspicion."[33] There was also, perhaps, not a little jealousy on Marx's part. He was notoriously touchy about any hint of ideological competition and by the early 1840s the young Engels had gained a name for himself. Despite the cloak of anonymity, his "Letters from Wuppertal," his pamphlet on "Schelling and Revelation," and much of his journalism for the *Telegraph für Deutschland* and then the *Rheinische Zeitung* had marked him out as an up-and-coming man in radical print. Trying hard to establish his own journalistic presence, Marx was not overly inclined to welcome the young Berlin officer.

In any case, Engels was about to leave Berlin. He had finished his military service in October 1842, receiving the standard approbation for his one year's volunteering and an acknowledgment that he "conducted himself very well during his period of service in respect both of morals and service."[34] Engels senior, though, was not convinced by such official commendation, and in a letter to his brother-in-law Karl Snethlage expressed grave concern about his radical heir's homecoming. "I have known since childhood his tendency to extremes and was convinced, although he never wrote to me about his views since he was in Bremen, that he would not keep to those ordinarily held." But he and Elise were not willing to compromise their own beliefs. "I shall make clear to him that merely for his sake or because of his presence I shall neither change nor conceal my views, either in respect of religion or politics; we shall continue entirely our former way of living and read the word of God and other Christian books in his presence." The anxious, pious father could only be patient: "His conversion must come from above. . . . Until then it is hard to bear having a son in the house who is like a black sheep in the flock and adopts a hostile attitude to the faith of his fathers." There was one possible solution: "I hope to be able to give him a fair amount of work, and wherever he may be I shall watch over him unnoticed with the greatest care so that he does not take any dangerous step."[35] The plan was to send Engels away to Manchester to look after the Ermen & Engels investment in Salford, where he would learn something of the "English commercial method" before returning to assist in the Engelskirchen factory. Surely the thunderous mills and dour merchants' parlors of "Cottonopolis" would prevent any further radicalization. It was another forlorn hope. On his way to Manchester, Engels encountered communism.

The historian Eric Hobsbawm has written of how late Marx and Engels arrived at communism; they were equally slow when it came to socialism.[36] In the 1830s and early 1840s, even though the terms were often used interchangeably, socialism and communism constituted relatively distinct philosophical traditions, each with its own intellectual and political lineage and both having flourished long before the arrival of our two Prussian protagonists.[37] The origins of socialism are particularly slippery and, in variant forms, can be traced back to any number of sources: to Plato's *Republic*, to the spiritual equality proclaimed by the Old Testament prophet Micah, the brotherly love preached by Jesus of Nazareth, the utopianism of Sir Thomas More and Tommaso Campanella, or to the radical leveling of the Putney Debates.[38] But in its modern form socialism emerges out of the religious and ideological ferment of the French Revolution. In the 1790s and early 1800s, the search for a new *pouvoir spirituelle* after the fall of the Roman Catholic Church and extensive de-Christianization across France led to the development of a number of identifiably socialist sects.

One of the first was founded by Count Claude Henri de Rouvroy de Saint-Simon, the aristocratic French war hero turned revolutionary partisan turned property speculator turned scourge of the idle rich. A descendant of the court chronicler of Louis XIV's Versailles, Saint-Simon believed that society was entering a new, critical phase of science and industry that required new forms of governance and worship. He called for a "science of mankind" that would understand societies as "bodies organised . . . like physiological phenomena."[39] This rational approach to the management of human affairs would avoid precisely the kind of anarchy France had experienced during the 1790s, but for it to succeed power had to be transferred from the hapless, nepotistic elites of the ancien régime to a hierarchy of industrialists, scientists, engineers, and artists. They alone would be able to plan a society "in which all individuals will be classed according to their capacities and remunerated according to their work." Politics would become an exact discipline, changing "from the conjectured to the positive, from metaphysics to physics."[40] The political act of "governing" would give way to the objective process of "administering" society so every individual could realize his potential. As Saint-Simon put it, in a phrase that Marx would later so successfully adapt, "From each according to his abilities, from each ability according to his work."

At the core of Saint-Simon's ideal society was an ethic of industry. Saint-Simon's heroes were the "industrial class" (*les industriels*), producers, not parasites. His enemies were the traditional rulers of France—the aristocracy, clergy, government officials (*les oisifs*, he called them)—as well as the "idlers," or "consumers," of the new bourgeoisie, who inherited wealth or leeched off the workers. In the coming scientific era, man would stop exploiting man and would instead unite to exploit nature. Existing patterns of private property, inheritance, and competition would be abolished as society collectively, harmoniously put its shoulder to the wheel. "All men will work; they will regard themselves as laborers attached to one workshop whose efforts will be directed to guide human intelligence according to my divine foresight. The Supreme Council of Newton will direct their works."[41]

And what was this Supreme Council of Newton? Saint-Simon conceived it as the governing body of the new society, a gathering of savants—"men of genius"—who would act as "torches illuminating mankind." This elite technocracy would preside over a *chambre d'invention* (manned by two hundred engineers and a hundred artists), a *chambre d'examination* (a hundred biologists, a hundred physicists, a hundred chemists) and a *chambre d'exécution* (the leading industrialists and entrepreneurs of the day). Just as Isaac Newton had reordered the universe around the principle of gravitational attraction, so the Supreme Council, chaired by a mathematician, would ensure society's smooth running along equally applicable universal laws.

In *The New Christianity* (1825), Saint-Simon took these ideas further to urge a secular religion of humanity. From the efficient governance of society would spring a new spirit of human harmony based on return to the fundamental "principle of Christian morality": brotherly love. From this followed the mission to "improve the moral and physical existence of the poorest class," a goal that could never be achieved under the iniquitous, wasteful, and inhuman system of competition that underpinned modern capitalism.[42] It was this promise of moral regeneration and spiritual growth through collective action that inspired the Saint-Simonian sects and their popular gospel of fraternity. If only mankind united together, Saint-Simon was convinced its productive energies could be channeled to create a New Harmony here on earth.

Saint-Simon's vision of a postcapitalist, post-Christian utopia was shared by the other leading French socialist of the early nineteenth century, Charles Fourier. One of the more likeable characters within the progressive pantheon, he was born in 1772 to a prosperous cloth merchant and spent his life as a silk broker and commercial salesman in southern France, notably in the silk-weaving districts of Lyon. "I am a child of the marketplace," he explained, "born and brought up in mercantile establishments. I have witnessed the infamies of commerce with my own eyes."[43] Fourier's socialism, however, was not simply the product of experience. Describing himself as a new Columbus, he claimed after a year spent studying natural sciences at the Bibliothèque Nationale to have discovered the true science of mankind, which would, at a stroke, end the misery, exploitation, and unhappiness of modern civilization. He recounted it all in his bizarre 1808 opus, *The Theory of the Four Movements.*

Between accounts of lemonade seas and mating planets, Fourier offered a simple proposition: men and women were governed by their natural, God-given passions. In fact, each individual could be slotted into precisely 810 different personality types, drawn from twelve passions, and lived in a world governed by the four movements of social, animal, organic, and material that constituted the general system of nature (as something of a sociological Linnaeus, Fourier was very good at lists). To attempt to repress these passions was the terrible mistake of contemporary society: "Nature driven out through the door comes back through the window." But this was exactly what nineteenth-century bourgeois France was doing with artificial constructs like monogamous marriage, which in true Newtonian fashion produced unwarranted counterpassions "as malignant as the natural passions would have been benign." The equal and opposite reaction to church-sanctioned monogamy, for example, could be seen in the thirty-two different types of adultery evident in France. In Fourier's harmonious society, citizens would be allowed full sexual freedom, starting and ending relationships as they desired. Women would have control over reproduction and children would be given the opportunity to choose between biological or adoptive fathers.[44] It was the same with economics as with sex. The subversion of benign passions had turned ambition into avarice, leached work of all joy, and allowed the exploitative, parasitic middlemen to flourish. Revolted by the unemployment, poverty, and hunger of 1790s Marseilles, Fourier blamed the deadly vice of capitalism: "It is falsehood with all of its paraphernalia, bankruptcy, speculation, usury, and cheating of every kind."[45] He especially despised the merchant class, who neither toiled nor spun but walked away with vast paper-money profits.

Capitalism's greatest crime, though, was that it sullied the soul of man by denying him pleasure—more specifically that it reserved pleasure for the rich. Since money was required to obtain such luxuries as good food, love, and art, only the rich could revel in the kind of delights that many others—such as Fourier—longed for.[46] This iniquitous state of affairs was bolstered by the Roman Catholic Church's hypocritical creed of abstention and holy poverty. Fourier, the frustrated, lonely traveling salesman, saw little virtue in impecuniousness or the restrictions of a monogamous married life.

Traditional politics had no answer to these human sufferings. There was no program of reform or economic adjustment that addressed the unnatural repressions of modern society. So the answer was to abandon the existing social order and reorganize humanity in a series of autonomous communities, known as phalansteries. These were to be based on the science of "passionate attraction": on the truths of human nature rather than moralists' projections. Each phalanstery was organized to cater for each different personality type, bringing the ideal population to 1,620. The guarantee of a "sexual minimum" for all residents would remove the frustrations and desires that distorted "amorous" relationships in patriarchal bourgeois society. Fourier delighted in describing the kind of highly choreographed orgies—modeled on a sensuous inversion of the Catholic Mass—that would take place in the phalanstery catering to every form of sexual inclination (including incest).

Alongside a "sexual minimum" came a "social minimum." Just as Fourier would restore respect to sexual love, so his system would revive the dignity of work. The problem of modern employment was that it, too, denied man the fulfillment of his natural passions—assigning him to tasks that were both monotonous and ill-suited to particular capacities. In the phalanstery, by contrast, residents would be able to work at up to eight different jobs a day in spontaneously formed groups of friends and lovers. This unleashing of abilities would produce an outpouring of talent as men and women marched to the fields, factories, workshops, studios, and kitchens, eager to fulfill their industrious enthusiasms. Fourier, contra the Catholic Church, did not think human beings were born to suffer. The creation of new communities would allow man to flourish in accordance with his innate passions.

Nowhere in Saint-Simon and Fourier are there demands for radical equality ("a social poison," in Fourier's words) or calls for the violent seizure of power in the name of "the people." Their socialism was a noble, frequently eccentric, but fundamentally inspiring vision of human fulfillment. Indeed, given their experience of and attitude toward the blood and horror of the French Revolution, both thinkers displayed very little interest in violently challenging existing social systems. Instead, they urged a program of gradual moral reform led by harmonious communities separated from the inequalities and injustices of existing society. As Engels put it, "Society presented nothing but wrongs; to remove these was the task of reason. It was necessary, then, to discover a new and more perfect system of social order and to impose this upon society from without by propaganda, and, wherever it was possible, by the example of model experiments."[47] America witnessed the most practical achievement of the Fourierist vision with the establishment of a series of communities at Brook Farm, Massachusetts; La Reunion in Dallas County, Texas; and Raritan Bay Union in New Jersey. These phalansteries fell rather short, however, when it came to converting the rest of American society to the Fourierist project. Such failings would allow Engels to belittle Saint-Simon and Fourier (along with Robert Owen) as "utopian socialists" in contrast to Marx and his rigorous, practical "scientific socialism." While Engels would later reveal a profound indebtedness to Fourier's analysis of bourgeois marriage and greatly admired his social criticism ("Fourier inexorably exposes the hypocrisy of respectable society, the contradiction between its theory and its practice, the dullness of its entire mode of life"), he criticized the utopians' failure to understand the function of the proletariat or the revolutionary ratchet of history: "These new social systems were foredoomed as Utopian; the more completely they were worked out in detail, the more they could not avoid drifting off into pure phantasies."[48]

Early-nineteenth-century France harbored other ideologues equally impatient with this rarefied nonsense of personality types and passions. These were the communists. Led by the likes of Étienne Cabet and Louis-Auguste Blanqui, they outlawed Parisian sects, active during the 1830s, concerning themselves much more with direct political change than with social analysis. While Cabet advocated the path of peaceful transition to "a society founded on the basis of the most perfect equality," Blanqui urged a revolution and lionized the martyrdom of "Gracchus" Babeuf, who in the name of the people had mounted a doomed rebellion in 1796 against the inequality and poverty of postrevolutionary France. Supported by sections of the disgruntled Parisian working class, the "Babouvists," or "communists" (a term that gained its wider currency in the early 1840s), wanted to reshape existing society, not retreat to phalansteries or communes. They called for a revival of the revolutionary republican tradition, demanding an end to inheritance and the abolition of private property and envisioning "a great national community of goods" to follow in the aftermath of revolution. A botched attempt by Blanqui and his supporters in 1839 to usher in the new Jerusalem by force resulted in a sentence of life imprisonment—from which he was intermittently released. Marx and Engels, enjoying their boozy evenings in Berlin and Bonn debating Hegelian philosophy, had little to do with these earnest early communists. But one German who did associate with them was the so-called communist rabbi, or, as Engels would describe him, the "first Communist of the party": Moses Hess.

Like Marx and Engels, Hess was a child of the Rhineland, born in Bonn in 1812 when the city was under Napoleonic occupation and, as Isaiah Berlin puts it, "the gates of the Jewish ghetto were flung wide open, and its inmates, after centuries of being driven in upon themselves, were permitted to emerge into the light of day."[49] He shared with Marx an impressive Semitic heritage, with rabbis on both parents' sides. His father, however, had sought a life outside the synagogue as a sugar refiner in Cologne, and Hess was left in the care of his "extremely orthodox" maternal grandfather, who brought him up on stories of the Jews' expulsion from Israel. "The strict old man's snow-white beard would be drenched with tears at this reading; we children, too, of course, could not prevent ourselves from weeping and sobbing."[50]

While Hess never fully freed himself this emotional inheritance, he did lose his faith. "My main problem was, naturally, religion: from it I moved later on to the principles of ethics. First to be examined was my positive religion [i.e., Judaism]. It collapsed. . . . Nothing, nothing remained. I was the most miserable person in the world. I became an atheist. The world became a burden and a curse to me. I looked at it as a cadaver."[51] Just as Engels's father had little patience for Friedrich's romanticism, so Hess's had no use for his son's melancholic introspection and pressured him to join the family refining business. But Hess was reluctant to participate in what he saw as the moral compromises of commerce and he fled for a year of European travel. Isaiah Berlin affectionately describes him at this time as "a generous, high-minded, kindly, touchingly pure-hearted, enthusiastic, not over-astute young man, ready, indeed eager, to suffer for his ideas, filled with love of humanity, optimisim, a passion for abstractions, and aversion from the world of practical affairs towards which the more hard-headed members of his family were trying to steer him."[52]

It was in Paris, in the early 1830s, that he discovered a cure for his atheism among the communist secret societies and increasingly outlandish Saint-Simonians. Like Engels before him, and many thousands after him, Hess filled the gap left by his abandoned religious heritage with the new socialist creed of humanity. He recounted his intellectual conversion in *The Sacred History of Mankind* (1837), which highlighted the growing social disparity between "pauperism" and an "aristocracy of wealth" and posited a Babouvist-inspired community of goods as the answer. The book was one of the earliest expressions of communist thought in Germany and enjoyed a favorable reception in liberal Rhineland circles. Long before Marx and Engels had codified their views, Hess and, following him, the artisan communist Wilhelm Weitling, were introducing German audiences to the idea of a radical, egalitarian communist future in which the spiritual and social crises of the day would be resolved.

Hess's real breakthrough came when he attached these communist ideas to Young Hegelian thinking. Indispensable to that process was the entrancing figure of August von Cieszkowski. Described by his biographer as "a sort of Polish Alexander Herzen," Cieszkowski was a wealthy, cultivated aristocrat educated at Cracow and then Berlin, where he participated in the Young Hegelian struggle against Schelling.[53] His military background inspired in Cieszkowski a demand for action and he soon lost interest in the endlessly arcane Hegelian philosophizing. In 1838, he published *Prolegomena to Historiosophy*, which sought to turn Hegel's work from an analytical tool into a socially oriented plan for change. The dialectic, he suggested, was entering a new age of synthesis where thought would have to be combined with action. What Europe needed was "a philosophy of practical activity, of 'praxis,' exercising a direct influence on social life and developing the future in the realm of concrete activity."[54] The futile, beer-soaked discussion so beloved by the Young Hegelians had to be rechanneled into a program of practical reform.

Hess was immediately taken by Cieszkowski's writings. "The time has come for the philosophy of spirit to become a philosophy of action," he proclaimed. Returning to Ludwig Feuerbach's stress on the need to end religious alienation, Hess developed his thinking a stage further. Of course, Hess agreed, man could regain his essence only by ending his subservience to a Christian deity. But such a radical shift should not be attempted on an individual basis; what was needed was a broader, communal process. "Theology is anthropology. That is true, but it is not the whole truth. The being of man, it must be added, is social, the co-operation of the various individuals towards a common aim . . . and the true doctrine of man, the true humanism, is the theory of human sociability. That is to say, anthropology is socialism."[55] For what socialism or communism promised (and Hess, like Marx and Engels, used the terms interchangeably) was heaven on earth: everything that in Christianity had been represented prophetically would come to pass in a truly humane society founded upon the eternal laws of love and reason.[56]

To reach this sublime state of cooperation a confrontation with the contemporary capitalist system—the cause of so many modern ills—was urgently needed. Hess called for the abolition of private property and, with it, an end to the alienating effects brought about by the money economy. Only then could the culture of egotism and competition be curtailed and, in its place, a new sociability based on freedom and human fellowship arise. In the great historical movement toward socialism, each member of what he called the European triarchy—France, England, and Germany—had a specific role to play. Germany was to provide the philosophical foundations of communism, France was already well advanced with the political activism, and industrializing England was to gather the social kindling. "The antagonism between poverty and the aristocracy of money will reach a revolutionary level only in England, just as that opposition between spiritualism and materialism could reach its culmination only in France and the antagonism between state and church could reach its apex only in Germany."[57]

Hess was among the first to introduce this "social question"—the human costs of industrial capitalism—into the political dynamic. In an article entitled "On the Approaching Catastrophe in England," Hess explained how the gathering storm was the product of powerful socioeconomic climacterics:

> The objective causes that will provoke a catastrophe in England are not of a political character. Industry passing from the hands of the people into those of the capitalists, the trade that used to be carried out on a small scale by small traders more and more being controlled by large scale capitalists, adventurers and swindlers, land property concentrated by the laws of heredity in the hands of aristocratic usurers . . . all these conditions that exist everywhere, but principally in England and which constitute, if not the exclusive, at least the principal and essential causes of the catastrophe that threatens us, have a social and not a political character.[58]

Increasingly, Hess's practical, socially oriented theorizing was drawing the Young Hegelians in an overtly communist direction. By the autumn of 1842, according to Engels, some of the Young Hegelian "party" (within which he included himself) "contended for the insufficiency of political change and declared their opinion to be that a *social* revolution based upon common property, was the only state of mankind agreeing with their abstract principles."[59]

What was equally obvious was that England—with its vast manufactories, wealthy mill owners, and hideously brutalized proletariat—was all set to stage the "approaching catastrophe": "The English are the nation of praxis, more than any other nation. England is to our century what France has been to the previous one."[60] And it was to England that Friedrich Engels was now heading. Before departing, he called on Moses Hess himself, with whom he had begun a correspondence. Hess recalled the visit in a letter to his friend the Jewish poet Berthold Auerbach. Engels arrived, he wrote, as a shy, naïve, "'first year' revolutionary" (*ein Anno I Revolutionär*) of the French Revolution, Montagnard type. By the time he had finished his tutorial with Hess and continued on his way to England, Engels the Young Hegelian had been converted into "an extremely eager communist."[61]

3

MANCHESTER IN
BLACK AND WHITE

On 27 August 1842, an advertisement appeared on the front page of the *Manchester Guardian*. Beneath an announcement by William Ashworth, "beerseller of Heywood," that he would "not be answerable for any debt or debts that my wife, Ann Ashworth, may contract after this day," the firm of Ermen & Engels expressed "their deep sense of obligation not only to the authorities, police, and special constables, but also to their kind neighbours, for the very efficient and preventive measures adopted, and ready assistance given, to afford protection to their works, and the people in their employ, during the late disturbances." What was more, "E. & E. beg to add, that these feelings are fully shared in by their people, to whom it is only due further to state, that they have without exception exhibited the best disposition and conduct during the recent general turn out." In short, Engels's father and business partner wished to thank the British state for crushing the so-called Plug Plot riots, the most invigorating display of working-class dissent since the Peterloo massacre of 1819 saw thousands of prodemocracy campaigners fall under the sabres of the Manchester yeomanry.[1]

The months before the Plug Plot riots were ones of increasing poverty and political disenchantment across Manchester. "Any man who passes through the district observing the condition of the people, will at once perceive the deep and ravaging distress that prevails, laying industry prostrate, desolating families, and spreading abroad discontent and misery where recently happiness and content were enjoyed," reported the *Manchester Times* in July 1842.[2] But such accounts of despair in Lancashire's cotton slums had little impact on the landowners, industrialists, and merchants sitting in session at Westminster. Earlier that summer, MPs had summarily rejected a million-strong petition requesting universal male franchise when it was presented by the working-class Chartist movement, whose six-point People's Charter advocated a democratic transformation of British governance. And now the parliamentarians were displaying equal disdain for the human cost of the "hungry 40s."

In fact, Manchester's millocrats had exploited working-class disarray in the aftermath of the petition's rejection to drive through a series of 50 percent wage cuts. In response, the mill workers headed out to the Lancashire moors for mass rallies, renewed demands for the charter, and raised again the familiar cry of "A fair day's wage for a fair day's work." Strikes followed in the mills and coal pits of the surrounding villages of Ashton and Hyde, with workers giving the riots their moniker by pulling the boiler plugs from factory steam engines. Disturbances flared in Bolton, and by the morning of Wednesday, 10 August 1842, some ten thousand men and women were ominously circling the vast mills of Manchester's Ancoats district. Despondent, armed, and increasingly violent, the workers looted shops, torched factories, and attacked the police.

Much to the admiration of the Ermen & Engels directors, the response of the authorities was swift and effective. The Riot Act was read, allowing for an immediate dispersal of the crowds, the army was mobilized, and special constables were sworn in from the middle classes, including members of the German merchant community who marched "through the city with their cigars in their mouths and thick truncheons in their hands."[3] The rioters were rounded up and detained and, by late August, Manchester resembled an occupied city with two thousand troops brought in by train.[4] "In the streets there were unmistakable signs of alarm on the part of the authorities," recalled the Chartist

Thomas Cooper. "Troops of cavalry were going up and down the principal thoroughfares, accompanied by pieces of artillery, drawn by horses."[5] In the face of such military bravado, and amid the early signs of an economic upturn, the protests quieted.

But the Plug Plot riots were merely the surface fury of a much deeper social malaise rooted in the increasing disparity between a prospering bourgeoisie and an impoverished proletariat. "The modern art of manufacture has reached its perfection in Manchester," Engles noted. "The effects of modern manufacture upon the working class must necessarily develop here most freely and perfectly." Accordingly, "the enemies are dividing gradually into two great camps—the bourgeoisie on the one hand, the workers on the other."[6] And no one thought they had seen the last of the struggle.

This city of social division would become Engels's home for some two decades and inspire him to write one of the greatest chronicles of the industrial experience, *The Condition of the Working Class in England* (1845). And it was in mid-1840s Manchester—amid the warehouses, mills, stock exchanges, slums, and public houses—that Engels would make a series of intellectual and ideological advances crucial to the development of Marxism. Lancashire delivered to Engels the essential data to flesh out his philosophy. If Berlin, with its lecture halls and beer-room debates, had been a city of the mind, then Manchester was a city of matter. Along Deansgate and Great Ducie Street, in the Salford rookeries and Oxford Road enclaves, Engels harvested the "facts, facts, facts" of industrial England, to devastating effect. Communism took a step forward as Engels connected his German philosophical inheritance to the class fissures and merciless capitalism he saw at work on the streets of London, Leeds, and Manchester. Hess's theorizing became flesh as Engels realized that communism offered the only credible answer to such a grievous social state. And while the French might have grasped this truth "politically" and the Germans "philosophically," Engels believed the English were being forced toward this conclusion "practically, by the rapid increase of misery, demoralization, and pauperism in their own country."[7]

In Manchester it had been tangibly brought to my notice that the economic facts which have so far played no role or only a contemptible one
in historiography are, at least in the modern world, a decisive historical
force. I learned that economic factors were the basic cause of the clash
between different classes in society. And I realized that in a highly
industrialized country like England the clash of social classes lay at the
very root of the rivalry between parties and were of fundamental significance in tracing the course of modern political history.[8]

Yet such advances in understanding did nothing to alleviate the awkward tension of Engels's own status: residing in Manchester on the pay
of his father, he was there as a bourgeois apprentice, a mill owner. He
was charged with learning the business and figuring out how to extract
maximum value from the proletariat at a time when his politics were
taking him in a very different direction. The young Engels, it seems fair
to say, did not wholly share the sentiments of his fellow Ermen & Engels
managers when it came to crushing working-class resistance.

So much of what we think we know about Victorian Manchester is itself
the product of Engels and his lacerating prose. Written when he was just
twenty-four, *The Condition of the Working Class* would in the twentieth
century come to serve as literary shorthand for the horror, exploitation,
and class conflict of urban industrial Europe. However, Engels's work
forms part of a much broader literature—some known, some unfamiliar
to Engels himself—on the industrial city and Manchester in particular.
"As you enter Manchester from Rusholme, the town at the lower end of
Oxford-road has the appearance of one dense volume of smoke, more
forbidding than the entrance to Dante's inferno," wrote the cooperative
pioneer George Jacob Holyoake in a typical response to the city. "It
struck me that were it not for previous knowledge, no man would have
the courage to enter it."[9]

To the Victorian mind, "Cottonopolis" stood for all the horrors of
modernity: it was the "shock-city" of the Industrial Revolution, an awful
metonym for the terrifying transformations of the age of steam. Be-

tween 1800 and 1841, the population of Manchester and adjacent Salford grew from 95,000 to over 310,000, driven by a booming textile industry that flourished—as in Barmen and Elberfeld—thanks to a culture of innovation and enterprise, reserves of labor power, and a damp climate essential for spinning cotton yarn. The entrepreneur and inventor Richard Arkwright—who had pioneered cotton production along the Derwent valley with his innovative use of mechanization and water power to drive his looms—was the first to use steam power for the purpose of cotton spinning in Manchester in the late 1780s. By 1816, his Shudehill mill had been joined by another eighty-five steam-powered factories employing almost twelve thousand men, women, and children. By 1830, there were more than 550 cotton mills in Lancashire, with well over a hundred thousand workers.

Unlike the surrounding towns of Oldham, Ashton, and Stalybridge, Manchester was more than just a cotton capital. It was a marketplace, a distribution hub, and a center of finance dependent as much on its construction industry and mercantile connections with neighboring towns as on its cotton mills. Manchester's wealthiest citizens were as likely to be bankers, brewers, or merchants as the mill owners of Victorian lore.[10] Nonetheless, the Cottonopolis image, with its stark contrasts of misery and Midas-like riches, made the city a magnet for those wishing to decipher the meaning of industrialization. Here was a demonstration of just what the age of steam had in store for European civilization. In 1833, for instance, Alexis de Tocqueville, fresh from his studies of democracy in America, turned to "this new Hades." Approaching the city, de Tocqueville noted "thirty or forty factories rising on the top of hills," spewing out their foul waste. In fact, he heard Manchester before he saw it as no visitor could escape the "crunching wheels of machinery, the shriek of steam from boilers, the regular beat of the looms," and "the noise of furnaces." Inside the sprawling city he found—in an echo of Engels at Wuppertal—"fetid, muddy waters, stained with a thousand colours by the factories they pass." And yet, "from this foul drain the greatest stream of human industry flows out to fertilise the whole world. From this filthy sewer pure gold flows."[11]

The French observer was not alone. Because of their commercial connections as well as official requests for industrial intelligence (from Prussian bureaucrats increasingly perturbed by Britain's surging prosperity), German visitors such as the historian Frederick von Raumer, the author Johanna Schopenhauer, the ministerial official Johann Georg May, even Otto von Bismarck were thick on the ground in the Manchester districts of Hulme, Chorlton, and Ardwick. May was mesmerized by the 'hundreds of factories in Manchester which tower up to five and six storeys in height. The huge chimneys at the side of these buildings belch forth black coal vapours and this tells us that powerful steam engines are used here. . . . The houses are blackened by it."[12] A few years later a French visitor, the liberal journalist Léon Faucher, was similarly appalled by "the fogs which exhale from this marshy district, and the clouds of smoke vomited forth from the numberless chimneys." Equally disgusting to him was the state of the waterways: "The river which runs through Manchester is so filled with waste dye matter that it looks like a dye-vat. The whole scene is one of melancholy."[13]

The scenes inside the factory were no less infernal. Manchester was renowned for its work ethic. "Hast thou heard, with sound ears," asked the Victorian sage Thomas Carlyle, "the awakening of a Manchester, on Monday morning, at half-past five by the clock; the rushing-off of its thousand mills, like the boom of an Atlantic tide, ten-thousand times ten-thousand spools and spindles all set humming there,—it is perhaps if thou knew it well, sublime as a Niagara, or more so."[14] The mill owners, as we shall see, were especially keen on effective time management. When the future poet laureate Robert Southey visited one Manchester factory, he was proudly informed by the owner, "There is no idleness among us." The child workers came in at 5:00 a.m., had half an hour for breakfast and half an hour for dinner, and left at 6:00 p.m.—at which point they were replaced by the next shift of children. "The wheel never stands still."[15] The result, according to the German travel writer Johann Georg Kohl, was a new race of humans: "In long rows on every side, and in every direction hurried forward thousands of men, women and children. They spoke not a word, but huddling up their frozen hands in their cotton clothes, they hastened on, clap, clap, along the pavement, to their dreary and monotonous occupation."[16] The French historian Hippolyte

Taine thought Manchester resembled nothing more than "a great jerry-built barracks, a 'work-house' for 400,000 people, a hard-labour penal establishment." The penning together of thousands of workmen carrying out mindless, regimented tasks, "hands active, feet motionless, all day and every day," appalled him. "Could there be any kind of life more outraged, more opposed to man's natural instincts?"[17]

Alongside the favella tourism of the day, there was also a highly developed canon of indigenous urban criticism, which Engels devoured. One of the most eloquent testimonials came from James Phillips Kay, the physician to the city-center Ardwick and Ancoats Dispensary. His 1832 polemic, *The Moral and Physical Condition of the Working Classes Employed in the Cotton Manufacture in Manchester,* was a part-Christian, part-medical critique of the misery he confronted on his cholera rounds in "the close alleys, the crowded courts, the overpopulated habitations of wretchedness, where pauperism and disease congregate round the source of social discontent and political disorder."[18] Like Engels, Kay was morally affronted by Manchester's extreme suffering in the face of such unprecedented prosperity—"a slumbering giant . . . in the midst of so much opulence." Accompanying such personal accounts were the official publications of civil servant Edwin Chadwick, whose *Report on the Sanitary Conditions of the Labouring Population of Great Britain* (1842) gave a stark assessment of the effects of rapid industrialization on public health: "The annual slaughter in England and Wales from preventable causes of typhus which attacks persons in the vigour of life, appears to be double the amount of what was suffered by the Allied Armies in the battle of Waterloo."[19] Manchester also came in for particularly strong censure from the city's assistant poor-law commissioner, Dr. Richard Baron Howard, who described how whole streets were "unpaved and without drains or main-sewers" and were "so covered with refuse and excrementitious matter as to be almost impassable from depth of mud, and intolerable from stench. . . . In many of these places are to be seen privies in the most disgusting state of filth, open cesspools, obstructed drains, ditches full of stagnant water, dunghills, pigsties etc., from which the most abominable odours are emitted."[20]

There lurked in the medical terminology of the day moral miasmas as well as sanitary ones. While Manchester's working classes were notorious for their irreligion (or, worse, Catholicism, among the Irish), sexual promiscuity, drunkenness, and general depravity, the city's middle classes were equally infamous for their vulgar materialism. "The all-absorbing feeling of the bulk of the inhabitants is a desire to acquire wealth; and everything is deemed worthless in their estimation, that has not the accomplishment of this object for its end," commented one resident. The Manchester man, it was said, "hears more music in the ever-lasting motion of the loom than he would in the songs of the lark or the nightingale. For him philosophy has no attraction, poetry no enchantment; mountains, rocks, vales and streams excite not his delight or admiration; genius shrinks at his approach."[21] As even the usually loyal *Manchester Guardian* was forced to admit, "If the English are held to be a nation entirely of shopkeepers, Manchester is supposed to be always behind the counter, and to view men and measures through an atmosphere of cotton."[22] The German visitors concurred: "Work, profit and greed seem to be the only thoughts here. . . . One reads figures, nothing but figures on all the faces here."[23]

The raw monetary divide between the proletariat and the bourgeoisie signified an unbridgeable social chasm. Canon Richard Parkinson noted of Manchester that there was "no town in the world where the distance between the rich and the poor is so great." In fact, there was "far less personal communication between the master cotton spinner and his workmen" than between "the Duke of Wellington and the humblest labourer on his estate."[24] This close-quartered urban division—physical proximity coexisting with a yawning social disparity—forcibly struck Léon Faucher, who described how in Manchester there were "two towns in one: in the one portion, there is space, fresh air, and provision for health; and in the other, every thing which poisons and abridges existence."[25] In 1845, Benjamin Disraeli placed this sense of class separation at the heart of his manifesto-cum-novel *Sybil; or, The Two Nations*. Within one city, he lamented, the rich and the poor now lived as two entirely different nations "between whom there is no intercourse and no sympathy; who are as ignorant of each other's habits, thoughts and feelings, as if they were dwellers in different zones, or inhabitants of different planets . . . formed by different breeding," fed by different food, and governed by different laws.[26] It was a striking depiction of imminent class conflict from the most fastidious of Tory voices.

Of course, Manchester was not the only city to undergo such critical inspection. Similar accounts could be told of Glasgow, Liverpool, Birmingham, and Bradford. There was likewise a well-developed European literature of urban discovery exposing the shantytowns, hidden tribes, and amoral underbelly of Lyon, Paris, Berlin, and Hamburg. But Manchester was something else: a symbol of the ne plus ultra of industrialization. It was an extraordinary urban phenomenon—akin to the Chinese boom cities or vast African megalopolises of today—that attracted intellectuals, activists, philosophers, even artists. They all wanted to *experience* and capture this terrifying future. But it was Friedrich Engels's gift to paint the city's social crisis upon an altogether grander historical canvas.

"Is a revolution in England possible or even probable? This is the question on which the future of England depends."[27] Disembarking onto the London docks in 1842, Engels was overwhelmed by "the masses of buildings, the wharves on both sides, . . . the countless ships along both shores. . . . All this is so vast, so impressive, that a man cannot collect himself, but is lost in the marvel of England's greatness." But fueled by Moses Hess's predictions of an English social crisis, he was on the lookout for any sign of the impending upheaval.[28] Instantly he alighted upon that class of proletarians who had to pay the price for such commercial greatness and who, he would come to argue, were the class destined to dismantle the unjust system. "For although industry makes a country rich, it also creates a class of unpropertied, absolutely poor people, a class which lives from hand to mouth, which multiplies rapidly, and which cannot afterwards be abolished," he wrote in a series of articles for Marx's *Rheinische Zeitung* that indicated that their relationship was slowly progressing from the early chill. Faced with the awful costs of industrialization, Engels was shifting away from Young Hegelian notions of *Geist*, consciousness, and freedom to the earthy language of economic reality. "The slightest fluctuation in trade leaves thousands of workers destitute; their modest savings are soon used up and then they are in danger of starving to death. And a crisis of this kind is bound to occur again in a few years' time."[29]

But before the revolution, there was his father's work to be done. The firm of Ermen & Engels had been established in 1837 when Friedrich Engels senior took the money he had received from selling his part of the family firm and invested it in the Ermen brothers' enterprise. The guiding force behind the company, Dutch-born Peter Ermen, had come to Manchester in the mid-1820s and worked his way up from being a doubler in a small factory to establishing a multinational cotton thread business run with the help of his brothers Anthony and Gottfried. Investment by Engels senior allowed the company to open a new mill in Salford for the production of cotton thread. This district to the west of Manchester was renowned for its fine-count mercerized cotton and its weaving, and the mill—next to Weaste station, alongside the Manchester and Liverpool railway line—was ideally situated both for bringing raw cotton from the Mersey docks and for drawing water from the nearby River Irwell for bleaching and dyeing. Patriotically christened Victoria Mill in honor of the young queen then ascending the throne, the new factory churned out thread bearing its trademark of three red towers, the arms reportedly granted to the Ermens' sixteenth-century ancestors. This was where Engels joined a 400-strong workforce, starting off among the cotton-spinning machines "in the throstle-room."[30] Though we don't know exactly where he lived, it seems his residence was close by in the Eccles neighborhood where he once witnessed a battle between the police and the brickmakers of Pauling & Henfrey. Local legend also has it that he was a regular at Salford's Crescent public house, and F. R. Johnston, the Eccles historian, has even suggested Engels tried to form "a Communist cell based at the Grapes Hotel."[31] The Weaste mill, later reincarnated as the Winterbottom Bookcloth Company, lasted until the 1960s, when the construction of a motorway necessitated the demolition of what was by then an industrio-socialist footnote.[32]

Working for the family firm while living within a community exploited by cotton capitalism quickly made the contradictions of Engels's position painfully apparent. As he put it in a heartfelt letter to Marx some years later, "Huckstering is too beastly. . . . Most beastly of all is the fact of being, not only a bourgeois, but actually a manufacturer, a bourgeois who actively takes sides against the proletariat. A few days in my old man's factory have sufficed to bring me face to face with this beastliness, which I had rather overlooked."[33] But even if he worked for the bourgeoisie, Engels didn't have to socialize with them: "I forsook the company and the dinner-parties, the port-wine and champagne of the middle classes, and devoted my leisure-hours almost exclusively to the intercourse with plain working men."[34] His first call was to the plain working men of the Owenite Hall of Science.

Robert Owen was the final member of Engels's "utopian socialist" triumvirate, joining Charles Fourier and Saint-Simon in the pantheon of dreamers—all of them, as he would later see it, marred by an inadequate appreciation of the historical rigors of scientific socialism. Yet Owen himself could lay claim to a far more practical understanding of social justice than either Marx or Engels ever could. A textile manufacturer by trade and marriage, he had attempted to turn his New Lanark factories in Scotland into a model of equitable employment and community cohesion. Owen's starting point was a belief that conditioning, not character, was the key to man. Original sin was a fallacy and what was required instead was an educational and social ethos that would draw out the cooperative best in mankind. At New Lanark, Owen operated a beneficent commercial dictatorship: he cut working hours, eliminated underage employment, restricted alcohol sales, improved living conditions, and introduced free primary education. In *A New View of Society; or, Essays on the Principle of the Formation of the Human Character* (1813–14), he detailed how his approach could be applied to society at large. The book helped to drive through the 1819 Cotton Mills and Factories Act limiting the working day in the textile industry for nine- to sixteen-year-olds to twelve hours.

Yet no matter how many ameliorative acts of Parliament were passed, politics as usual could never provide the answer to the structural poverty that afflicted Britain in the years following the Napoleonic wars. The underlying fault, Owen decided, lay with organized Christianity, which kept man in a backward state of superstition, and with the competitive ethos of society (exemplified by the attachment to private property), which corrupted the nature of man. Straying a long way from his industrial reform roots, Owen now advocated a wholesale moral revolution: this meant retreating from the evils of the "old immoral world" and, as with Fourier, creating new communities, built around agriculture and industry, where education and cooperation would kick-start the regenerative process. "The children are not tormented with religious and theological controversies, nor with Greek and Latin," Engels wrote admiringly of the early Owenite settlement at Queen Farm in Hampshire. "instead they become better acquainted with nature, their own bodies and their intellectual capacities. . . . Their moral education is restricted to the application of the one principle: Do not do to others what you would not have them do to you, in other words, the practice of complete equality and brotherly love."[35] Just as with Fourier's phalansteries and the Saint-Simonian sects, however, planned Owenite communities proved expensive and short-lived in both England and the United States.

Another faction of Owenite socialism, whose adherents grouped themselves together under the aegis of the British Association for the Promotion of Co-operative Knowledge, was more productive. Its criticisms were particularly aimed at modern competition. "The selfish feeling in man may fairly be called the competitive principle," announced the leading Owenite William Lovett, "since it causes him to compete with others, for the gratification of his wants and propensities. Whereas the co-operative may be said to be the social feeling that prompts him to acts of benevolence and brotherly affection." An economy based on the competitive system was thus inherently inequitable and unstable: wealth was concentrated, trade cycles became more extreme, and poverty deepened. While Robert Owen himself increasingly focused his efforts on reforming religion and ending "the unnatural and artificial union of the sexes" in marriage, his followers concentrated on developing a political program based on cooperation and a moral sense of value: wages would be determined by labor time and just transfer (in essence, a fair day's wage for a fair day's work) rather than the exploitative "doctrine of wages" in which value is dictated by the vagaries of the market and employer whim. The Owenites established a series of cooperative shops in London and Brighton, 'labor exchanges' for the direct marketing of goods, trade unions to advance the cause of labor, and a network of Halls of Science (under the banner of "The Association of All Classes of All Nations") to promote the ways of socialism, fellowship, and reason.

One of the largest and most active branches of the association, with 440 members and a dedicated Hall of Science, was initially located in Salford; as interest in socialism surged across the northwest, it relocated in 1840 to grander premises in Manchester's Campfield neighborhood. Léon Faucher remembered it as

> an immense building . . . raised exclusively by the savings of the mechanics and artisans, at a cost of £7,000, and which contains a lecture-hall—the finest and most spacious in the town. It is tenanted by the disciples of Mr. Owen. In addition to Sunday lectures upon the doctrines of Socialism, they possess a day and Sunday-school, and increase the number of their adherents by oratorios and festivals—by rural excursions, and by providing cheap and innocent recreation for the working classes. . . . The large sums of money they raise, prove that they belong to the wealthier portion of the working classes. Their audiences on Sunday evenings are generally crowded.[36]

Generous estimates put Manchester's "socialist community" at between eight and ten thousand during the 1840s, with an impressive three thousand filling the hall on Sunday evenings—Friedrich Engels among them. Accustomed to the drunken Barmen artisan, he was most struck by the articulateness of the British working classes: "At first one cannot get over one's surprise on hearing in the Hall of Science the most ordinary workers speaking with a clear understanding on political, religious and social affairs."[37] Indeed, he often heard "working men, whose fustian jackets scarcely held together, speak upon geological, astronomical and other subjects, with more knowledge than most 'cultivated' bourgeois in Germany possess." This was, he thought, the product of their voracious literary culture, with Rousseau, Voltaire, and Paine all firm favorites among Manchester's working but not its middle classes. "Byron and Shelley are read almost exclusively by the lower classes; no 'respectable' person could have the works of the latter on his desk without his coming into the most terrible disrepute."[38]

As with so many variants of socialism, the Owenites too subsumed into their practice the rites and rituals of Christian worship. "In their form, these meetings partly resemble church gatherings; in the gallery a choir accompanied by an orchestra sings social hymns," Engels noted. "These consist of semi-religious or wholly religious melodies with communist words, during which the audience stands." The sermons were of an altogether higher quality than the rantings of Krummacher. "Then, quite nonchalantly, without removing his hat, a lecturer comes on to the platform . . . and then sits down and delivers his address, which usually gives much occasion for laughter, for in those speeches the English intellect expresses itself in superabundant humour." At other times, the Owenite gatherings were simply social occasions for workers and the lower-middle classes: Sunday evening parties "of the usual supper of tea and sandwiches; on working days dances and concerts are often held in the hall, where people have a very jolly time."[39]

Once in a while, a crowd puller would be booked. In late 1843, it was the celebrated mesmerist Spencer Hall, who, in front of a skeptical audience of materialist Owenites, "undertook magnetico-phrenological performances with a young woman in order to prove thereby the existence of God, the immortality of the soul, and the incorrectness of materialism." Engels was clearly gripped by the demonstration and, on returning from the hall, attempted to conduct a similar experiment in this pseudoscience for himself: "A wide-awake young boy twelve years old offered himself as subject. Gently gazing into his eyes, or stroking, sent him without difficulty into the hypnotic condition. . . . Apart from muscular rigidity and loss of sensation, which were easy to produce, we found also a state of complete passivity of the will bound up with a peculiar hypersensitivity of sensation." However, the cofounder of dialectical materialism was not easily fooled by such hocus-pocus: "We discovered in the great toe an organ of drunkenness which only had to be touched in order to cause the finest drunken comedy to be enacted. But it must be well understood, no organ showed a trace of action until the patient was given to understand what was expected of him; the boy soon perfected himself by practice to such an extent that the merest indication sufficed."[40]

Of greater intellectual value was the Owenite lecturer John Watts. A ribbon weaver and former assistant secretary of the Coventry Mechanics' Institute, Watts was an Owenite missionary and fierce critic of the school of "political economy," which he identified with the works of Adam Smith and Thomas Malthus and their ethos of free trade, division of labor and laissez-faire. Engels would learn much from this "outstanding man" and his moral critique of competition. "The nature of trade is evil," Watts wrote in his influential tract *The Facts and Fictions of Political Economists* (1842), "and to it more than to aught else, we owe what we have of natural depravity." The capitalist system of values and money wages—held in place by manufacturers and mill owners whose control of the means of production gave them the whip hand when it came to negotiating with labor—was the root cause of the economic crisis gripping industrial Britain. It sought to deny the truth that "labour is the source of all wealth." Watts's solution was to return to a preindustrial, cooperative system of exchange—"i.e., a fixed return for labour, a return in kind, a certain and invariable proportion of the produce." At the same time, contra Adam Smith, he railed against the deadening effects of the division of labor ("It cannot admit of long question, whether, the clipping of the wire, or the pointing or heading of a pin, be fit employment for the life of a rational being") and the hideous state of factory life ("Is this condition so much better than that of the negroes, that it deserves no exhibition of philanthropy, that it demands no sympathy? Yet the tendency of our Political Economy in the doctrine of wages, is to perpetuate this state of things").[41]

Despite their undoubted strength within Manchester, by the late 1830s the Owenites were a waning force in national working-class politics. Their place had been taken by the Chartists, with their easily understood six-point demand: universal manhood suffrage, secret ballots, annual elections, equally populated constituencies, the payment of salaries, together with the abolition of a minimum property requirement for MPs (so allowing for working-class representatives). In contrast to the utopian ambitions of the Owenites, the charter was a practical attempt to find a political solution to working-class difficulties. It found its warmest reception in Lancashire, where the Manchester Political Union organized torchlight marches and "monster rallies" on Kersal Moor— the Mons Sacer of Chartism. In September 1838, some thirty thousand turned out under their trade union banners to hear the Chartist leader Feargus O'Connor declaim that "universal franchise" was "the only principle which can stop the flowing of human blood. . . . You will never be represented until every man is entrusted with that which nature has imprinted in the breast of every man, namely, the power of self-defence as implied in the vote of every individual."[42] But such popular shows of force served only to heighten establishment fears. In 1839 and again in 1842, the Chartists' petitions were rejected by the House of Commons. Such obvious contempt radicalized Chartist opinion, sparking a move away from middle-class alliances and a heated internal debate as to the merits of moral versus physical force.

In one sense, the 1842 Plug Plot riots were an expression of Chartism's political impotence. Nevertheless, Engels had few doubts as to the movement's significance. While modern interpretations tend to view Chartism as an outgrowth of radical eighteenth-century politics that presaged demands for political transparency and a moral economy, to Engels's eyes it was "a class movement" pure and simple, encapsulating the working-class "collective consciousness."[43] He wanted to learn as much from it as possible and managed to gain two separate introductions to the movement. His first came from George Julian Harney, Chartism's enfant terrible, who was firmly on the radical side of the movement, advocating the use of physical force and enjoying riling his conservative comrades by flaunting the red cap of liberty at public meetings. In and out of jail, endlessly feuding with fellow Chartists, and ultimately expelled from the party, the Robespierre-admiring Harney remained convinced that insurrection was the surest route to achieve the demands of the charter.[44] Decades later, Harney remembered how Engels— "a tall, handsome young man, with a countenance of almost boyish youthfulness"—sought him out at his Leeds office. "He told me he was a constant reader of *The Northern Star* [the Chartist paper] and took a keen interest in the Chartist movement. Thus began our friendship."[45] As ever with Marx and Engels, the friendship would prove rocky, but it lasted—through an intermittent correspondence—for half a century, during which Harney provided one of the more memorable assessments of Manchester. "I am not surprised to find you expressing your disgust at Manchester," he wrote to Engels in 1850. "It is a damned dirty den of muckworms. I would rather be hanged in London than die a natural death in Manchester."[46]

Engels's other main contact in the party was James Leach, the Manchester handloom weaver turned Chartist activist. Before being elected as South Lancashire's delegate to the National Charter Association, Leach, according to Engels, "worked for years in various branches of industry, in mills and coal-mines, and is known to me personally as an honest, trustworthy, and capable man."[47] He was also regarded as a "terror, not only to the cotton lords, but every other humbug"—a well-deserved reputation judging by his anonymous 1844 polemic, *Stubborn Facts from the Factories by a Manchester Operative*. Dedicated to "the working classes," it was a firsthand indictment of the pernicious practices of mill owners, from deducting wages for minor workplace infractions to fining pregnant women for sitting down, manipulating clocks, employing "infants of a tender age," and forcing female workers into prostitution. Much of this evidence would find its way into Engels's book—along with the insight that the modern state was merely a front for bourgeois class interests: "The working classes will ever look upon this [the state] as no better than a *brigand* system, that thus allows the employers to assume a power over the Law, and by their nefarious plotting, first create what they are pleased to term offences, and then punish them. They are both law makers, judges, and jurors."[48] As Marx and Engels would later put it in *The Communist Manifesto*, "The executive of the modern State is but a committee for managing the common affairs of the whole bourgeoisie."[49]

Despite these close friendships and his own personal enthusiasm for Chartism, Engels did not think the solution to Britain's crisis lay with the six points. First of all, their socialism, in contrast to the advanced ideas on the Continent (among the Fourierists, Saint-Simonians, or Moses Hess and his circle), was "very little developed" but, more importantly, "social evils cannot be cured by People's Charters."[50] Something altogether more fundamental than democratic tinkering was required. It was a sentiment majestically enunciated by another British mentor to the young Engels, Thomas Carlyle.

Sage, polemicist, and reactionary, Carlyle was the only British intellectual whom Engels truly admired, in part perhaps because of his Germanophilia. Carlyle's earliest work, when he was a critic for the *Edinburgh Review*, had been a translation of the German poet Johann Paul Richter and from there he went on to immerse himself in the work of Goethe (with whom he regularly corresponded), Schiller, and Herder, acting as a kind of cultural importer bringing German romanticism to a British audience. Imbued with nostalgia for a lost world of feudal heroism, Carlyle was drawn to contrast the miserable state of industrial England with the nation's romantic medieval past, before mournfully concluding that 'this is not a Religious age. Only the material, the immediately practical, not the divine and spiritual, is important to us."[51] The nineteenth century was "the mechanical age," in which the social bonds that traditionally connected man to man had fallen apart in the quest for material riches: "We call it a Society; and go about professing openly the totalest separation, isolation. Our life is not a mutual helpfulness; but rather, cloaked under due laws-of-war, named 'fair competition' and so forth, it is a mutual hostility. We have profoundly forgotten everywhere that *Cash-payment* is not the sole relation of human beings."[52] In this view, demands for the charter and other political quick fixes—which Carlyle dismissed as "Morrison's Pills," after a voguish quack doctor of the day— would make no real difference to the so-called condition of England. The solution, for Carlyle, was a combination of renewed religiosity and quasi-dictatorial leadership. On the walls of his Cheyne Row drawing room, Carlyle gave pride of place to portraits of Oliver Cromwell and Martin Luther's parents.

In an 1844 review of *Past and Present*, Carlyle's work contrasting medieval and modern Britain, Engels (still then aligning himself with the radical wing of the Young Hegelians) responded: "We too are concerned with combating the lack of principle, the inner emptiness, the spiritual deadness, the untruthfulness of the age." Religion, however, was certainly not the answer: "We want to put an end to atheism, as Carlyle portrays it, by giving back to man the substance he has lost through religion; not as divine but as human substance, and this whole process of giving back is no more than simply the awakening of self-consciousness."[53] Carlyle's defining weakness, according to Engels, was that he had read German literature but not philosophy. Goethe without Feuerbach got you only so far. Yet Engels admired both Carlyle's extraordinary prose style—"Carlyle treated the English language as though it were completely raw material which he had to cast utterly afresh"—and his Olympian denunciation of the misery wrought by capitalist society.[54] In *The Condition of the Working Class*, Engels used the same historical metaphors as Carlyle (contrasting the position of a factory hand unfavorably with that of a Saxon serf under the lash of a Norman baron and highlighting the hypocrisy of liberal "freedom," which meant little more than liberty to die by starvation), and relied on the same official sources. He also frequently quoted "the sage of Chelsea" directly. "The relation of the manufacturer to his operatives has nothing human in it; it is purely economic," Engels wrote in a chapter on industrial relations taken straight from "Signs of the Times" (1829), Carlyle's epic denunciation of mechanical, industrial England. "The manufacturer is capital, the operative labour. . . . He [the manufacturer] insists, as Carlyle says, that 'cash payment is the only nexus between man and man.'"[55]

Carlyle's condemnations of "the mechanical age," the Owenites' call for moral renewal, the six points of the people's Charter, and Watts's and Leach's attacks on competition were all instrumental to Engels's ideological evolution, but he was not in Manchester to read books. He was there to confront the *reality* of working-class life, to forsake "the company and the dinner-parties, the port-wine and champagne" for the fellowship of "plain working men." But who would guide this boyish German explorer through the proletarian netherworld? One streetwalking companion was fellow socialist émigré George Weerth, then unhappily clerking in Bradford, "the most disgusting manufacturing town in England." To Weerth's horror, this woolen boomtown had "no theatre, no social life, no decent hotel, no reading room, and no civilized human beings—only Yorkshiremen in torn frock coats, shabby hats and gloomy faces." To escape the Yorkshire philistinism, he would set out across the Pennines to visit his friend and ideological ally in Lancashire, and the two would wander about investigating the sprawling Manchester.[56] In addition, Engels had the personal attentions of a native of the city. A vital link to outcast Manchester, Mary Burns was the first great love of Engels's life.

"She was a very pretty, witty, and altogether charming girl. . . . Of course, she was a Manchester (Irish) factory girl, quite uneducated, though she could read and write a little, but my parents . . . were very fond of her, and always spoke of her with the greatest affection."[57] Eleanor Marx's sketchy, secondhand childhood memories are, sadly, some of the fullest accounts we have of Engels's Mary. Born sometime between April 1822 and January 1823, Mary was the daughter of the Irish dyer and factory hand Michael Burns, who came to Manchester in the 1820s and took Mary Conroy as his first wife. At the time of the 1841 census, Michael surfaces as the husband of his second wife, Mary Tuomey, and living in grim conditions just off Deansgate—but without his daughters Mary and Lydia (known as Lizzy) Burns. A decade on, Michael and the second Mrs. Burns had disappeared into the workhouse on New Bridge Street, after which he became just another Manchester mortality statistic for 1858.[58] Mary, however, was prospering.

We know that Engels met her in the early months of 1843, but there is much debate as to the exact nature of the encounter. With no obvious evidence, Edmund Wilson asserts that Mary operated a "self-actor" machine in the Ermen & Engels mill.[59] Similarly, the socialist Max Beer, who met Engels in the 1890s, declares that Engels "lived, in free union, with an Irish girl of the people, Mary Burns, who had worked in his father's factory."[60] Historian Heinrich Gemkow more vaguely describes

Mary Burns "work[ing] in one of the city's many cotton factories."[61] Engels himself, however, was never particularly complimentary about the quality of his father's female employees: "I do not remember to have seen one single tall, well-built girl; they were all short, dumpy, and badly-formed, decidedly ugly in the whole development of the figure."[62] More probable, according to the Manchester chronicler Roy Whitfield, is that Mary and Lizzy worked in a Manchester mill before becoming domestic servants, when they might have caught Engels's roving eye. Historians Edmund and Ruth Frow, by contrast, provide an altogether more romantic legend, which has Engels meeting Mary at a reception in the Owenite Hall of Science, where she was selling oranges.[63] This version certainly helps to explain (but just a little too easily) George Weerth's idiosyncratic poem "Mary," which recounts—in deliciously labored verse—the life of a vivacious young Fenian girl selling oranges on the Liverpool docks:

> From Ireland with the tide she came,
> She came from Tipperary;
> Warm, impetuous blood in her vein,
> The young lass, Mary.
> And when she boldly sprang ashore,
> A cry from the sailors arose:
> "The lass Mary, thank the Lord,
> Is just like a wild rose!"[64]

The conjectures surrounding Mary are so varied because of the paucity of sources. She herself was illiterate, and Engels later burned much of the correspondence from this period of his life. In addition, Engels himself was never especially keen to publicize his relationship with Mary. There were no missives about her to his "goose" Marie. He had to maintain his social position within Manchester and he had to keep up good relations with his censorious parents; living in "free union" with an illiterate Irish factory girl could not be expected to achieve either. There might also have been some sense of political embarrassment stemming from the disparity in their class status, for one of the many socialist charges laid against the cotton lords was their almost feudal exploitation of female workers. Engels himself touched upon it in *The Condition*: "It is, besides, a matter of course that factory servitude, like any other, and to an even higher degree, confers the *ius primae noctis* upon the master. . . . His mill is also his harem."[65] Even if Mary was no longer an employee of Ermen & Engels or had never been one, this kind of sexualized power relationship of the bourgeois and the proletarian, the mill owner and the mill hand, was widely frowned upon in socialist circles.

Whatever the social niceties or details of the original encounter, Engels and Mary were in each other's arms over 1843–44. And while there was, as later letters testify, deep affection between them there was also, for Engels, a very helpful entrée into the dark continent of industrial Manchester. Taking him by the hand, Mary Burns acted as his Persephone, profoundly enriching Engels's appreciation of capitalist society. "She introduced him to the life of the immigrant Irish community in Manchester," as one historian puts it. "She escorted him on excursions through districts which would otherwise have been unsafe for any stranger to enter; she was a source of information about factory and domestic conditions endured by working people."[66] Behind Engels's communist theory was Mary's material reality.

Friedrich Engels's two worlds—the Manchester of the mill owner and the Manchester of Mary Burns—deeply influenced the shift in his focus from philosophy to political economy and would have a marked effect on the emerging shape of Marxism. Uniquely situated, he was able to fuse his firsthand understanding of industrial capitalism and working-class Chartist politics with the Young Hegelian tradition. "German Socialism and Communism have grown, more than any other, from theoretical premises," Engels noted censoriously. "We German theoreticians still knew much too little of the real world to be driven directly by the real conditions to reforms of this 'bad reality.'"[67] In "Outlines of a Critique of Political Economy," a seminal 1843 article for the *Deutsch-Französische Jahrbücher* (Marx's latest newspaper), he displayed the riches of his Manchester experience by dropping the Berlin theorizing in favor of a hardheaded empirical analysis of the economic contradictions and social crises coming Europe's way. The article showed the impact of James Watts's lectures in the critique, framed in tellingly biblical terms, of competition and market manipulation: "This political economy or science of enrichment born of the merchants' mutual envy and greed, bears on its brow the mark of the most detestable selfishness." An all-consuming beast, capitalism necessitated the continuing, unending expansion of the British economy or the terrible alternative of debilitating trade crises as the inherently unstable market system retrenched. This explained Britain's unquenchable thirst for colonies—"You have civilized the ends of the earth to win new terrain for the deployment of your vile avarice"—and the ever-greater domestic concentrations of wealth. With every periodic trade crisis and resulting collapse in credit, the small capitalist and struggling middle class went to the wall. "The middle classes must increasingly disappear until the world is divided into millionaires and paupers, into large landowners and poor farm labourers." At some point all these tensions were bound to come to a bloody climax.[68]

Engels's most remarkable ideological advance came when he applied the Young Hegelian notion of alienation to the realm of political economy. Feuerbach had discussed alienation solely in terms of religious sentiments: "Man . . . projects his essence into objectivity and then makes himself an object of this projected image of himself." But for Engels it wasn't just Christianity that involved a denial of man's nature: competitive capitalism, through its systems of property, money, and exchange, involved an equally disfiguring process of alienation from the authentic human essence. Under capitalism, man was divorced from himself and became the slave of things. "Through this theory [of Adam Smith, Thomas Malthus, and political economy] we have come to know the deepest degradation of mankind, their dependence on the conditions of competition. It has shown us how in the last instance private property has turned man into a commodity whose production and destruction also depend solely on demand."[69] This insight was garnered not only from Feuerbach and Hess but from watching the thousands hunting for work outside the mill gates of Ancoats, condemned to poverty by the slightest trade fluctuations.

What drove this process of alienation, what stood at the root of political economy—and what the Owenites, Fourierists, and Chartists had all overlooked—was private property. This was the essential thesis of Engels's "Outlines." It owed not a little to his recent reading of *What Is Property?* (1840) by the French socialist-cum-anarchist Pierre-Joseph Proudhon, who had answered that question with the celebrated response "It is theft." It was private property in the form of unearned interest from usury and rents from land that, Proudhon suggested, enabled one man to exploit another and underpinned the iniquities of modern capitalism. Proudhon's stress on individual labor and ownership, alongside his conviction that political equality necessitated the abolition of private property, struck an immediate chord with the young Engels (despite the unacceptably anarchist trajectory of Proudhon's thinking). "The right of private property, the consequences of this institution, competition, immorality, misery, are here developed with a power of intellect, and real scientific research, which I never since found united in a single volume," he wrote of Proudhon's book for the Owenite journal *The New Moral World.*[70]

Engels took the conception of private property much further than Proudhon himself had allowed. For Engels it encompassed all the myriad features of political economy—"e.g., wages, trade, value, price, money"— that he had seen at work in Manchester.[71] He concluded that private property was the essential prerequisite of capitalism and it, too, had to be eliminated: "If we abandon private property, then all these unnatural divisions disappear." Discord and individualism would melt away and the true nature of profit and value would be clarified: "Labour becomes its own reward, and the true significance of the wages of labour, hitherto alienated, comes to light—namely, the significance of labour for the determination of the production costs of a thing." The elimination of private property and thence personal avarice would ultimately conclude, in Hegelian fashion, with the end of history and the arrival of communism, "the great transformation to which the century is moving—the reconciliation of mankind with nature and with itself."[72] All this in a short, precocious article by a scarcely known twenty-three-year-old apprentice manufacturer. No wonder, in his Left Bank apartment, Marx was bewitched by this "brilliant essay."[73] But "Outlines" was just a foretaste of Engels's true monument to Manchester.

I have read your book again and I have realized that I am not getting any younger. What power, what incisiveness and what passion drove you to work in those days. That was a time when you were never worried by academic scholarly reservations! Those were the days when you made the reader feel that your theories would become hard facts if not tomorrow then at any rate on the day after. Yet that very illusion gave the whole work a human warmth and a touch of humour that makes our later writings—where "black and white" have become "grey and grey"— seem positively distasteful.[74]

So wrote Marx to Engels almost twenty years after the publication of *The Condition of the Working Class in England*. And he was right. Today, the book's tone of uncompromising passion assures its status as one of the most celebrated polemics in Western literature as well as a leading text— alongside Disraeli's *Sybil; or, The Two Nations*, Dickens's *Hard Times*, and Elizabeth Gaskell's *Mary Barton*—in the "condition of England" canon. But what separates Engels's work from those novels (with their milky Christian hopes for an irenic absolution of class division) is its relentless condemnatory tone. *The Condition* challenged the reader, as few other contemporary accounts dared, with the full, unvarnished horrors of laissez-faire industrialization and urbanization. "I shall be presenting the English with a fine bill of indictment," Engels announced midcomposition. "I accuse the English bourgeoisie before the entire world of murder, robbery and other crimes on a massive scale."[75] Mixing history and statistics, the work races across a range of subjects, from "The Great Towns" to "Irish Immigration" to "The Mining Proletariat," each of them encompassing a litany of crimes to be laid at the feet of the bourgeoisie. Alongside his own firsthand narratives and those culled from James Leach, Engels especially enjoyed deploying the reams of official documentation (the so-called Blue Books) coming out of Whitehall: "I always preferred to present proof from Liberal sources in order to defeat the liberal bourgeoisie by casting their own words in their teeth."[76] It was a polemical trick that Marx would perfect in *Das Kapital*. Thus *The Condition* is full of factory commission reports, court records, articles from the *Manchester Guardian* and *Liverpool Mercury*, and spurious accounts of merry industrializing England from liberal propagandists such as Peter Gaskell and Andrew Ure.

The Condition's strengths lie both in its intellectual rigor and in its empirical richness. What leap off the page are the detailed accounts of the Manchester Engels had seen with Mary Burns: its stink, noise, grime, and human horror. As the German social democrat Wilhelm Liebknecht would later put it, "Friedrich Engels had a clear bright head, free from any romantic or sentimental haze, that did not see men and things through coloured glasses or a misty atmosphere but always in clear bright air, with clear bright eyes, not remaining on the surface but seeing to the bottom of things, piercing them through and through."[77] The Condition was a shining product of this intellectual incisiveness, but it also manifested some obvious journalistic license and a fierce urge to contrast the "phantasms" and "theoretical twaddle" of the Young Hegelians with "real, live things."[78] This combination of political philosophy with material reality would set the precedent for much of Engels's polemical work. "A knowledge of proletarian conditions is absolutely necessary to provide solid ground for socialist theories," he declared.[79]

His rhetorical blows, Engels wrote in the preface, "though aimed at the panniers, are meant for the donkey, namely the German bourgeoisie."[80] For it was only a matter of time before the social crisis wrought by industrialization made its way onto the Continent. "While the conditions of existence of Germany's proletariat have not assumed the classical form that they have in England, we nevertheless have, at bottom, the same social order, which sooner or later must necessarily reach the same extremes as it has already attained across the North Sea, unless the intelligence of the nation brings about the adoption of measures that will provide a new basis for the whole social system."[81] Written back at his parents' house in Barmen in late 1844, The Condition was published in Leipzig in 1845 and aimed for a German audience (it was translated into English for an American edition only in 1885 and then made its way to the British market in 1892). The work was a tour de force of urban industrial horror. In a passage that recalls his earlier account of Barmen's waterways in "Letters from Wuppertal," Engels ascends Ducie Bridge to record a view "characteristic for the whole district": "At the bottom flows, or rather stagnates, the Irk, a narrow, coal-black, foul-smelling stream, full of débris and refuse, which it deposits on the lower right bank. In dry weather, a long string of the most disgusting blackish green slime pools are left standing on this bank, from the depths of which bubbles of miasmatic gas constantly arise and give forth a stench unendurable even on the bridge forty or fifty feet above the surface of the stream." Close by, Engels retraces the steps of James Phillips Kay inside some unsanitary hovels: "In one of these courts there stands directly at the entrance, at the end of the covered passage, a privy without a door, so dirty that the inhabitants can pass into and out of the court only by passing through foul pools of stagnant urine and excrement." All around are hundreds more of these "cattle-sheds for human beings" where men are reduced to the state of animals. Hundreds cramp into dank cellars, pigs share sties with children, railways slash through neighborhoods, and privies, rivers, and water supplies all seem to merge into one deadly mix:

> Such is the Old Town of Manchester, and on re-reading my description, I am forced to admit that instead of being exaggerated, it is far from black enough to convey a true impression of the filth, ruin, and uninhabitableness, the defiance of all considerations of cleanliness, ventilation, and health which characterise the construction of this single district, containing at least 20–30,000 inhabitants. And such a district exists in the heart of the second city of England, the first manufacturing city of the world.[82]

There was worse to come. The south side of the city, just off Oxford Road, was where some of Manchester's 40,000 Irish immigrants huddled. Mary Burns's confreres were the most exploited, lowly paid, and abused of all the city's residents; the most lumpen of the proletariat:

> The cottages are old, dirty, and of the smallest sort, the streets uneven, fallen into ruts and in part without drains or pavement; masses of refuse, offal and sickening filth lie among standing pools in all directions. . . .
> The race that lives in these ruinous cottages, behind broken windows,

mended with oilskin, sprung doors, and rotten door-posts, or in dark, wet cellars, in measureless filth and stench, in this atmosphere penned in as if with a purpose, this race must really have reached the lowest stage of humanity.[83]

Despite having "Tipperary" Mary Burns as his guide, Engels unquestioningly acceded to the mid-Victorian caricature (much of it codified by Thomas Carlyle) of the immature, drunken, filthy Irish. Ignoring both the differences within Manchester's highly varied Irish community and their vital contribution to the Chartist movement (under the leadership of Feargus O'Connor and James Bronterre O'Brien), Engels depicted them en masse as a dissolute group. "The Irishman," Engels explained, "is a carefree, cheerful, potato-eating child of nature," wholly unable to deal with the "mechanical, egoistic, ice-cold hurly-burly of the English factory towns."[84] Inevitably, he swiftly descended into alcohol and depravity: "The southern facile character of the Irishman, his crudity, which places him but little above the savage, his contempt for all humane enjoyments, . . . his filth and poverty, all favour drunkenness." His other weakness was livestock: "The Irishman loves his pig as the Arab his horse. . . . He eats and sleeps with it, his children play with it, ride upon it, roll in the dirt with it."[85] Since their minimal sustenance requirements inevitably forced down local wage rates, the Irish effect on urban life was far from benign. In every part of the economy where these "wild Milesians" competed for jobs, impoverishment was the end result.

It was the primitive, brutish nature of the Irish that allowed them to cope with the terrible demands of industrial employment. With almost vicarious pleasure, Engels systematically listed the maiming and physical disfigurements that accompanied life on the factory floor. "The knees are bent inward and backwards, the ankles deformed and thick, and the spinal column often bent forwards or to one side," he wrote of the effects of the long hours spent in the cotton mill. In the mining industry, the labor of transporting coal and ironstone was so punishing that children's puberty was unnaturally delayed. And then there was the tyranny of time management: "The slavery in which the bourgeoisie holds the proletariat chained, is nowhere more conspicuous than in the factory system." Engels had before him a copy of factory regulations "according to which every operative who comes three minutes too late, forfeits the wages for a quarter of an hour, and every one who comes twenty minutes too late, for a quarter of a day. Every one who remains absent until breakfast forfeits a shilling on Monday, and sixpence every other day of the week, etc." But, as James Leach had first revealed, time was a variable phenomenon: "Operatives find the factory clock moved forward a quarter of an hour and the doors shut, while the clerk moves about with the fines-book inside, noting the many names of the absentees." All of which meant that, in the radical idiom of the day, the working classes were "worse slaves than the Negroes in America, for they are more sharply watched, and yet it is demanded of them that they shall live like human beings, shall think and feel like men!"[86]

The filthy housing, the debilitating hand-to-mouth existence, and the workplace's mental and physical torture—"Women made unfit for childbearing, children deformed, men enfeebled, limbs crushed, whole generations wrecked, afflicted with disease and infirmity, purely to fill the purses of the bourgeoisie"—forced a wretched retreat into drinking and prostitution.[87] This was certainly the case in Sheffield, Engels noted: "The younger generation spend the whole of Sunday lying in the street tossing coins or dog-fighting, and go regularly to the gin palace. . . . No wonder, then, that, as all witnesses testify, early, unbridled sexual intercourse, youthful prostitution, beginning with persons of 14–15 years, is extraordinarily frequent in Sheffield. Crimes of a savage and desperate sort are of common occurrence." The predicament facing the residents of the industrial city was exactly the sort of social disintegration Carlyle had warned of: "The brutal indifference, the unfeeling isolation of each in his private interest becomes the more repellent and offensive. . . . The dissolution of mankind into monads, of which each one has a separate essence, and a separate purpose, the world of atoms, is here carried out to its utmost extreme."[88] And what did the middle classes think of this wretched state of society? "I once went into Manchester with such a bourgeois, and spoke to him of the bad, unwholesome method of building, the frightful condition of the working people's quarters, and asserted that I had never seen so ill-built a city. The man listened quietly to the end, and said at the corner where we parted: 'And yet there is a great deal of money made here; good morning, sir.'"[89]

On the surface, Engels's Manchester appeared to have no purpose or structure—"a planless, knotted chaos of houses"—but in reality there existed a terrible logic behind the city's suffocating form. As Marx in *Das Kapital* would go beneath the bourgeois mirage of freedom and equality to depict capitalism's "hidden abode of production," so Engels, a good Hegelian, transcended the appearance of the city to elucidate its true essence. Yes, slum tenements went up haphazardly on the crumbling riverbanks and railways sliced through old neighborhoods, but these developments were part of an urban form that perfectly reflected the class divisions of industrial society. Like few before him, Engels appreciated the city's spatial dynamics—its streets, houses, factories, and warehouses—as expressions of social and political power. The struggle between the bourgeoisie and the proletariat was not limited to the throstle rooms or Chartist rallies; it was right there in the street layouts, the transport systems, and the urban planning process: "The town itself is peculiarly built, so that a person may live in it for years, and go in and out daily without coming into contact with a working people's quarter or even with workers. . . . This arises chiefly from the fact, that by unconscious tacit agreement, as well as with outspoken conscious determination, the working people's quarters are sharply separated from the sections of the city reserved for the middle class." The social divides wrought by private property were visible in the very flagstones of the city.

Engels's analysis of class zoning begins with the main thoroughfare of Deansgate, where the merchant princes and cotton lords came to make their deals. In the 1840s, like today, the road was a retail and commercial attraction lined with high-end shops and showy warehouses designed in Italianate style and used as much for corporate display as for storage. And, as with so many other modern city centers, "the whole district is abandoned by dwellers, and is lonely and deserted at night; only watchmen and policemen traverse its narrow lanes with their dark lanterns." But surrounding it, in the inner suburbs, lay the "unmixed working people's quarters" of Manchester proper, "stretching like a girdle . . . around the commercial district." And beyond that, outside this girdle, in the suburbs, "lives the middle bourgeoisie . . . in regularly laid out streets in the vicinity of the working quarters, especially in Chorlton and the lower lying portions of Cheetham Hill; the upper bourgeoisie in remoter villas with gardens in Chorlton and Ardwick, or on the breezy heights of Cheetham Hill, Broughton, and Pendleton, in free, wholesome country air, in fine, comfortable homes." The finest part of the arrangement was that

> the members of this money aristocracy can take the shortest road through the middle of all the labouring districts to their places of business, without ever seeing that they are in the midst of the grimy misery that lurks to the right and the left. For the thoroughfares leading from the Exchange in all directions out of the city are lined, on both sides, with an almost unbroken series of shops, and are so kept in the hands of the middle and lower bourgeoisie, which, out of self-interest, cares for a decent and cleanly external appearance. . . . They [the shops] suffice to conceal from the eyes of the wealthy men and women of strong stomachs and weak nerves the misery and grime which form the complement to their wealth.[90]

Engels, who in Barmen had shared his neighborhood with the local dyers and weavers, declared himself properly shocked: "I have never seen so systematic a shutting out of the working class from the thoroughfares, so tender a concealment of everything which might affront the eye and the nerves of the bourgeois, as in Manchester." He was convinced this manipulation of urban form was not accidental: "I cannot help feeling that the liberal manufacturers, the bigwigs of Manchester, are not so innocent after all, in the matter of this sensitive method of construction."[91] Of course, this notion of two nations in one city was a familiar one, and Leon Faucher, among others, had already pointed out Manchester's geography of class division. But no one before Engels had managed to describe it with such acute percipience.

Engels established a mode of reading the city through an entirely different lens: an appreciation that class power was the ultimate determinant of urban form. It was a subject that he would return to some thirty years later in an analysis of Second Empire Paris, which, thanks to the urban improvements of Baron Georges-Eugène Haussmann, had been transformed from a decaying medieval city into a metropolis worthy of Emperor Napoleon III. Markets were erected, sewers dug, trees planted, churches and museums redecorated, and, most crucially, a series of boulevards driven through the traditional working-class arrondissements. In the process, some twenty-seven thousand houses were demolished and tens of thousands of workers either forced or priced out of the city center. No matter how the scheme was dressed up—whether it was presented as an improvement to public health or to transport—it was far more obviously an example of class-based urban planning in which the fabric of the city constituted a reification of bourgeois values. Engels termed it simply "Haussmann":

> By "Haussmann" I mean the practice which has now become general of making breaches in the working class quarters of our big towns, and particularly in those which are centrally situated, quite apart from whether this is done from considerations of public health and for beautifying the town, or owing to the demand for big centrally situated business premises, or owing to traffic requirements, such as the laying down of railways, streets, etc. No matter how different the reasons may be, the result is everywhere the same: the scandalous alleys and lanes disappear to the accompaniment of lavish self-praise from the bourgeoisie on account of this tremendous success, but they appear again immediately somewhere else and often in the immediate neighborhood.[92]

Critics and biographers have often suggested that Engels simply walked the streets of 1840s Manchester, notebook in hand, writing down what he saw with little premeditation. According to Steven Marcus, "Engels was choosing to write about his own experience: to contend with it, to exploit it, to clarify it, and in some literal sense to create it and thereby himself. For in transforming his experiences into language he was at once both generating and discovering their structure."[93] Similarly, historian Simon Gunn describes how "Engels developed a style of grimly detailed reportage in order to extract meaning from the profusion of sense impressions."[94] Manchester historian Jonathan Schofield goes even further in stressing that Lancashire reshaped Engels's thinking and, with it, the nature of communism. "Without Manchester there would have been no Soviet Union," he declares. "And the history of the 20th century would have been very different."[95]

Much of this approach falls into a broader conception of Engels as the socially acute but philosophically naïve reporter, the Marx collaborator whose only real achievement was to provide the data on capitalist conditions. Yet, following his 1842 "conversion" to communism, Engels came to Manchester with a clear idea of the political significance of industrial society. He was so drawn to this city—"where the modern art of manufacture has reached its perfection"—precisely because it promised to validate the communism he had learned from Moses Hess, with its prediction of social revolution. Manchester's role was to confirm, not create the theory. Which meant that, despite The Condition's dark vividness, what set it apart from other urban travel literature of the time was not its descriptive resonance but its polemical power.

This explains the book's curious opening, with its epic account of British industrialization—"a history which has no counter-part in the annals of humanity." With this sweeping narrative, Engels affirmed his belief in Hess's "Triarchy," with each leading European nation playing its role in the march toward communism: "The industrial revolution [is] of the same importance for England as the political revolution for France, and the philosophical revolution for Germany."[96] Engels revealed how the dynamic of industrialization inexorably dismantled the old economy of guilds and apprenticeships in favor of class division, of "great capitalists and working men who had no prospect of rising above their class." For the great crime of the British Industrial Revolution was that, thanks to the system of private property, the technological and economic progress of the nineteenth century had not brought about the equitable enrichment of man. Industrial capitalism had promised an abundance of riches and an end to the Malthusian specter of famine, but these were denied to the people by forms of property ownership that only entrenched inequality. Instead of leading to broad societal prosperity, industrialization had produced the proletarian—"who has nothing but his two hands, who consumes today what he earned yesterday, who is subject to every possible chance, and has not the slightest guarantee for being able to learn the barest necessities of life, whom every crisis, every whim of his employer may deprive of bread, this proletarian is placed in the most revolting, inhuman position conceivable for a human being."[97] This notion of social class as economically determined would, in time, become one of Marxism's most influential propositions.

These desperate, miserable proletarians, born of Britain's breakneck industrialization, are the callow heroes of *The Condition*. Despite the bucolic, "idyllic simplicity" of preindustrial peasant life—of farmers and fields, maypoles and harvesting—"intellectually, they [the peasants] were dead," according to Engels. "They were comfortable in their silent vegetation, and but for the industrial revolution they would never have emerged from this existence, which, cosily romantic as it was, was nevertheless not worthy of human beings."[98] It is only once the working classes have been ripped from their villages and the idiocy of rural life and herded into factories that they come to appreciate their purpose as a proletariat. And here Engels provides one of the earliest accounts of the historic function of the proletariat as the harbingers of the communist revolution. Crucial to that role was their wretched existence within the city. Engels's breakthrough in "Outlines of a Critique of Political Economy," that capitalism alienated man from his human essence, provided the essential ideological preamble. Now, his trawl through the slums of Salford and Little Ireland was an attempt, as Gareth Stedman Jones puts it, "to validate, both metaphorically and literally, the Feuerbachian conception of the ontological loss of humanity associated with religious alienation and—in the radical communist gloss added by Young Hegelians—with the establishment of money and private property."[99] In the industrial city, man was reduced to a beast of burden—hence the ubiquitous animalistic imagery, the endless swine and cattle, that suffuses Engels's text. As *The Condition* notes of Manchester's working-class accommodation, "in such dwellings only a physically degenerate race, robbed of all humanity, degraded, reduced morally and physically to bestiality, could feel comfortable and at home."[100]

Such suffering was, however, necessary. It was only once the impoverished masses reached their lowest ebb, once their very humanity had been taken from them, that they began to realize their class consciousness. "Here humanity attains its most complete development and its most brutish; here civilization works its miracles, and civilized man is turned back almost into a savage," as de Tocqueville described the process.[101] As the birthplace of the labor movement, the city was thus both the scene of immense sacrifice and the origin of redemption: through exploitation came ultimate liberation. As Engels later put it in "The Housing Question," "Only the proletariat created by modern large-scale industry, liberated from all inherited fetters including those which chained it to the land, and herded together in the big cities, is in a position to accomplish the great social transformation which put an end to all class exploitation and all class rule."[102]

Through their planning of the city, the middle classes had hoped to put the working classes out of sight and out of mind. But with the proletariat cooped up in their slums, the spatial configuration of the city only accelerated the nurturing of class consciousness. Thus Manchester was the scene of middle-class triumph and its doom. Every factory, slum, and workhouse was a bourgeois memento mori: their glistening cities were tombs of the living dead. "The middle class dwells upon a soil that is honeycombed, and may any day collapse," Engels proclaimed. From Glasgow to London, revolution was inevitable, "a revolution in comparison with which the French Revolution, and the year 1794, will prove to have been child's play."[103]

This sense of the city's purpose underlies Engels's seemingly rambling descriptions of 1840s Manchester. This was not simply a feuilleton but a politically persuasive work of supple propaganda. Everything had an ideological role to play: the landscape, the people, and the industry. Hence, in Engels's account, we never hear the working class speak; nor is there any sense of the multiple divisions within Manchester's laboring masses—the street cleaners as distinct from the cotton spinners, Tories from Liberals, Catholics from Protestants. The nuances of Manchester's multiple economies—distribution, services, construction, and retail in addition to the cotton mills—are subtly elided for an overarching urban confrontation between monolithic labor and capital. Similarly, the city's rich working-class civil society—mechanics' institutes, friendly societies and workingmen's clubs, political parties and chapels—is entirely absent. Instead, Engels offers one undifferentiated proletarian mass eager to fulfill its historic destiny.

This focus on the historic role of the proletariat significantly distinguishes Engels's thinking from the Owenite and Chartist movements, which had little sense of the broader socioeconomic forces that had given rise to the working class. Nor did their schemes for New Harmonies, phalansteries, or charters take account of the social revolution required: "They acknowledge no historical development, and wish to place the nation in a state of Communism at once, overnight, instead of continuing political action until the goal is won and the movement can dissolve. . . . They preach instead a philanthropy and universal love far more unfruitful for the present state of England. . . . They are too abstract, too metaphysical, and accomplish little."[104] What was needed was practicable action, a union of Chartism and socialism—and, with that, the march of history toward communism. "The revolution must come; it is already too late to bring about a peaceful solution," Engels declared. The one hope was to lessen the accompanying violence by converting as much of the proletariat to communism as possible: "In proportion as the proletariat absorbs socialistic and communistic elements, will the revolution diminish in bloodshed, revenge, and savagery." For even if the specific task of delivering the communist future belonged to the proletariat, the new society would embrace every class as old antagonisms melted away. "Communism is a question of humanity and not of the workers alone."[105]

With the clash between the proletariat and the bourgeoisie resolved in the communist future, the site of this struggle—the modern big city—would be rendered obsolete "by the abolition of the capitalist mode of production."[106] The cities might have witnessed the birth of the labor movement, but that movement's triumph would resolve the old antithesis between town and country. In later works, Engels predicted that modern industrial techniques and a planned economy meant that commercial concentrations in urban areas would prove unnecessary. In turn, the poor sanitation and degraded environment—"the present poisoning of the air, water and land"—would be alleviated by the town-country fusion. And so we have the irony that Engels, the great apostle of urban radicalism, ended his days advocating a technocratic future devoid of civic life: "Abolition of the antithesis between town and country is not merely possible. It has become a direct necessity of industrial production itself, just as it has become a necessity of agricultural production and, besides, of public health. . . . It is true that in the huge towns civilisation has bequeathed us a heritage which it will take much time and trouble to get rid of. But it must and will be got rid of, however protracted a process it may be."[107]

The impact of *The Condition of the Working Class* was immediately apparent within German radical circles. "As far as I know, I was the first to describe in German . . . the social conditions created by modern large-scale industry," Engels later recalled proudly, "to provide an actual basis for German socialism, which was then arising and was expending itself in empty phrases."[108] According to one Elberfeld communist, "Friedrich Engels's book, which abases all sacrosanct nonsense and iniquity, lies openly in taverns."[109] Most bourgeois reviews, including the one in the local *Barmen Zeitung*, were scathing, but the Prussian statistician Friedrich Ludwig von Reden provided one exception, writing that the work deserved "particular attention both for its subject and its thoroughness and accuracy." He was especially impressed by Engels's "visibly truthful representation of the English bourgeoisie's attitude towards the proletariat: the despotism it practised in all important social issues, on the one hand, and the rage and frustrated bitterness of the propertyless on the other."[110] Marx, as we have seen, was entranced by the book and its helpful accumulation of data, from the mill owners' manipulation of factory clocks to the physical condition of the laborers to the cotton industry's economic history. It was a source to which he turned again and again for concrete evidence of capitalism's inhumanity. "As far as concerns the period from the beginning of large-scale industry in England down to the year 1845 I shall only touch upon this here and there, referring the reader for fuller details to Friedrich Engels's *Condition of the Working Class*," he wrote in an early note to the first volume of *Das Kapital*. "The fullness of Engels's insight into the nature of the capitalist method of production has been shown by the factory reports, the reports on mines, etc., that have appeared since the publication of his book."[111]

But Engels contributed more than just facts. While Marxist scholars rarely give it full credit, *The Condition of the Working Class* (together with "Outlines of a Critique of Political Economy") was a pioneering text of communist theory. Engels had, in the words of Wilhelm Liebknecht, "de-Hegeled" himself: the human injustices he witnessed at first hand in industrializing Manchester took him beyond the "mere abstract knowledge" of his Berlin days. With astonishing intellectual maturity, the twenty-four-year-old Engels applied the Young Hegelian notion of alienation to the material realities of Victorian Britain and thereby crafted the ideological architecture of scientific socialism. The germ of theoretical communism he took from Moses Hess had flowered in his Manchester days. So much of what would later be regarded as mainstream Marxist thought—the nature of class division, the inherent instability of modern industrial capitalism, the creation by the bourgeoisie of their own gravediggers, the inevitability of socialist revolution—was first embedded in Engels's brilliant polemic.[112] Yet *The Condition* was also to be Engels's last substantive work of socialist ideology for thirty years. By the summer of 1844, Engels's apprenticeship in Manchester had come to an end, and the son and heir to Ermen & Engels returned home to Barmen. On his way back, he stopped off in Paris for an altogether warmer meeting with Karl Marx. From then on, Engels's life's work was given over to managing "Moor."

4

"A LITTLE PATIENCE AND SOME TERRORISM"

In the final moments of *Old Goriot*, Honoré de Balzac's acid chronicle of bourgeois Paris, young Rastignac steps forward to confront the French capital: "Lights were beginning to twinkle here and there. His gaze fixed almost avidly upon the space that lay between the column of the Place Vendôme and the dome of the Invalides; there lay the splendid world that he had wished to gain. He eyed that humming hive with a look that foretold its despoliation, as if he already felt on his lips the sweetness of its honey, and said with superb defiance, 'It's war between us now!'"

Paris provided the glittering stage for the next phase of Engels's life. It was a city, he thought, whose "population combines a passion for pleasure with a passion for historical action like no other people." Like Rastignac, the ambitious, intellectually voracious, and libidinous Engels wanted to taste all of the city's delights. After the philistinism of Barmen and the smoggy drizzle of Manchester, Paris offered countless opportunities for a young man of means. As Balzac marveled, "Paris is an ocean. Throw in the plummet, you will never reach bottom. Survey it; describe it. However conscientious your survey and careful your chart, however numerous and concerned to learn the truth the explorers of this sea may be, there will always be a virgin realm, an unknown cavern, flowers, pearls, monsters, things undreamed of, overlooked by the literary divers."[1]

Engels was not alone in wanting to master this metropolis. For radicals, intellectuals, artists, and philosophers, Paris was, as Walter Benjamin said, "the capital of the nineteenth century." The Young Hegelian Arnold Ruge called it "the great laboratory where world history is formed and has its ever fresh source. It is in Paris that we shall live our victories and our defeats. Even our philosophy, the field where we are in advance of our time, will only be able to triumph when proclaimed in Paris and impregnated with the French spirit."[2] True to Moses Hess's European triarchy, Paris's role was to draw on its revolutionary essence and provide the vital spark in the struggle for communism. To the material injustices of England and the philosophical advances of Germany, France would add the political dynamite, "the crowing of the Gallic cock," as Marx excitedly called it.

More immediately, Paris provided the backdrop for the formation of the modern Communist League, the political vehicle that Marx and Engels alighted on for the furtherance of their philosophy. It was here that Engels learned the dark arts of machine politics: amid the capital's boarding houses and workshops, he started to craft the movement that would culminate in the worldwide Communist Party. Accompanying the politics—the vote rigging and procedural maneuverings—came Engels's collaboration with Marx on the nineteenth century's most celebrated polemic, *The Communist Manifesto*. It all began over drinks at the Café de la Régence—a bar that had once served Benjamin Franklin, Louis Napoleon, and Voltaire himself now played host to an increasingly dissolute pair of young Prussian philosophers.

Karl and a pregnant Jenny Marx had arrived in Paris in October 1843 after the demise of his newspaper, the *Rheinische Zeitung*. No less a reader than Tsar Nicholas I had complained of the paper's anti-Russian tone and forced the Prussian authorities to revoke its printing license. Marx's fellow editor Arnold Ruge suggested they leave Prussia to pursue their journalistic careers in France, at the newly formed *Deutsch-Französische Jahrbücher*. But within weeks, Ruge, who had sunk a great deal of his own money into the paper, was already regretting his suggestion as Marx's lack of editorial discipline became apparent: "He finishes nothing, breaks off everything and plunges ever afresh into an endless sea of books."[3] And the division between the two was more than just temperamental. Soon after arriving in Paris, Marx began to distance himself from Ruge's Young Hegelian, by more clearly defining himself as a communist and embracing the activist elements of the Parisian working class. "You should be present at one of the meetings of French workers so that you could believe the youthful freshness and nobility prevailing amongst these toil-worn people," he wrote to Feuerbach in August 1844. "It is among these 'barbarians' of our civilized society that history is preparing the practical element for the emancipation of man."[4] In addition, his study of the French Revolution and his detailed reading of Adam Smith's and David Ricardo's classic works of political economy (as well as Engels's "Outlines of a Critique of Political Economy") led Marx to shift his focus from the problem of religious alienation to the material realities of capitalist society. "The years 1843–45 [were] the most decisive in his life," declares Isaiah Berlin. "In Paris he underwent his final intellectual transformation."[5]

Less concerned with a critique of Hegelianism, Marx was increasingly interested in the division of labor and the influence Carlyle's cash nexus had on the nature of man. Like Engels in his observation of Manchester laborers, Marx saw that class-based capitalism progressively alienated man from himself. And, like Engels, he regarded the solution to this crisis of alienation as lying in the property-less hands of the very class created by capitalism, the proletariat. It was their historic function to return man to himself ("human emancipation") by transcending the iniquity that underlay political economy, the system of private property. "Communism is the positive abolition of private property and thus of human self-alienation and therefore the real re-appropriation of the human essence by and for man," Marx wrote.[6] This obvious philosophical like-mindedness meant that by the time Marx and Engels downed their aperitifs at the Café de la Régence the memory of their chilly 1842 meeting at the *Rheinische Zeitung* offices had faded. Now, over ten beer-soaked days, they formed the emotional and ideological bond that would last a lifetime. "When I visited Marx in Paris in the summer of 1844, our complete agreement in all theoretical fields became evident and our joint work dates from that time," recalled Engels.[7]

What was the nature of this meeting of minds, this companionship that in the words of Lenin "surpassed the most moving stories of human friendship among the ancients"?[8] Unpersuasively, Edmund Wilson claims that Marx provided "the paternal authority" that Engels had rejected in his own father. Alternatively, Francis Wheen describes Engels as serving Marx "as a kind of substitute mother." In a less Freudian fashion, their relationship is perhaps best seen as one of affectionate first cousins. While sharing a Rhenish-Prussian background, the two men displayed markedly different but mutually supportive characteristics. "Engels had a brighter, less contorted, and more harmonious disposition: physically and intellectually he was more elastic and resilient," was how biographer Gustav Mayer judged it.[9] Certainly, there was less of the "dragon" about Engels—less "Moorish" impetuosity, intellectual self-absorption, and personal indignation at the human cost of capitalism. Engels was both more aloof and also more rigorously empirical than his distracted, tormented collaborator. Marx's son-in-law Paul Lafargue called Engels "methodical as an old maid."[10] Physically, too, Engels was far more robust than the blister- and boil-ridden Marx, whose personal and financial stresses could be read like an angry Braille across his body. Much has been made of how these differing characteristics revealed themselves in the handwriting of the two men, with Engels's studious, symmetrical script (decorated here and there by a neat, humorous illustration) offering a marked contrast to Marx's furious, blotch-marked scribbling. Yet, in a neat metaphor for their friendship, it was often only Engels who could decipher Marx's meaning.

For the next forty years, their relationship barely faltered even amid the most wretched of circumstances. "Money, knowledge—everything was in common between them. . . . Engels extended his friendship to the whole of Marx's family: Marx's daughters were as children to him, they called him their second father. This friendship lasted beyond the grave," was how Lafargue described it.[11] Fundamental to this friendship was a division of responsibility: from the Paris days onward, Engels recognized Marx's superior ability to provide the ideological grounding of "our outlook." He accepted this intellectual demotion in a typically candid, matter-of-fact manner. "I cannot deny that both before and during my forty years' collaboration with Marx I had a certain independent share in laying the foundations of the theory," Engels wrote after his friend's death. "But the greater part of its leading basic principles ... belongs to Marx. . . . Marx was a genius; we others were at best talented. Without him the theory would not be by far what it is today. It therefore rightly bears his name."[12] This faith in Marx's genius was what convinced Engels to step back, sacrifice the development of his own ideas, and play "second fiddle" to "so splendid a first fiddle as Marx."[13] And the devoted Engels could never understand how anyone would have acted differently, "how anyone can be envious of genius; it's something so very special that we, who have not got it, know it to be unattainable right from the start; but to be envious of anything like that one must have to be frightfully small-minded."[14] Crucially, Engels never needed to be converted to Marx's thinking. He had, according to Marx, "arrived by another road . . . at the same result as I" and was thus equally committed to exploring the theoretical and political implications of their philosophical stance. The only difference, in Engels's words, was that "Marx stood higher, saw further, and took a wider and quicker view than all the rest of us."[15]

The first fruit of their relationship was a pamphlet entitled *A Critique of Critical Criticism: Against Bruno Bauer and Co.* (1845). This short work revealed their shared impatience, in the wake of their Manchester and Paris experiences, with the idealistic remnants of the Young Hegelian school and served as a public proclamation of Marx and Engels's newly held materialism. "In direct contrast to German philosophy which descends from heaven to earth, here it is a matter of ascending from earth to heaven," as they later codified this philosophical breach. "That is to say, not of setting out from what men say, imagine, conceive . . . in order to arrive at men in the flesh; but setting out from real, active men, and on the basis of their real life-process demonstrating the development of the ideological reflexes and echoes of the life process."[16]

In line with their new thinking, Marx and Engels now portrayed idealist philosophizing as "formulae, nothing but formulae," and denounced the Bauers' Berlin circle as a self-indulgent impediment to progressive social change. "A war has been declared against those of the German philosophers, who refuse to draw from their mere theories practical inferences, and who contend that man has nothing to do but to speculate upon metaphysical questions," as Engels later put it with increasing stridency.[17] Leaving behind the "beer literati," Marx and Engels wanted to focus on social and economic conditions, not chase the Hegelian shadows of Idea and Spirit. "Real humanism has no more dangerous enemy in Germany than spiritualism or speculative idealism, which substitutes 'self-consciousness' or the 'spirit' for the real individual man," they declared.[18] Marx's reading of political economy and Engels's time in the cotton mills of Manchester had revealed to both men the defining role of private property in shaping modern society. It was material reality, not "faded, widowed Hegelian philosophy" that determined social structures, and, if evidence were needed, one had only to consult the past. In an early, tentative exploration of the materialist interpretation of history, Engels countered the role of the Hegelian Idea in history by stressing the real contribution of flesh and blood humanity. "History does nothing, has no 'enormous wealth,' wages no battles," he wrote in criticism of Bruno Bauer. "It is not 'history' but living human beings who own possessions, take action and fight battles. There is no independent entity called 'history,' using mankind to attain its ends: history is simply the purposeful activity of human beings."[19]

Despite its grandiose theme, the *Critique* was initially conceived as merely a short squib against Bauer and company, and Engels quickly churned out his draft before leaving Paris for Barmen in September 1844. "Good-bye for the present, dear Karl," Engels wrote on his departure, "I have not been able to recapture the mood of cheerfulness and goodwill I experienced during the ten days I spent with you."[20] Foolishly, he left the manuscript behind with "dear Karl," and it soon accumulated the telltale signs of Marx's stylistic incontinence. First of all, there was the length. "The fact that you enlarged the *Critical Criticism* to twenty sheets surprised me not a little," Engels remarked. "If you have retained my name on the title page it will look odd since I wrote barely 1½ sheets." And then there was the disproportionate space given to denouncing political foes: "The supreme contempt we two evince towards the *Literatur-Zeitung* is in glaring contrast to the sheets we devote to it." The pamphlet's growth was also an early omen of Marx's crippling weakness for distracting himself from more substantive projects. "Do try and finish your political economy book, even if there's much in it that you yourself are still dissatisfied with, it doesn't really matter; minds are ripe and we must strike while the iron is hot," Engels pleaded in what would, over the following decades, become a wearily familiar refrain. "Do as I do, set yourself a date by which you will *definitely have finished*, and make sure it gets into print quickly." Finally, there was the journalistic knack of a catchy title: in mock reference to the Bauer circle, Marx had crassly rechristened the pamphlet *The Holy Family; or Critique of Critical Criticism. Against Bruno Bauer and Co.* "Its new title . . . will probably get me into hot water with my pious and already highly incensed parents," Engels noted, "though you could not have known that."[21]

Even prior to the publication of *The Holy Family*, the situation at the Engels home was hardly harmonious. Despite a two-year absence and his agreement to return to "huckstering" in the family firm, Engels's relations with his father were strained. Both of them found that atheistic communism and evangelical Protestantism did not rub along well. "I can't eat, drink, sleep, let out a fart, without being confronted by this same accursed lamb-of-God expression," Engels complained to Marx. "Today the whole tribe went toddling off to Communion. . . . This morning the doleful expressions surpassed themselves. To make matters worse I spent yesterday evening with [Moses] Hess in Elberfeld, where we held forth about communism until two in the morning. Today, of course, long faces over my late return, hints that I might have been in jail." The situation was not helped by his sister Marie's engagement to another communist, Emil Blank: "Of course, the house is now in a hellish state of turmoil."[22] Those good pietists Friedrich and Elise were probably asking themselves where it had all gone wrong.

None of these domestic ructions diverted Engels from his missionary work. On his return journey from Paris through the Rhineland, he had been highly encouraged by the advanced state of socialist sentiment. "I spent three days in Cologne and marveled at the tremendous propaganda we had put out there," he wrote in a letter to Marx. Even along the Wupper valley, that Zion of obscurantists, there were signs of progress: "This promises to be first-rate soil for our principles. In Barmen the police inspector is a communist. The day before yesterday I was called on by a former schoolfellow, a grammar school teacher, who's been thoroughly bitten although he's had no contact whatever with communists."[23] In an article for the Owenite journal *The New Moral World*, Engels reported on "the rapidity with which Socialism has progressed in this country." Gilding the lily somewhat, Engels announced that "Socialism is the question of the day in Germany. . . . You cannot go on board a steamer, or into a railway carriage, or mail-coach, without meeting somebody who has imbibed at least some Social idea, and who agrees with you, that something must be done to reorganize society." He went so far as to suggest that "among my own family—and it is a very pious and loyal one—I count six or more, each of whom has been converted without being influenced by the remainder."[24] As a result of such successes, "the clerical gentry have been preaching against us. . . . For the present they confine themselves to the atheism of the young, but I hope this will soon be followed by a philippic against communism."[25]

Engels was particularly excited by the growing number of agricultural uprisings and industrial strikes across the German states, the most celebrated of which was the revolt of Silesian weavers in Peterswaldau in June 1844. After years of impoverishment caused by international and technological competition, these formerly wealthy and independent artisans stormed the local cotton mills in desperation. Similar riots erupted across Silesia and Bohemia as "the social question"—what to do about poverty and exploitation in the face of accelerating industrialization—started to dominate public discourse. The Silesian weavers gained particular notoriety thanks to Heinrich Heine's sorrowful "Song of the Silesian Weavers." As the workers chant a lament for the "old Germany," they weave a shroud for their vanishing society:

> The crack of the loom and the shuttle's flight;
> We weave all day and we weave all night.

Germany, we're weaving your coffin-sheet;
Still weaving, ever weaving!

Engels translated the verses into English and proudly announced that "Heinrich Heine, the most eminent of all living German poets, has joined our ranks."[26]

Engels's political strategy was to channel this growing concern in an explicitly communist direction through a series of public lectures and debates he organized together with his old mentor Moses Hess. The first, in February 1845, was held at the popular Zweibrücker Hof in Elberfeld and attended by the liberal elite of the town. Addressing an audience numbering some two hundred and including the directors of local manufacturing and commercial firms, members of the court of law, and even the attorney general, Engels outlined the principles of communism and invited the audience to respond. Only members of the working class—the handmaidens of the communist future, but not yet allowed into Elberfeld's finer drinking establishments— were absent from the discussion of their predicament. Engels thought the evening, which began with a reading of Shelley, an astounding success. "All Elberfeld and Barmen, from the financial aristocracy to *épicerie*, was represented, only the proletariat being excluded.... The ensuing discussion lasted until one o'clock. The subject is a tremendous draw. All the talk is of communism and every day brings us new supporters."[27]

One Elberfeld resident remembered the evening slightly differently:

In order to make the thing look harmless, some harpists had been engaged. At the beginning of the meeting, poems based on social themes were read. Then Hess and "Friedrich Oswald" began their speeches. In the audience were manufacturers who had come for a thrill; they expressed their annoyance by laughter and jeers. The defense of capitalist society was left to the director of the local theater. The more violently he attacked the possibility of communism, the more enthusiastically the notables drank his health.[28]

Engels enjoyed the rough-and-tumble of public speaking: "Standing up in front of real, live people and holding forth to them directly and straightforwardly, so that they see and hear you is something quite different from engaging in this devilishly abstract quill-pushing with an abstract audience in one's 'mind's eye.'" In his speeches, Engels emphasized the iniquitous nature of capitalist society and the inevitability of its descent into class conflict as the divide between rich and poor widened and the middling classes were squeezed out of existence: "The ruin of the small middle class, that estate which constituted the main foundation of states during the last century, is the first result of this struggle. Daily we see how this class in society is crushed by the power of capital."[29] As the waste, bankruptcies, and unemployment inherent in the capitalist mode of production mount up, as a result of cyclical trade crises and market failures, he argued, society would come to demand its reorganization along more rational principles of distribution and exchange. That future would necessitate a form of communism where competition was eliminated, with capital and labor efficiently allocated through a central authority. Crime would disappear, the tensions between individual and society would dissolve, and productivity would skyrocket as industrial advances were marshaled for the good of all rather than the profits of the few: "The greatest saving of labour power lies in the fusing of the individual powers into social collective power and in the kind of organization which is based on this concentration of powers hitherto opposed to one another."[30] In soothing tones, Engels explained the series of practical policies that would lead to this communist future: universal childhood education, followed by a reorganization of the poor relief system and a progressive tax on capital. "So you see, gentlemen, there is no intention of introducing common ownership overnight and against the will of the nation. What we are trying to do is to establish the aim and the ways and means of advancing towards it," he reassured the conservative-minded Elberfeld elite.[31] Indeed, it was almost a question of old-fashioned paternalism. "We must make it our business to contribute our share towards humanizing the condition of the modern helots," the young manufacturing heir suggested.[32]

Despite the conciliatory message, Engels's sermonizing brought him to the attention of the authorities. The mayor of Elberfeld threatened to withdraw the license of any hotel keeper who provided a further meeting venue. He also dispatched a letter to the Rhineland president, Freiherr von Spiegel-Borlinghausen, recounting the subversive debates and pointing to Hess and Engels as the organizers. The security services, too, became involved. "Friedrich Engels of Barmen is a quite reliable man, but he has a son who is a rabid communist and wanders about as a man of letters; it is possible that his name is Frederick," noted a police report to the Ministry of the Interior.[33] On the basis of such intelligence the Prussian interior minister issued a decree banning all communist meetings in Elberfeld-Barmen. The unfortunate travails of Engels senior and his disreputable son were soon the talk of polite Barmen society. One Wuppertal notable, Georg Gottfried Gervinus, remarked on the looming perils of communist indoctrination in a letter to his friend Otto Freiherr von Rutenberg. He used Engels as stark evidence "of how they are reeling in a young merchant and converting him to their philosophy." He recounted a conversation with Engels père: "The father is very unhappy about his experience with his son; he told me: 'You can't imagine how much this grieves a father: first my father endowed the Protestant parish in Barmen, then I built a church and now my son is tearing it down.'—I replied: 'That's the story of our times.' "[34]

Engels's father was indeed furious about his son's political activities. As an unrepentant Engels described the scene to Marx, "My public appearance as a communist has fostered in him bourgeois fanaticism of truly splendid proportions."[35] And in response to Engels's latest announcement that he would not continue in the family firm after all, the patriarch curtailed his allowance, leaving the aspirant revolutionary "leading a real dog's life" and moping around the house. "He is now at terrible variance with his family," Engels's Bradford friend George Weerth reported. "He is considered godless and impious, and the rich father will not give his son another *pfennig* for his keep."[36] So in the autumn of 1844, Engels retreated to his study to work on *The Condition of the Working Class in England*. But that too aroused suspicion: "If I sit in my room and work—on communism, of course, as they know—the same expression." By this time, Marx had been deported from Paris as a political undesirable and was scrabbling together an exile's living in Brussels. Out of his devotion, Engels promised to give his new friend the book's advance; then, catching wind of police plans to have him arrested and keen not to embarrass his parents any further in the eyes of the Barmen bourgeoisie, he decided to join Marx in Belgium. It was a momentous step: by the time he stepped across the Belgian border in spring 1845 it was clear he would not easily be allowed back into Prussia—not even for Marie's wedding to Emil. "As you know, of all my brothers and sisters, I loved you the best and you were the one in whom I always had most confidence," he wrote to his disappointed "goose" that May.[37]

No sooner had Engels met up with Marx than the two of them left Belgium for a study trip to England. There, Engels reacquainted himself with Mary Burns (who would return with them to the Continent), while Marx immersed himself in political economy, reading the works of various liberal economists and boning up on official government publications. Their favored reading spot was a bay window seat in Manchester's seventeenth-century Chetham's Library, whose hundred thousand volumes they plundered for political and social data. "In the last few days I have often been sitting at the quadrilateral desk in the small bow window where we sat 24 years ago," Engels wrote to Marx in 1870. "I like this place very much; because of its coloured window the weather is always fine there."[38] The thick oak desk and stained-glass window are still there today, though now they look out on the youthful bustle of the Chetham School of Music and are overlooked by the skyscrapers, hotels, and cranes of corporate Manchester. The library acts as a popular shrine for communist pilgrims seeking some kind of direct physical connection to the founding fathers. According to one tour guide, "Whenever I bring people from the Chinese consulate here and get out the old books that Marx and Engels touched, they weep."[39]

This time, Engels didn't stay long in Manchester, and he and Marx were back in Belgium by late summer 1845. The following months were among the happiest the two spent together: living side by side in neighboring Brussels apartments with their respective partners, they debated, laughed and drank long into the night. "When I informed my wife of your very philosophical system of writing in couples till 3 or 4 o'clock in the morning, she protested that such philosophy would not suit her," the Chartist George Julian Harney joked to Engels in March 1846, "and that if she was in Brussels she would get up a *pronunciamento* amongst your wives."[40] Brussels offered Engels the opportunity to devote himself entirely to socialism. There was no threat of "huckstering" in Belgium—instead, there were intoxicating evenings spent in the bars with Marx, Moses Hess, George Weerth (who was delighted to exchange Bradford for Brussels), Stephan Born, the poet Ferdinand Freiligrath, and the journalist Karl Heinzen. Michael Bakunin, the Russian aristocrat and future anarchist, was left out of the circle, and he bitterly described to his friend Georg Herwegh how "the Germans, those craftsmen Bornstedt [editor of the prodemocracy paper *Deutsch-Brüsseler Zeitung*], Marx, and Engels—especially Marx—are plotting their usual mischief here. Vanity, malice, squabbles, theoretical intolerance and practical cowardice, endless theorizing about life, activity, and simplicity, and in practice a total absence of life, action, or simplicity. . . . The single word *bourgeois* has become an epithet which they repeat *ad nauseam*, though they themselves are ingrained bourgeois from head to foot."[41]

There was one social difficulty in this otherwise gregarious émigré scene: "the small English woman from Manchester," in George Weerth's words. Described in correspondence of the period as either Engels's "mistress" or his "wife," Mary Burns was clearly not to everyone's taste. Some socialists harbored an ideological objection to her relationship with Engels, resenting the wealthy mill owner's son parading his proletarian lover through the salons of Brussels. According to Stephan Born, it was "over-confident of Engels to bring his mistress into this circle, which was frequented primarily by workers, thus invoking the accusation often made against rich sons of factory owners: namely, that they know how to draw the daughters of the common people into the service of their friends."[42] And it wasn't just Mary. Engels had a habit of introducing his other lovers—among whom a "Mademoiselle Josephine" and a "Mademoiselle Félicie" featured prominently—into the socialist circle. It was not a practice that Jenny Marx, daughter of the high-ranking

Baron Ludwig von Westphalen and herself something of a bluestocking, ever felt comfortable with. The Marxes, in the words of Max Beer, "never in their heart of hearts regarded Engels and his female companions as their equals. . . . Marx, one of the greatest revolutionists that ever lived, was in point of moral rectitude as conservative and punctilious as his Rabbinic forebears."[43] This puritanism—or snobbery or moral rectitude—came to a head when Engels arrived with his current paramour at one of the numerous gala evenings the socialists put on in Brussels. Stephan Born was there:

> Among those present were Marx and his wife and Engels and his . . . lady friend. The two couples were separated by a large room. When I approached Marx to greet him and his wife, he gave me a look and a meaningful smile that let me know that his wife strictly refused all contact with this . . . lady friend. The noble woman was intransigent when it came to honouring *mores*. If anyone had had the impertinence to demand of her that she make a concession in this regard, she would have refused indignantly.[44]

It is worth noting that Born recounted this scene many decades after the event and long after he had fallen out with both Marx and Engels. Eleanor Marx, who was not there, always disputed what she called "the idiotic Brussels story." "To begin with, a person must have known my parents very little to ascribe to them the sleek-headed 'morality' of the petit-bourgeois," she wrote in a long letter to the German socialist Karl Kautsky after the death of Engels. "I know that occasionally the General [Engels] *did* turn up with queer acquaintances of the other sex, but, so far as I could ever learn, this only amused my mother, who had a rare sense of humor, and absolutely no middle-class hypocritical 'propriety.'"[45]

Out of this tight-knit, sometimes tense social circle something very great emerged: *The German Ideology.* Jointly written by Marx and Engels, the book was not published in their lifetimes; it was famously abandoned "to the gnawing criticism of the mice" and gained a readership only in 1932. But the book achieved its purpose of providing the authors an opportunity to clarify their thoughts, and it signaled a further step along the road from idealism to materialism, another conscious act of distancing from the Young Hegelian heritage. As often happened with Marx and Engels, they staked out their position by bludgeoning an ideological rival—the thinker in their sights this time being the philosopher Max Stirner. And, equally typically, the level of abuse he sustained was precisely commensurate with the intellectual debt that Marx and Engels owed him.

An influential member of Berlin's Young Hegelian fraternity, Stirner had been unconvinced by Feuerbach's critique of Hegelianism. Feuerbach had suggested that idealistic philosophy—that is, Hegelianism— was little better than Christian theology: both demanded that man worship something outside of himself, be it the Hegelian *Geist* or the Christian God, and therefore both impoverished man's spiritual state. The solution, according to Feuerbach, was for man to "worship humanity," so to speak. But Stirner thought that Feuerbach's critique of Hegel was equally applicable to Feuerbach himself: Feuerbach, like Hegel, had simply elevated another enslaving theophany in place of the Christian deity. In Hegel's case it had been Spirit and in Feuerbach's case "Man with a capital M," but in Stirner's judgment this "HUMAN religion is only the latest metamorphosis of the Christian religion." By contrast, Stirner's *The Ego and Its Own* (1845) advocated absolute egoism, completely free of any of the alienating effects of devotion to God, Man, Spirit, or State. It was a supremely atheistic, solipsistic, and ultimately nihilistic ethos in which the egoist "does not look upon himself as a tool of the idea or a vessel of God, he recognizes no calling, he does not fancy that he exists for the further development of mankind and that he must contribute his mite to it, but he lives himself out, careless of how well or ill humanity may fare thereby."[46] While Marx and Engels had no interest in Stirner's advocacy of personal rebellion or in the ahistoric nature of his individual man, their materialist inclinations were bolstered by his critique of Feuerbach's humanistic philosophy as little better than updated religion. But where Stirner remained committed to a morality of the self, they were determined to move from his philosophy of individualism to the politics of mass action. As Engels put it in a rather strained explanatory letter to Marx, "We must take our departure from the Ego, the empirical, flesh-and-blood individual, if we are not, like Stirner, to remain stuck at this point but rather proceed to raise ourselves to 'man.' . . . In short we must take our departure from empiricism and materialism if our concepts, and notably our 'man,' are to be something real; we must deduce the general from the particular, not from itself or, *à la* Hegel, from thin air."[47]

This materialist ambition underpinned *The German Ideology*, which spelled out for the first time Marx and Engels's view of social structures—religion, class, political systems—as the product of economic and technological forces. "The production of ideas, of conceptions, of consciousness, is at first directly interwoven with the material activity and the material intercourse of men. It is not consciousness that determines life, but life that determines consciousness."[48] Each stage of production, from the primitive communism of early man to medieval feudalism to the industrial capitalism of the nineteenth century, resulted in different "forms of intercourse" in society. The most notable of these was the property system, which trailed in its wake social class, political forms, religion, even cultural movements. As Marx later put it, "Social relations are closely bound up with productive forces. In acquiring new productive forces men change their mode of production; and in changing their mode of production, in changing the way of earning their living, they change all their social relations. The hand-mill gives you society with the feudal lord; the steam-mill society with the industrial capitalist."[49]

The materialist interpretation of history suggested that each civilization was ultimately an expression of the modes of production that molded it: the political and ideological superstructure was determined by the economic base as mediated by its rules of property ownership, so-called relations of production. This was especially true when it came to the political superstructure of the state, which was simply "the form in which the individuals of a ruling class assert their common interests, and in which the whole civil society of an epoch is epitomized."[50] However, at a certain stage of development (for example, the rising bourgeoisie clashing with the medieval monarchy of King Charles I during the English Civil War), the material forces of production come into conflict with existing property relations and their accompanying political, social, and ideological superstructure—and then the moment is ripe for revolution. When the political systems were out of kilter with the economic fundamentals, then the former would have to readjust themselves to the latter in a series of often painful transformations. None of which meant that political change was either spontaneous or automatic. Given the inevitable opposition of the ruling elite, progress could be achieved only by fighting for it, through political organizations, mass movements, and practical agitation. Neither the English Commonwealth nor the French republic was handed over willingly. "A revolution is necessary, therefore, not only because the ruling class cannot be overthrown in any other way," Marx and Engels explained, "but also because the class overthrowing it can succeed only by revolution in getting rid of all the traditional muck and become capable of establishing society anew."[51]

The German Ideology made plain for the first time that the historic driver of such epochal shifts was class struggle. In the specific case of the industrialized 1840s, it would fall to the new proletarian class to instigate the revolution and usher in a communist future, which promised not only their liberation but a change in the entire human condition. As competition and private property gave way to communism men would regain "control of exchange, production and the mode of their mutual relationship" and "the alienation between men and their products" would dissolve. In contrast to capitalist society, where the division of labor forces each man into "a particular, exclusive sphere of activity," communist society would regulate production and thereby ensure that "nobody has one exclusive sphere of activity but each can become accomplished in any branch he wishes, . . . to do one thing today and another tomorrow, to hunt in the morning, fish in the afternoon, rear cattle in the evening, criticize after dinner, just as I have a mind without ever becoming hunter, fisherman, cowboy or critic."[52] But this enviable future needed to somehow be ushered in.

"The philosophers have only *interpreted* the world in various ways; the point is to *change* it," Marx declared in his 1845 "Theses on Feuerbach."

The vehicle that he and Engels lit upon for delivering this change was the Bund der Gerechten, the League of the Just. Founded in Paris in the 1830s, the league was part of an underground communist society run by émigré German tailors whose political inspiration could be traced back to the radical egalitarianism of Babeuf. In 1839, they collaborated with Louis-Auguste Blanqui in a doomed uprising that saw Blanqui jailed while three other leaders of the league crossed the English Channel in search of political asylum. "I came to know all three of them in London in 1843," Engels recalled. He was most impressed by Karl Schapper—a man "of gigantic stature, resolute and energetic, always ready to risk civil existence and life, he was a model of the professional revolutionary."[53] Schapper, together with the shoemaker Heinrich Bauer and the watchmaker Joseph Moll ("these three real men," as Engels called them) established the German Workers' Educational Society in February 1840 in Great Windmill Street, Soho, as a front organization for the league. Most likely because of their continuing link to the Blanquists—which came with a shared belief in plots, conspiracies, and putsches—Engels declined to join the league in 1843. However, he and Marx held a series of meetings with league members during their 1845 trip to England, as part of an attempt to develop an international society of socialists, or "Fraternal Democrats." Back in Brussels, they pursued this work with the establishment of a German Workers' Association and a Communist Correspondence Committee to coordinate socialist agitation and worker education across Europe. The League of the Just was to act as the recognized English arm of the movement.

Politically, the immediate aim of the Communist Correspondence Committee was the furtherance of democracy. "Democracy nowadays is communism: democracy has become the proletarian principle, the principle of the masses," Engels explained.[54] Ultimately, democracy would lead to the political rule of the proletariat and thence to communism. Indeed, the winning of suffrage rights would itself constitute a revolutionary event. "Communism and communists were not binding words," recalled Stephan Born, one of the founding members of the committee. "Indeed, people hardly talked about them. Much more pertinent was the increasingly significant movement to reform electoral law in France."[55]

To destroy feudalism and move toward a democratic state, an alliance with the middle class was an unfortunate necessity. "To overthrow the nobility, another class is required, with wider interests, greater property and more determined courage: the bourgeoisie."[56] From 1845 to the revolutions of 1848, Marx and Engels were unshakeable in their support for the establishment (by force if necessary) of bourgeois power and liberal democracy as a way station to communism. There could be no overnight dictatorship of the proletariat; instead, the situation demanded a long process of political engagement and commitment to a bourgeois-democratic revolution. "In a party one must support everything which helps towards progress, and have no truck with any tedious moral scruples," the committee declared in almost Stalinist terms.[57] However, the bourgeoisie was not to get too comfortable with this alliance. As Engels warned on the eve of 1848, "So just fight bravely on, most gracious masters of capital! We need you for the present; here and there we even need you as rulers. You have to clear the vestiges of the Middle Ages and of absolute monarchy out of our path. . . . In recompense whereof you shall be allowed to rule for a short time. . . . But do not forget that 'The hangman stands at the door!' "[58]

Not everyone within the European communist movement was willing to join hands with the bourgeoisie, even temporarily. Some yearned for an immediate proletarian revolution, with its promise of rapturous human fulfillment, and regarded Marx and Engels's strategy as little better than weak-willed gradualism. Their leader was the itinerant tailor Wilhelm Weitling, who had fled France for Switzerland and Austria after the 1839 Blanquist uprising. There he established outposts of the League of the Just and nurtured an enthusiastic plebeian following. There wasn't much of Adam Smith, David Ricardo, or Jeremy Bentham in Weitling's earthy politics. Instead, his doctrine encompassed a highly emotional mix of Babouvist communism, chiliastic Christianity, and millenarian populism. Following the work of the Christian radical Felicité de Lamennais, Weitling urged installing communism by physical force with the help of a 40,000-strong army of ex-convicts. A prelapsarian community of goods, fellowship, and societal harmony would then ensue, ushered in by the Christlike figure of Weitling himself. While

Marx and Engels struggled with the intricacies of industrial capitalism and modern modes of production, Weitling revived the apocalyptic politics of the sixteenth-century Münster Anabaptists and their gory attempts to usher in the Second Coming. He liked to connect himself to communist martyrology, revealing to his audience the still livid scars he had suffered at the hands of Prussian jailors. Much to Marx and Engels's fury, Weitling's giddy blend of evangelism and protocommunism attracted thousands of dedicated followers across the Continent. And the more Weitling was persecuted by official authorities, the brighter his halo of righteous martyrdom burned. "He was now the great man, the prophet, driven from country to country," Engels sneered, "who carried a prescription for the realization of heaven on earth ready-made in his pocket, and who imagined that everybody was out to steal it from him."[59]

Unsurprisingly, the continental socialist establishment was aghast at Weitling's facile approach. In London, the "real men" of the league gave him short shrift and so in 1846 he turned up in Brussels hoping to win over the Communist Correspondence Committee. It was to be a bruising encounter since Marx and Engels were always eager to denounce an ideological competitor. "The tailor-agitator Weitling was a handsome fair-headed young man in a coat of elegant cut, a coquettishly trimmed small beard, more like a commercial traveler than the stern, embittered worker that I had expected to meet," recalled Pavel Annenkov, a Russian observer of the Brussels meeting. The ideologues gathered around a "small green table," he reported. "Marx sat at one end of it with a pencil in his hand and his leonine head bent over a sheet of paper, while Engels, his inseparable fellow-worker and comrade in propaganda, tall and erect, as dignified and serious as an Englishman, made the opening speech. He spoke of the necessity for people who have devoted themselves to transforming labour of explaining their views to one another and agreeing on a single common doctrine that could be a banner for all their followers who lacked the time and opportunity to study theory." But before he could expound any further, Marx—full of pent-up fury at Weitling's pretensions—sprang up and demanded, "Tell us, Weitling, you who have made such a noise in Germany with your preaching: on what grounds do you justify your activity and what do you intend to base it on in the future?" When Weitling, who liked to deal in abstractions and biblical imagery, failed to respond with the requisite level of scientific rigor, Marx hit the table and screamed, "Ignorance never yet helped anybody!"[60]

It wasn't enough just to crush Weitling; his acolytes also had to be exposed. Chief among them was Hermann Kriege, who had tried to disseminate Weitling's views to the German community in America through his editorship of the New York–based *Der Volks-Tribun.* "He founded a paper in which, in the name of the League, he preached an effusive communism of starry-eyed love, based on 'love' and overflowing with love," Engels complained. In the face of such ideological deviation, it was clearly far more important to enforce party purity than to hunt after broad public support. As a result of Kriege's political depredations, the Brussels Communist Correspondence Committee (at this stage only eighteen men) decided as one of its first public acts to expel a founding member. The "Circular against Kriege," signed by Engels, accused him of "childish pomposity," "fantastic emotionalism," damage to workers' morale, and unacceptable deviation from the official communist "line." Kriege's crime, like Weitling's, was a hopeless inability to realize that a "revolutionary movement of world-historical importance" had to be built on more than just vague aspirations about "the great spirit of community" and the "religion of love." The communism of Marx and Engels was a methodical, increasingly rigorous process dependent upon the historical actions of the proletariat in emancipating society. "And Communism," Engels declared, "now no longer meant the concoction, by means of the imagination, of an ideal society as perfect as possible, but insight into the nature, the conditions and the consequent general aims of the struggle waged by the proletariat."[61] It wasn't enough simply to will it; the proletariat needed to understand their function in delivering the future. So Kriege's errors had to be silenced and Engels "let fly with a circular that did not fail to have its effect." Soon after, "Kriege vanished from the League scene."[62] What the next 150 years brought in terms of expulsions, denunciations, and political purges within left-wing parties is grimly foreshadowed in this chilling three-point circular. And, from the outset, Engels was in the vanguard: over the decades, he would express his love and loyalty to Marx by gleefully enforcing party discipline, pursuing ideological heretics, and generally playing the Grand Inquisitor when it came to upholding the true communist faith.

In addition to Weitling's rudimentary communism, another menace to Marx and Engels's dominance of Continental communism was the "true," or "philosophical," socialism that revolved around the French philosopher Pierre-Joseph Proudhon. Initially, Marx—like Engels—had been impressed by Proudhon and his 1840 work, *What Is Property?* Proudhon had taught Marx that the solution to the iniquity of private property did not lie, as Weitling suggested, in some mystical "community of goods." Instead, Proudhon proposed the abolition of all income not derived from productive work and the establishment of a system of fair exchange in which goods were equitably traded on the basis of the labour embodied in them. Marx was so enamored of Proudhon's approach that in May 1846 he invited him to join the Communist Correspondence Committee as the French representative. Engels added a postscript expressing the earnest hope that Proudhon would "approve of the scheme" they had proposed and would "be kind enough not to deny" his cooperation. But Marx couldn't resist another little addition and the committee's mask of harmonious cooperation suddenly dropped: "I must now denounce to you Mr Grün of Paris. The man is nothing more than a literary swindler, a species of charlatan, who seeks to traffic in modern ideas."[63]

Unfortunately, the Brussels agitators had overreached. Proudhon was a close ally of Karl Grün, the German émigré and leading popularizer of so-called true socialism, and he wrote back clearly judging the measure of Marx and Engels's political absolutism. "Let us by all means collaborate in trying to discover the laws of society . . . but for God's sake, after we have demolished all the dogmatisms a priori, let us not of all things attempt in our turn to instill another kind of doctrine into the people. . . . Let us not set ourselves up as the leaders of a new intolerance, let us not pose as the apostles of a new religion—even though this religion be the religion of logic, the religion of reason itself."[64] Marx and Engels did not take criticism well, and the next few months saw a veritable sea of bile hurled at Proudhon. The attack culminated in Marx's blistering pamphlet *The Poverty of Philosophy* (a characteristically chiasmatic response to Proudhon's *Philosophy of Poverty*), which excoriated Proudhon's petit bourgeois philosophizing, utopian plans for labor exchanges, and crippling inability to appreciate the historic role of the proletariat in ending capitalist relations. To Marx and Engels's mind, this was the trouble with Grün and Proudhon's notion of "true socialism": it was a philosophy that ignored the historic calling of the working class and failed to grip the seismic societal leap demanded by communism. The "true socialists" could not see beyond the existing bourgeois settlement, while their entire approach "presupposed the existence of bourgeois society, with its corresponding economic conditions of existence, and the political constitution adapted thereto."[65] Indeed, its parochial attempts to preserve a petit bourgeois quality of life in the face of international competition only hindered the advent of the final communist triumph. It was a philosophy wedded to a romantic notion of preindustrial cooperation and cravenly catering to the narrow needs of an artisan class impoverished by accelerating industrialization. At least Weitling's messianic egalitarianism appreciated the historic enormity of the communist project, in contrast to the facile tinkering of "true socialism." Yet however compelling Marx's philosophical critique, Proudhon and Grün's allies were well dug in among the Paris working class, where their politically feasible program of cooperation, fair pricing, and universal employment enjoyed popular support. So that was where Engels, the Grand Inquisitor, was forced to take the fight.

"The scent of the great Revolution and of the July Revolution was still in the air," wrote Stephan Born of 1840s Paris. "Unlike in Germany, where nothing of the sort existed at the time, the workers of Paris already formed a distinct opposition to the ruling bourgeoisie."[66] Engels's posting to Paris in August 1846 came with a clear brief: to win over these workers to the League of the Just and prevent any proletarians falling into the hands of either Grün's "true socialists" or Weitling's "tailor communists."

The French metropolis was just as seductive and dangerous as Balzac's Rastignac had described. And like industrializing Manchester, it was increasingly regarded as a divided city. Historically, Paris had always prided itself on the geographical intimacy of differing social classes—"a palace opposite a stable and a cathedral next to a chicken-run," according to one U.S. visitor. But now the rich were separating themselves off from the poor, leaving behind neighborhoods peopled by a dangerous residuum. Among the most notorious was the horribly overcrowded Île de la Cité—"a labyrinth of obscure, crooked, and narrow streets, which extends from the Palais de Justice to Notre Dame"—which provided the opening scene for Eugène Sue's best-selling potboiler, *The Mysteries of Paris* (1842).[67] While the western enclaves of Paris cocooned themselves in wealth and privilege, the filthy faubourgs of the center and the east housed the city's increasingly restive *classes dangereuses*. Novelists of the era delighted in portraying their capital as a hideous, decaying old harridan. The heroism of the revolution was progressively tarnished both by the awful reality of disease, prostitution, and crime and by the shallow vulgarity of mercantile bourgeois culture. The political economist Victor Considérant described Paris in 1848 as "a great manufactory of putrefaction in which poverty, plague . . . and disease labour in concert and where sunlight barely ever enters. [It is] a foul hole where plants wilt and perish and four out of seven children die within their first years."[68]

Scratching out a living just above this lumpen proletariat were the skilled workers of the émigré communities. It was to them that Engels directed his attention. The Industrial Revolution had come late to France, but by the 1840s the economy was at last starting to pick up. The expansion of the defense sector and the increase in railway construction, together with the development of cotton, silk, and mineral industries, led to a surge in industrial production and foreign exports. Within Paris, however, the workshop system of manufacture continued to hold out against the production line of the factory. Skilled workers in small firms selling into a fashion-oriented market dictated much of the city's employment patterns. In 1848, Paris had 350,000 workers, with one-third of these engaged in the textile trades and much of the remainder divided between construction, the furniture trade, jewelry, metallurgy, and domestic service. A large part of the workforce was made up of Germans—Engels described them as being "everywhere." By the late 1840s, there were some sixty thousand of them, and such was their strength that in certain Parisian quarters barely a word of French was to be heard.[69]

The competition for their political affiliation was keen. France had, as we have seen, long been a center of socialist thought and, after the early years of Fourier and Saint-Simon, radical politics resurfaced in the 1840s on the back of "the social question"—the poverty, unemployment, and urban divisions coming in the wake of industrialization. Proudhon was joined by Louis Blanc, Étienne Cabet, Pierre Leroux, and George Sand, all offering visions of a new society that ranged from Owenite-style cooperation to full-blooded communism. The theorizing found its keenest audience among the exploited, impoverished German community—so much so that in 1843 the Prussian government launched an inquiry into the extent of the danger posed by expatriate Germans. One consequence was Marx's expulsion from France in 1845. "We must purge Paris of German philosophers!" was King Louis-Philippe's understandable reaction to the subversive pamphleteering infecting his capital.

Engels entered this competitive political market supported only by his self-confidence (and a grudging revival of his father's allowance). He gamely set to work trying to rid the Parisian working class of the deviant socialist strains of Grün and Weitling. His target was the so-called Straubingers, the German artisans and journeymen inclined to "true socialism," who resided in the Saint-Antoine manufacturing district. For students of entryism, Engels's tactics at the Straubingers' weekly political meetings are textbook stuff, a brutally successful medley of threats, divide and rule, denunciations, and ideological bullying. "By dint of a little patience and some terrorism I have emerged victorious with the great majority behind me," he boasted to Marx, recounting how he "went into action, so intimidating old Eisermann [a joiner and member of the League of the Just] that he no longer turns up." The one worry Engels had was the primitive level of ideological understanding he found amongst the Straubingers: "The fellows are horribly ignorant." The problem was that their relative prosperity was hindering their development of class consciousness: "There is no competition among them, wages remain constantly at the same wretched level; the struggle with the master, far from turning on the question of wages, is concerned with 'journeymen's pride,' etc." Ideally, Engels would have had them a great deal poorer and desperate.

At the next meeting, Engels decided to set out the real meaning of communism to these myopically contented workers. Here began his career as one of the most prolific and intelligible popularizers of Marxist doctrine. Its aims, he explained, were clear:

1. to ensure that the interests of the proletariat prevail, as opposed to those of the bourgeoisie,
2. to do so by abolishing private property,
3. to recognize no means of attaining these aims other than democratic revolution by force.

He then called a vote on the aims, so as quickly to determine whether the Straubingers were committed communists or merely a fanciful debating society on which he would not waste any more time. "At the beginning I had nearly the whole clique against me and at the end only Eisermann and the three other Grünians," Engels reported. He denounced the antiproletarian, petit bourgeois sentiments of Grün and his disciples in such strident tones that the meeting eventually acceded to his definition of communism by a majority of 13–2, which gives some sense both of Engels's debating skills and of the intimacy of the gatherings.[70]

In Paris, as in Elberfeld, his achievements did not go unnoticed by the authorities. Among those taking an interest were the city police, who used the growing number of social disturbances in the Saint-Antoine neighborhood as a pretext to crack down on the subversive Straubinger cells. Grün's followers fingered Engels as the agitator, and he soon had a collection of various spies and informers trailing him across Paris. Perhaps tiring of the nightly debates and votes on procedural motions, Engels used this police harassment as a welcome excuse to exchange socialist study evenings for a plunge into Paris's carnal delights. "If the suspicious individuals who have been following me for the past fortnight are really informers, as I am convinced some of them are, the Prefecture must of late have given out a great many entrance tickets to the *bals* Montesquieu, Valentino, Prado, etc.," he told Marx. "I am indebted to Mr Delessert [prefect of the Paris police] for some delicious encounters with grisettes and for a great deal of pleasure, since I wanted to take advantage of the days and nights which might well be my last in Paris."[71]

Now in his midtwenties, Engels was a well-versed lothario whose silky good looks and raffish demeanor had earned him a string of lovers. No sooner had he left the earthy embrace of Mary Burns in Manchester than he was writing to Marx of "a love affair" he had "to clear up."[72] By January 1845, it had come "to a fearful end," he reported. "I'll spare you the boring details, nothing more can be done about it, and I've already been through enough over it as it is."[73] In Brussels over the summer he was back with his "wife," Mary, but during the autumn in Paris prudish Stephan Born was aghast at his companion's bacchanalian urges and his attendance at "the wildest burlesques at the theater of the Palais Royal."[74] Engels took a series of mistresses (apparently his "insolent manner" was found to "work well with the female sex"), spent boozy evenings with a louche cadre of artists, and, like so many others of his class and epoch, had no compunction about paying for sex. Barely one year later he would condemn prostitution as "the most tangible exploitation—one directly attacking the physical body—of the proletariat by the bourgeoisie," but no such reservations concerned him now.[75] "It is absolutely essential that you get out of boring Brussels for once and come to Paris, and I for my part have a great desire to go carousing with you," he urged family man Marx. "If I had an income of 5000 francs I would do nothing but work and amuse myself with women until I went to pieces. If there were no Frenchwomen, life wouldn't be worth living. But so long as there are grisettes, well and good!"[76] Happily for Engels, when it came to female relationships the personal and the ideological fused gratifyingly together: he had a strong libido, a love for the company of women, and also an innate distaste for the bourgeois morality of marriage and monogamy. In time these inclinations would develop into a coherent theory of socialist feminism, but in his midtwenties they were just part of a young man's gleeful enjoyment of Parisian night life.

There was a darker aspect to Engels's womanizing. Since the start of his friendship with Marx, Engels's attitude toward Moses Hess had been hardening. He increasingly disparaged the "communist rabbi" who had first brought him into the socialist current as an ideologically confused ditherer whose growing sympathy for Grün's "true socialism" provided clear evidence of his suspect tendencies. Like a pair of playground bullies, Marx and Engels decided to make the political personal by directing their attention toward Hess's wife. According to Cologne police reports, Sibylle Hess was a former prostitute turned seamstress. Hess had rescued her from the gutter as much out of political conviction as emotional attachment. "He wished to perform an act expressive of the need for love among men and for equality between them," according to Isaiah Berlin. Sibylle, however, apparently had a wandering eye.[77]

In July 1846, Engels agreed to help Hess by smuggling the passportless Mrs. Hess across the border from Brussels into France. No sooner had the two arrived in Paris than Engels was dropping her name in a series of unchivalrous letters to Marx. "Mrs Hess is on the look-out for a husband. She doesn't give a fig for Hess. If there should happen to be someone suitable, apply to Madame Gsell, Faubourg Saint-Antoine. There's no hurry since the competition isn't keen." By September, it seemed Engels had taken the conjugal role upon himself, and shortly thereafter he wrote to Marx of having consigned Mrs. Hess, "cursing and swearing," back to the "furthest end of the Faubourg St. Antoine." What gave him special pleasure was that the unknowingly cuckolded Hess (now little more than a Falstaff figure to Engels's Prince Hal) was at the same time trying to renew their friendship. When Hess eventually turned up in Paris in January 1847, Engels crowed, "My treatment of him was so cold and scornful that he will have no desire to return. All I did for him was to give him some advice about the clap he had brought with him from Germany." Unsurprisingly, when Hess discovered Engels's seduction of his wife, the friendship ended. Now Hess returned to Brussels and began to trash his one-time protégé. Engels, for his part, adopted an air of lofty nonchalance: "Moses brandishing his pistols, parading his horns before the whole of Brussels . . . must have been exquisite," he wrote to Marx. What certainly did unsettle Engels, however, was Hess's "preposterous lie about rape." This was, he assured his friend, utter nonsense. "I can provide him with enough earlier, concurrent, and later details to send him reeling. For only last July here in Paris this Balaam's she-ass made me, *in optima forma*, a declaration of love mingled with resignation, and confided to me the most intimate nocturnal secrets of her ménage! Her rage with me is unrequited love, pure and simple." Boorishly, he went on to suggest that "the horned Siegfried" was "perfectly at liberty . . . to avenge himself on all my present, past and future mistresses," which he helpfully listed. But if Hess wanted to take this matter of honor further, then Engels, who learned his dueling among the wealthy of Bremen, would "give him fair play."[78]

Did Engels really rape Moses Hess's wife? With his self-styled "insolent manner," Engels was certainly something of a sexual predator during his time in Paris, but it seems unlikely he would have resorted to violence. Most likely, the two had an affair—driven partly by Engels's desire to humiliate Moses Hess—that went sour. Nonetheless, there exists a rather curious passage in an 1898 letter from Eleanor Marx to Karl Kautsky in which she mentions that one Paris incident involving Engels was unusually hushed up within the otherwise open-minded Marx household: "That there was a woman in the case I *did* most certainly know, and from some words I heard, apparently a rather disreputable one at that. But what it all was—except that it was an episode to be passed over and covered up—I don't know." It was, she assured herself and Kautsky, "some silly young fellow's nonsense."[79]

Impressively, Engels made some political headway amid his skirt chasing. In June 1847, the League of the Just held a congress in London that Marx and Engels were invited to as new members. The meeting's purpose was for Schapper, Bauer, and Moll to join forces with the Brussels committee, dropping the old secret society mentality for a more open political program. With Marx's finances at another characteristic low, the Brussels contingent was represented by the German teacher and communist Wilhelm Wolff while Engels had to battle through a meeting of the Paris branch to ensure his selection as its representative. "I realised

that it would be very difficult to get Engels nominated, though he hoped
to be," Stephan Born recalled. "There was strong opposition to him. I
succeeded in getting him elected only by asking—against the rules—
that those who were against, not for, the candidate raise their hands.
This trick strikes me as loathsome today. 'Well done,' Engels said to me
as we went home."[80]

The congress represented a seminal moment in the development of
the Communist Party. Delegates agreed to rename the League of the Just
the Communist League and replace the motto "All men are brothers"
with the altogether more bombastic "Working Men of All Countries,
Unite!" Engels was tasked with drawing up a "revolutionary catechism"
for the league that would showcase its politico-philosophical stance. The
result was the "Draft of a Communist Confession of Faith," whose very
title revealed the blend of religious zealotry and personal commitment
that marked the early communist movement:

QUESTION 1: *Are you a Communist?*
ANSWER: Yes
QUESTION 2: *What is the aim of the Communists?*
ANSWER: To organise society in such a way that every member of it can
    develop and use all his capabilities and powers in complete freedom
    and without thereby infringing on the basic conditions of society.
QUESTION 3: *How do you wish to achieve this?*
ANSWER: By the elimination of private property and its replacement by
    community of property.[81]

The draft confession, running to almost two dozen questions, was a
compromise document that displayed much of the "true," or utopian,
socialism Marx and Engels abhorred—even including an uncharacteris-
tically wishy-washy passage about how "every individual strives to be
happy. The happiness of the individual is inseparable from the happiness
of all."[82] But the confession also contained inklings of the very brilliant
popularizing touch that would culminate in *The Communist Manifesto*.
The coming of the proletariat and their historic function in ushering in
the socialist revolution were at the core of the catechism. Engels's text

was also replete with the materialist interpretation of history and society that he and Marx had been developing over the previous five years. Political revolution, the document declared, was contingent upon a disjuncture between property relations and the mode of production; that is, the likelihood of revolt depended on whether the political and social superstructure was in accordance with the economic base. But this contingency did not exclude communists from fighting to bring the desired condition into existence: "If, in the end, the oppressed proletariat is thus driven into a revolution, then we will defend the cause of the proletariat just as well by our deeds as now by our words." The first step along the path to "the political liberation of the proletariat" was the securing of "a democratic constitution." After that would come the limiting of private property, universal state education and even some reforms to the marriage system.[83]

With the congress concluded, Engels threw himself into an intensive round of shuttle diplomacy from which Marx was excluded, given his numerous official travel bans. Engels went from London to Brussels to shore up the Marxist position against rival German factions attempting to usurp the communist network, then back to Paris to pitch the "Confession of Faith" to the local Communist League branches. "I at once set up a propaganda community and I rush round speechifying," he reported to Marx from Paris. "I was immediately elected to the district [Committee of the Communist League] and have been entrusted with the correspondence." To get the committee to adopt the "Confession" Engels had to outmaneuver Moses Hess, who was hawking an alternative version. Once again, Engels's political skills came to the fore as he played "an infernal trick on Mosi": "Last Friday at the district I dealt with this [Hess's version], point by point, and was not yet halfway through when the lads declared themselves *satisfaits*. Completely unopposed, I got them to entrust me with the task of drafting a new one which will be discussed next Friday by the district and will be sent to London behind the backs of the committees. Naturally not a soul must know about this, otherwise we shall all be unseated and there'll be the deuce of a row."[84]

The next draft of the catechism, composed by Engels in October 1847 in preparation for the second Communist League congress, scheduled for that November, was entitled "Principles of Communism." While much of the text resembled the "Confession," there was a perceptible ratcheting up of the materialism and downplaying of the earlier, utopian socialism. There was also a more open call for proletarian revolution as well as a new emphasis on the global character of capitalism and worker solidarity. "So if now in England or France the workers liberate themselves," Engels expounded, "this must lead to revolutions in all other countries, which sooner or later will also bring about the liberation of the workers in those countries." But until that day the processes of globalized capitalism were to be embraced: "Precisely that quality of large-scale industry which in present society produces all misery and all trade crises is the very quality which under a different social organisation will destroy that same misery and these disastrous fluctuations." In *The German Ideology*, Engels proclaimed that when the social order "no longer corresponds to the existing conditions" revolution results. In the "Principles of Communism," Engels retained the commitment to the abolition of private property and the inauguration of a democratic constitution but now offered an expanded list of transitional steps toward socialism. One of these, in something of a throwback to the Fourierist and Owenite traditions, was a pledge to erect "large palaces on national estates as common dwellings for communities of citizens engaged in industry as well as agriculture, combining the advantages of both urban and rural life without the one-sidedness and disadvantage of either." Engels also suggested that the coming communist order would transform relations between the sexes, since "it abolishes private property and educates children communally, thus destroying the twin foundation of hitherto existing marriage—the dependence through private property of the wife upon the husband and of the children upon the parents."[85]

Unpublished until 1914, "Principles of Communism" was to become the basis of *The Communist Manifesto*. "This congress must be a decisive one," Engels urged Marx before they traveled together to the meeting in London. "Give a little thought to the Confession of Faith. I think we would do best to abandon the catechetical form and call the thing Communist Manifesto." At the headquarters of the German Workers' Education

Association, above the Red Lion pub in Great Windmill Street, the "Principles" was picked apart by the second congress over the course of an exhausting ten days in November 1847. But Marx carried the meeting. "His speech was brief, convincing and compelling in its logic," reported Engels. "He never said a superfluous word; every sentence contained an idea and every idea was an essential link in the chain of his argument."[86] By the end, "all contradiction and doubt were finally over and done with, the new basic principles were adopted unanimously, and Marx and I were commissioned to draw up the Manifesto. This was done immediately afterwards."[87]

From the rough, sometimes leaden drafts of the "Confession of Faith" and "Principles of Communism" emerged the seamless prose of *The Communist Manifesto*. "This irresistible combination of utopian confidence, moral passion, hard-edged analysis, and—not least—a dark literary eloquence was eventually to become perhaps the best-known and certainly the most widely translated pamphlet of the nineteenth century," in the fine words of Eric Hobsbawm. Marx and Engels had begun working on the manifesto together in London and continued in Brussels, but it was Marx who delivered the final edition and it is this gratifying absence of a committee consensus that makes the *Manifesto* read so well. From its epic opening lines—"A spectre is haunting Europe—the spectre of Communism"—to its challenging finale—"The proletarians have nothing to lose but their chains. They have a world to win. WORKING MEN OF ALL COUNTRIES, UNITE!"—it is a polemic written in one heroic breath. Yet much of the hard intellectual grind, in league meetings and drafting sessions, had been done by Engels. The German socialist leader Wilhelm Liebknecht had it right: "What was supplied by one, what by the other? An idle question! It is of one mold, and Marx and Engels are one soul—as inseparable in *The Communist Manifesto* as they remained to their death in all their working and planning."[88]

The *Manifesto* was perhaps most obviously indebted to Engels's previous work in its account of the emergence of the proletariat, "a class of labourers, who live only so long as they find work, and who find work only so long as their labour increases capital." This socioeconomic narrative, premised heavily on the role of the Industrial Revolution in moving society toward communism, could have come straight from *The Condition of the Working Class in England*. The unique history of the English proletariat suddenly became in the *Manifesto* a universal template of working-class development.[89] The *Manifesto* restated and reemphasized many ideas that Engels had already outlined. It blasted the immoral nature of bourgeois society, which "has pitilessly torn asunder the motley feudal ties that bound man to his 'natural superiors,' and has left remaining no other nexus between man and man than naked self-interest, than callous 'cash-payment' "; it revealed the class bias of bourgeois government, where "the executive of the modern State is but a committee for managing the common affairs of the whole bourgeoisie"; it pointed out the deadly irony of the bourgeoisie producing, above all, "its own grave-diggers." And it reiterated the core communist demand, which could be "summed up in the single sentence: Abolition of private property."

Marx did drop some of Engels's hobbyhorses, including plans for agrico-industrial communes, and any suggestion of the end of marriage (a familiar target for communist critics). In their place, he offered the kind of rhetorical flights that Engels could never master:

> It [the bourgeoisie] has been the first to show what man's activity can bring about. It has accomplished wonders far surpassing Egyptian pyramids, Roman aqueducts, and Gothic cathedrals; it has conducted expeditions that put in the shade all former Exoduses of nations and crusades.
>
> The bourgeoisie cannot exist without constantly revolutionizing the instruments of production, and thereby the relations of production, and with them the whole relations of society. . . . All fixed, fast-frozen relations, with their train of ancient and venerable prejudices and opinions, are swept away, all new-formed ones become antiquated before they can ossify. All that is solid melts into air, all that is holy is profaned, and man is at last compelled to face with sober senses his real conditions of life, and his relations with his kind.[90]

Despite such extravagant predictions, on its publication the *Manifesto* made no impact at all. It came off the London presses of the German

Workers' Educational Society in February 1848 to a resounding "conspiracy of silence." A few hundred members of the Communist League read it perhaps and an English translation was serialized in Harney's *Red Republican* in 1850, but the booklet was neither widely on sale nor yet obviously influential. This was, not least, because history was already overtaking it. Marx's bourgeoisie, which had achieved so much, was about to add another notch to its belt: the extinguishing of the monarchy of King Louis-Philippe of France. On the morning of 24 February 1848, Alexis de Tocqueville walked out of his Parisian town house, turned his face to the chill wind, and declared he could "scent revolution in the air." By the afternoon, with the Boulevard des Capucines caked in blood and trees along the Champs-Elysées being felled for barricades, the July monarchy of 1830 melted into air. "Our age, the age of democracy, is breaking," Engels exclaimed. "The flames of the Tuileries and the Palais Royal are the dawn of the proletariat."[91] The Gallic cock was crowing; Paris was fulfilling its destiny. Revolution had arrived.

5

THE INFINITELY RICH
'48 HARVEST

"At half-past twelve at night, the train arrived, with the glorious news of Thursday's revolution, and the whole mass of people shouted, in one sudden outburst of enthusiasm, Vive la République!" Engels wrote excitedly of the events gripping Europe in March 1848.[1] As the French monarchy crumbled, Marx and Engels were in the wrong place at the wrong time, milling around a Brussels train station snatching at the latest tidbits of intelligence. It was to be a familiar pattern over the next eighteen months as the two aspirant insurgents chased the tail of the great 1848 revolutions across the Continent—sometimes catching it, occasionally pulling it, but more often being led by it. It was a period laden with promise and ridden with frustration.

From Marx and Engels's hopeful perspective, the startling events of 1848 looked to be a textbook bourgeois-democratic revolution. Europe's archaic political and legal systems were out of sync with the ever-quickening capitalist modes of production and would be forced to adjust themselves to the new economic realities. Given the mismatch between the industrializing base and the feudal superstructure, a revolution led by the rising bourgeoisie was the obvious next step. Then after the middle classes had done the dirty work of disposing of the old world, the bourgeois revolution would, in turn, be succeeded by the rule of the proletariat.

After all the talk of the last decade—"formulae, nothing but formulae"—1848 offered the tantalizing prospect of praxis and the chance to give history a helping hand. Leaving little to the inevitability of progress, Marx and Engels sought to accelerate the coming revolution through an exhaustive program of political organization, newspaper propaganda, and, eventually, military insurrection. As *The Communist Manifesto* came off the presses, Marx and Engels crisscrossed Europe from Brussels to Berne, Paris to Cologne, dodging arrest warrants and Prussian spies to urge the destruction of Europe's ancien régime.

Engels himself would leave the battlefield of 1848 particularly gratified: the self-styled Montagnard, student fencer, and barrack-room boxer at last personally got to experience some frontline military action. Fulfilling a boy's dream of adventure, he raised the red flag over his hometown of Barmen and launched raiding parties against Prussian infantry troops, before fleeing, under fire, through the Black Forest. It was a blooding on the barricades, a personal investment in the life-and-death struggle for revolution. Over the coming decades, Engels would rarely allow friends or enemies to forget it.

Whatever the personal heroics, the cumbersome reality was that the 1848–49 revolutions—in Denmark, Sicily, Sardinia, Piedmont, France, Prussia, Saxony, Hungary, and Austria—were far from Marx and Engels's idealized class uprising. Instead, they were driven by a multiplicity of motives ranging from economic insecurity to national identity to republican demands for an end to monarchy and democratic self-government. These uprisings, *frondes*, rebellions, or revolutions—call them what you will—were also subject to rapid reversal, depending upon the level of worker support, radical leadership, and strength of the reactionary fight back. Such shifting, ultimately unfulfilled ambitions led the historian A. J. P. Taylor to describe 1848 as the turning point when Europe "failed to turn." For Marx and Engels, this much-vaunted "age of democracy" was a time of personal disappointment and ideological reevaluation.

The epic storm that broke over Europe in the spring of 1848 began with a cloud no bigger than a man's hand, in the city of Palermo, where simmering discontent with the Bourbon king Ferdinand II and his aloof, Naples-based regime led to rioting in January. Dissatisfied with decades of distant, aggressive Neapolitan rule, leading Sicilian families played on widespread economic distress to promote the restoration of their autonomous pre-1816 Parliament. Well-organized street demonstrations quickly spilled over into attacks on the police; soon the barricades went up, the king's troops deserted their barracks for the mainland, and the Bourbon dynasty was deposed. Within weeks, a provisional government was formed and a new parliament elected.

Sicily was the first to go, but stresses were apparent in royal courts across Europe as social pressures piled up and falling revenues necessitated the calling of parliaments. These national assemblies typically had the power to replenish royal funds through levying taxes but now, in return, politicians were demanding constitutional reform. This was the era of "prerevolution," or *Vormärz*, in which ill-defined expectations abounded in newspapers and parliaments across the Continent's capitals. A decade of poor harvests—with the attendant high grain prices, economic depression, and specter of famine—exacerbated the instability. Widespread crop failures in 1845 had had a devastating effect on numerous rural economies, while an advancing credit crunch saw a collapse of confidence in urban markets, a crisis in the banking sector, and a decline in businesses' ability to trade. Food prices rose, disposable incomes fell, and unemployment mounted. All of which fostered a popular dissatisfaction with the monarchies that had ruled Europe since the 1815 Vienna conference. But as Marx had predicted, it would take the crowing of the Gallic cock to transform such sullen resentment into a European conflagration.

France's February Revolution of 1848 placed the Parisian workers in the forefront of European communism. In the wake of the Palermo uprising, French radicals organized outdoor banquets—a tradition of popular discontent dating back to the French Revolution—in support of universal manhood suffrage and economic reform. Against a backdrop of renewed nostalgia for the great events of 1789, revolutionary anthems were belted out by Parisian theater crowds and chanted menacingly outside society balls. King Louis-Philippe's much-reviled prime minister, the liberal historian François Guizot, reacted to the crisis by banning the banquets and calling out the National Guard. It did no good: on 23 February 1848, Guizot was offered up as a political sacrifice to the mob. The next day Louis-Philippe himself abdicated and fled to England. Events soon succumbed to Parisian street tradition and, after the accidental shooting of protestors by nervous soldiers, the capital embarked on its familiar choreography of revolution.

Marx and Engels, stuck in Belgium, were desperate to make sure that Brussels did not miss out on this revolutionary impetus sweeping the Continent—or, as they put it in a letter to Julian Harney, they wanted the locals "to obtain through the ways proper to Belgian political institutions the advantages which the French people have won." To Marx's mind such "peaceful but vigorous agitation" meant arranging meetings outside the town hall, drawing up petitions to the town council, and covertly buying arms for Belgian workers with money collected from his late father's estate.[2] The wily King Leopold I, however, had no desire to follow Louis-Philippe's flight across the Channel, and the Belgian police quickly clamped down on their troublesome German guests. On 3 March 1848, Marx was ordered to quit the kingdom within twenty-four hours. Engels followed not long after.

As befitted the capital of the nineteenth century, Paris was the trigger for uprisings across Europe as the promise of liberty and democracy, nationalism, and republicanism challenged the conservative settlement—of monarchy and ancien régime autarchy—that had dictated Continental politics since the defeat of Napoleon at the battle of Waterloo. To radicals, the eruption of bread riots and rural rebellions provided a glorious opportunity to drive home constitutional reform and national self-determination. At the beginning of March 1848, the Austrian diet in Vienna was hijacked by student activists and workers. Barricades were swiftly erected, followed by a bloody counterattack by Habsburg troops—but even that could not save Austrian chancellor Klemens von Metternich, the very embodiment of ancien régime arrogance, who was forced to flee for England. As the Habsburg monarchy tottered, the northern states of Italy rose up, with the urban poor of Lombardy, Piedmont, Venice, and Milan leading the rebellion. Milan was to suffer a particularly fierce fight back by the Austrians, under Marshal Radetzky: during the celebrated Five Days, 1,500 barricades went up overnight and the city's narrow streets became the setting for savage urban warfare. But it was to Paris, the laboratory of revolution and now host to the Second Republic, that Marx and Engels headed.

The city that had once harassed and deported them now embraced Marx, Engels, and the executive committee of the Communist League with official ardor. A provisional government was in place, staffed by a cadre of moderate republicans, such as the socialist philosopher Louis Blanc and the radical journalist Ferdinand Flocon, to whose paper, *La Réforme,* Engels had contributed. They were proud to welcome the communist revolutionaries and Engels, more used to being harried by police informers, reveled in the change of circumstance. "Recently I lunched at the Tuileries, in the Prince de Joinville's suite, with old Imbert who was a refugee in Brussels and is now Governor of the Tuileries," he boasted to his brother-in-law Emil Blank.[3] True to form, the remainder of the letter was filled with a denunciation of the prevarications, stupidity, and weaknesses of the newly installed administration.

For all its glamour and official hospitality, Paris was only a holding post. As he explained in a letter to Marx, in his heart Engels yearned for Germany. "If only Frederick William IV digs his heels in! Then all will be won and in a few months' time we'll have the German revolution. If he only sticks to his feudal forms! But the devil only knows what this capricious and crazy individual will do."[4] Engels was not alone in hoping to transplant the revolution back to the homeland: Paris's vast German émigré community was equally keen to cross the Rhine and inaugurate their longed-for democratic republic. To that end, a German legion of artisan volunteers had emerged from the Parisian faubourgs ready to march on Prussia and launch a series of military attacks. The provisional French government was understandably more than happy to see the back of these Straubinger troublemakers and offered them a subsidy of fifty centimes a day to help them get to the frontier.

Marx and Engels were certain this hapless scheme of direct attack was doomed to fail—which it duly did. They preferred a more considered approach, which they outlined in "Demands of the Communist Party in Germany." Curiously, given the immediacy of *The Communist Manifesto*'s tone, the "Demands" did not argue for immediate revolution or an all-out assault on private property. Instead, it set out the case for bourgeois revolution—a complex process that could not be ushered in overnight by some clumsy brigade of bumbling émigrés. The priority was to remove Germany's Junker classes from political and military power and then work toward a bourgeois republic based on manhood suffrage, freedom of the press, rule of law, and parliamentary authority. At this stage, the Communist League's hope was to unite Germany's bourgeoisie, petite bourgeoisie, working classes, and even peasantry in a grand democratic coalition. The proposed strategy called for propaganda and organization rather than violent political action. To prepare the ground, Marx and Engels founded the German Workers' Club, which surreptitiously sent to the Rhineland some three hundred communist activists.

They found the ground already well prepared. Part of the phenomenon of 1848 was the rapidity with which popular politics responded to events across Europe as the steam train and the telegraph ensured the fast movement not just of troops and armaments but also of information and ideas. Telegrams and an expanding newspaper industry offered continuous coverage of the events, and the torching of the Paris Tuileries in February 1848 was all the encouragement the angry, radicalized German masses needed. As elsewhere in Europe, a series of crop failures combined with a downturn in the business cycle had led to substantial increases in the price of foodstuffs alongside a falling standard of living. Famines in rural areas, bread riots in cities, and growing unemployment produced a treacherous political terrain for the aristocratic administrations of princely Germany. In Bavaria, news of the February Revolution led to the swift replacement of King Ludwig I (who had ignored widespread peasant distress for the bawdy delights of his mistress, Lola Montez) with his son Maximilian II. In Saxony, King Friedrich August II gave in to demands for a reform-minded "March ministry" with an expansion of suffrage and the summoning of a national assembly. Across the German states, "public meeting democracy" flourished as petitions were drawn up, monster rallies were held, and vast crowds of journeymen, peasants, workers, and students picketed town halls and palaces. According to historian James J. Sheehan, "With the possible exception of the months immediately prior to World War I, there is no other period in German history so full of spontaneous social action and dramatic political possibilities."[5]

Revolution officially arrived in Prussia in March 1848. Berlin had suffered particularly badly from the economic downturn, with the collapse in manufacturing leading to dramatic and dangerous levels of unemployment. In turn, the usual run of petitions, rallies, and meetings had steadily grown into a threatening array of encampments and anti-military skirmishing across the capital. Contrary to popular expectation, King Friedrich Wilhelm IV did not dig his heels in but wisely looked to steer a course through the rebellion, easing censorship and offering (as in Saxony) a progressive "March ministry" package of constitutional reforms. When the concessions were announced, the mood in Berlin instantly lightened, with cheering crowds thronging into Palace Square to catch sight of their benign sovereign. While Friedrich Wilhelm was soaking up the applause, his less enlightened military commanders were planning to clear the square with a squadron of dragoons. As the troops closed in, the guns of two officers accidentally discharged. No one was hurt, but the capital's febrile crowds—rightly suspicious of Berlin's officer class—thought the army had turned on them. They responded with barricades and makeshift missiles, inaugurating one of Europe's bloodiest March revolutions. In a single day, over three hundred protestors (mostly artisans and laborers employed on public works projects) were killed and the military suffered nearly a hundred casualties. In the aftermath of the massacre, Friedrich Wilhelm was forced to inspect the dead. As he and his wife, Queen Elisabeth, stood, "white with fear," in front of the crowds, she is said to have whispered, "All that is missing is the guillotine."[6] To avoid such a fate, the king ceded further ground. He withdrew his troops from the city and issued a humiliating royal address promising greater liberalization of the Prussian state. He also declared his support for the convening of an all-German National Assembly as a step toward unification and liberal democracy.

With the monarchy in retreat, the time was ripe for Marx and Engels's bourgeois revolution. Instead of heading to the bloodied streets of Berlin—a city they did not remember fondly for "its cringing petty bourgeoisie" and "mass of bureaucrats, aristocrats and court riff-raff"—they chose to reenter German politics in the Rhineland city of Cologne. Marx still had useful connections there from his days in the newspaper industry; besides, the city's accelerating industrialization, expanding proletariat, and wealthy manufacturing elite made it "in every respect the most advanced part of Germany at that time."[7] The urban, industrial Rhineland was destined to be in the forefront of the impending revolution, and its relaxed censorship regime made it the perfect base for Marx's scheme to revive the *Rheinische Zeitung.*

Yet the location was not without its difficulties. Chief among them was Andreas Gottschalk, a butcher's son and gifted doctor who ministered to slum dwellers. Gottschalk had bravely led the March revolution in Cologne by invading the town council and demanding voting reforms, abolition of the standing army, and freedom of the press. For his troubles, he was arrested and jailed before being released in the aftermath of the Berlin riots. By the time Marx and Engels arrived, Gottschalk stood at the head of an eight-thousand-member Workers' Association and was able to dictate much of the city's politics. Naturally, such proletarian authenticity infuriated Marx, who responded by founding a competing workers' organization, known as the Democratic Society. This was a blatant attempt to split the city's working-class movement, though in fairness the split had some grounding in real ideological differences. Gottschalk was a follower of Moses Hess, Karl Grün, and the "true socialist" school of thought, which advocated a peaceful reordering of the capitalist system toward an equitable mode of exchange. Ignoring much of Marx and Engels's communism, Gottschalk's socialism avoided the dynamic of class struggle or the historical progression toward proletarian revolution. Instead, the Workers' Association subscribed to a mixture of cooperation and mutualism based on a harmonious ideal of humanity beyond party politics. It was a program that Marx and Engels variously dismissed as petit bourgeois, utopian, and naïve.

Ironically, such a stance actually made the true socialists *more* antagonistic to the ruling bourgeoisie than Marx and Engels were, since they saw no need for an intervening period of bourgeois-democratic rule. They wanted to move straight from the remnants of a feudal polity to socialism. "You have never been serious about the emancipation of the repressed," Gottschalk taunted the two Prussian intellectuals. "The misery of the worker, the hunger of the poor has for you only a scientific, a doctrinaire interest. . . . You do not believe in the revolt of the working people, whose rising flood begins already to prepare the destruction of capital, you do not believe in the permanence of the revolution, you do not even believe in the capacity for revolution."[8] The pursuit of constitutional government was, in the words of Karl Grün, "an egotistical wish of the possessing classes" that the "true socialists" would have nothing to do with. They boycotted the approaching elections for the all-German National Assembly—a decision that instantly placed the Workers' Association on a collision course with Marx and Engels's carefully crafted plans for a revolution of the bourgeois-democratic kind.[9]

Having returned to Prussia to deliver a bourgeois democracy as part of the transition toward communism, Marx and Engels were in no mood for any indulgent nonsense about worker cooperatives. Backward, feudal Germany—in contrast, say, to advanced, industrial England with its developed working class—was not yet ready for a proletarian revolution. Their hostility to such futile scheming became quickly evident in the pages of Marx's newly founded paper, *Neue Rheinische Zeitung*, which gave ostentatiously little space to covering strikes, radical congresses, and any other signs of proletarian insurrection. Indeed, so hostile was the *Neue Rheinische Zeitung* to the city's radical working class that historian Oscar J. Hammen even suggests the paper was produced using casual printing labor with wages far lower than its reactionary rival, the *Kölnische Zeitung.*[10] Marx and Engels's political strategy was clear: to turn the *Neue Rheinische Zeitung* into "the organ of the democratic movement," but according to Engels, "a democracy which everywhere emphasized in every point the specific proletarian character which it could not yet inscribe once for all on its banner."[11] In the long run, the democratic initiatives would help bring the proletariat to greater consciousness arming them with the political tools to take on the bourgeoisie when the time was right. Week in and week out, the paper hurled insults at Prussian bureaucrats and Junker aristocrats, but the reforms it was arguing for were fairly modest, centered on universal suffrage, the dismantling of feudalism, and assistance for the unemployed. For all of Marx's fiery journalese, the paper was in fact advocating a very moderate, bourgeois-friendly program as a first stage to revolution. And this proved a great commercial success as the paper's sales surged to almost five thousand copies per day.

Given their middle-of-the-road, liberal-democratic stance, Marx and Engels thought it would not be too hard to drum up some investment for the paper from the region's middle classes. With an altogether misplaced confidence, Engels was dispatched to Barmen to butter up the Wupper valley bourgeoisie. It was another difficult homecoming. "C. and A. Ermen were quaking visibly when I walked into their office today," he reported mischievously to Emil Blank. Unsurprisingly, the fund-raising was not a success: the Barmen bourgeoisie were well aware of the communist program: "The fact is, *au fond*, that even these radical bourgeois here see us as their future main enemies and have no intention of putting into our hands weapons which we would very shortly turn against themselves." Engels then pointlessly asked his family to help fund the *Neue Rheinische Zeitung.* His uncle August was a notable reactionary on the Barmen town council and his brother Hermann the commander of a troop of the counterrevolutionary Home Guard. As for his father: "Nothing whatever is to be got out of my old man. To him even the *Kölner Zeitung* [another reactionary paper] is a hotbed of agitation and sooner than present us with 1,000 talers, he would pepper us with a thousand balls of grape."[12]

The few investors whom Marx and Engels did entice into supporting the publication deserted en masse after Engels used the first issue to deliver a sarcastic diatribe against the newly elected National Assembly sitting in Frankfurt. As he wrote in his history of the Communist League, "By the end of the month we no longer had any [investors] at all."[13] But the paper somehow struggled on, with Marx providing the bulk of the German political coverage and Engels concerning himself mainly with foreign and military matters. And despite the fears of its shareholders, the *Neue Rheinische Zeitung* was in principle extremely supportive of the Frankfurt assembly. Marx and Engels just wanted the assembly's representatives to go further and faster in transforming Germany into a unitary bourgeois state, the requisite first step toward revolution. The problem was the assembly's "parliamentary cretinism," with its endless, introspective debates and dizzying array of verbose lawyers, officials, and academics. After one unproductive session, Engels dismissed the assembly as "nothing but a stage where old and worn-out political characters exhibited their involuntary ludicrousness and their impotence of thought as well as action."[14] The dragged-out proceedings were not without cost: the precious moment of revolution had to be seized quickly if Germany's scattered states and principalities were to be molded into a single bourgeois republic. As the Frankfurt delegates speechified about procedures and protocol, the forces of reaction were regrouping. In Paris, they had already struck.

The political honeymoon of the provisional government in Paris did not last long. Deteriorating public finances had forced the republican administration to raise taxes and the April 1848 elections to France's Constituent Assembly saw a resurgence of conservative opinion loyal to the deposed monarchy. The socialist and republican candidates did poorly at the polls, winning barely 100 of the 876 seats at stake. Once in power, the conservatives swiftly acted to dismantle the "national workshop" plan that had been a cornerstone of the provisional government. The policy had been conceived as "true socialism" in action, with unemployed male residents of Paris offered either decently paid public works–type jobs (available at various workshops around the capital to which they applied in person) or generous unemployment benefits. But the system was quickly overwhelmed by tens of thousands of workers, idlers, and opportunists moving to Paris hoping to profit from this gigantic system of welfare relief. Confronting ruinous costs, a residuum of well-paid loafers, and the fury of private employers forced to hike wages to compete, the newly conservative assembly announced its intention to close the workshop system, forcing unemployed workers to enlist in the army or return to their low-paid jobs in the provinces. Fearing a popular backlash, it also enacted a series of measures against radical political clubs and the newly popular open-air banquets. In June 1848, the government issued an ultimatum to Paris's 120,000-odd workers receiving financial support, enlist or go home. In the impoverished eastern faubourgs of the city, the workers responded with street riots under the banners of "Work or Death!" and "Bread or Death!" By the following morning, the towering barricades were up again.[15]

Infuriatingly, as the revolution flared anew Engels was stuck in Cologne. Geographical distance did not however, put a damper on his breathless reports on Parisian events for the *Neue Rheinische Zeitung*, written as if the bullets were whizzing past him. For Engels, what was so invigorating about June 1848, in contrast to February, was that the insurrection was "purely a workers' uprising" as France moved from a bourgeois to a proletarian revolution with delicious alacrity. More than that, it was a moment of international proletarian solidarity. "The people are not standing on the barricades as in February singing '*Mourir pour la patrie*,'" he wrote. "The workers of June 23 are fighting for their existence and the fatherland has lost all meaning for them." Comparing the uprising to the great slave revolts of ancient Rome, Engels the Jacobin manqué celebrated a "Paris bathed in blood" and admired how the 50,000-strong insurrection was "growing into the greatest revolution that has ever taken place, into a revolution of proletariat versus the bourgeoisie."[16] In his *Class Struggles in France*, Marx would later claim the June Days amounted to "the war between labour and capital." While modern scholarship is generally skeptical about the level of proletarian involvement in the uprising (seeing it more as a traditional artisan-led revolt), there is no doubt about the naked class antagonism of the government's response.

The counterattack was overseen by Louis-Eugène Cavaignac, a bloodthirsty Algiers veteran who had recently been appointed minister of war. It was a gruesome affair: Cavaignac's troops cleared the boulevards with cavalry charges, peppered barricades with grapeshot, and concluded the day with a barrage of shells and incendiary Congreve rockets. On the other side of the German border, Engels recounted it all, drawing on secondhand sources, in prose dripping with socialist martyrology. "A strong detachment of the national guard made a flanking attack upon the barricade of the rue de Clery," he wrote in the *Neue Rheinische Zeitung* on 28 June 1848:

> Most of the barricade's defenders withdrew. Only seven men and two women, two beautiful young *grisettes*, remained at their post. One of the seven mounts the barricades carrying a flag. The others open fire. The national guard replies and the standard-bearer falls. Then a *grisette*, a tall, beautiful, neatly-dressed girl with bare arms, grasps the flag, climbs over the barricade and advances upon the national guard. The firing continues and the bourgeois members of the national guard shoot down the girl just as she has come close to their bayonets. The other *grisette* immediately jumps forward, grasps the flag, raises the head of her companion and when she finds her dead, furiously throws stones at the national guard. She, too, falls under the bullets of the bourgeoisie.[17]

Anarchy on the streets of Paris played perfectly into the hands of embattled authorities across Europe. By late summer, Prussia's reactionaries were becoming much bolder in countering the liberal ambitions of the National Assembly, marching troops through radical neighborhoods and clamping down on republican and socialist clubs. The staff of the *Neue Rheinische Zeitung* faced constant harassment, with Marx and Engels brought before the magistrates on an almost weekly basis to be charged with either "insulting or libelling the Chief Public Prosecutor," "incitement to revolt," or various other acts of subversion. The Cologne workers responded to the growing force of counterrevolution by establishing a Committee of Public Safety and then organizing a mass meeting on Fühlinger Heide, near Worringen, a heath to the north of Cologne. Traveling on barges with red flags fluttering at the prow, some eight thousand workers and socialists journeyed up the Rhine on 17 September to hear a rousing address by Engels in which he vowed that in the coming struggle with the Prussian authorities the people of Cologne were "ready to sacrifice their lives and property."[18] Ten days later, the city was placed under martial law. Public gatherings were banned, the civic militia was disbanded, and all newspapers were suspended.

Luckily for him, Marx had not taken part in the Worringen meetings. But warrants for high treason were issued for the rest of the *Neue Rheinische Zeitung* editorial board. Wilhelm Wolff fled for the Bavarian Palatinate, George Weerth made for Bingen in Hesse-Darmstadt, Karl Schapper (part of the original Communist League triumvirate) went straight to jail. Cologne's chief public prosecutor was especially keen to get his hands on the "merchant" Friedrich Engels, described in the arrest warrant as having an "ordinary" forehead, a "well-proportioned" mouth, "good" teeth, an "oval" face, a "healthy" complexion, and a "slender" figure. Unfortunately, Engels's mother caught sight of the warrant in the *Kölnische Zeitung* over her morning coffee. "Now you have really gone too far," the mortified Elise upbraided her son. "So often have I begged you to proceed no further but you have paid more heed to other people, to strangers, and have taken no account of your mother's pleas. God alone knows what I have felt and suffered of late." The public humiliation was enough to break a mother's heart: "I can think of nothing else but you and then I often see you as a little boy still, playing near me. How happy I used to be then and what hopes did I not pin upon you." The only solution was for him to get away from the dangerous influence of his friends and start a new life in commerce across the Atlantic: "Dear Friedrich, if the words of a poor, sorrowing mother still mean anything to you, then follow your father's advice, go to America and abandon the course you have pursued hitherto. With your knowledge you will surely succeed in finding a position in a good firm."[19] She could hardly have known him less.

Like Wolff and Weerth, Engels was now on the run. After stopping briefly in Barmen (where, thankfully, his parents were absent), he left for Brussels. But the Belgian authorities were all too familiar with his type. When the police heard about the arrival of Engels and his fellow communist Ernst Dronke, a newspaper reported, "the inspector took them to the Town Hall and from there to the prison of the Petits-Carmes, whence after an hour or two they were transported in a sealed carriage to the Southern Railway Station."[20] On 5 October 1848, using their mandate to disperse "vagabonds"—a favored tactic for dealing with communists—the Belgian police unceremoniously dumped the two freedom fighters on a train to Paris. As Engels and Dronke traveled through the night, Europe was alight: the struggle between the forces of revolution and counterrevolution was intensifying across the Continent. In France, Louis Napoleon was beginning his march to power; in Vienna, imperial troops were moving in the heavy artillery to shell the revolutionaries out of Parliament; in Prague, the Czech rising had been crushed by Habsburg forces, who were soon to turn their attentions to reinvading northern Italy; in Berlin, the Prussian army was on the verge of retaking the city; and in Cologne, Marx's *Neue Rheinische Zeitung* was demanding "revolutionary terrorism" as the only way to avenge "the useless butcheries of the June and October days."[21] And what did Friedrich Engels do to help see in the promised proletariat dawn? Did he return to the struggle? Propagandize in Paris? Support a workers' defense fund? No, he got away from it all on a walking holiday.

His journey began in Paris—and his heart instantly sank when he saw the effects on the capital of Cavaignac's fusillade: "Paris was dead, it was no longer Paris. On the boulevards, no one but the bourgeoisie and police spies; the dance-halls and theatres deserted. . . . It was the Paris of 1847 again, but without the spirit, without the life, without the fire and the ferment which the workers brought to everything in those days."[22] He had to leave. Turning his back on this "beautiful corpse" of a city, Engels headed into *la France profonde*. The twenty-eight-year-old fugitive had had enough, it seems, of the demands of revolution. The sensuous, almost Fourierist side of his character reasserted itself and he abandoned the tedious demands of insurgent life for an escapade through the sexual and gastronomic riches of rural France.

Engels chronicled this meandering journey from Paris to Geneva in a self-conscious feuilleton reminiscent of the most purple prose of his teenage years. Within this unpublished travelogue there are some flashes of political commentary, such as when he encounters some former denizens of the Parisian national workshops—now forcibly returned to the provinces—and is horrified by their fallen ideological state. "Not a trace of concern with the interests of their class and with current political issues which touch the workers so closely," he comments. "They appeared not to read any papers any more. . . . They were already on the point of turning into rustics, and they had only been there for two months."[23] But the body of the journal is less exercised about politics and far more concerned with wine, women, and the natural beauty of the Loire valley. "The avenue is lined with elms, ashes, acacias or chestnuts," he says of the countryside. "The valley floor comprises luxuriant pastures and fertile fields, amongst stubble a second harvest of the richest clover was sprouting."

At times the entries are reminiscent of nothing so much as an upmarket wine-tour brochure: "What a diversity, from Bordeaux to Burgundy, . . . from Petit Macon or Chablis to Chambertin, . . . and from that to sparkling champagne! . . . With a few bottles one can experience every intermediate state from a Musard quadrille to the Marseillaise, from the exultation of the cancan to the tempestuous fever heat of revolution, and then finally with a bottle of champagne one can again drift into the merriest carnival mood in the world!" As revolutionaries are offering up their lives on barricades across Europe, Engels allows himself a small joke on entering the town of Auxerre "robed in red":

> It was not just one hall here but the whole town which was decorated in red. . . . Dark-red streams filled even the gutters and bespattered the paving stones, and a sinister-looking blackish, foaming red liquid was being carried about the streets in great tubs by sinister bearded men. The red republic with all its horrors appeared to be working continuously. . . . But the red republic of Auxerre was most innocent, it was the red republic of the Burgundian wine-harvest.

Would his fellow revolutionaries have appreciated the joke? Never mind: "The 1848 harvest was so infinitely rich, . . . better than '46, perhaps even better than '34!" Ever the taxonomist, Engels found as much variation in the women he encountered in France's vineyards as in the local wine. His personal preference was for "the cleanly-washed, smoothly-combed, slimly-built Burgundian women from Saint-Bris and Vermenton" rather than "those earthily dirty, tousled young Molossian buffaloes between the Seine and the Loire." All in all, he was not overly selective in his favors. It was an interlude of simple pleasures: "lying in the grass with the vintners and their girls, eating grapes, drinking wine, chatting and laughing, then marching up the hill."[24]

By the time the well-satiated Engels crossed the French border into Switzerland in early November, the counterrevolution in Germany was on its way to overturning the advances of March 1848. Friedrich Wilhelm IV had abandoned his reforms for the reactionary strategy of General Brandenburg, who marched the army back from Potsdam into Berlin, adjourned the Prussian parliament, banned radical newspapers, and declared martial law. Unsurprisingly, Engels was not keen on returning to Cologne, where he would face charges of high treason. Instead, he hunkered down in Berne (assisted by secret funds from his mother, who worried about his catching a cold in the Swiss winter), halfheartedly involved himself in the local Workers' Association, and spent most of his time catching up on the revolutionary events he had missed while lolling about the Burgundian fields.

Engels was particularly interested in the Hungarian uprising led by Lajos Kossuth. This nationalist rebellion against the Austro-Habsburg monarchy had been fermenting since the late eighteenth century, when a romantic resurgence of Magyar culture had combined with an increasingly vocal prejudice against the millions of transnational Slavs resident within the Habsburg Empire. Over the decades this cultural renaissance developed into a cohesive political and social reform movement, led by an enlightened Hungarian nobility championing national determination free from Austrian interference. Inspired by the upheavals in Paris and Vienna, Kossuth and his fellow nobles took control of the Diet in a bloodless revolution, enacted a series of antifeudal "March laws," and restored Hungarian sovereignty. Hungary had never been the unitary ethnic state of romantic imagination, however, and the Magyar upsurge met with resistance not only from the Habsburg forces but also from the disaffected Slav, Croat, and Romanian minorities. The winter of 1848–49 witnessed a series of dramatic battles between an Austro-Croation coalition and Kossuth's nationalist, Magyar army, culminating in the capture of Buda-Pest by the Hungarians.[25] The campaign had multiple attractions for Engels. Despite his earlier criticism of Thomas Carlyle's "great man" theory of history, he was bewitched by heroic military statesmen, with Wellington, Napoleon, and Cromwell as particular heroes. Similarly, he regarded Kossuth as "a truly revolutionary figure" fighting for an obviously righteous cause. Ignoring widespread opinion that the Hungarian nobles were little more than an aristocratic *fronde*, Engels championed the Magyar cause for its nationalist ambitions, republican spirit, and military strategy—all essential for overthrowing ancien régime monarchies and marshaling a bourgeois-democratic revolution.

In a rather less pleasant vein, he also supported the Magyar's anti-Slav prejudice. Abandoning for the moment his materialist analysis of class for a decidedly unscientific mix of racial and nationalist opinion, Engels branded the Slavs part of that subgroup of humanity he labeled "historyless" or "nonhistoric" peoples, prone to interfere with revolutionary progress and so needing to be eliminated. Engels had earlier alluded to this specious ethnophilosophy in the run-up to the September 1848 Cologne rallies, when the Rhineland was in an uproar about the armistice of Malmö—a humiliating treaty forcing Prussia to retreat from the duchy of Schleswig and agree to its annexation by Denmark. For revolutionary nationalists hoping for a united Germany, it was a debilitating setback and Engels used the treaty controversy as an excuse to berate the "brutal, sordid, piratical, Old Norse national traits" that made up Scandinavian culture, with its "perpetual drunkenness and wild beserk frenzy alternating with tearful sentimentality." Behind this boorish stereotyping was a more unnerving argument in favor of Prussia's ethnonational claim over the duchies. "By the same right under which France took Flanders, Lorraine and Alsace, and will sooner or later take Belgium—by that same right Germany takes over Schleswig; it is the right of civilization as against barbarism, progress as against stability," Engels wrote in an article for the *Neue Rheinische Zeitung*.[26]

The Ukrainian historian Roman Rosdolsky long ago suggested that Engels owed his theory of "nonhistoric" people to Hegel, whose *Philosophy of Mind* argued that only those people who were able to establish a state—thanks to inherent "natural and spiritual abilities"—could be regarded as part of historical progress. "A nation with no state formation . . . has, strictly speaking, no history," Hegel declared, "like the nations which existed before the rise of states and others which still exist in a condition of savagery."[27] It was an arbitrary division that laid down only the vaguest criteria for what constituted "national viability"—which seemed to center mainly around the capacity to produce a bourgeoisie and, with it, entrepreneurs, capitalists, and workers—but it allowed Engels to dismiss various stateless peoples as nonhistoric and, in their opposition to a Marxian notion of progress toward unified nation-state, inherently counterrevolutionary. Among these he included the Bretons in France, the Gaels in Scotland, the Basques in Spain, and, of course, the Slavs. "There is no country in Europe which does not have in some corner or other one or several ruined fragments of peoples," he wrote in an essay on "The Magyar Struggle." And it was no surprise that "these residual fragments of people always become fanatical standard-bearers of counter-revolution and remain so until their complete extirpation or loss of their national character, just as their whole existence in general is itself a protest against a great historical revolution."[28] Perhaps the best example of this struggle between ancient ethnicities and historic progress was taking place in North America, where the United States was wrenching control of California, Texas, and other territories from Mexico. Engels was wholly in favor of this colonial land grab. Is it in any way unfortunate, asked Engels, "that splendid California has been taken away from the lazy Mexicans, who could not do anything with it?" Were the Mexicans capable of exploiting gold mines, building cities up the Pacific coastline, constructing railways, and transforming global trade? Not a bit of it. "The 'independence' of a few Spanish Californians and Texans may suffer because of it, in some places 'justice' and other moral principles may be violated; but what does that matter compared to such facts of world-historic significance?"[29]

For Engels, the subjugation of "nonhistoric" people was especially appropriate in the case of the Slavs, who had committed the ultimate counterrevolutionary crime of allying themselves with both the imperial Habsburgs and tsarist Russia against Kossuth's Magyars. In words that many dictators would echo in the twentieth century, Engels advocated a policy of ethnic cleansing in the service of progress and history. "I am enough of an authoritarian to regard the existence of such aborigines in the heart of Europe as an anachronism," he wrote of the Slavs in a letter to the German socialist theoretician Eduard Bernstein. "They and their right of cattle stealing will have to be mercilessly sacrificed to the interest of the European proletariat."[30] It was an ugly, brutal ideology and there is something deeply chilling about the ease with which Engels made the transition from his sybaritic wine-tasting tour to calling for "bloody revenge on the Slav barbarian" in the span of just a few weeks. "The next world war will result in the disappearance from the face of the earth not only of reactionary classes and dynasties, but also of entire reactionary peoples," he blithely wrote in the *Neue Rheinische Zeitung.* "And that, too, is a step forward."[31]

By December 1848, Engels had had enough of standing on the sidelines of revolution and wanted to return to "the movement." "Now that Gottschalk and [Friedrich] Anneke [coleader of the Cologne Workers' Association] have been acquitted, shan't I be able to come back soon?" he wrote plaintively to Marx in Cologne, testing the legal waters. The attractions of a reflective life in Berne—"lazing about in foreign parts"— had started to pale. "I am rapidly coming to the conclusion that detention for questioning in Cologne is better than life in free Switzerland." And despite General Brandenburg's best efforts, the Rhenish revolutionary spirit had not completely succumbed to Prussian revanchism. Indeed, to keep the democratic flame alive, a left-wing faction of the Frankfurt National Assembly had recently formed the Central March Association to defend the liberal settlement of March '48, and by the spring of 1849 it had over half a million members. The struggle was far from over.

Meanwhile, the *Neue Rheinische Zeitung* had found its true voice after Marx took the paper in a more obviously left-wing direction. Now openly blaming the weak-willed bourgeoisie for the "failure" of the revolution, Marx looked to develop an independent political line for the working classes that would be distinct from the bourgeois-democratic movement. The working class–middle class alliance of 1848 clearly had to be recalibrated and a more obvious route to proletarian rule set out. For Engels, Marx's achievements on the *Neue Rheinische Zeitung* constituted perhaps his finest hour: "No German newspaper, before or since, has ever had the same power and influence or been able to electrify the proletariat masses as effectively as the *Neue Rheinische Zeitung*. And that it owed above all to Marx."[32] Engels was delighted with the paper's militant turn and, in one of his first articles after returning to Cologne in January 1849, he reproached himself and his fellow activists for their naïveté about the bourgeoisie: "Why after the revolution in France and in Germany did we show so much generosity, magnanimity, consideration and kind-heartedness, if we did not wish the bourgeois again to raise its head and betray us, and the calculating counter-revolution to plant its foot on our neck?"[33]

Inspired by Kossuth's impressive military strikes against the overwhelming Habsburg forces, Engels now sought to import the insurgent tactics of Hungary into Germany. His vision in early 1849 was for Frankfurt and southern Germany to rise up in revolt and join the Magyar rebellion to create a broader revolutionary coalition against the reactionary monarchies of Germany and Austria. It was a strategy that would require a sophisticated use of guerrilla tactics since the Rhenish revolutionaries could never hope to beat the Prussian army in open battle. The lessons from Hungary were clear: "Mass uprising, revolutionary war, guerrilla detachments everywhere—that is the only means by which a small nation can overcome a large one, by which a less strong army can be put in a position to resist a stronger and better organized one."[34] And now was the moment to act. In March 1849, the parliamentary cretins in Frankfurt had finally done something historic by voting to adopt a full-fledged imperial constitution, bringing together all the constituent states of Germany under one federal authority. This seismic political decision lay the groundwork for a genuine constitutional monarchy, with a single currency, tariff structure, and unified defense policy. But it all rested on the willingness of the Prussian king, Friedrich Wilhelm IV, to rule within the parameters of a constitutional monarchy and in concert with a democratic parliament. Needless to say, the great feudal sovereign and faithful believer in the divine right of kings was having none of it. "This so-called crown is not really a crown at all, but actually a dog-collar, with which they want to leash me to the revolution of 1848," was his haughty response to the parliament's offer.[35]

For the Central March Association and other radical groups, the proposed imperial constitution represented everything they had struggled for. They were not going to let it slip away lightly. As Rhenish Westphalia rose up in support of the constitution, Friedrich Wilhelm unleashed the Prussian *Landwehr* on the workers. By April 1849, revolution was once again in the air in western and southern Germany, as militant communists and socialists assumed leadership posts previously occupied by middle-class democrats and constitutionalists inclined more to negotiation than to confrontation. As a political solution began to seem more and more unlikely, violent unrest resurfaced. "Everywhere the people are organizing themselves into companies, electing leaders, providing themselves with arms and ammunition," Engels reported excitedly.[36] On 3 May, Dresden erupted after the king of Saxony, Augustus II, closed the state parliament and joined Friedrich Wilhelm in refusing to recognize the imperial constitution. Workers and revolutionaries flooded onto the streets to battle both Saxon and Prussian troops. Among those manning the barricades were Engels's former Berlin classmate Michael Bakunin, now an active anarchist; the prudish, precious Stephan Born, who had spent the previous months running a workers' brotherhood in Berlin; and Richard Wagner, the newly appointed conductor of the Dresden opera. The Rhineland took its cue from the south: Düsseldorf, Iserlohn, Solingen, and even the Wupper valley joined the rebellion. After all his research into revolutionary warfare, after his youthful articles denouncing Prussian conservatism and long evenings spent with Moses Hess outlining the promise of communism to guffawing industrialists, Engels was certain the moment of revolution had arrived. "The *Neue Rheinische Zeitung*, too, was represented at the Elberfeld barricades," as Engels, the native child of the Wupper, proudly put it.[37]

• • •

In May 1849, with opposition to the Prussian authorities spreading through the Rhineland, workers in Elberfeld gathered in a beer hall overlooking the city to hear rousing speeches from democrats and radicals urging a campaign of resistance. The result was the formation of a revolutionary militia, which the local civic guard wisely demurred from disarming. When a troop of soldiers arrived from Düsseldorf to challenge the insubordination, the mayor ordered them back. They refused and by 10 May the county commissioner had fled and Elberfeld was in a state of armed revolt.[38] "From the middle of Kipdorf and lower Hofkamp everything was closed off with barricades," Alexander Pagenstecher, an Elberfeld surgeon, recalled. "There were fellows busy repairing and reinforcing the old barricades and setting up new ones."[39] To coordinate the resistance, the Elberfeld Political Club established a Committee of Public Safety that included (to the disgust of the more zealous activists) members of the existing city council.

Into this delicate situation stepped Engels. Adhering closely to protocol, on his arrival in Elberfeld—"with two cases of cartridges which had been captured by the Solingen workers at the storming of the arsenal of Gräfrath"—he reported to the committee. Aware of his revolutionary reputation, the members wanted to know precisely what his motives were. Engels replied falsely that he had been sent by the Cologne workers and innocently suggested he might be able to provide some military assistance against the inevitable Prussian response. But, far more importantly, "having been born in the Berg Country, he considered it a matter of honour to be there when the first armed uprising of the people of the Berg Country took place." And the good burghers of Elberfeld had no need to worry about his red, radical politics. "He said that he desired to concern himself exclusively with military matters and to have nothing to do with the political character of the movement."[40] Unwisely taken in, the committee gave him the task of inspecting the barricades, positioning artillery installations, and completing the fortifications. Drawing together a company of sappers, Engels reconfigured various defenses, strengthening all possible entry points along the narrow Wupper valley.[41] But there was little chance that this "dyed in the wool" radical would fail to exploit the revolutionary promise of the Elberfeld barricades.

"After I had climbed over the barricade by the Haspeler Bridge, which was armed with three or four small Nuremberg-caliber salute cannons, I was stopped in front of the nearby house that acted as a barrier," the worried Pagenstecher continued. "It had been transformed into a sentry room, and Dr. Engels from Barmen was in command."[42] Engels had decorated the site in a suitable manner: "On the barricade by the mayor's house, a piece of red material torn from one of his curtains had been put up, and young men had made themselves sashes and bands from this same material; these signs were taken as proof that all of this was for the republic—the red one, naturally."[43] At the Committee for Public Safety, the penny finally dropped: just as they had feared, this was the red-radical takeover, instigated by the town's most infamous communist. "When the flags of the red republic finally fluttered on the barricades in our bleak streets, scales fell from the eyes of our well-meaning Elber-felders," was how one local paper reviewed the events of May 1849.[44]

A loving array of myths and legends surround Engels's time on the Elberfeld barricades. The finest is the story of Friedrich Engels senior encountering his rebel son directing the gunners on the Haspeler Bridge. As reported by local resident and Barmen manufacturer Friedrich von Eynern, the fraught meeting between the "barricade-mounting son" and the "old, dignified factory owner" (on his way to church, no less) feels almost too pathos-ridden for reality.[45] And, indeed, evidence for this encounter seems fairly thin. Similarly, Alexander Pagenstecher suggests that Engels was involved in the capture and holding for ransom of an Elberfeld minister, Daniel von der Heydt, along with his mother and brother. Again, apart from the aggrieved Pagenstecher, the supporting sources are sketchy. What is certainly true is that Engels's time in Elber-feld was both brief and widely resented. To one member of the Commit-tee for Public Safety, a barrister named Höchster, Engels was "a dreamer, one of those who ruin everything."[46] And his replacement of the Ger-man tricolor with the red flag did not go down well at all. According to a fellow insurrectionist, the drawing instructor Joseph Körner, "people were so upset early the next morning that a counterinsurrection and Engels's maltreatment could be avoided only through the speedy clear-ing away of the red scraps and Engels's 'removal from the city.'"[47] It was up to Höchster to deliver the ultimatum: he approached Engels and stated (in Engels's version) that, "although there was absolutely nothing to be said against his behaviour, nevertheless his presence evoked the utmost alarm of the Elberfeld bourgeoisie; they were afraid that at any moment he would proclaim a red republic and that by and large they wished him to leave."[48]

Engels was furious and demanded "that the above-mentioned request should be presented to him in black and white, over the signatures of all members of the Committee for Public Safety." If this was an attempt to call the committee's bluff, it failed miserably, as the members swiftly returned with a signed statement, which, to deepen the public humiliation, they posted around Elberfeld: "WHILE FULLY APPRECIATING *THE ACTIVITY HITHERTO SHOWN IN THIS TOWN BY CITIZEN FRIEDRICH ENGELS OF BARMEN, RECENTLY RESIDENT IN COLOGNE, IT IS REQUESTED THAT HE SHOULD FROM TODAY LEAVE THE PRECINCTS OF THE LOCAL MUNICIPALITY* SINCE HIS PRESENCE COULD GIVE RISE TO MISUNDERSTANDINGS AS TO THE CHARACTER OF THE MOVEMENT." The message could not have been clearer. According to Engels, "The armed workers and volunteer corps were highly indignant at the decision of the Committee for Public Safety. They demanded that Engels should remain and said they would 'protect him with their lives.'"[49] But, selfless to the end, Engels accepted the verdict and decided to leave Elberfeld. With his departure, the town returned to its habitual moderation. When, one week later, Prussian forces arrived ready to storm the Wupper valley, they found the barricades dismantled, red flags and all. As Engels left Elberfeld he received a final stinging rebuke, a letter from his brother-in-law Adolf von Griesheim that gave full vent to the repeated humiliations Engels had caused his family—public arrest warrants, police searches of the family home, and endless neighborhood gossip. "If you had a family and worried about them like me," Griesheim wrote, "you would change your restless life and, in the friendly circle of your loved ones, you would gain more from this short life than you ever can receive from a heartless gang of cowardly, ungrateful troublemakers. . . . It is as if you still have this thankless idea of sacrificing yourself for irredeemable Mankind, to become a social Christ and to devote all your egoism to achieving this goal."[50]

With another arrest warrant out for Engels ("special characteristics: speaks very rapidly and is short-sighted") and the *Neue Rheinische Zeitung* firmly shut down after a melodramatic final edition printed in red ink, the communist influence over the German uprising looked finished. But as long as the chance for revolution remained, Marx and Engels refused to give up. They trudged from Cologne to Frankfurt and thence to Baden, Speyer, Kaiserslautern, and Bingen, in support supposedly of the armed struggle for the imperial constitution but in reality of the rebellion as a vehicle for more radical political demands. In Engels's opinion the last remaining chance of insurgency lay in the southwest corner of Germany, in Baden-Palatinate. As he reported, "The entire people were united in their hatred for a government that broke its word, engaged in duplicity and cruelly persecuted its political adversaries. The reactionary classes, the nobility, the bureaucracy and the big bourgeoisie were few in numbers."[51]

Unfortunately, Baden's revolutionary aspirations were being steadily eroded by the timid leadership of local lawyer Lorenz Peter Brentano, who could not quite shed his fear of committing high treason. Moreover, Brentano's group seemed to suffer from a distinct lack of revolutionary rigor. "People yawned and chatted, told anecdotes and made bad jokes and strategic plans and went from one office to another trying as well as they could to kill time," was how Engels described the hapless scene in his account of the struggle, *The Campaign for the German Imperial Constitution*. As ever, Marx and Engels let their views be known about the incompetence of those in charge. At one point, Engels was so precise in his analysis of the leadership's weaknesses and so explicit in describing the coming Prussian onslaught that he was arrested as a spy on the grounds that only an enemy of the revolution could be quite so damaging to morale. After spending a day in jail, he was released thanks to the intervention of various communist activists. Seeing no real hope, at this point Marx abandoned the Baden insurgency and headed back to Paris.

Engels was ready to do the same when August von Willich, a former Prussian officer and now a rebel commander, marched into Kaiserslautern with a volunteer company of eight hundred worker and student soldiers. "Since I had no intention of letting slip the opportunity of gaining some military education," Engels recounted, "I too buckled on a broadsword and went off to join Willich."[52] Quickly commissioned as Willich's aide-de-camp, Engels regarded his commander as one of the few figures of any worth within the Baden-Palatinate revolutionary army. In battle, he found him "brave, cool-headed and adroit, and able to appreciate a situation quickly and accurately." Outside the war zone, he considered him a terrible bore—"*plus ou moins* tedious ideologist and a true socialist."[53] Nevertheless, after his enforced exit from Elberfeld, here was a chance for real combat as the Prussian forces started to encircle this last redoubt of the 1848 revolution.

"Every man thinks meanly of himself for not having been a soldier, or not having been at sea," claimed Samuel Johnson. And Engels certainly thought a great deal more of himself for having been in combat. In a long letter to Jenny Marx in the aftermath of the Baden campaign, Engels was practically strutting. "The whistle of bullets is really quite a trivial matter," he reported insouciantly, "and though, throughout the campaign, a great deal of cowardice was in evidence, I did not see as many as a dozen men whose conduct was cowardly in battle."[54] Engels was involved in four engagements altogether, "two of them fairly important," but most of his time was spent in a futile alternation of skirmish and retreat. "We had scarcely climbed the bushy slope when we came to an open field from the opposite wooded edge of which Prussian riflemen were loosing off their elongated bullets at us. I fetched up a few more of the volunteers, who were scrambling around the slope helpless and rather nervous, posted them with as much cover as possible and took a closer look at the terrain," reads a fairly typical account in Engels's *Campaign*.[55] And while he had a great deal of admiration for Willich, some of the officers, and the worker corps within the company, he had the autodidact's total disdain for the student contingent: "During the course of the entire campaign the students generally showed themselves to be malcontent and timid young gentlemen; they always wanted to be let into all the plans of operation, complained about sore feet and grumbled when the campaign did not afford all the comforts of a holiday trip."[56]

It was at the Rastatt fortress, along the River Murg, on the very western edges of Germany, that Engels fought in the largest battle of the campaign—and discovered, as he put it to Jenny, "that the much-vaunted bravery under fire is quite the most ordinary quality one can possess."[57] Facing a Prussian force some four times the size of the 13,000-man revolutionary force, Engels fought with mettle and distinction. He led a workers' company of Willich's troops into battle with the First Prussian Army Corps and took part in a series of skirmishes along the Murg. Indeed, throughout the campaign Engels was widely praised by fellow soldiers for his willingness to join in with the troops and for his "energy and courage" in battle.[58] But systematically outgunned and outmaneuvered by the Prussian army, Willich's men had no chance of winning. Rastatt proved a bloody defeat, with the Communist League's founding member Joseph Moll among the many fallen.

In the wake of the rout, the straggling remnants of the revolutionary army retreated south through the Black Forest toward the Swiss border. While Willich and Engels argued for making a last stand, they could no longer command the support of the battered, exhausted, hungry troops. "We marched through Lottstetten to the frontier, bivouacked that night still on German soil, discharged our rifles on the morning of the 12th [of July] and then set foot on Swiss territory, the last of the army of Baden and the Palatinate to do so," he reported.[59] From its hapless beginnings through to its divided leadership and woeful logistics, the Baden-Palatinate campaign was a doomed enterprise. For Engels, however, it served a vital purpose: he had tasted blood and could now look any fellow revolutionary in the eye. "*Enfin*, I came through the whole thing unscathed," he told Jenny Marx, "and *au bout du compte*, it was as well that one member of the *Neue Rheinische Zeitung* was present, since the entire pack of democratic blackguards were in Baden and the Palatinate, and are now bragging about the heroic deeds they never performed."[60] Marx, too, realized the campaign's significance in terms of their public image: "Had you not taken part in the actual fighting, we couldn't have put forward our views about that frolic," he wrote from Paris. Marx now urged Engels to write up this authentic episode of revolutionary endeavor as swiftly as possible. He was positive "the thing will sell and bring you money."[61]

Back in safe but dull Switzerland along with thousands of other political refugees seeking asylum, Engels followed Marx's advice and churned out *The Campaign for the German Imperial Constitution*. It aimed simultaneously to cement his reputation for heroic conduct under fire and establish the contours of the post-1848 blame game. The unredeemed villains of the piece, castigated for having allowed the entire '48 harvest to go to waste, were the bourgeoisie who led the workers down the garden path of insurgency and then abandoned them the minute the counterrevolution surfaced. In a blistering opening chapter, Engels branded them "faint-hearted, cautious and calculating as soon as the slightest danger approaches; aghast, alarmed and wavering as soon as the movement it provoked is seized upon and taken up seriously by other classes." There was no failure on the part of the radical democrats, the communists, or the proletariat. Instead, it was the "stab in the back" from the bourgeoisie that had betrayed the promise of revolution. In the coming months, Engels's contempt for bourgeois prevarication—"as soon as there is the slightest chance of a return to anarchy, i.e., of the real, decisive struggle, it [the bourgeoisie] retreats from the scene in fear and trembling"—would harden into political ideology.[62] After Europe's failure to turn, Marx and Engels realized that the two-step model of a bourgeois-democratic revolution followed later by a proletarian takeover was something they would need to rethink in its entirety. And now they had the time to do so.

Marx had been in Paris only a month when the forces of reaction caught up with him. Threatened by the authorities with banishment to "the Pontine marshes of Brittany," he chose exile in London. "So you must leave for London at once," he wrote to Engels, now festering in Lausanne. "In any case your safety demands it. The Prussians would shoot you twice over: (1) because of Baden; (2) because of Elberfeld. And why stay in a Switzerland where you can do nothing. . . . In London we shall get down to business."[63] But it was not easy for a wanted man in an era of counterrevolutionary resurgence to make his way across a still-smoldering Europe. France and Germany were out of bounds, so he headed for Genoa via Piedmont to catch a ride to London aboard the *Cornish Diamond*. Hurrying to Marx's side, Engels, the bloodied veteran of the Baden campaign, joined a diaspora of émigrés, exiles, revolutionaries, and communists huddled together in the capital of the one country that had so spectacularly failed to rise to the '48 revolution. Far removed from the turmoil of the Continent, conservative mid-Victorian England was to be his home for the next forty years.

6

MANCHESTER IN
SHADES OF GRAY

On Saturday I went out fox-hunting—seven hours in the saddle. That sort of thing always keeps me in a state of devilish excitement for several days; it's the greatest physical pleasure I know. I saw only two out of the whole field who were better horsemen than myself, but then they were also better mounted. This will really put my health to rights. At least twenty of the chaps fell off or came down, two horses were done for, one fox killed (I was in AT THE DEATH).[1]

Barely a decade after raising the red flag over the Barmen barricades, Friedrich Engels seemed to have undergone a startling character change. The revolutionary of '49 was now a stalwart of Manchester society: riding out with the Cheshire Hunt, a member of the Albert Club and the Brazenose Club, a resident of a salubrious city suburb, and a respectable, hardworking employee of Ermen & Engels, with good prospects of making partnership. "I am very glad you have left and are well on the way to becoming a great COTTON LORD," Jenny Marx wrote admiringly to her husband's friend.[2] It seemed Elise and Friedrich Engels might finally rest easy as their black sheep son settled into his rightful place within the family firm. Had he, like so many other young radicals, turned from firebrand to fogey? Or was it, like "Oswald," just another front?

In truth, the middle decades of Engels's life were a wretched time. Exiled back to Manchester, humiliatingly forced to return to Ermen & Engels, the two decades he spent in the cotton trade constituted an era of nervous, sapping sacrifice. Karl Marx called them Engels's years of Sturm und Drang—and he was not a little to blame. Heroically, between 1850 and 1870 Engels abandoned much of what gave his life meaning— intellectual inquiry, political activism, collaboration with Marx—to serve the cause of scientific socialism. "The two of us form a partnership together," Marx soothingly explained, "in which I spend my time on the theoretical and party side of the business," while Engels's job was to provide the financial support by busying himself at commerce.[3] To support Marx, his growing family, and, most important of all, the writing of *Das Kapital*, Engels willingly offered up his own financial security, his philosophical researches, and even his good name. The Manchester years demanded a heavy price of the self-appointed second fiddle.

"If any one had conceived the idea of writing from the outside the inner history of the political émigrés and exiles from the year 1848 in London, what a melancholy page he would have added to the records of contemporary man," the Russian exile Alexander Herzen wrote in his memoirs. "What sufferings, what privations, what tears, . . . and what triviality, what narrowness, what poverty of intellectual powers, of resources, of understanding, what obstinacy in wrangling, what pettiness of wounded vanity."[4]

When Engels stepped off the *Cornish Diamond* in 1849 and rented some rooms in Chelsea and then Soho, he reentered precisely this scene, the pettiness and politicking made worse by the ever-present Prussian spies. "We cannot make a single step without being followed by them wherever we go," Engels publicly protested to the *Spectator* in June 1850. "We cannot get into an omnibus or enter a coffee-house without being favoured with the company of at least one of these unknown friends. . . . The majority of them look anything but clean and respectable."[5] Meanwhile, the days passed with selection battles for the Communist League Central Committee, fights over the membership of the London German

Workers' Educational Society, and a tussle over dispersing charitable funds for impoverished émigrés. Marx and Engels had quickly reverted to type, undermining the existing German Refugee Relief Committee and establishing their own Social Democratic Relief Committee for German Refugees. After fleeing Prussian sharpshooters and enduring the ennui of Switzerland, this rats-in-a-sack politics was a welcome return to the good times Engels remembered from Brussels and Paris. "All in all, things are going quite well here," he wrote to his publisher friend Jakob Schabelitz in Paris. "[Gustav] Struve and [Karl] Heinzen are intriguing with all and sundry against the Workers' Society and ourselves, but without success. They, together with some wailers of moderate persuasion who have been thrown out of our society, form a select club at which Heinzen airs his grievances about the noxious doctrines of the communists."[6] Happy days.

This beery, smoke-filled world centered on Great Windmill Street amused itself in a political time warp. "After every unsuccessful revolution or counter-revolution, feverish activity develops among the émigrés who escaped abroad," Engels later wrote.

> Party groups of various shades are formed, which accuse each other of having driven the cart into the mud, of treason and of all other possible mortal sins. They also maintain close ties with the homeland, organize, conspire, print leaflets and newspapers, swear that it will start over again within the next 24 hours, that victory is certain and, in the wake of this expectation, distribute government posts. Naturally, disappointment follows disappointment, . . . recriminations accumulate and result in general bickering.[7]

The enormity of the 1848 failure—the collapse of a bourgeois-democratic revolution in the face of an ancien régime reaction—and the dominance of counterrevolutionary sentiment on the Continent had simply failed to sink in. The Great Windmill Street communists still believed the overthrow of monarchism was imminent. "The revolution is advancing so rapidly, that every one *must* see its approach," Engels confidently predicted of the French political scene in March 1850 (as

Bonaparte's Second Empire lurked in the wings).[8] Marx and Engels hoped to use the moment's breathing space to reaffirm their demands for a more organized, autonomous working-class movement. The "stab in the back" thesis they had been promoting since the failure of the Continental revolutions—the willingness of a liberal bourgeoisie to sacrifice the workers' cause at the first hint of a settlement with the ruling classes—now became the basis of a broader political strategy. In their 1850 "Address of the Central Authority to the League," Marx and Engels explained how only a system of workers' associations could exploit the political gains of the coming revolution without falling into the trap of a liberal alliance. "In a word, from the first moment of victory, mistrust must be directed no longer against the defeated reactionary party, but against the workers' previous allies," they enjoined.[9] What this necessitated, in a phrase Leon Trotsky would later appropriate, was a "permanent revolution" and a far more aggressive proletarian commitment to grabbing the levers of power. To avoid any prospect of bourgeois consolidation, there could be no period of calm after the initial democratic revolution.

Yet, at the same time, the revolution could not be rushed if the socio-economic fundamentals were not in place. And just as it had done in Cologne, this political hesitancy placed them at odds with the broader membership of the Communist League. In London the league was led by by Karl Schapper and Engels's old commander August Willich, both of whom advocated immediate military action. To Marx and Engels, this was tin-pot terrorism and a premature threat to the communist cause. In addition to which, Marx could not abide Willich's cocky bravado and war veteran aura (nothing infuriated him more than authentic revolutionary credentials). Naturally, he ended up challenging the decorated class warrior to a duel and then, in a fit of pique, transferring the Central Board of the Communist League back to Germany.

But the disagreements were not confined to Willich and Schapper. Marx and Engels also couldn't get on with the German community leaders Gottfried Kinkel and Arnold Ruge, their supposed old friend from Berlin days. Nor did they care for Struve and Heinzen, for the exiled Italian nationalist Giuseppe Mazzini, the French socialists Louis Blanc and Alexandre-Auguste Ledru-Rollin, their one-time hero Lajos

Kossuth, or even their Chartist ally Julian Harney. Endlessly obdurate, Engels embraced the prospect of complete political isolation. "At long last we again have the opportunity—the first time in ages—to show that we need neither popularity, nor the SUPPORT of any party in any country," he wrote to Marx. Their role as communist ideologues was to chart the march of history and highlight the contradictions of capitalism, in order to prepare the proletariat for their approaching revolutionary duty. This political loneliness seemed to appeal to Engels's instinctive, almost puritanical ardor for sacrifice and martyrdom. "How can people like us, who shun official appointments like the plague, fit into a 'party'?" he asked Marx.[10]

What was less appealing was the poverty that accompanied the London sojourn. Jenny Marx had followed her husband across the Channel in September 1849 with their three small children and a fourth on the way—Heinrich Guido (nicknamed "Fawksey"), who earned his incendiary soubriquet by being born on 5 November 1849. But with only irregular funds from freelance journalism, niggardly publishing contracts, and a doomed attempt to relaunch the *Neue Rheinische Zeitung*, Marx was in no position to support his family. Jenny Marx later described this period as one of "great hardship, continual acute privations, and real misery."[11] Crammed together with undernourished brothers and sisters in a series of shabby flats, Guido suffered an infancy of wretched privation and fatigue. "Since coming into the world, he has never slept a whole night through—at most, two or three hours. Latterly, too, there have been violent convulsions, so that the child has been hovering constantly between death and a miserable life. In his pain he sucked so hard that I got a sore on my breast—an open sore; often blood would spurt into his little, trembling mouth," Jenny wrote in a desperate fund-raising letter to their Communist friend Joseph Weydemeyer.[12] For a lady of Jenny von Westphalen's lineage, there was also the indignity of being harried across London by bakers, butchers, milkmen, and bailiffs as Marx dodged bills and schemed his way into new lodgings. It was a debilitating and humiliating time, and young Guido suffered the effects. "Just a line or two to let you know that our little gunpowder-plotter, Fawksey, died at ten o'clock this morning," Marx wrote to Engels in November 1850. "You can imagine what it is like here. . . . If you happen to feel so inclined, drop a few lines to my wife. She is quite distracted."[13] Jenny and Karl Marx were to lose two other children, Franziska and Edgar ("Colonel Musch"), to the same noxious mix of poverty, damp, and disease.

Lodging on Macclesfield Street, down the road from Marx's flat on Dean Street in Soho, Engels was in no better shape financially as he worked to drum up support for the refugee community and pursued various publishing contracts. While he lacked Marx's brood of dependents, he faced a similar absence of money, since his usually indulgent parents had finally cut off the financial tap after one arrest warrant too many. "It might be convenient to send you money to live on," Elise wrote after another request, "but I find quite extraordinary your demand that I should give financial support to a son who is attempting to spread ideas and principles which I regard as sinful."[14] Facing diminishing opportunities in Soho and increasingly anxious about Marx's desperate situation, Engels readied himself for the inevitable: the only way he could feed himself, help Marx, and assist their cause was to bend the knee, reconcile with his family, and return to commerce. His sister Marie deftly managed the family diplomacy. "The thought has come to us that you may perhaps wish to enter business seriously for the time being, in order to ensure yourself an income; you might drop it as soon as your party has a reasonable chance of success and resume your work for the party," she wrote in an elegantly crafted letter sent with the blessing of her parents.[15] His rejoining the firm might not be pleasant, his father added, but it would be useful for the family business. With few other options available, Engels agreed to the deal on a temporary basis, so he might return to the barricades when the workers' revolution called. His father, he wrote, "will need me here for three years at least, and I have entered into no long-term obligations, not even for three years, nor was I asked for any, either with regard to my writing, or to my staying here in case of a revolution. This would appear to be far from his mind, so secure do these people now feel!"[16] As well they might: Engels ended up working nineteen years for the family firm.

· · ·

The failure of the '48 revolutions had been mourned nowhere more keenly than in Manchester. The farrago of Kennington Common—where the Chartist dream of marching on Parliament to press home the six points fell victim to public inertia, government repression, and rain—signaled the collapse of English working-class radicalism. The 150,000 demonstrators for democracy had been met by 85,000 special constables, 7,000 troops, 5,000 police, 1,200 Chelsea pensioners, and even the Duke of Wellington. It was a drizzly, sodden affair with the Chartists reduced to scurrying across the Thames in cabs to present their petition to Parliament. While Europe's capitals had gone up in flames, the class-conscious English proletariat had spectacularly failed to rise. Among the mills and moors of Lancashire, where the Chartist call for social and political reform had resounded most loudly, the disappointment was most evident. But it was all in tune with a changing city.

The 1846 repeal of the Corn Laws—an import tariff, introduced in the aftermath of the Napoleonic wars to keep the price of corn artificially high, that long attracted opprobrium as a subsidy for the landed elite—had marked the triumph of the so-called Manchester School, with its philosophy of free trade, minimal state intervention, open markets, and democracy. Loosely marshaled under the leadership of two members of Parliament, John Bright and Richard Cobden, this consciously middle-class political movement pressed for an end to protective tariffs and costly state expenditure (often connected to imperialism) but had no great affinity with the interests of organized labor. And Manchester, the city that had once portended a terrifying future of class warfare, industrial unrest, and proletarian revolution, was the movement's spiritual home. In the face of the mid-Victorian economic boom, the "shock city" of the Industrial Revolution was transformed into a middle-class imperium. For "Cottonopolis" this would be the age not of lockouts, strikes, and torch-lit rallies but of baths and washhouses, libraries and parks, Mechanics' Institutes and Friendly Societies.

As Engels retraced his steps, *The Condition of the Working Class* already felt dated. In place of Little Ireland, there were signs everywhere of the new mercantile order: well-endowed chapels, multistory warehouses modeled on Renaissance palazzi, and, most symbolic of all, the foundations of the Free Trade Hall, callously erected on the site of the 1819 Peterloo massacre, to commemorate the Corn Law victory. Modeled on the Gran Guardia Vecchia in Verona, the hall was in A. J. P. Taylor's words, "dedicated, like the United States of America, to a proposition—one as noble and beneficent as any ever made. . . . The men of Manchester had brought down the nobility and gentry of England in a bloodless, but decisive, Crécy. The Free Trade Hall was the symbol of their triumph."[17] Radical Manchester had been rendered so harmless that in October 1851 the city was deemed fit for a queen. Victoria and Albert's civic progression, across Victoria Bridge and passing under a canopy of Italianate arches before bestowing various honors on the council, was transformed into a pageant of bourgeois pride and provincial self-regard. The meaning of Manchester—commerce, religious toleration, civil society, political self-government—was now granted royal approbation. The city had shown itself, according to the *Manchester Guardian*, as a "community based upon the orderly, sober and peaceful industry of the middle classes."[18]

For Engels, this bourgeois self-satisfaction made for an awful welcoming party. Even his old friend and mentor the Owenite lecturer John Watts had thrown in his lot with the enveloping smug liberalism. "Recently I went to see John Watts; the fellow seems skilled in sharp practice and now has a much larger shop in Deansgate," Engels wrote to Marx. "He has become a consummate radical mediocrity. . . . From a few instances he gave me, it transpired that he knows very well how to boost his tailoring business by parading his bourgeois liberalism."[19] Most shameful of all, Watts was selling that great agora of radical intent, the Owenite Hall of Science, to provide space for a new library and reading room. "The free traders here are exploiting the prosperity or semi-prosperity to buy the proletariat, with John Watts for broker."[20]

Former Chartist Thomas Cooper was similarly disturbed by the bourgeois tendencies of his erstwhile comrades. "In our old Chartist time, it is true, Lancashire working men were in rags by thousands; and many of them often lacked food. But their intelligence was demonstrated wherever you went," he wrote in his autobiography. "You could see them in groups discussing the great doctrine of political justice. . . . Now, you will see no such groups in Lancashire. But you will hear well dressed working men talking, as they walk with their hands in their pockets, of 'Co-operatives' and their shares in them, or in building societies."[21] Miserably, Engels noted the progress of this embourgeoisification. "The English proletariat is actually becoming more and more bourgeois, so that the ultimate aim of this most bourgeois of all nations would appear to be the possession, alongside the bourgeoisie, of a bourgeois aristocracy and a bourgeois proletariat," he grumbled.[22] In the early 1850s, Engels put some faith in the leadership of the socialist Ernest Jones and his attempts to resuscitate the Chartist cadaver. He was even minded "to start up a small club with these fellows, or organise regular meetings to discuss the *Manifesto* with them."[23] But after Jones failed to subscribe to the Marx-Engels canon in its entirety and agreed to one too many compromises with middle-class reformers, Engels disowned him. "The English proletariat's revolutionary energy has completely evaporated," he concluded in 1863.[24]

Driving the mid-Victorian boom and sapping proletariat ambition was a resurgent cotton industry. Profits were up owing to new markets in America, Australia, and China, while improvements in technology ensured sustained productivity gains. The economic upswing was particularly evident in Lancashire, where wage rates and employment both rose; the county's two thousand mills kept their 300,000 power looms beating day and night. In 1860, at the zenith of its power, the cotton industry accounted for almost 40 percent of the total value of British exports. Thanks to the invention of the sewing machine, which increased demand for its specific type of sewing thread, Ermen & Engels took a profitable chunk of that trade. The firm's fortunes received another boost in 1851 when Godfrey Ermen patented an invention for the polishing of cotton thread that allowed it to market its product under the exclusive banner of "Diamond Thread." With surging orders, the company moved offices to 7 Southgate (into a warehouse overlooking the courtyard of the

Golden Lion public house) and purchased another mill—Bencliffe Mill in Little Bolton, Eccles—in addition to its Victoria Mill at Salford.

Behind the healthy balance sheet, there was the usual corporate in-fighting. Ermen & Engels was owned by four partners—Peter, Godfrey, and Anthony Ermen, together with Friedrich Engels senior. The Manchester branch of this Anglo-German conglomerate was run by Peter and Godfrey Ermen while Engels senior spent his time at the Engels-kirchen factory in the Rhineland. Besides running Ermen & Engels, Peter and Godfrey also operated a printing mill and bleach works business. This company, Ermen Brothers, was technically independent of Ermen & Engels, but it was run from the same office and just happened to be one of Ermen & Engels's leading suppliers. Engels senior was convinced he was being cheated by this cozy arrangement, and he wanted his son—employed simply as a corresponding clerk and general assistant—to unpick the company finances and expose any sharp practice.

The Ermens, understandably, were not overly delighted at the prospect of an internal auditor on the staff and made life as difficult as possible for their new clerk. They remembered well Engels's apprenticeship in the office eight years earlier, when "he worked for the firm as little as possible and spent most of his time at political meetings and on studying the social conditions in Manchester."[25] And now, in Engels's words, Peter Ermen was "going round in circles like a fox that has left its brush in a trap, and [is] trying to make things too hot for me here—the stupid devil imagines he could annoy me!" Meanwhile the Ermens had their own problems, with Peter and Godfrey jockeying for control of the firm. "See that you entrench yourself firmly between the two warring brothers," was Jenny Marx's advice on office politics for Engels, after he posted her a large parcel of cotton thread. "Their tussle is bound to place you in a position of indispensability vis-à-vis your respected Papa, and in my mind's eye I already see you as Friedrich Engels Junior and partner of the Senior."[26]

What no one had expected was just how industrious and effective Engels would prove at his job. He went through the books, tried to untangle Ermen & Engels from Ermen Brothers, and generally looked after the Engels family concern with exemplary diligence. "My old man is enchanted with my business letters and he regards me remaining here as a great sacrifice on my part," the unlikely capitalist informed Marx.[27] Indeed, father and son were well on their way to a rapprochement. In June 1851, they met in Manchester for the first time since the apocryphal Barmen bridge incident. "I think it is probably better that you should not be together all the time, for you can't always be talking business, and it is better to avoid politics, on which you have such different views," was his nervous mother's advice prior to the reunion.[28] She was right. The trip was generally deemed a success, but Engels thought that "had my old man stayed here a few days longer we'd have been at each other's throats. . . . On the last day of his visit, for example, he sought to take advantage of the presence of one of the Ermens . . . to indulge himself at my expense by intoning a dithyramb in praise of Prussia's institutions. A word or two and a furious look were, of course, enough to bring him back to heel."[29]

Despite improved family relations, the fun of goading the Ermen brothers, and even the initial intellectual challenge of bookkeeping, there was no avoiding the reality that Engels had returned to the beastly business of huckstering. His letters of the time are filled with references to "accursed commerce" and "filthy commerce" as office life perpetually impinged on his scholarship, journalism, and socialism. It was a dull, tedious existence. "I drink rum and water, swot and spend my time 'twixt twist and tedium,'" he wrote to his friend Ernst Dronke in 1851. To Marx he was even franker: "I am bored to death here."[30] Politically, the job also had its costs since Engels's position as a bourgeois mill owner obviously risked compromising his and Marx's standing within the communist world. "You wait and see, the louts will be saying, what's that Engels after, how can he speak in our name and tell us what to do, the fellow's up there in Manchester exploiting the workers, etc. To be sure, I don't give a damn about it now, but it's bound to come," he confided to Marx.[31] And such charges were certainly leveled at him. Friedrich von Eynern, for example, a young Barmen industrialist and family friend, visited Engels in 1860, took him on a walking tour of Wales (during which

Engels sang verses of Heine's *Die Heimkehr*), and peppered him with questions. "Encouraged by his debating ways," Eyern recalled,

> I had not failed to point out to him that his position as a manufacturer, as co-owner of one of the period's worst "big capitalist businesses," must put him at sharp odds with his theories, if he didn't practically utilize his considerable means to help the "disowned" entrusted to his direct care. However, since according to his teachings the goals of universal economic freedom could be achieved only through the systematic cooperation of the international labor force, he dismissed such trifling help as pointless and disruptive to all circles of the movement. He showed no inclination to allow any limits to be placed on the basic freedom of his existence: to use his private earnings by himself, as he saw fit.[32]

The criticisms were not without foundation since, when it came to the "direct care" of his employees, Engels could be something of a bully. "Godfrey has taken on three fellows for me who are absolutely hopeless. . . . I shall have to sack one or two of them," he wrote to Marx in 1865 in a spirited defense of flexible labor laws. A month later, one of the fellows was dismissed following an administrative error: "That was the last straw as far as his slovenliness was concerned, and he was sacked."[33] To be fair, in contrast to the clerks, the more obviously working-class mill hands of Ermen & Engels were said to enjoy better working conditions than the average. A report from the 1871 annual meeting of the Sick and Burial Society at Bencliffe—where the second Ermen & Engels mill was located—referred to "the stream of clean and well-dressed young women passing through the village" and commented that "in few mills were the hands so profitably and regularly employed."[34]

Engels's own employment was equally profitable. For all the banality and self-loathing the job entailed, it provided a sizable salary beginning at £100 per year plus an annual "expenses and entertainment allowance" of £200. From the mid-1850s, Engels was also entitled to a 5 percent profit share, which grew to 7.5 percent by the end of the decade. In 1856, Engels's cut of the company profits stood at £408; this increased to some

£978 by 1860, thereby taking his annual wage over £1,000—which is not far off $150,000 in today's money.*

Still, the awkward truth was that Engels's lucrative income was the direct result of his exploitation of the labor power of the Manchester proletariat. The very evils that he and Marx had decried funded their lifestyles and philosophy. Engels was always more perturbed by this political contradiction than Marx (often the chief beneficiary of Ermen & Engels's market dominance), but he still cashed the check. The obvious defense was that without the money from the mill workers Engels could never have funded Marx's seminal advances in the scientific analysis of capitalism. "The opponents of the working class would, of course, have preferred Engels to give up his job and renounce his income," was the later official communist line on Engels's profiteering. "He would have been unable to support Marx in this case, *Das Kapital* would not have been written, and the process of the working classes becoming politically and theoretically independent would have been delayed." But, thankfully, "Engels looked on the profits he made as a factory owner and merchant as a contribution toward the working class's fight for emancipation, and used them accordingly all his life."[35]

In the very first letter we have from Engels in Manchester to Marx in London, he is already promising to send part of his salary. There was never any explicit agreement between Engels and Marx that his toiling in the cotton trade would fund Marx's intellectual exertions for the communist cause, just an implicit recognition that this was how their partnership would work. And the money cascaded south like a spring torrent for the rest of Engels's professional life. There were post office orders, postage stamps, five-pound notes, a few pounds pilfered from the Ermen & Engels cash box when Godfrey Ermen was out of the office, and then far more weighty sums when payday arrived. In addition, there

---

* To provide some kind of context, the social commentator Dudley Baxter analyzed the 1861 census to produce a class analysis of mid-Victorian England relative to income. To scrape into the middle class was to earn over the taxable threshold of £100, with parsons, army officers, doctors, civil servants, and barristers usually operating in the £250–£350 salary range. Baxter thought that to join the comfortable upper middle classes one had to take home an annual salary of £1,000–£5,000. In contrast to Engels's riches, another great Victorian writer, Anthony Trollope, was having to get by on £140 a year at his day job as a post office clerk.

were generous hampers, crates of wine, and birthday presents for the girls. "Dear Mr. Engels," as Jenny was apt to address him, was regularly allocating over half his annual income to the Marx family—a total of £3,000–£4,000 ($450,000–$600,000 in today's terms) over the twenty-year period he was employed. Yet it was never enough. "I assure you that I would rather have had my thumb cut off than write this letter to you. It is truly soul-destroying to be dependent for half one's life," begins a typical letter from Marx pleading for an emergency loan.[36] "Considering the great efforts—greater, even, than you can manage—that you make on my behalf, I need hardly say how much I detest perpetually boring you with my lamentations," starts another. "The last money you sent me, plus a borrowed pound, went to pay the school bill—so that there shouldn't be twice the amount owing in January. The butcher and *épicier* made me give them IOUs, one for £10, the other for £12, due on 9 January."[37] When Marx was in an especially cowardly frame of mind, he had his wife write the begging letter. "It is for me a hateful task to have to write to you about money matters. You have already helped us all too often. But this time I have no other recourse, no other way out," Jenny pleaded in April 1853. "Can you send us something? The baker warned us that there'd be no more bread after Friday."[38]

As numerous biographers have pointed out, Marx was not poor. In the measured judgment of Marx biographer David McLellan, "his difficulties resulted less from real poverty than from a desire to preserve appearances, coupled with an inability to husband his financial resources."[39] The subsidy from Engels, combined with income from journalism, book deals, and the odd inheritance totaled some £200 per annum, which meant that—after the needy Soho years—his financial position was far sounder than that of many middle-class families. But Marx was terrible with money ("I don't suppose anyone has ever written about 'money' when so short of the stuff") and went from feast to famine in a hopeless cycle of financial gorging and retrenchment. With every windfall, the family moved to a new and larger house—from Soho to Kentish Town to Chalk Farm—with the costs adding up for Engels to sort out. "It is true my house is beyond my means, and we have, moreover, lived better this year than was the case before," Marx wrote to Engels after an upgrade to fashionable Maitland Park Road. "But it is the only way for the children to establish themselves socially with a view to securing their future. . . . Even from a merely commercial point of view, to run a purely proletarian house-hold would not be appropriate in the circumstances."[40] Here was the rub: Karl and Jenny Marx were far more concerned about keeping up appearances, marrying their daughters well, and holding their place in polite society—in short, being bourgeois—than the bohemian Engels ever was. "For the sake of the children," Jenny Marx explained defensively, and without acknowledging Engels's generosity, "we had already adopted a regular, respectable middle class life. Everything conspired to bring about a bourgeois existence, and to enmesh us in it."[41] Marx himself, the prophet-philosopher, was never going to sully himself with a profession to support his family, so it was Engels who was chained to the office treadmill to fund their aspirational lifestyle. Which is why it is wrong to paint Marx as a real-life Mr. Micawber desperately hoping something would turn up; thanks to Engels, he always *knew* something would turn up. "Karl was tremendously pleased when he heard the postman's portentous double KNOCK," Jenny wrote to their benefactor in 1854. "'*Voilà* Frederick, £2, we're saved!' He cried."[42] No wonder that, behind his back, Marx called Engels "Mr. Chitty."

Accompanying the flow of cash was a gripping correspondence. While both Marx and Engels desperately resented the distance between them after their years spent at close quarters in Paris, Brussels, and Cologne, posterity has been the beneficiary. The 1850s and 1860s represent the golden years of their letter writing, as they exploited the mid-Victorian postal revolution—of Penny Blacks, post offices, and postboxes—to the full. A letter posted in Manchester before midnight would reach Marx the following day by 1:00 p.m.; a letter sent by 9:00 a.m. would be in his hands by 6:00 p.m. the same day. And this cache of letters provides an unequaled insight into their individual neuroses, frustrations, passions, and disappointments. Stories of royal flatulence, cuckolded émigrés, and drinking marathons abound—in the words of Francis Wheen, "a gamey stew of history and gossip, political economy and schoolboy smut, high ideals and low intimacies."[43] The letters are also a telling commentary on the depth of affection between the two men as they provided each other consolation in bereavement, encouragement in work, and criticism of political strategy. The mail carried as well a touching exchange of photographs. For Engels at his office and Marx in his study, the post was a highlight of the day. "The two friends wrote to each other almost every day," Eleanor Marx recalled, "and I can remember how often Moor, as we called our father at home, used to talk to the letters as though their writer were there. 'No, that's not the way it is'; 'You're right there,' etc., etc. But what I remember best is how Moor used sometimes to laugh over Engels's letters until tears ran down his cheeks."[44]

A large chunk of the early Manchester–London correspondence focused on the tantalizing prospect of an economic crash. Marx and Engels's conflict with the Willich-Schapper faction in the Communist League was partly driven by their conviction, as good materialists, that revolution could occur only given the appropriate economic circumstances. Attempts at insurrections and putsches were doomed if the socioeconomic preconditions were not in place—as the events of 1848–49 had so frustratingly shown. What revolutionary socialism required was advance warning of financial collapse so the activists could be prepared for the political consequences. And luckily the movement had a man stationed behind enemy lines: from his seat in the counting houses of Cottonopolis, Engels became the main source of intelligence on the state of international capitalism.

"Speculation in railways is again reaching dazzling heights—since 1 January most shares have risen by 40%, and the worst ones more than any. Ça promet!" he reported to Marx six months into the job. Clearly, capitalism's denouement was just around the corner. The East India market was overstocked, while the British cloth industry was being hit hard by a flood of cheap cotton. "If the Crash in the market coincides with such a gigantic crop, things will be cheery indeed. Peter Ermen is already fouling his breeches at the very thought of it, and the little tree-frog's a pretty good barometer," Engels wrote in July 1851. With bankruptcies starting to pick up in London and Liverpool and overproduction glutting the market, Engels was adamant the crash would arrive by

March 1852.⁴⁵ "All this is guess-work," he allowed on March 2, slightly revising his forecast. "We could just as well have it in September. It should, though, be a fine how-d'ye-do, for never before has such a mass of goods of all descriptions been pushed onto the market, nor have there ever been such colossal means of production." The only possible fly in the ointment was a strike by the Amalgamated Society of Engineers seeking improved working conditions, which was holding up machine building. Engels, the champion of the workers, thought such irredeemably selfish behavior might "hold it [the crash] up for at least a month."⁴⁶ And yet as April followed March and 1852 bowed to 1853, the day of reckoning was somehow never quite at hand. Instead, production increased, exports surged, wages rose, standards of living improved, and the mid-Victorian boom ground inexplicably on.

By September 1856, the prophet of the Manchester Exchange had rediscovered his voice. "This time there'll be a *dies irae* such as has never been seen before; the whole of Europe's industry in ruins, all markets over-stocked, . . . all the propertied classes in the soup, complete bankruptcy of the bourgeoisie, war and profligacy to the nth degree." At last, Engels was partly right: overproduction in the textile markets, combined with an unexpected hike in the cost of raw material, had led to a collapse of confidence in the cotton industry, followed by a run on the banks and a spate of commercial insolvencies. The global economy, from America to India via Britain and Germany, was shaken as sugar, coffee, cotton, and silk prices plummeted. "The American Crash is superb and not yet over by a long chalk," Engels wrote rapturously in October 1857. "The repercussion in England would appear to have begun with the Liverpool Borough Bank. *Tant mieux.* That means that for the next 3 or 4 years, commerce will again be in a bad way. *Nous avons maintenant de la chance.*" The conditions for revolution were ripe; they had to strike! "A period of chronic pressure is needed to get the people's blood up." It was now clearer than ever that 1848 had been a false dawn, but this was the real thing, "a case of do or die." Nevertheless, two months into the crash, the proletariat was still failing to realize its calling. "There are as yet few signs of revolution, for the long period of prosperity has been fearfully demoralizing," Engels noted gloomily in December 1857. And by the following spring, business had picked up again, thanks to developing markets in India and China.[47]

Engels's last and best hope lay with the American Civil War. In April 1861, Union forces started to blockade Southern ports, ratcheting up the cost of freight, insurance, and, above all, the price of middling New Orleans cotton, with serious consequences for production and employment in the UK. Imports from the American South fell from 2.6 million bales in 1860 to less than 72,000 in 1862. Hundreds of thousands of Lancashire operatives, valiantly supporting the ideals of Abraham Lincoln and the antislave North, were cut back to part-time and then fired. Their reduced earnings started to undermine the wider northwest economy as shops closed, savings dwindled, and food riots broke out. By November 1862, almost 200,000 workers across Lancashire were receiving support from various relief committees. Modern economic historians now suggest the Lancashire "cotton famine" was caused as much by an oversaturated global market as by the Civil War embargo but either way the results were the same. "You will readily understand that all the philistines are in a cold sweat," Engels reported in April 1865 as the Liverpool import-export industry shuddered and 125,000 unemployed mill hands wandered the Manchester streets. "A lot of people in Scotland are finished as well, and one fine day it's bound to be the turn of the banks, and that'd be the end of the matter."[48] Like many other cotton-based businesses, Ermen & Engels was directly affected: it introduced half-time in the mills, watched profits evaporate as unwanted stock piled up, and even slashed directors' salaries. For Engels, no matter the personal costs, this was another chance for revolution. "The distress up here is gradually becoming acute," he noted as cases of malnutrition, pneumonia, typhoid, and tuberculosis mounted. "I imagine by next month the working people themselves will have had enough of sitting about with a look of passive misery on their faces."[49]

In fact, the exact opposite occurred. The Manchester cotton workers were to become a symbol of the mid-Victorian consensus, patted on the head for the dignified resolve with which they endured their poverty. It was an exemplary display of self-control in the interests of a greater moral calling: "The leaders of the operative class are in general strongly favourable to the Northern policy, firm in their hatred of slavery, and firm in their faith in democracy," wrote R. Arthur Arnold in his *History of the Cotton Famine*.[50] One government inspector thought that "at no period in the history of manufactures have sufferings so sudden and so severe been borne with so much silent resignation and so much patient self-respect."[51] Instead of rioting, the factory hands accepted the vagaries of the global marketplace with unwavering stoicism and, to Victorian official opinion, it seemed that the respectable, self-helping working class had at last come of age. John Watts, the former radical turned bourgeois apologist, thought such endurance revealed the beneficial influence of Sunday schools, improving literature, and cooperative sentiments.[52] Everything Engels had first feared about the Manchester proletariat's disinclination toward class struggle was being proved horribly right.

With revolution postponed, Engels returned to his day job—or, rather, jobs, since Marx now called upon Engels to carry out the only piece of professional employment for which he was personally contracted. In early 1851, Charles Dana, a former Fourierist and now managing director of the progressive, antislavery *New York Daily Tribune*, asked Marx to contribute articles to the paper on English and European affairs. Marx's grasp of written English was so poor, however, that Engels had to translate the texts from German into English—which all too often meant just writing them himself. "If you could possibly let me have an article on conditions in Germany by Friday morning, that would make a splendid beginning," Marx loftily wrote to his friend on receiving news of his assignment.[53] To which Engels obediently answered, "Write and tell me soon what sort of thing it should be—whether you wish it to stand on its own or to be one of a series, and (2) what attitudes I should adopt."[54] The pay—at £2 per article—was impressive and the newspaper had over 200,000 U.S. readers, but Marx clearly thought it grubby work for a philosopher. "The continual newspaper muck annoys me," he fumed when actually forced to write his own articles. "It takes a lot of time, disperses my efforts and in the final analysis is nothing."[55] But it was all right for his harried comrade slogging away in Manchester. "Engels really has too much work," Marx explained majestically to his

American friend Adolf Cluss, "but being a veritable walking encyclopaedia, he's capable, drunk or sober, of working at any hour of the day or
night, is a fast writer and devilish quick on the uptake."[56]

He was not wrong. Engels was a gifted journalist, able to turn around
text on most topics to length and on time. "This evening I shall translate
the final part of your article and shall do the article on 'Germany' tomorrow or Thursday," reads a typically dutiful Engels response.[57] But it
was hackwork and very few of the *New York Daily Tribune* articles rose
to the usual heights of Engels's intellect. Back and forth the letters sped
between Manchester and London with translations, suggestions for new
articles, pleas for information on unknown subjects, demands for brev-
ity ("You really must stop making your articles so long. Dana can't possibly want more than 1–1.5 columns"), stylistic criticisms ("You must
colour your war-articles a little more seeing that you are writing for a
general newspaper"), and urgent requests to make sure the copy made
the Liverpool steamer.[58] But Marx was always happy to take full credit.
"How do you like my husband creating a stir with your article throughout western, eastern and southern America?" asked Jenny indelicately
after Engels's multiple installments on the history of 1848–49, *Revolution and Counter-Revolution in Germany*, were well received by the *Tribune* readership.

The traffic was not all one way, of course. The letters also reveal the
degree to which Marx shared the development of his thinking on *Das
Kapital* with Engels. Much of the initial impetus for the book had come
from Engels himself. As early as 1851 he was chiding Marx that "the
main thing is that you should once again make a public debut with a
substantial book. . . . It's absolutely essential to break the spell created by
your prolonged absence from the German book market."[59] Nine years
later, with still no obvious sign of publication in the offing, Engels re-
minded him of the "paramount importance" of the work, which he was
needlessly holding up with minor intellectual quibbles. "The *main* thing
is that it should be written and published; the weaknesses which you
think of will never be discovered by those donkeys; and if an unsettled
period sets in what will you be left with if the whole thing is interrupted
before you get *Capital* finished as a whole?"[60]

Eventually, at his daily perch at seat 07 in the British Museum Reading Room, Marx got down to writing his opus—and soon started pestering Engels with requests for technical data. While the British Museum had much to offer, when it came to understanding the functioning of capitalism it was no substitute for the realities of the Manchester cotton trade. "I have now reached a point in my work on economics where I need some practical advice from you, since I cannot find anything relevant in the theoretical writings," Marx wrote in January 1858. "It concerns the *circulation* of capital—its various forms in the various businesses; its effects on profit and prices. If you could give me some information on this, then it will be very welcome." There followed a series of questions on machinery costs and depreciation rates, the allocation of capital within the firm, and the calculation of turnover in the company bookkeeping. "The theoretical laws for this are very simple and self-evident. But it is good to have an idea of how it works in practice."[61] Over the next five years, the requests for real-life information kept coming. "Could you inform me of all the different types of workers employed, e.g., at your mill and in what proportion to each other?" Marx inquired in 1862. "For in my book I need an example showing that, in mechanical workshops, the division of labour, as forming the basis of manufacture and as described by A[dam] Smith, does not exist. . . . All that is needed is an example of some kind."[62] Engels's years at Ermen & Engels provided the empirical foundations of *Das Kapital*. "Since practice is better than all theory, I would ask you to describe to me *very precisely* (with examples) how you run your business," began another round of queries.[63]

Engels's contribution went beyond the statistical as he became the sounding board for Marx's emerging economic philosophy. "Let me say a word or two about what will, in the text, be a lengthy and complex affair, so that you may LET ME HAVE YOUR OPINION on it," Marx began a letter of 2 August 1862. He then launched into an explanation of the difference between constant capital (machinery) and variable capital (labor), offering an early draft of the "surplus value" theory of employee exploitation, which would become a core part of *Das Kapital*. Engels responded in kind, raising a number of methodological objections to the way in which Marx was calculating the value of a factory worker's labor and its relative compensation in labor-wage rates. But Marx rarely enjoyed too close a questioning and breezily replied that any such criticisms could not properly be treated "prior to the 3rd book. . . . If I wished to refute all such objections in advance, I should spoil the whole dialectical method of exposition."[64]

For all the reams of correspondence concerning *Das Kapital,* pursuing such complex themes on paper could sometimes prove too trying. "Can't you come down for a few days?" Marx asked on 20 August 1862. "In my critique I have demolished so much of the old stuff that there are a number of points I should like to consult you about before I proceed. Discussing these matters in writing is tedious both for you and for me." And even the sprightly Engels could find Marx's requests for enlightenment a little arduous after a day in the office. "What with the cotton bother, the theory of rent has really proved too abstract for me," he replied wearily in September 1862. "I shall have to consider the thing when I eventually get a little more peace and quiet."[65]

Amid this profusion of intellectual, professional, and personal material, there is an uncomfortable silence in the correspondence about Engels's most generous sacrifice. "In the early summer of 1851 there occurred an event which I shall not touch upon further, although it brought about a great increase in our private and public sorrows," was how Jenny Marx alluded to the delicate history of Henry Frederick Demuth.[66] The boy's mother, Helene "Lenchen" Demuth, known as "Nim," had long been a live-in housekeeper for the Marx family. Even in the Marxes' most cramped Soho lodgings, the family always found a place for Nim. Indeed, it was that very intimacy that sparked the crisis: when Jenny Marx traveled to the Continent in 1850 on a family fund-raising mission, Marx took advantage of the twenty-eight-year-old housemaid. And on 23 June 1851, their progeny, Freddy Demuth, duly entered the world to no great acclaim.

He was Marx's son, but the birth certificate remained blank and it was Engels who unofficially acknowledged paternity. For the good of Marx's marriage and the broader political cause (émigré groups enjoyed

nothing more than discrediting enemies via sexual scandal), Engels allowed Marx's son to take his Christian name and, in the process, sully
his own good name. Marx behaved abominably when it came to Freddy's
upbringing, packing him off to unsympathetic foster parents in East
London. He never received a proper education or enjoyed the kind of
intellectual upbringing—the Shakespeare dramas, boisterous picnics on
Hampstead Heath, socialist banter—Marx bestowed on his other children. Freddy spent his professional life as a skilled fitter and turner and
member of the Associated Society of Engineers, and his political life as a
member of the Hackney Labor Party. When Engels later moved to London and, after Marx's death, hired Nim as his own housekeeper, Freddy
and his son Harry used the tradesman's entrance to visit—in Harry's
recollection—"a motherly sort of person" in "a basement." Engels, however, was always careful to absent himself on such occasions.

Only Marx's daughter Eleanor (or "Tussy," as she was now known
within the family) seemed moved by Freddy's plight. "It may be that I
am very 'sentimental'—but I can't help feeling that Freddy has had great
injustice all through his life," she wrote in 1892. Nor could she account
for the hostile and distant attitude of Engels towards his "son" when he
was, in all other respects, so generous and warmhearted to everyone in
their extended familial circle. On Engels's deathbed, to Tussy's horror,
all was revealed. In an 1898 letter now located in the Amsterdam archives of the International Institute for Social History, Engels's final
housekeeper and companion, Louise Freyberger, describes how on the
eve of his death Engels confided to Tussy the real identity of Freddy's
father. "General [Engels] gave us . . . permission to make use of the information only if he should be accused of treating Freddy shabbily,"
Freyberger wrote. "He said he would not want his name slandered, especially as it could no longer do anyone any good." In the succeeding years,
Tussy tried desperately to repair the damage by befriending Freddy, who
would prove one of her most trusted and sympathetic correspondents.
By then, however, Engels's ill repute as a shoddy father was well established. The sordid episode is a telling indication of the personal sacrifices
Engels was willing to endure to protect his friend and expedite the
march of socialism.[67]

Such lies were just part of the miasma of subterfuge that enveloped his middle decades. For Engels led little short of a double life: by day the respectable cotton lord, a frock-coated member of the upper middle class; by night the revolutionary socialist, an ardent disciple of the low life. To retain his office job, support Marx, and keep the communist cause afloat, Engels was forced to maintain a facade of painful propriety. The effort of living in two worlds was exhausting, and the contradiction between public commitments and personal beliefs eventually sent Engels spiraling toward illness, depression, and breakdown.

The anchors of his private life, his real life, were his long-time lover, Mary Burns, and her sister Lizzy. To retain his place within Manchester society and avoid the disapproval of his parents, however, Engels felt compelled to hide his relationship with the Irish sisters from colleagues and family alike. (A letter from his troublesome brother-in-law Adolf von Griesheim complaining about the connection and its damaging effects on the Engelses' social standing suggests such secrecy was not wholly successful.)[68] On his arrival in Manchester, Engels boarded with an "old witch of a landlady," Mrs. Isabella Tatham, at 70 Great Ducie Street in the Strangeways district, close to where the hulking Victorian jail now stands. Joining him in this insalubrious establishment were a cobbler, a waste dealer, and a silversmith-cum-salesman. After briefly renting some more expensive lodgings to convince his visiting father he was spending his allowance wisely (rather than funneling it to Marx), in March 1853 Engels moved in with the Burns sisters. Thanks to Roy Whitfield's meticulous reconstruction of Engels's Manchester years, we know that the poor-rate books for the districts of Chorlton-on-Medlock and Moss Side show a certain Frederick Mann Burns (a very Engels-style pun) as the occupant of 17 Burlington Street and then 27 Cecil Street.[69] But in April 1854, disaster struck. "The philistines have got to know that I'm living with Mary," a furious Engels reported to Marx, and he was driven back into "private lodgings again."[70]

From 1854 onwards, after the discovery of his proletarian ménage, the cash-strapped Engels was forced to run two separate premises, one public and private: he took an official residence at 5 Walmer Street in Rusholme—for entertaining business associates, correspondence, and reasons of bourgeois propriety—while hiding the Burns sisters at Cecil Street. In 1858, he moved his official base to Thorncliffe Grove, which is where the 1861 census has him down as a "short-sighted Prussian merchant."[71] Meanwhile, he rehoused the sisters in two smaller, jerry-built houses in the expanding working-class suburbs of Hulme and Ardwick. The rate book has the occupants of these addresses—7 Rial Street and 252 Hyde Road—living under the pseudonyms Frederick and Mary Boardman, together with a certain "Elizabeth Byrne." Deftly, Engels had managed to locate his lover and her sister just half a mile from his official residence.

These were only the first of numerous properties Engels would surreptitiously take for the Burnses over the next fifteen years. "I'm living with Mary nearly all the time now so as to spend as little money as possible," he explained to Marx in 1862. "I can't dispense with my lodgings, otherwise I should move in with her altogether." But it wasn't easy. "You are right, I am very broke," Engels responded later that year to another financial demand from Marx. "In the hope that, by leading a domesticated life in Hyde Road, I shall be able to make good the deficiency, I enclose herewith a £5 note."[72] In 1864, the caravan moved on again, after Engels fell out with his Thorncliffe Grove housemaid; he relocated his public residence to a flat in Dover Street, in the affluent Oxford Road neighborhood, and his unofficial one to nearby Mornington Street. Keeping the different addresses going and making sure no one breached the borders between his public and private lives were all unwelcome additions to Engels's workload, and he complained endlessly about the expense and annoyance. Yet one also gets the sense that the aggressively independent Engels enjoyed the freedom of maneuver these two distinct worlds provided.

It was in his private, unofficial surroundings that the revolutionary could reveal himself. Here Engels gathered together a regular coterie of socialist believers and intellectual sparring partners to drink beer, discuss the latest philosophical advances, and lament the bourgeois compromise they saw all around them. Wilhelm Wolff ("Lupus"), the Brussels communist turned tutor to the children of middle-class Manchester, was a close friend. "For several years Wolff was the only comrade I had in Manchester with the same views as myself," Engels later recalled. "No wonder that we met almost daily and that I had more than ample opportunity of admiring his almost instinctively correct assessment of current events."[73] George Weerth, back clerking in "beastly" Bradford, was again part of the circle before commerce took him abroad to Havana. Another favorite was Darmstadt-born Carl Schorlemmer, a lecturer in organic chemistry at Owens College, who was a fellow of the Royal Society and an expert on paraffin hydrocarbons—which, much to Engels's amusement, frequently exploded, leaving burns on his "bruised and battered face."[74] Schorlemmer was also a committed socialist who was trusted enough by Marx and Engels to correct proofs for *Das Kapital*. On a Saturday night, he could be found alongside Engels propping up the bar of the Thatched House Tavern in Newmarket Place, around the corner from the Royal Exchange.[75]

Engels's other great companion and Dover Street flatmate was Samuel Moore, a failed cotton trader who became a barrister and a Marxist (honored with the task of translating *Das Kapital* into English) before incongruously concluding his professional life in Asaba as chief justice of the territories of the Royal Niger Company. Alongside these fixed friends, there was a smattering of German émigrés, unemployed communists, and distant cousins, plus occasional visits from Marx himself. Sometimes the boozy evenings could get out of hand: "At a drunken gathering," Engels reported, "[I] was insulted by an Englishman I didn't know; I hit out at him with the umbrella I was carrying and the ferrule got him in the eye." Unfortunately for Engels, the Englishman in question took him to court on charges of assault, demanding £55 in compensation and costs. Engels reluctantly paid the sum, in the desperate hope of avoiding "a public scandal and a ROW with my old man."[76]

Engels's public life was a world away from such barroom brawls. The Cheshire Hounds—one of the grandest meets in Victorian Britain, "composed of the first gentlemen in that aristocratic county"—dated from 1763, when the Honorable John Smith-Barry brought together a pack of hounds from the Belvoir and Milton bloodlines. And they met, according to the *Field*, in some of England's most hunt-friendly settings:

"Cheshire abounds with parks, and mansions, and the aristocracy have from time immemorial been most devoted patrons of fox-hunting; indeed there is no county in England where that feeling can prevail more universally among the higher classes."[77] From Tatton Hall, just south of Manchester, to Crewe Hall, to the east of Crewe; from Norton Priory, alongside the River Mersey, to Alderley Park, just outside Macclesfield, the Cheshire Hounds crisscrossed the county two to three times a week during the November to April season. But it was not a cheap hobby: the annual subscription fee to the Cheshire Hunt Covert Fund, as it was known, was £10 while yearly stabling fees could approach £70 (taking the costs into the region of $12,000 in today's money). Then there was the price of a good hunter. "I saw Murray the horse-dealer on Saturday and asked him if he had anything . . . carrying 14 stone with hounds at about £70. He seemed to think he had," began a note to Engels from one James Wood Lomax, who seems to have been his horse agent.[78] Thankfully, when it came to funding respectable activities like hunting, he could always draw on the resources of his father. "For my Christmas present my old man gave me the money to buy a horse and as there was a good one going, I bought it last week," Engels wrote to Marx in 1857. "But I'm exceedingly vexed that I should be keeping a horse while you and your family are down on your luck in London."[79]

It is unclear who first introduced Engels to the Cheshire Hounds, but he soon became a fixture in the field alongside some of England's most elevated nobility. As Paul Lafargue, Marx's son-in-law, remembered it: "He was an excellent rider and had his own hunter for the fox chase; when the neighboring gentry and aristocracy sent out invitations to all riders in the district according to the ancient feudal custom he never failed to attend."[80*] Engels tried to justify his hobby on revolutionary

---

* In 2004, when the Labor government introduced legislation to ban foxhunting, Engels's membership in the Cheshire Hunt was cited in its defense. "The idea of joining the class war with fox hunting is pathetic as well as nasty, as was very well demonstrated by no less an authority on both subjects than Friedrich Engels," Lord Gilmour of Craigmillar told the House of Lords during a debate on the Hunting Bill. "I think that shows that, at least in some ways, old communism was much more sensible than new Labour." And Engels was not the only Victorian left-winger with a penchant for the saddle: Michael Sadler, leader of the Factory Reform movement; Joseph Arch, the farmworkers' leader; and Robert Applegarth, the general secretary of the Carpenters and Joiners all rode to hounds.

grounds as "the best school of all" for warfare. Indeed, he thought one of the few saving graces of the British cavalry was its background in chasing old Charlie. "Being, most of them, passionate huntsmen, they possess that instinctive and rapid appreciation of advantage of ground, which the practice of hunting is sure to impart," he wrote in a review of British military strategy.[81] But however he dressed it up, what clearly aroused Engels was the visceral thrill of the chase. And he was never afraid to front the field. "He was always among the leaders in clearing ditches, hedges and other obstacles," Larfargue reported.[82] "Let me tell you that yesterday I took my horse over a hedge and bank measuring 5 feet and some inches, the highest jump I've ever done," Engels boasted to a sedentary Marx festering in the British Museum. Even with a nasty bout of piles, Engels would happily put himself through a twenty-eight-mile hack in pursuit of his quarry. Indeed, over the years he obviously developed something of a bloodlust. "Yesterday I let myself be talked into attending a coursing meeting at which hares are hunted with greyhounds, and spent seven hours in the saddle. All in all, it did me a power of good though it kept me from my work."[83]

Engels's other pursuits were noticeably less savage. "Everyone up here is an art lover just now and the talk is all of the pictures at the exhibition," he wrote to Marx in the summer of 1857, having visited the celebrated Art Treasures Exhibition at Trafford Park and fallen for Titian's portrait of Ariosto. "*S'il y a moyen*, you and your wife ought to come up this summer and see the thing."[84] The gallery going fitted right in with Engel's life as a leading Manchester merchant—a sophisticated, high-bourgeois world of dinners, clubs, charitable events, and networking focused around the respectable German quarter near his Thorncliffe Grove and Dover Street residences. Manchester had been a mecca for Prussian merchants since the 1780s, and by 1870 there were some 150 German business houses operating in the city and over a thousand residents of German birth. The most elevated of this community congregated nightly at the Schiller Anstalt (Institute) on Oxford Street.[85] The institute had its origins in an 1859 festival commemorating the centenary of Friedrich Schiller's birth, and its mission was to give the German community a club for socializing and a little bit of cultural comfort from the homeland. By the mid-1860s, it boasted three hundred members, a four-thousand-volume library, a skittle alley and billiard room, a gymnasium, a well-stocked reading room, and a prodigiously busy calendar of events ranging from male choir concerts to public lecture series to amateur dramatics productions. Engels joined in 1861 and immediately fell out with the management over an overdue-book notice from the librarian: "When I had read this missive, it was as though I had been suddenly transported home." And not for nostalgic reasons. "It was as though, instead of a communication from the Librarian of the Schiller Institute, I were holding a peremptory summons from a German inspector of police ordering me, on pain of a heavy penalty, to make amends for some kind of violation 'within 24 hours.' "[86] For Engels, the recipient of any number of police summons, an innocent library fine was altogether too reminiscent of the heavy-handed Prussian state.

Overdue notices didn't keep him away for long. Engels soon entered enthusiastically into the institute's business, was elected to the governing body, and finally voted chairman. There, he proved himself a good committee man, introducing beer into the directors' meetings, chairing numerous subcommittees, and successfully overseeing the purchase of six thousand volumes from the Manchester Subscription Library.[87] But the following year, Engels was out altogether after the institute extended an invitation to the well-known science popularizer Karl Vogt. Unbeknownst to the inviting committee, Vogt featured prominently on Marx and Engels's extensive blacklist as a suspected Bonapartist spy, and Engels immediately resigned.

Luckily, he had a number of other institutions to patronize. Together with Samuel Moore, he was a member of the Albert Club, "christened appropriately after the husband of our most gracious Queen." Renowned for its smoking room—"We believe it to be, without exception, the best room of the kind in Manchester"—the club housed an equally impressive array of card rooms, private dining rooms, and billiard tables. Its membership list, filled with names like Schaub, Schreider, von Lindelof, and König, revealed the high proportion of Germans in the club—almost 50 percent.[88] In addition, Engels belonged to the Athenaeum, the Brazenose Club, the Manchester Foreign Library, and even the Royal Exchange. "So now you're a member of the Exchange, and altogether respectable. My congratulations," Marx wrote with a light pasting of sarcasm. "Some time I should like to hear you howling amidst that pack of wolves."[89] Despite this heavy schedule of lectures, dinners, and concerts, Engels remained contemptuous of the provincialism of Manchester life. "For six months past I have not had a single opportunity to make use of my acknowledged gift for mixing a lobster salad—*quelle horreur*; it makes one quite rusty," spoke the original champagne communist.[90]

By the mid-1850s, the workload and strains of his double life were beginning to test even Engels's endurance. "I now have three lads to keep in control and am forever checking, correcting, telling off and giving orders," he complained to Marx in 1856. "Add to this the running battle with manufacturers over bad yarn or late delivery, and my own work." The mountain of business correspondence, along with the competing demands of his father and Godfrey Ermen, meant that Engels was having "to slave away in the office until 8 o'clock each evening and can't start work till 10 o'clock, after supper." His journalism was suffering, his attempt to learn Russian was stalled, and he had made little headway with his socialist theorizing. "This summer things have got to be reorganized," he announced in March 1857.[91] Yet at that moment Marx decided to pile on the pressure by accepting a ridiculous—if lucrative—contract to contribute to Charles Dana's latest publishing scheme, *The New American Cyclopaedia*. Engels was, of course, delighted with the money Marx would earn—"Now everything is going to be alright again"—but he was the one who would have to do the legwork for this tedious reference book. By early summer 1857, Engels's body was giving way. "I'm sitting at home with linseed poultices on the left-hand side of my face in the hope of getting the better of a nasty abscess. . . . I have had continual trouble with my face for the past month—first toothache, then a swollen cheek, then more toothache and now the whole thing has blossomed out into a furuncle." By midsummer, he was suffering from exhaustion and full-blown glandular fever (a worrying development in Victorian England) and being nursed by his sister Marie. "I'm one of your really miserable figures, stooped, lame and weak and—for example as at present—beside myself with pain."[92] And what was Marx's response to his friend's debilitating illness? "As you will understand, nothing could be more distasteful to me than TO PRESS UPON YOU while you are ill," but he needed the *Cyclopaedia* articles—and quick. It was only when Engels suffered a total collapse that Marx eased up on the demands. "The chief thing for you at present is naturally to recover your health. I shall have to see how I can put Dana off again," he wrote sheepishly in July 1857.

It would be wrong, though, to suggest that Marx did not care about Engels's health. Indeed, discussions of illness, medication, therapies, and doctors often constituted the most detailed and impassioned parts of their correspondence. Like any good hypochondriacs, the two of them positively reveled in their ailments. "How are things in regard to 'coughing'?" was an early inquiry when Marx learned of Engels's condition. After pursuing some "meticulous medical studies" in the British Museum (always keen to put off the writing of *Das Kapital* if at all possible), Marx asked Engels to "let me know whether you are taking iron. In cases such as yours, as in many others, iron has proved stronger than the affliction."[93] Engels was unconvinced and replied with a lengthy disquisition on the merits of iron versus cod-liver oil, before revealing a personal preference for the Norwegian variety of the latter. But this was an exception: usually it was Marx's health problems that held center place— his series of psychosomatic illnesses (from liver complaints to headaches to insomnia) as well as the all too real struggle against the boils that took apart his body like land mines. A small hint of the miseries Marx endured is given by an 1866 letter he sent to Engels after the carbuncles had encircled his crotch: "The itching and scratching between my testis and posterior over the past 2½ years and the consequent peeling of the skin have been more aggravating to my constitution than anything else." Marx's preferred remedy was to go at every eruption with a razor until the blood and pus spurted forth. Engels advocated a less invasive strategy involving phosphate of lime—or at least some arsenic. He even solicited advice from a new friend he had made in Manchester, the pediatrician Edward Gumpert, who had used arsenic "in one case of carbuncles and one of very virulent furunculosis and achieved a complete cure in approximately 3 months."[94]

Engels's own recovery from glandular fever was due less to medical attention than to the economic crash devastating Manchester in 1857. Seeing Peter Ermen and the other tree-frogs fouling their breeches as cotton prices tumbled was just the tonic: "The general appearance of the Exchange here was truly delightful last week. The fellows are utterly infuriated by my sudden and inexplicable onset of high spirits."[95] He was still fragile, however, and the death of his father in March 1860 brought on a relapse. What affected Engels was not so much the loss—his filial affection being notably tepid—but the ensuing family dispute over the Ermen & Engels finances. Godfrey Ermen wasted no time in trying to lever Engels junior out of the firm. Relations quickly broke down at the Southgate office as Engels tried desperately to negotiate his future and hold on to his job. Up against the Ermen's business acumen, "while physically so indisposed that I was incapable of making one single urgent decision in a sound frame of mind and with faculties unimpaired," he knew he would be unable to secure a decent settlement. Humiliatingly, he called in his brother Emil—"clear of eye, firm of resolve and in full command of the situation"—to do the deal and secure his prospects.[96]

Worse was to come. His brothers Rudolf and Hermann seized the moment to carve Engels—the eldest son and heir—out of the lucrative family business in Engelskirchen while his beloved mother fell ill with a suspected case of typhoid. "For seven weeks now I've been living in a state of continual tension and excitation which has now reached a climax—never has it been so bad," Engels wrote to Marx in May 1860.[97] Outmaneuvered by his brothers, Engels agreed to a wholly inequitable settlement—forcing him to cede all rights to the German component of Ermen & Engels—to please his ailing mother. "Mother dear, I have swallowed all this and much more for your sake. Not for anything in this world would I contribute in the smallest way towards embittering the evening of your life with family disputes over inheritance," her firstborn wrote lovingly. "I might acquire a hundred other businesses, but never a second mother." But he wanted her to know that "it was extremely disagreeable for me to have to withdraw from the family business in this way."[98] What Engels walked away with, in exchange for his brothers' placing £10,000 in the Manchester firm, was a commitment to a partnership in Ermen & Engels by 1864. Given his enfeebled state, it was all he could hope for.

1. Friedrich and Elise Engels: a model of bourgeois parental rectitude.

2. "Zion of the obscurantists." Engels's hometown of Barmen in the early 1800s.

3. Georg Wilhelm Friedrich Hegel at the
University of Berlin in 1828, sowing his dragon seeds.

4. "With one blow it pulverized the
contradiction." Ludwig Feuerbach,
author of *The Essence of Christianity*.

5. "The wild black boar,"
"the wicked knave," "the Moor."
A young Karl Marx.

6. "I am very busy at present with philosophy and critical theology."
Self-portrait of Engels the questing intellectual, aged nineteen.

7. Design from the mill of John Marshall & Sons depicting the civilizing wonders of the cotton trade, circa 1821.

8. Reels from the Ermen & Engels mill with their three towers trademark.

9. "The Juggernaut of capital." The Ermen & Engels mill in Weaste, alongside the Manchester–Liverpool railway line.

10. Oswald the Montagnard. Portrait of Engels the romantic visionary, 1840.

11. Face-to-face with the proletariat. Child labor in the Victorian cotton industry.

12. "And yet there is a great deal of money made here; good morning, sir."
The wealth of mid-Victorian Manchester.

13. Engels's other world. The Albert Club on Dover Street, Manchester, renowned for its smoking room, card rooms, and billiard tables.

14. "The quadrilateral desk in the small bow window." Chetham's Library, Manchester, where Marx and Engels spent the summer of 1845 reading up on political economy.

15. The 1848 revolution. Dresden in revolt against the king of Saxony. Among the rioters were Michael Bakunin and Richard Wagner.

16. Berlin's March revolution. "All that is missing is the guillotine," muttered Queen Elisabeth.

17. "Composed of the first gentlemen in that aristocratic county."
A meet of the Cheshire Hounds, by Henry Calvert.

18. "What Art was to the ancient world, Science is to the modern; the
distinctive faculty." Physicist James Joule (*left*) and chemist John Dalton
face each other across the impressive entrance to Manchester Town Hall.

19. Engels as the second father and the giver of good things. "The General" with Marx and his daughters—(*left to right*) Laura, Eleanor, Jenny—on holiday in 1864.

20. The much-indulged
Laura Marx.

21. Lizzy Burns, the only
Mrs. Friedrich Engels—of "genuine
Irish proletarian blood" with
"passionate feelings for her class."

22. Eleanor Marx,
the beloved and
doomed "Tussy."

23. "The Grand Lama of the Regent's Park Road" in 1891.

24. The mecca of international socialism. Engels's study
at No. 122 Regent's Park Road as it looks today.

25. Hampstead Heath—"London's Chimborazo"—the regular venue
for picnics and constitutional hikes by "the old Londoners."

26. The Paris Commune, the "dictatorship of the proletariat." Barricade at the Faubourg St. Antoine during the Commune, 18 March 1871.

27. A panorama of the fires in Paris during the Commune, May 1871.

28. "The greatest event to have taken place in England since the last Reform Bills." Striking dockers march through the London streets in 1889.

29. Engels thought the dockers' political cohesion and proletarian class consciousness heralded "the beginning of a complete revolution in the East End." Posing for a photograph, with float, 1889.

30. The global reach of Friedrich Engels. A poster in
Havana, Cuba, commemorating the 130th anniversary
of *The Communist Manifesto*, circa 1978.

31. An icon of colonial resistance. Engels, alongside Marx and Lenin,
on a war-torn mural in Addis Ababa, Ethiopia, 1991.

7

AN END TO HUCKSTERING

Incredibly, between housing the Burns sisters, clerking at Ermen & Engels, and riding to the Cheshire Hounds, Engels managed to make some significant contributions to the Marxist canon. The first of these was a further development of the concept of "historical materialism," as outlined in *The German Ideology*. For Engels, this approach to studying the past—which pointed to modes of production as determining property relations and thence the broader contours of society—was one of Marx's seminal achievements. Marx had discovered, Engels wrote, "the great law of motion of history"—"that the whole of history hitherto is a history of class struggles, that in all the manifold and complicated political struggles the only thing at issue has been the social and political rule of classes of society," and consequently that "the conception and ideas of each historical period are most simply to be explained from the economic conditions of life and from the social and political relations of the period, which are in turn determined by these economic conditions."[1] Or, as Marx himself put it in his preface to *A Contribution to the Critique of Political Economy*, "The mode of production in material life determines the social, political and intellectual life processes in general. . . . It is not the consciousness of men that determines their being, but, on the contrary, their social being that determines their consciousness."[2]

All of which helped to explain the phenomenon of false consciousness ("a consciousness that is spurious"), whereby the true, materialist motives behind a political or intellectual shift in history—the Reformation, say, or romanticism—were attributed wrongly to the autonomous role of ideas or religion rather than to the inescapable workings of socioeconomic forces. Similarly, to analyze political economy without regard to the true nature of exploitation, as Adam Smith and David Ricardo had done, yielded only a partial understanding, a false consciousness of the present, compromised by its failure to delve below the political superstructure of ideas to the materialist base of society.

In *The German Ideology*, Marx and Engels had considered contemporary capitalist society from a materialist perspective. Now they turned their attentions to the past, arguing that it was a period's economic condition (the base)—its level of technology, division of labor, means of production, and so on—that molded its law, ideologies, religion, even its art and science (the superstructure). Certainly, historical actors as individuals had free will and could make choices. But what Marx and Engels were concerned with was mass phenomena and social change as the product of numerous individual decisions motivated by structural economic conditions. As Engels put it, "The will is determined by passion or deliberation. But the levers which immediately determine passion or deliberation are of very different kinds." Marx, again, had the more vivid phrasing. "Men make their own history, but they do not make it just as they please," he wrote in *The Eighteenth Brumaire of Louis Bonaparte*. "They do not make it under circumstances chosen by themselves, but under circumstances directly found, given and transmitted from the past. The tradition of all the dead generations weighs like a nightmare on the brain of the living."[3] Marx and Engels did away with Carlyle's "great man" view of history: "The fact that such and such a man, and he alone, should arise at a particular time in any given country, is, of course, purely fortuitous."[4] In the absence of a Napoleon, someone else would simply have taken his place. Instead of great men, class and class warfare (master/slave, lord/serf, capitalist/worker)—themselves the product of historical developments of the modes of production—became the defining factors in Marxist historiography. As Hegel had traced the march of Spirit through the pages of history, now Marx and Engels charted the rise and fall of class struggle within an equally teleological framework. History was a story of both bondage and liberation, a battle that would continue until the final redemptive triumph of the proletariat brought an end to class warfare—indeed, the end of history itself.

Engels was an early practitioner of this discipline, not least because the approach was heavily influenced by the pioneering account of economic history he first provided in *The Condition of the Working Class in England*. His narrative of the Industrial Revolution had presaged changes in the mode of production—the division of labor, the move toward mechanization, the collapse of household economies, the end of guild regulations—as the essential element in understanding the political, religious, and cultural attitudes of the era. But in his final years he would worry that the strategy had been debased by lesser minds wanting to reduce everything to narrow economic causes. "According to the materialist view of history, the determining factor in history is, *in the final analysis*, the production and reproduction of actual life," he wrote in a letter to a series of theoretical inquiries from a Berlin student, Joseph Bloc von Boegnik, in 1890. "More than that was never maintained by Marx or myself. Now if someone distorts this by declaring the economic moment to be the only determining factor, he changes that proposition into a meaningless, abstract, ridiculous piece of jargon." In the same letter, Engels went on to introduce a new variable into the historical materialist template by suggesting that the superstructure—those ephemeral forms of law, philosophy, and religion—somehow had a "reciprocal influence" on the economic structure and thus on historical development: "All these factors also have a bearing on the course of the historical struggles of which, in many cases, they largely determine the form. It is in the interaction of all these factors and amidst an unending multitude of fortuities . . . that the economic trend ultimately asserts itself as something inevitable." History, he now suggested in a significant reappraisal of Marxist historiographic thinking, was a lot more fluid than the materialist stereotype would have it. For the dialectical process was not

simply a question of cause and effect but the mutual interaction of opposites: so, while the economic context was "ultimately decisive," Engels
now thought that politics, culture, even "tradition" could play a part in
shaping man's decisions and history. The past was "made in such a way
that the ultimate result is invariably produced by the clash of many individual wills of which each in turn has been made what it is by a wide
variety of living conditions." Such were the caveats introduced into the
notion of historical materialism that it seemed almost devalued as a
credible intellectual tool, let alone a political one. By then aged seventy
and firmly ensconced as Europe's leading communist seer, Engels was in
a reflective mode, conceding that the battle against idealist history might
have earlier led him and Marx to overemphasize the materialist component. "If some younger writers attribute more importance to the economic aspect than is its due, Marx and I are to some extent to blame. We
had to stress this leading principle in the face of opponents who denied
it, and we did not always have the time, space or opportunity to do justice to the other factors that interacted upon each other," he wrote in a
passage full of special pleading. He no doubt realized that his historical
theorem was in danger of becoming either a banal truism (in the sense
that one should, of course, take some account of the economic context of
a period) or an indefensible species of economic reductionism.[5]

In 1850s Manchester, Engels was as yet untroubled by such nuances.
Indeed, he penned a positively bludgeoning work of historical materialism, *The Peasant War in Germany* (1850), which attempted to explicate
"the political structure of Germany at that time, the revolts against it,
and the contemporary political and religious theories not as causes but
as results of the stage of development of agriculture, industry, roads and
waterways, commerce in commodities and money then obtaining."[6] His
aim, in fact, was an old-fashioned plundering of history (as well as of the
recent work of historian Wilhelm Zimmerman) to assist in current political battles—in this case, framing the 1520s peasant wars as inspiration for the German radicals discouraged by the 1848–49 setbacks: "In
the face of the slackening that has now ensued almost everywhere after
two years of struggle, it is high time to remind the German people of the

clumsy yet powerful and tenacious figures of the Great Peasant War."[7] He did so with all the crassness of a year-zero materialist.

Ironically, the hero of Engels's history was a Carlylean great man, the "magnificent figure" of the Protestant radical Thomas Müntzer. An itinerant mystic in the German chiliastic tradition, Müntzer attempted in the early 1520s to combine the radical wing of the Reformation with a traditional peasants' revolt to form a "Christian League" of the godly against the godless. His emphasis on the suffering of God, his stress on social equality alongside spiritual equality, and his attack on the "burgher reformation" of Martin Luther galvanized an impoverished peasantry angry at high clerical tithes and unpopular land reforms. Trained in the priesthood, a student at Wittenberg, and for many years a preacher in Allstedt, Prague, and Zwickau, Müntzer proposed a vision of social reform profoundly marked by his Protestant theology. But Engels was having none of that. Of course "the class struggles of those days were clothed in religious shibboleths," he allowed, but one could not forget the materialist underpinnings.[8] Accordingly, Engels went on to recount in fastidious detail the economic fundamentals of early-sixteenth-century German society and how class divisions—among the feudal nobility, the bourgeois Protestant reformers, and the peasantry—shaped this revolutionary epoch. Müntzer was merely able to bring the plebeian elements to a recognition of their class consciousness: properly understood, he was an embryonic Marxist agitator successfully marshaling the most advanced section of the peasantry toward class warfare. "As Müntzer's religious philosophy approached atheism, so his political programme approached communism. . . . By the kingdom of God, Müntzer meant a society with no class differences, no private property and no state authority independent of, and foreign to, the members of society."[9] His misfortune was to have gotten ahead of the modes of production: "The worst thing that can befall the leader of an extreme party is to be compelled to assume power at a time when the movement is not yet ripe."[10] Despite Müntzer's heroic oratory and political organization, neither the feudal social system nor its agricultural economy was ready for revolutionary communism. And so, on the fields of Frankenhausen in eastern Germany in 1525, Müntzer's ragtag peasant army was put to the sword by Luther's allies. Engels's familiar refrain of the bourgeois "stab in the back" proved only too accurate.

The failures of 1525 and 1848–49 were not just the result of the disjunction between economic base and political superstructure; extensive military blunders also played a role. The study of warfare thus became a second area of academic interest for Engels. Within months of moving to Manchester, he was writing to his old German communist ally Joseph Weydemeyer in Frankfurt, asking for some books on military history (which he later acquired by buying up the library of a retired Prussian military officer) so that he could learn enough military science "to be able to join in theoretical discussion without making too much of a fool of myself."[11] Warfare became Engels's "special subject" and with typical rigor he immersed himself in studying the function of leadership, the nature of strategy, and the role of topography, technology, and army morale. Despite his theoretical aversion to "great men," Engels couldn't help himself when it came to the great generals. He admired Garibaldi and Napier with schoolboy ardor, but it was the Manichean clash between Napoleon and Wellington that truly bewitched him. Against every one of his materialist inclinations, Engels revered the hero of Waterloo—"He would be a genius if common sense were not incapable of rising to the heights of genius"—and in 1852 publicly lamented the passing of Britain's most reactionary general-politician.[12]

The years spent studying military history reaped dividends in the mid-1850s when the Crimean peninsula became a miserable quagmire for Russian, British, and French troops. Engels began a successful second career as one of England's leading armchair generals and he even hoped his military punditry might offer a route out of Manchester. As soon as war broke out in 1854, he immediately fired off a job application to the editor of the *Daily News*. "Perhaps I am not mistaken in supposing that at the present moment an offer to contribute to the military department of your paper may meet with some favour," he wrote, going on to provide a short military résumé—beginning with his service in the

Prussian artillery and building up to his "active service during the insurrectionary war in South Germany." While he hoped the Russians would get a sound beating, he promised to mix his politics up "as little as possible with military criticism." But despite such assurances, the job never materialized. "It's all off with the *Daily News*," he wrote angrily to Marx as he saw another lifeline out of Ermen & Engels slipping from his grasp. Everything seemed settled—the fee, the proofs, the terms—and then "the answer finally arrives saying that the articles are too professional" and he should approach a specialized military journal. In a rare burst of pure fury, Engels blamed German émigré gossips in London for belittling his military experience and ruining his chances: "Nothing was easier than to represent Engels, the MILITARY MAN, as no more than a former one-year volunteer, a communist and a clerk by trade, thus putting a stop to everything."[13] All the horrible huckstering indignity of his position flooded back to taunt him. But while there is little proof of any whispering campaign against him, there is abundant evidence in the *Daily Tribune* column he wrote for Marx of the dry, overanalytical tone of his military journalism. His account of the Charge of the Light Brigade, one of the most gory and dramatic moments in the entire campaign, is a case in point. After describing how "the Earl of Cardigan led his light brigade up a valley opposite his position," Engels matter-of-factly recounts its obliteration: "Of the 700 men that advanced, not 200 came back in a fighting condition. The light cavalry brigade may be considered destroyed, until reformed by fresh arrivals."[14] It was small wonder the *Daily News* passed on such leaden copy.

Mercifully, Engels's style matured, and in the late 1850s the growing tension between Prussia, Austria, and France over the issue of Italian unification allowed him to reenter the field with an anonymous pamphlet entitled *Po and Rhine*. With a deft overview of political intelligence, alpine geography, and war readiness, Engels outlined what Prussia's stance should be in the face of the various military scenarios a Franco-Austrian war might present. "Have read it all," Marx wrote on receiving the paper. "Exceedingly clever; the political side is also splendidly done and that was damned difficult. The pamphlet will have a great success."[15] And so it did, garnering adulatory coverage in the

German and Austrian press and, it was rumored, being bought in bulk by General Giuseppe Garibaldi. Indeed, *Po and Rhine* was so well informed that its anonymous author was the object of numerous HQ guessing games. "Your pamphlet is considered in high, if not the highest, military circles (including, *inter alia*, that of Prince Charles Frederick) to be the product of an anonymous Prussian general," a delighted Marx reported back to Engels.[16] But, frustratingly, the Manchester clerk remained unknown.

The looming hostilities between France and Austria were just one of the dramatic consequences of Bonaparte's rise to power. From the outset of his reign, Napoleon III was keen to extend the dominion of imperial France, and by the late 1850s (after a botched assassination attempt with tenuous British connections) some in Britain's military staff thought his ambition might entail an invasion of England. Following a highly jingoistic press campaign, on 12 May 1859 Britain's local volunteer corps— last called up to repel Napoleon I in 1804—was reassembled to counter the new Bonapartist threat. In a remarkable act of spontaneous military association, 170,000 volunteers signed up on behalf of the British people, with "Irish Corps," "Artisans Corps," "Borough Guards," and even a "Press Guard" springing into action.[17] As Lord Palmerston erected a series of forts (his so-called Follies) along the English Channel to prevent an invasionary fleet, Britain's parade grounds and parks resounded with the ill-disciplined step of the volunteer corps and their rousing anti-French songs. Engels had always been confident of the martial spirit of the British people—"Nowhere are there more hunters and poachers, i.e., semi-trained light infantry and sharpshooters"—and he enthusiastically endorsed this grassroots resistance movement against the reactionary Bonapartist regime.[18] He was especially supportive of the training the volunteers received. For if the veteran of Baden had learned anything as he fled through the Black Forest, it was the importance of logistical support, a proper chain of command, and basic military skills. "Experience teaches us that no matter how intense the patriotism of the masses may be, the fact that they, as a general thing, have no arms, and do not know how to use them if they had, renders their disposition in an emergency of very little value," he wrote in an article for the *Daily Tribune* melodramatically entitled "Could the French Sack London?"[19] Happily, the authorities were well on their way to countering such a prospect with a highly effective inspection and drilling program. "All in all, the experiment is to be regarded, after three years, as completely successful," Engels stated in 1862. "Almost without any expense to the Government, England has created an organized army of 163,000 men for the country's defence."[20] His enthusiasm was only tempered when, on a railway journey from London back to Manchester, he "had the added pleasure of a rifle-bullet shattering the window and flying through the carriage not 12 inches from my chest: some volunteer probably wished to demonstrate yet again that he ought not to be entrusted with a firearm."[21]

Engels's support for the volunteers was another example of his occasional class confusion as an intense anti-Bonapartism got the better of his communist ideology. While the corps were indeed the first line of resistance against a French invasion, they were also an inherently reactionary force. For it was not the workers who signed up en masse but only those persons who could furnish their own arms, "defray all expenses," and be available for up to twenty-four days' training per year. The Preston Volunteer Corps was notable for the "total absence of the working-class element," while the Fortieth (Manchester) Lancashire Rifle Volunteers was overwhelmingly made up of "gentlemen," tradesmen, clerks, and artisans.[22] This was a rich man's army, led by local aristocrats and industrialists; indeed, working-class radicals in Rochdale and Oldham branded it a "Tory device" for diverting attention from political reform. The volunteer corps was, in fact, another component of the bourgeois dominance of mid-Victorian Britain: a middle-class voluntarist association subtly confirming existing class stratification. Engels, who instinctively took the view of the officers, remained entirely blind to the subaltern component, focused as he was on military preparedness against the Bonapartist enemy.[23]

To the intense disappointment of the volunteers, no doubt, Bonaparte's game plan never involved crossing the Channel. Instead, he set himself on a collision course with Continental Europe's other expansive power, Bismarck's Prussia. The chancellor of the North German Confederation had already gone to war against Austria in 1866 over the convoluted question of Schleswig-Holstein, and by the end of the decade a clash with France looked unavoidable. Engels had underestimated Bismarck's determination at the start of the Iron Chancellor's rise to power and, in a notable misjudgment, even thought Austria would win the 1866 tussle. But by July 1870, he no longer harbored any misapprehensions about Bismarck's bellicosity, ambition, and strategic prowess. As it turned out, the Franco-Prussian War would prove the high point of Engels's career as a military pundit.

This time he had a proper outlet for his views, Marx having set him up as a military commentator for the middle-brow London paper the *Pall Mall Gazette.* Still obviously smarting from the *Daily News* debacle, Engels offered only a lukewarm response to the offer of work: "I suppose I would like to write two articles weekly on the war for the *Pall Mall Gazette* for good cash payment." His initial columns, charting the routing of Bonaparte's forces by the Prussians, were based on reports from the front and on a cross-section of European papers. But at the end of July, Engels got a scoop on German troop maneuvers with the deployment of his friend Edward Gumpert's cousin, "a company commander in the 77th regiment." As a result, he accurately predicted that one of the first major engagements between French and Prussian forces would take place near Saarbrucken. "Enclosed you will find the plan of the Prussian campaign. Please get a CAB immediately and take it round to the *Pall Mall Gazette,* so that it can come out on Monday evening," Engels, desperate for his exclusive, commanded Marx. "It will make me and the *Pall Mall Gazette* tremendously famous. Delay is now fatal for articles of this sort." He was proved right when all the London papers—from the *Times* to the *Spectator*—followed up the story. "If the war lasts a certain time, you will soon be acknowledged as the foremost military authority in London," Marx wrote back with pride.[24] Engels's authority grew further when in August 1870 he forecast the defeat of the French troops at Sedan and the capture of Bonaparte. Again and again, Engels called it right and so earned his Marx family moniker, "General Staff"—or just "The General." The nickname instantly stuck and was soon adopted by the broader socialist fraternity. For it captured not only Engels's command of military policy but his physical forbearance, remarkable self-discipline, personal reliability, strategic sensibility, and, above all, utter dedication to achieving his and Marx's objectives. And as the years went by and Marx's powers began to fade, Engels's rigid commitment to their cause bore all the hallmarks of a general's intent.

There was more to Engels's analysis than audits of firepower and strategy. Thanks to Lenin's later reprints of some of Engels's *New York Daily Tribune* articles on insurrection, he is often regarded as a pioneer theorist of guerrilla warfare. Engels did, indeed, describe insurrection as "an art quite as much as war," with its own particular rules: "Act with the greatest determination, and on the offensive. The defensive is the death of every armed rising. . . . Surprise your antagonists while their forces are scattering, prepare new successes, however small but daily. . . . Force your enemies to a retreat before they can collect their strength against you; in the words of Danton, the greatest master of revolution policy yet known, *de l'audace, de l'audace, encore de l'audace!*"[25] But Engels remained at root deeply skeptical of guerrilla combat in part because of his unhappy Baden experience but largely because he favored a materialist approach to military science.

In the materialist view the British had bungled the Crimean campaign and Bonaparte had been smashed by Bismarck because their respective military structures reflected their antiquated socioeconomic fundamentals. To Engels, warfare was another component of the superstructure—like religion, politics, law, or culture—and, as such, it was determined by the economic base. "Armaments, social composition, organization, tactics and strategy are above all dependent on the level of production and communications that has been reached." Warfare had only assumed its modern form in the years following the French Revolution, Engels suggested, when the rising bourgeoisie and the emancipated peasantry produced the money and men for the colossal war machines of the nineteenth century. Thus the development of various European armies was a product of these nations' socioeconomic development—their class systems, technological capacity, property relations—in which "the influence of commanders of genius is at most restricted to adapting the methods of fighting to the new weapons and fighters."[26] An obvious example of the military's dependence on technological achievement was the modern battleship, which was "not only a product, but at the same time a specimen, of modern large-scale industry, a floating factory."[27]

In the case of the British army, the state of its troops also exposed an outdated political system in all its corrupt finery. "Like old England herself, a mass of rampant abuses, the organization of the English army is rotten to the core," Engels wrote of the Crimean forces, going on to list the selling of commissions, absence of professionalism, officer and soldier class divisions, and the unnatural enthusiasm for corporal punishment that flourished in Her Majesty's regiments.[28] In materialist terms, the disastrous Charge of the Light Brigade was due less to the Earl of Cardigan's individual failures in the field and more to the British elite's failure to adjust to the modern industrial era. The incompetence, the needless casualties, "the miserable leadership of the British army [are] the inevitable result of rule by an antiquated oligarchy."[29]

Since so much of the warfare Engels reported on was imperial in origin, he naturally began to think more broadly about the nature of colonialism. In the twentieth century, Marx and Engels's writings on this topic would prove among their most enduring political legacies, with "freedom fighters" from Mao to Ho Chi Minh to Castro embracing Marxism as an essential component of colonial liberation. Just as with their conversion to communism, Marx and Engels came late to these ideas. While a critique of the brutality and cronyism of imperialism had been a staple part of British radicalism since Thomas Paine and William Cobbett, Engels had been more noteworthy for his high-handed dismissal of those "nonhistoric" peoples—those ethnic remnants fighting the tide of history, as the Slavs had during the 1848 revolutions—who had resisted colonial aggression. "The conquest of Algeria is an important and fortunate fact for the progress of civilization," he had written in 1848. "And if we may regret that the liberty of the Bedouins of the desert has been destroyed, we must not forget that these same Bedouins were a nation of robbers." We should remember, he went on, that "the modern bourgeois, with civilization, industry, order and at least relative enlightenment following him, is preferable to the feudal lord or to the marauding robber."[30]

The benefits of capitalist imperialism—the forcible induction of backward peoples into the flow of history, thus setting them on their way to class consciousness, class struggle, and all the rest—outweighed the unfortunate acts of the invasionary forces. As Marx and Engels put it in *The Communist Manifesto,* "The cheap prices of its [capitalism's] commodities are the heavy artillery with which it batters down all Chinese walls, with which it forces the barbarians' intensely obstinate hatred of foreigners to capitulate."

This was certainly their view in regard to south Asia. "Indian society has no history at all, at least no known history," Marx wrote in an article that drew on the thinking of the political economists James Mill and Jean-Baptiste Say, as well as Hegel, to categorize the people of the subcontinent as stationary, nonhistoric, and in need of forcible liberation. "What we call its history, is but the history of the successive intruders who founded their empires on the passive basis of that unresisting and unchanging society." Therefore, the British Empire had to fulfill a double mission in India: "one destructive, the other regenerating—the annihilation of old Asiatic society, and the laying of the material foundations of Western society in Asia."[31] Similarly, Engels the mill owner, more than aware of the threat posed by south Asian industry, spoke with positive relish of India's "native handicrafts . . . finally being crushed by English competition."[32] When it came to the Indian Mutiny (or First War of Independence) of 1857, Marx was quick to place the account of atrocities in the context of decades of imperial abuse: "However infamous the conduct of the Sepoys, it is only the reflex, in a concentrated form, of England's own conduct in India."[33] But neither Marx nor Engels felt fully able to support the struggle for independence since the demands of economic progress and imperial modernity superceded any narrow Indian rights to self-governance.

On the other hand, for over a decade Marx and Engels had condemned the oppression of Poland by Germany and Russia as both a denial of democratic self-determination and an ugly chauvinism that undermined proletarian sensibility in the aggressor nations. "A people that oppresses others cannot emancipate itself," wrote Engels. "The power it needs to oppress others is ultimately always turned against itself."[34] The cause of Poland was the cause of the German working class, both men declared; Poland would never shake off the shackles of feudalism until the German workers shed their colonial mindset and realized their common cause with the Polish people. At some point during the late 1850s, Marx and Engels extended their belief in the shared fortunes of working-class solidarity and national liberation from the "old, cultured nations" of the West to non-European peoples. At the same time, they reinterpreted the economics of colonialism. Whereas Marx and Engels previously regarded colonialism as an important aid to primitive capitalist accumulation, they now saw it as an iniquitous component of global capitalism whereby raw material and unprotected markets shored up the ruling classes of the metropole. Rather than a force of modernization, colonialism was a tool of bourgeois hegemony. It was, after all, the push by British commerce into virgin colonial markets that had prevented the great crash of 1857 from spiraling into revolution.

As Engels abandoned his notion of nonhistoric peoples, he began to endorse the principle of colonial resistance. Whereas he would once have championed every advance of European civilization, by 1860 he supported the Chinese in their struggle against the British during the Second Opium War. He was also shocked at the brutality of Governor Edward Eyre's troops during the Morant Bay rebellion ("Every post brings news of worse atrocities in Jamaica. The letters from the English officers about their heroic deeds against unarmed niggers are beyond words") and sarcastically praised the grotesque atrocities of "Belgium's humane, civilizing Association Internationale" in the African Congo.[35] In a complete reversal, he even celebrated the resistance of "Arab and Kabyle tribes" in Algeria (surely, the marauding Bedouin of old?) while condemning France's "barbarous system of warfare . . . against all the dictates of humanity, civilization, and Christianity."[36] In countries that were "inhabited by a native population, which are simply subjugated, India, Algiers, the Dutch, Portuguese, and Spanish possessions," Engels now advocated a program of revolutionary working-class insurgency that would lead "as rapidly as possible towards independence." By the 1870s, the Marxist vision of proletarian-led colonial resistance that would prove so inspirational in the twentieth century was finally in place.[37]

However assiduously Engels tried to cordon off his professional from his political life, there was one contradiction in this newly progressive colonial stance that he could not resolve. As a part owner of Ermen & Engels, he was a knowing accomplice in the commercial-imperial complex. The mid-Victorian boom in the Manchester cotton trade, which so enriched Engels personally, was fueled by a foreign export market that could not have functioned without the colonies. Cheap raw cotton came in from the slave plantations of the southern United States and was reexported as finished goods to the ends of empire. By 1858–59, India was the destination of 25.8 percent of British cotton exports (followed by America, Turkey, and China), boosting profits and helping to provide a vital counterweight to the usual cyclical depression. Meanwhile, Indian calico remained banned from European nations by penal tariffs, while Asian markets were forced to accept English imports. In the aftermath of the 1857 Indian mutiny, the final remnants of the subcontinent's cotton autonomy were crushed. The classic Manchester School beliefs in anti-imperialism and free trade were junked. Now the cotton lords urged the further subjugation of India and an expanded military budget to guarantee the continuation of favorable trading terms.[38] The mills and merchant world that Engels inhabited benefited hugely from this political settlement. Inevitably, he blamed the misguided English proletariat for pocketing the imperial lucre—"The workers gaily share the feast of England's monopoly of the world market and colonies"—but never quite dared question his own place within the colonial nexus.[39]

In the shattering winter of 1863 such hypocrisies were of little matter to Engels.

Dear Moor,

Mary is dead. Last night she went to bed early and, when Lizzy wanted to go to bed shortly before midnight, she found she had already died. Quite suddenly. Heart failure or an apoplectic stroke. I wasn't told this morning; on Monday evening she was still quite well. I simply can't convey what I feel. The poor girl loved me with all her heart.

Still weakened from his 1860 depression, Engels felt the sudden death of his lover as a terrible blow. For all his womanizing and raffish exterior, he was a devoted partner to Mary. They had been together—off and on—for twenty years, ever since the fresh-faced Young Hegelian first turned up in Manchester to work at the Salford mill. It was she who had provided his entrée into the Cottonopolis underworld, and it was with her and her sort that Engels had been most at ease. For Engels, her death felt as though "I was burying the last vestige of my youth." What was almost as unsettling was Marx's response to Mary's passing. He began his commiseration letter appropriately enough, announcing how "the news of Mary's death surprised no less than it dismayed me. She was so good-natured, witty and closely attached to you." Having cleared his throat, he then launched into an extraordinarily self-centered tirade about his own bad luck—expensive school fees, rent demands—in a wholly misjudged jokey morose tone. "It is dreadfully selfish of me to tell you about these *horreurs* at this time. But it's a homeopathic remedy. One calamity is a distraction from the other," he wrote before signing off with a cheery "*Salut!*" Perhaps because Marx had never accepted Mary as a social equal or worthy companion to the General, he thought her death was of little importance. Engels was staggered by his callousness, and the letter brought about the greatest breach of their friendship. "You will find it quite in order that, this time, my own misfortune and the frosty view you took of it should have made it positively impossible for me to reply to you any sooner," he replied after a five-day hiatus. Even Engels's "philistine acquaintances"—the ones he had spent years hiding Mary from—had displayed greater sympathy and affection than his dearest friend. "You thought it a fit moment to assert the superiority of your 'dispassionate turn of mind.' *Soit!*"

Marx was suitably shamed. "It was very wrong of me to write you that letter, and I regretted it as soon as it had gone off. However, what happened was in no sense due to heartlessness," he responded a week later, offering as an excuse the wretched state of his household. Although awkwardly couched, this constituted a rare apology from Marx and the bruised Engels accepted it with alacrity. "Thank you for being so candid," he wrote back, "One can't live with a woman for years on end without being fearfully affected by her death. . . . When your letter arrived she had not been buried. . . . Your last letter made up for it and I'm glad that, in losing Mary, I didn't also lose my oldest and best friend." The row passed, and to reaffirm their friendship Engels pilfered £100 from the Ermen & Engels accounts to bail Marx out.[40]

Engels was not one to dwell on the past: he forgave Marx and slowly got over Mary. By the autumn of 1864, there were a growing number of inquiries from Marx as to the health and happiness of "Madame Lizzy." It was a common enough Victorian practice for a man to move on from a deceased wife to her spinster sister, and at some point over those eighteen months Engels did precisely that by upgrading Lizzy Burns from housekeeper to lover. We know much more about Lizzy than about Mary, mainly due to the "staunch friendship" she struck up with Tussy Marx. "She was quite illiterate and could not read or write," was how Tussy described her in a letter to Karl Kautsky, "but she was as true, as honest, and in some ways as fine-souled a woman as you could meet. . . . It is true she and Mary in later years both drank to excess: but my parents always said this was as much the fault of Engels as of the two women."[41] Engels, meanwhile, chose to emphasize Lizzy's working-class qualities, describing her as of "genuine Irish proletarian blood" and, in a touchy acknowledgment of her illiteracy, asserting that "her passionate feelings for her class, a feeling that was inborn, was of immeasurably greater value to me . . . than anything of which the priggishness and sophistry of the 'heddicated' and 'sensitive' daughters of the bourgeoisie might have been capable."[42]

The first notable consequence of Lizzy's succeeding the more prickly Mary was much improved relations between the Marx and Engels households. Whereas Marx himself had generally ignored the existence of Mary, his letters were now replete with "my best compliments to Mrs Burns" and other such pleasantries. Engels, in turn, was far more open about his companionship with Lizzy, calling her "my dear spouse" and forwarding her best regards—and the odd shamrock—to Mrs. Marx and the daughters. The Marx sisters—Laura, Jenny, and Tussy (as Eleanor was known)—were the key to this blossoming friendship. From an early age, Tussy had adored her "uncle Angel"; as one biographer put it,

"She looked upon him as a second father: the giver of good things. From him had flowed wine and stamps and jolly letters all her childhood."[43] And now she included "Auntie" Lizzy within her embrace. In the summer of 1869, she spent a happy few weeks in Manchester with Engels and Lizzy, shopping, going to the theater, and strolling around the city. "I walk about a good deal with Tussy and as many of the family, humane and canine, as I can induce to go with us," Engels wrote to Jenny Marx, her mother, "Tussy, Lizzy, Mary Ellen [or "Pumps," Lizzy's niece], myself and two dogs, and I am specially instructed to inform you that these two amiable ladies had two glasses of beer a-piece."[44] For despite her later disparaging comments about Lizzy's alcoholism, Tussy was not averse to a drop herself and enjoyed a freedom of conduct in Engels's house that was unknown in the more straitlaced Marx residence. One summer day it was so hot that, according to Tussy, the ladies of the house "laid down on the floor the whole day, drinking beer, claret, etc." which was how Engels found them when he came home: "Auntie [Lizzy Burns], Sarah [Parker, a servant], me and Ellen [Pumps] . . . all lying our full length on the floor with no stays, no boots and one petticoat and a cotton dress on and that was all."[45] Engels adored this louche, bohemian, female-dominated environment and often felt at his happiest around the various Marx daughters—he officiated at their weddings, he encouraged their journalism, he reveled in their philosophical-intellectual wordplay, and he gave their portraits pride of place on his "chimney-piece." Only this affection can explain the young Jenny Marx's ability to wheedle out of Engels his inner secrets in the highly popular mid-Victorian parlor game "Confessions." For a biographer, the result offers an invaluable character study:

> Favourite virtue: jollity;
> in a man: to mind his own business;
> in a woman: not to mislay things;
> Chief characteristic: knowing everything by half;
> Idea of happiness: Chateau Margaux 1848;
> Idea of misery: going to a dentist;
> The vice you excuse: excess of all sort;

The vice you detest: cant;

Your aversion: stuck-up, affected women;

The characters you most dislike: [Charles Haddon] Spurgeon [influential Baptist preacher];

Favourite occupation: chaffing and being chaffed;

Favourite hero: "none";

Favourite heroine: too many to name one;

Favourite poets: Renard the Fox, Shakespeare, Ariosto;

Favourite prose: Goethe, Lessing, Dr. Samuelson;

Favourite flower: bluebell;

Favourite colours: any one not Aniline [cotton dye];

Favourite dishes: "cold: salad; hot: Irish stew";

Favourite maxim: not to have any;

Motto: take it easy.[46]

Part of the attraction of Lizzy for the Marx girls was her Irish proletarian blood. Tussy and Lizzy, according to Engels, liked to spend their Manchester evenings "getting their tea ready . . . and after that there will be a reading of Irish novels which is likely to last until bedtime or nearly so, unless relieved by a bit of talk about the "convicted nation.'"[47] Engels might mock this melancholy as so Irish *aligorning*, but he was as susceptible to talk of "the benighted isle" as any of the Marx sorority. The two decades he had spent with the Burns sisters had turned his thinking on the Irish question in a far more sophisticated direction. The crass racial caricatures of the Irish he had once offered in *The Condition of the Working Class in England*—largely drawn from Thomas Carlyle—gave way to a far more sophisticated reading of Anglo-Irish relations, heavily enriched by his materialist and colonialist theorizing.

Most importantly of all, Engels visited the island in 1856, traveling with Mary Burns from Dublin to Galway, and in 1869 he returned with Lizzy and Tussy to visit the Wicklow mountains, Killarney, and Cork. Always the scholar, Engels planned to write a history of Ireland and set himself to studying Gaelic before filling fifteen notebooks with jottings on the country's law, geography, geology, economics, and folk songs. It was to be an epic account of the topographical, cultural, and economic struggle of a nation and a people for whom he had developed an unexpected empathy. "The weather, like the inhabitants, has a more acute character," ran one of the more purple passages of Engels's aborted history. "It moves in sharper, more sudden contrasts; the sky is like an Irish woman's face: here also rain and sunshine succeed each other suddenly and unexpectedly and there is none of the grey English boredom."[48]

Perhaps because the Irish peasantry had yet to let him down, he felt far more passionately about their exploitation than about that of the English working class. "I had never imagined famine could be so tangibly real," he wrote during his 1856 trip. "Whole villages are deserted; and there among them lie the splendid parks of the lesser landlords, who are almost the only people still living there, lawyers mostly. Famine, emigration and clearances between them have brought this about." The Westminster-induced potato famine, followed by the clearances—"the mass eviction of the Irish from house and home"—had produced a pasturage economy that decimated the agricultural proletariat. For unexplained reasons, Engels did not regard Britain's action as the progressive, modernizing intervention of a greater nation upon a backward, nonhistoric people but rather as unwarranted subjection. Indeed, Engels argued that Ireland had been reduced to the state "of a completely wretched nation" by systematic English plundering stretching back to the Norman Conquest.[49] And whereas he had previously sanctioned such aggression—in the case of the French and Algeria, for example—when it came to the Gaels his judgment was somehow different. Indeed, what made the Irish people heroic was their continued, if faltering, resistance to this English imperialism.

Long before Marx codified his thinking on Ireland and English radicalism, Engels connected British class structure with its imperial suzerainty across the Irish Sea. "Ireland may be regarded as the earliest English colony," he wrote, whereby "the English citizen's so-called freedom is based on the oppression of the colonies."[50] The riches Ireland offered, from the plantations of Queen Elizabeth I to the vast holdings of absentee British landowners, immeasurably strengthened the hand of the imperial ruling classes. The income derived from Irish properties enriched England's leading nobility and provided a vital kick start toward industrialization. "Ireland is the bulwark of the English landed aristocracy," as Marx later put it. "The *grand moyen* by which the English aristocracy maintains its domination in England itself." Additionally, the gutting of the Irish economy led hundreds of thousands of immigrants to Britain's industrial cities, where they undercut wages, impoverished the working class, and diverted the revolutionary spirit of the proletariat down chauvinist blind alleys. "In relation to the Irish worker, he [the English worker] feels himself to be a member of the ruling nation and therefore makes himself a tool of the aristocrats and capitalists against Ireland, thus strengthening their domination over himself," in Marx's words.[51] Just as the progress of the German working class depended upon the liberation of Poland, so revolution in Britain depended upon Irish independence. Ireland was England's weakest point and Irish republicanism would surely undermine the British Empire and unleash class war in England.

But, as ever, the political conditions were not yet quite right. Founded in March 1858, the Irish Republican Brotherhood, or "Fenians" (a reference to the Fianna army in the medieval saga of Fionn Mac Cumhail), was an Irish American secret society committed to the violent overthrow of British rule and the establishment of a democratic and independent Irish republic. Led by sons of middle-income farmers, shopkeepers, and small-town petit bourgeois, the movement was organized around "a mystic commitment to Ireland" as well as a "view of England as a satanic power on Earth" and a "belief that an independent Irish republic, 'virtually' established in the hearts of men, possessed a superior moral authority."[52] What this meant in practice was a series of doomed "risings" easily quelled by the British authorities, followed by a campaign of terrorist attacks, arson, and sabotage on the mainland. The most notorious actions were the blowing up of Clerkenwell Prison—which killed twelve innocent people—and the daring rescue of two Fenian activists, Thomas Kelly and Timothy Deasy, from a Manchester police van in 1867. Unfortunately, a British police sergeant was killed in the struggle around Kelly and Deasy. In the following days, police swooped down on five suspected Fenians, who were swiftly convicted of his murder.

Other things being equal, this was exactly the kind of self-defeating terrorism that Marx and Engels would have abhorred: an insurrectionary vanguard getting ahead of material conditions and consequently endangering the broader social revolution. But their opinion was swayed by Lizzy's passionate involvement in the Fenian cause: she was, as Engels later described her, "a revolutionary Irishwoman." Marx's son-in-law Paul Lafargue recalled that Lizzy was "in continual touch with the many Irishmen in Manchester and [was] always well informed of their conspiracies." He even suggested that "more than one Fenian found hospitality in Engels's house and it was thanks to his wife that the leader in the attempt to free the condemned Sinn Feiners [Kelly and Deasy] on their way to the scaffold was able to evade the police."[53] It was a story repeated by Max Beer, who described Engels's house as "the safest refuge of the Fenian fugitives from justice; the police had no inkling of their hiding-place."[54] There is little supporting evidence to prove that Lizzy was involved in the 1867 prison-van break, but the house on Hyde Road was tantilizingly close to the railway arch where, as Engels had it, "the great Fenian liberation battle was enacted." Maybe, just maybe, Lizzy and Engels helped some of the forty-strong Fenian mob slip away.

As a hapless terrorist outfit built around romantic nationalism, the Irish Republican Brotherhood needed above all a martyrology, and the execution of three of the five convicted Fenians—William Allen, Michael Larkin, and Michael O'Brien—provided just that. Engels correctly predicted it would "transform the liberation of Kelly and Deasy into an act of heroism, such as will now be sung at the cradle of every Irish child in Ireland, England and America. The Irish women will see to that as surely as did the Polish womenfolk."[55] Despite the much-needed halo it promised, the hanging of the three "Manchester martyrs" sent Lizzy, Tussy, and Jenny into collective mourning. "Jenny goes in black since the Manchester execution, and wears her Polish cross on a *green* ribbon," Marx reported. "I need hardly tell you that black and green are the prevailing colours in my house, too," Engels somewhat wearily replied.[56]

The response of the Manchester working class to the cause of Irish liberation was very different from that of the emotional Marx daughters. Rather than bring about a union with the IRB and proclaim their common cause against an exploitative ruling class, the Manchester workers went in exactly the opposite direction; the Fenian atrocities only added to the anti-Irish sentiment that had been festering in Manchester since the spike of Irish immigration in the early 1860s. When this combined with a broader distaste for the city's liberal millocracy in the wake of their parsimonious response to the cotton famine, the anti-Irish mood sparked an extraordinary Tory revival just in time for the newly enfranchised urban working class to cast their vote in the 1868 elections. For Engels, this was the final indignity: the promise of Manchester—the citadel of proletarian revolution—had vanished forever as the imperialist, reactionary Tory Party triumphed. "What do you say about these elections in the factory districts?" he asked Marx indignantly. "The proletariat has once again made an awful fool of itself. Manchester and Salford return 3 Tories against 2 Liberals. . . . Everywhere the proletariat are the rag, tag and bobtail of the official parties, and if any party has gained strength from the new voters, it is the Tories." The raw psephology of the situation was appalling: "It cannot be denied that the increase in working-class votes has brought the Tories more than their simple percentage, and has improved their relative position." Ireland, and the Irish question, had strengthened, not eviscerated, the English class structure.[57]

Still, in 1868, Engels could absorb such setbacks. The years of storm, stress, and accursed commerce had finally yielded some fruit. "The day that manuscript is sent off, I shall drink myself to kingdom come," Engels had promised Marx in 1865.[58] Inevitably, it would take another couple of years before the first volume of *Das Kapital*—"this economy shit"—was ready for the printers. But when it appeared the relief was tangible. The sacrifice, the boredom, the barren frustration of the Manchester years had all been worth it. "I am exceedingly gratified by this whole turn of events, firstly, for its own sake, secondly, for your sake in particular and your wife's, and thirdly, because it really is time things looked up," Engels wrote in a heartfelt letter to Marx. "There is nothing I long for so much as for release from this vile commerce, which is

completely demoralizing me with all the time it is wasting. For as long as
I am in it, I am good for nothing else." "Without you, I would never have
been able to bring the work to a conclusion," Marx wrote back with a
guilty air to his steadfast funder in May 1867, "and I can assure you it
always weighed like a nightmare on my conscience that you were allowing your fine energies to be squandered and to rust in commerce, chiefly
for my sake, and into the bargain, you had to share all my *petites misères*
as well."[59] But he chose not to dedicate the work to Engels. Instead, Marx
gave that honor to Wilhelm Wolff, who had died in 1864 and left him a
very welcome £843.

Engels's contribution to Marx's masterwork had been above and beyond the monetary. He had provided many of the book's core insights
into the actual workings of capital and labor (to which Marx added a
generous plundering of official reports) as well as its essential philosophy. He had also suggested a barrage of edits, clarifications, and rewrites,
taking his blue pencil to the gargantuan German manuscript that arrived in the summer of 1867. "The train of thought is continually interrupted by illustrations and the illustrated point never resumes at the end
of the illustration, so that one always leaps from the illustration of one
point straight into the exposition of another point," he rightly noted of
Marx's often chaotic style. "That is dreadfully tiring and even confusing
if one is not very attentive."[60] At times, the work felt too rushed ("The
piece you have inserted on Ireland was done in the most fearful haste,
and the material is not properly knocked into shape at all") and in other
passages the writing was too angry ("Sheet two in particular has the
marks of your carbuncles rather firmly stamped upon it").[61] Luckily,
Engels was one of the *very* few people from whom Marx was willing to
accept criticism.

The ultimate result was the foundational text of scientific socialism
and one of the classics of Western political thought. In the apposite
summary of Robert Skidelsky, *Das Kapital* combined "a dialectical theory of historical stages, a materialist theory of history (in which the
struggle of classes replaces Hegel's struggle of ideas in humanity's ascent), an economic and moral critique of capitalist civilization (embodied in the exploitation and alienation theses), an economic demonstration

that capitalism was bound to collapse (because of its contradictions), a call to revolutionary action, and a prediction (perhaps more an assurance) that communism would be the next—and final—historical stage."[62] At the intellectual crux of *Das Kapital* was the theory of surplus value (to Engels's mind, Marx's second monumental discovery after historical materialism), which was the alchemist's equation for explaining precisely how class exploitation occurs in a capitalist economy. For Marx, the enforced sale of the worker's labor power for less than the exchange value of the commodities produced by his labor power was the ratchet by which the bourgeoisie was progressively enriched and the proletariat steadily alienated from its own labor and humanity. In essence, Marx argued that if in six hours the worker produced enough output to cover his subsistence needs, then the output of the remaining six hours—of a twelve-hour day—was being expropriated by the capitalist for his own profit. This exploitative mode of production—the necessary result of a system based on private property—was unnatural, historically transient, and violently inequitable. The great hope of liberation promised by *Das Kapital* was that this form of capitalist iniquity would be destroyed by a class-conscious proletariat:

> Along with the constantly diminishing number of the magnates of capital, who usurp and monopolize all advantages of this process of transformation, grows the mass of misery, oppression, slavery, degradation, exploitation; but with this too grows the revolt of the working class, a class always increasing in numbers and disciplined, united, organized by the very mechanism of the process of capitalist production itself. The monopoly of capital becomes a fetter upon the mode of production, which has sprung up and flourished along with and under it. Centralization of the means of production and socialization of labour at last reach a point where they become incompatible with their capitalist integument. This integument is burst asunder. The knell of capitalist private property sounds. The expropriators are expropriated.

But the dry theory of surplus value was never going to be enough to popularize the communist cause, so Marx embellished the book with all the hellish detail of Victorian factory life that Engels had provided. The capitalists "mutilate the labourer into a fragment of a man, degrade him to the level of an appendage of a machine, destroy every remnant of charm in his work and turn it into a hated toil," was how he described the industrial process of "capitalist accumulation." "They transform his life-time into working-time, and drag his wife and child beneath the wheels of the Juggernaut of capital."[63] And yet one always has to remember that the funds that kept Marx afloat through *Das Kapital*'s long literary gestation, the money that powered this excoriating prose, came ultimately from the very same exploited labor power—the mill hands of Ermen & Engels, that Juggernaut of capital.

Since its first appearance, *Das Kapital* has been subject to numerous different readings—as a work of economics, political science, satire, literary Gothic, sociology, and all or none of the above. That tradition of multiple interpretations began with Engels himself. Having sacrificed seventeen years of his life for this opus he was determined to ensure it did not succumb to the usual conspiracy of silence. "I am convinced that the book will create a real stir from the moment it appears," he wrote to Marx in 1867, "but it will be very necessary to help the enthusiasm of the scientifically-inclined burghers and officials on to its feet and not to despise petty stratagems." Engels was always keen on petty stratagems and, with all the cunning of a seasoned public relations expert, he opened up his contact book to generate some decent coverage. "I hope you will be able to bring Karl Marx's book to the attention of the German-American press and of the workers," he wrote to his fellow 1848 veteran Hermann Meyer, then involved in the American communist movement. "The German press is still observing complete silence in respect of *Capital*, and it really is of the greatest importance that something should be said," he complained to Ludwig Kugelmann, a physician friend in Hanover. "We have a moral obligation to damned well get these articles into the papers, and as near simultaneously as possible, especially the European ones, and that includes the reactionary ones."[64]

In the end, he realized he would have to do it himself. "Do you think I should attack the thing from the bourgeois point of view, to get things under way?" he asked Marx.[65] They agreed that the best thing to attract attention was "to get the book denounced" and create a journalistic firestorm. The full panoply of media manipulation and literary salesmanship was put to work by Marx's most gifted publicist, and if Engels could not quite bring himself to denounce it he did churn out review after review for the English, American, and European press. For *Die Zukunft*, he assumed a lofty academic tone ("We acknowledge that we regard the new introduced category of surplus-value as an advance"); for the *Staatsanzeiger für Württemberg*, a more commercial slant ("German businessmen . . . will here find a copious source of instruction and will thank us for having directed their attention to it"); for the *Beobachter*, a suitably patriotic interpretation ("We may say that it is one of those achievements which do honour to the German spirit"); and for the *Demokratisches Wochenblatt*, his own true voice ("As long as there have been capitalists and workers on earth no book has appeared which is of as much importance for the workers as the one before us. The relation between capital and labour, the axis on which our entire present system of society turns, is here treated scientifically for the first time").[66]

Engels's contract with Godfrey Ermen was due to expire in June 1869 and both men wanted the uncomfortable partnership to end. The question was, at what price? Characteristically, Engels's first thought was for Marx's family finances. What debts were outstanding and "can you manage with £350 for your *usual* regular needs for a year," he asked his friend as he opened severance negotiations with Ermen. His aim was to secure a suitable rentier income for himself and guarantee the Marx family a healthy annual subsidy. Trying to pin Godfrey Ermen down was a stressful, "murky business" and Engels was forced to walk away with a less than optimal settlement. "If I had wished to drive things with G. Ermen to extremes, that is, risk a breach, and had then had to start something else, I think I could have squeezed out about £750 more," he explained to his brother Hermann. "But I had absolutely no interest in being tied to jolly old commerce for about another ten years."[67] Ermen knew his reluctant business partner was never going to set up a competitor firm and so drove a hard bargain, leaving Engels with a lump sum of £12,500 (roughly $2.4 million in today's terms). For a partnership in such a successful multinational business it was not a large amount, but Engels would take any price. At last, he had the chance to put the years of huckstering behind him. "Hurrah! Today *doux commerce* is at an end, and I am a free man," Engels announced to Marx on 1 July 1869. "Tussy and I celebrated my first free day this morning with a long walk in the fields."[68]

Shedding the misery of commercial life—with all the personal and ideological compromises it entailed—saw Engels reborn at the age of forty-nine. "Today is the first day of my freedom," the still dutiful son wrote to his mother. "This morning, instead of going into the gloomy city, I walked in this wonderful weather for a few hours in the fields; and at my desk, in a comfortably furnished room in which you can open the windows without the smoke making black stains everywhere, with flowers on the windowsills and trees in front of the house, one can work quite differently than in my gloomy room in the warehouse, looking out on to the courtyard of an ale-house."[69] But for all his joy, the leisured pursuits of a retired mill owner in the Manchester suburbs were never going to sustain Engels for long. After Lizzy had had one too many rows with what remained of her family, the couple decided to move to London in the late summer of 1870. "In the last eighteen years, I have been able to do as good as nothing *directly* for our cause, and have had to devote myself to bourgeois activities," Engels had earlier apologized to Friedrich Lessner, another 1848 veteran. All that was now set to change. Having endured the political abstinence of his wilderness years, Engels was hungry to return to Marx's side on the ideological barricades. "It will always be a pleasure for me to bash the same enemy on the same battlefield together with an old comrade like you," he promised Lessner.[70] The General was once more ready for action.

8

THE GRAND LAMA OF
THE REGENT'S PARK ROAD

Engels did not immediately take to London. "One accustoms oneself only with difficulty to the gloomy atmosphere and the mostly melancholy people, to the seclusion, the class divisions in social affairs, to the life in closed rooms that the climate prescribes," he wrote. "One has to tone down somewhat the spirit of life brought over from the Continent, to let the barometer of zest for life drop from 760 to 750 millimetres until one gradually begins to feel at home." Yet there were benefits to life in the low-skied capital: "One finds oneself slowly blending in and discovers that it has its good side, that the people generally are more straightforward and trustworthy than elsewhere, that for scholarly work no city is so suitable as London, and that the absence of annoyances from the police compensates for a great deal."[1]

In fact, London proved a perfect home for Engels as he settled back into his favored role as Marx's adviser and all-purpose propagandist. Immediately elected to the General Council of the International Working Men's Association (commonly known as the International), Engels got to work behind the scenes enforcing Marx's intellectual writ and stamping out ideological deviation. As the International's corresponding secretary for Belgium and then Italy, Spain, Portugal, and Denmark, Engels was de facto in charge of coordinating the proletarian struggle across the Continent. His passion for street politics, his organizing skills, and his ability to churn out barbed polemics made him the ideal choice to keep the European left's warring factions in order. In the words of the Austrian communist Victor Adler, Engels proved himself the "greatest tactician" of international socialism.

He managed this messy, fragmented movement from his study at 122 Regent's Park Road. "Every day, every post, brought to his house newspapers and letters in every European language," recalled Marx's son-in-law Paul Lafargue, "and it was astonishing how he found time, with all his other work, to look through, keep in order, and remember the chief contents of them all." Engels's extraordinary linguistic ability—he knew languages ranging from Russian to Portuguese to Romanian as well as regional dialects such as Provencal and Catalan—meant that as corresponding secretary he could reply in the tongue in which he had been addressed, and he made it a point of honor to do so. In addition, Engels was in charge of editing and authorizing the official publications of the Marxian canon: "When anything of his writings, or of Marx's writings, was to be translated into other languages, the translator always sent the translations to him for supervision and correction." Alongside the correspondence came the familiar flotsam and jetsam of émigrés, exiles, opportunists, and acolytes to whom Engels unfailingly opened his door. "It was like a little Tower of Babel business," according to Tussy's lover, Edward Aveling. "The Socialists from other countries made 122 Regent's Park Road their Mecca."[2]

Now that the social mores of bourgeois Manchester were of no concern, Engels was openly living with Lizzy not far from Marx and his family. Best of all, he was back in the political game, fighting the communist cause side by side with his lifelong collaborator. As their ideas spread across the rapidly industrializing regions of Europe and socialists parties formed wherever the authorities allowed, the opinions of "the old Londoners," as they became known, proved ever more influential.

Engels and Lizzy Burns owed their Primrose Hill location to the efforts of Jenny Marx. Sounding a little like Margaret Schlegel on first encountering Howards End, an excited Jenny wrote to Engels in July 1870 that she had "found a house, which charms all of us because of its wonderful open situation." She knew just what Engels would need: four, ideally five bedrooms, a study, two living rooms, a kitchen, and, given Lizzy's asthma, nothing on too steep a gradient. "All the front rooms have the finest and openest view and air. And round about, in the side streets, there are shops of all sorts, so your wife will be able to buy everything herself." The interior of the house boasted an impressive kitchen and a "very spacious bathroom with large bathtub." Jenny thought it best "if your wife came with you right away and saw for herself. You know we shall be very happy to have her with us." Engels himself was delighted with the choice—not for the interior design or shopping opportunities but because the location was "not quite ten minutes away from Marx." He agreed to the terms of the lease with the landlord, the Marquis de Rothwell, and after twenty years apart Marx and Engels were back around the corner from each other.[3]

Over the preceding thirty years, Primrose Hill had been subject to exactly the kind of class-based urban planning Engels had chronicled in *The Condition of the Working Class in England*. Previously a secluded district of cottages and farms on the edges of London, it had gained a rough reputation thanks to its proximity to Chalk Farm Tavern, an establishment notorious for prostitutes and brawls. But gentrification arrived in the mid-nineteenth century as Lord Southampton and the Eton College estate started to lay out a model village transforming the open fields into a series of terraced streets lined with detached and semidetached villas. Plans to build to the top of Primrose Hill itself were foiled only when the Crown Estate purchased the plot and turned the grazing pasture into an orderly, paved, and planted space for respectable middle-class recreation. With blue-chip developments and a well-tended park (where the primroses still bloomed), the area quickly became a pleasant middle-class neighborhood.

Alongside the developers, the railway had also been at work shaping Engels's new neighborhood. In Manchester, the contours of the city had been dictated by the land grab of the Leeds–Liverpool line; in Primrose Hill it was London–Birmingham. The track from Euston station (named

after a Suffolk village on one of Lord Southampton's estates) to Birmingham New Street defined the northern and eastern boundary just as the
Regent's Canal formed the southern edge. Behind the streets' fashionable neo-Regency veneer the London suburb was being hammered into
shape by the messy, dirty forces of industrialization. Along the edge of
the terraced streets, next to the railway lines, were vast sheds for refuel-
ing and cleaning the trains. Nearby stood the iconic Round House at
Chalk Farm, containing major engineering works. This was a noisy,
stinking, eye-watering environment, where "flakes of soot often an inch
across, like black gossamer lace, constantly floated about, settling everywhere." And with the trains came hundreds of engineers, signalmen,
lamp men, porters, shunters, and cleaners wafting into the neighborhood just like the smoke and steam of the bellowing train engines. They
provided tenants for the subdivided houses and thirsty custom for the
plentiful pubs.[4]

The four-story house at 122 Regent's Park Road still stands today,
marked with a blue plaque from the Greater London Council describing
Engels rather anodynely as a "political philosopher." The building was
converted into apartments during the 1960s, but walking around it one
can still get a feel of how it was laid out in the 1870s, with the kitchen
and bathroom in the basement and a morning room and dining room
on the first floor, separated by double doors. The second floor—which
most Victorians would have used as their drawing room—was converted
into Engels's vast study, an airy, well-lit studio with a polished Norwegian pine floor, ceiling-high bookcases, a magisterial fireplace, and tall
French windows looking out onto the noisy bustle of the street. Engels
was characteristically fastidious about his study, keeping it orderly and
uncluttered. "The rooms were more like reception rooms than a scholar's
study," according to one visitor. The two upper floors were given over to
bedrooms for himself, Lizzy, maidservants, Lizzy's niece Pumps, and
any passing houseguest. One such visitor was the German social democrat Eduard Bernstein, who was to become a regular at Regent's Park
Road during the 1880s. "Upstairs we soon began a political conversation, which often assumed a very lively character," Bernstein recalled of
a rambunctious evening at No. 122. "Engels' stormy temperament, which

concealed such a truly noble character, and many good qualities, revealed itself to us as unreservedly as the joyous conception of life peculiar to the Rhineland. 'Drink, young man!' And with these words, in the midst of a violent dispute, he kept on refilling my glass with Bordeaux, which he always had in the house."[5]

Despite his bohemian inclinations, Engels could never quite shake his Calvinist work ethic and he was a man of strict routine. Breakfast would be followed by a couple of hours of work and correspondence, and then came the highlight of the day, his visit to Marx on Maitland Park Road. "Engels came to see my father every day," Tussy remembered. "They sometimes went for a walk together but just as often they remained in my father's room, walking up and down, each on his side of the room, boring holes with his heel as he turned on it in his corner. . . . Frequently they walked up and down side by side in silence. Or again, each would talk about what was then mainly occupying him until they stood face to face and laughed aloud, admitting that they had been weighing opposite plans for the last half hour."[6] When they did go for a walk, it was a brisk hike of "one and a half German miles" up and around Hampstead Heath, where the Rhinelanders breathed in "more ozone than in the whole of Hanover." Engels would then return to Primrose Hill to send off any remaining letters by the 5:30 post and have an early dinner with Lizzy at 7:00. Then there was more reading, drinking, and chatting, after which a late "supper" and bed around 2:00 a.m.

This daily schedule had one exception. "On Sundays," recalled the communist exile August Bebel, "Engels would throw open his house. On those puritanical days when no merry men can bear life in London, Engels's house was open to all, and no one left before 2 or 3 in the morning." All and sundry—"socialists, critics and writers, . . . anybody who wanted to see Engels could just go"—were welcome at No. 122 for an afternoon of wine-fueled discussion assisted by "a fairly 'liberal' helping of meat and salad." The house speciality was a springtime bowl of *Maitrank*, a May wine flavored with woodruff. There would be German folk songs round the piano or Engels reciting his favorite poem, "The Vicar of Bray," while the cream of European socialism—from Karl Kautsky to William Morris to Wilhelm Liebknecht to Keir Hardie—all paid court to the man whom the British Marxist Henry Hyndman called the "grand Lama of the Regent's Park Road." It was just about as far as you could get from the seedy image of émigré anarchism—the world of dirty pubs, furtive meetings, and Soho porn shops—that Joseph Conrad conjured up in *The Secret Agent*. The lights were on, the shutters were open, and the Pilsener was flowing. The nights of the elections to the German Reichstag were a particularly riotous affair: "Engels laid in a huge cask of special German beer, laid on a special supper, invited his very intimates. Then, as the telegrams came pouring in from all parts of Germany far into the night, every telegram was torn open, its contents read aloud by the General, and if it was victory we drank, and if it was defeat we drank."[7] But the social pinnacle of the year was Christmas, which Engels, the noted atheist, celebrated with Prince Albert–like enthusiasm. "Christmas was kept by Engels after the English fashion, as Charles Dickens had so delightfully described it in *The Pickwick Papers*," Bernstein wrote in his memoirs.

> The room is decorated with green boughs of every kind, between which, in suitable places, the perfidious mistletoe peeps forth, which gives every man the right to kiss any person of the opposite sex who is standing beneath it or whom he can catch in passing. At table the principal dish is a mighty turkey, and if the exchequer will run to it this is supplemented by a great cooked ham. A few additional attractions—one of which, a sweet known as tipsy-cake, is, as the name denotes, prepared with brandy or sherry—make way for the dish of honour, the plum-pudding, which is served up, the room having been darkened, with burning rum. Each guest must receive his helping of pudding, liberally christened with good spirits, before the flame dies out. This lays a foundation which may well prove hazardous to those who do not measure their consumption of the accompanying wines.[8]

Given his extensive roster of communist visitors, it is no surprise that Engels was watched by an array of security forces. A January 1874 report to the prefecture in Paris describes Engels as "*l'ami et protégé de Karl Marx*" and "*un homme de lettres*." The police spy placed opposite No.

122, code-named "Blatford," was clearly concerned by Engels's activities and reported in August that *"Engels est très occupé,"* spending his days with *"beaucoup d'étrangers."* Over the coming years, according to the files, Engels flits in and out of the French government's concerns as "Jack" replaces Blatford and discovers a copy of the subversive magazine *Le Socialiste* in Engels's mail.[9] London's metropolitan police, nudging up in the shadows alongside the Parisian spooks, also took an interest. For Engels, who otherwise valued the absence of British state harassment, these hapless officers were a source of amusement rather than annoyance. "We have every evening a bobby promenading before the house," he noted in 1883, as he and Carl Schorlemmer hid giggling behind the shutters. "The imbeciles evidently think we are manufacturing dynamite, when in reality we are discussing whisky."[10]

In 1916 it was said that you could hear the guns of the Somme from the top of Primrose Hill. In 1871 the low thud of Otto von Bismarck's troops shelling Paris was indiscernible, but the wider reverberations of the Paris Commune were certainly felt along Regent's Park Road. At the outbreak of the Franco-Prussian War, Marx and Engels had been surreptitiously inclined to back the Prussians on the grounds that "Bismarck is doing a bit of our work, in *his own* way and without meaning to, but all the same he is doing it." Their loathing for Napoleon III was such that any means to dislodge him from power seemed worthy of support. Then they discovered that your enemy's enemy can turn out to be your enemy as well. "Due to the unexpected victories, chauvinism has gone horribly to the heads of the German philistines," Engels noted after Bismarck had defeated the French army at Sedan in September 1870. As the Bonapartist Second Empire collapsed and a new, more peaceable French government of national defense was sworn in, the Prussian army did not simply return to their barracks as the Primrose Hill communists had hoped they would. Instead, Bismarck demanded a massive indemnity, the handover of Alsace and Lorraine, and a victory march on the Champs-Elysées. "The fact is that you cannot see beyond the end of your noses," Engels wrote to his jingoistic brother Rudolf back in Engelskirchen. "You have made sure that for many years to come France (which after all lies on your border) will remain your enemy."[11] Bismarck's punitive postwar demands served only to galvanize the French, and tens of thousands joined the *levée en masse* to resume the fight against the Prussians. But the citizen army was no match for the well-trained and better-equipped Prussian troops, who steadily ground down the French patriots until all that remained was a battle for the capital, where the Paris National Guard stood fast. Instead of storming the city, the Prussians decided to dig in, hoping to starve the 2.2 million inhabitants into surrender. Under siege for weeks and then months, stoic Parisians famously held out by expanding their dietary regimen to include rats, dogs, cats, and then the entire contents of the city zoo, kangaroos and all. As the Prussian noose tightened around Paris, a political divide opened between France's moderate republican politicians and the revolutionaries inside the capital, with the former urging an armistice and the latter a death-or-glory counterattack. After four months of increasing suffering, the government finally surrendered. On 1 March 1871, the Prussians had their victory procession—a triumphant capstone to their earlier proclamation of a new German empire in the Versailles Hall of Mirrors—and then left a weakened, hungry, angry Paris to its own bloody devices.

While final treaty terms were hammered out, the government turned to its next task: enforcing discipline on a capital radicalized by the siege. On 18 March 1871, a contingent of French regular troops marched up Montmartre to reclaim a set of cannons from the Paris citizens' militia. Adolphe Thiers and his fellow moderates in the National Assembly had been increasingly concerned about the radical sentiments infecting the Parisian soldiery and their representative body, the Republican National Guard Federation (*fédérés*). Thiers had wanted them immediately disarmed after the Prussian departure. But when the government troops were confronted by the *fédérés*—intermingled with the working-class neighborhood's women and children—they lay down their guns and joined forces with the local residents. This symbolic moment of military populism was the spark Paris needed. Despite all of Baron Haussmann's urban improvements of the previous decades—the barrier-proof boulevards, the dispersal of working-class neighborhoods, the straight streets designed to facilitate the movement of troops—Paris was still the city of revolution. The barricades went up, the remaining government troops scurried back to Versailles, and a new city council was announced, with its title of "Paris Commune" consciously evoking the revolutionary Commune of 1792. "What resilience, what historical initiative, what a capacity for sacrifice in these Parisians," exclaimed Marx. "The present rising in Paris—even if it be crushed by the wolves, swine and vile curs of the old society—is the most glorious deed of our Party since the June [1848] insurrection in Paris."[12]

Early events seemed to confirm Marx's optimism. On 19 April, the Commune produced its "Declaration to the French People," which called for liberty of conscience, the right of permanent involvement by citizens in communal affairs, accountability of officers and magistrates (whose salaries were capped), the replacement of army and police by the National Guard, and the transfer of abandoned workshops or factories to "the co-operative association of the workers who were employed in them."[13] Engels was full of admiration: "As almost only workers, or recognized representatives of the workers, sat in the Commune, its decisions bore a decidedly proletarian character." Indeed, those brief, glorious weeks represented an exemplary "dictatorship of the proletariat" (understood more in the classical Roman rather than the Continental twentieth-century sense) and, as such, they were a model for all aspirant social revolutionaries.

Yet inside the Hôtel de Ville, the class imperative was never quite so pure. The Commune had a marked bias toward skilled manual and white-collar workers, diluting the proletarian character of the group. To add to the confusion, there were also a number of competing political philosophies at work. Proudhonist sentiments had always found a warm reception among Parisian artisans and petty tradesmen, and the Commune's plan for worker cooperatives was obviously indebted to this lineage. At the same time, the Commune's most militant revolutionaries were Jacobins and Blanquists set on violent insurrection rather than "Marxists"—although many were also members of the International

Working Men's Association. In addition, there was a strongly civic republican edge to the Communards' thinking, a commitment to building a "democratic and social" republic—Paris ruled by and for Parisians without interference from the external political powers that had historically betrayed their city.

This promiscuity of thought ultimately proved useful for Marx and Engels: when things went wrong, there was someone else to blame. It was the absence of a properly organized revolutionary workers' party, they later claimed, that kept the Communards from launching an assault on the reactionary government forces at Versailles and made them hopelessly reticent about seizing the Bank of France. Instead, they hunkered down for another siege, which lasted barely a month before government troops bludgeoned their way into the capital in late May 1871. Against this force of 120,000, the Communards—even with their barricades and guerrilla tactics—did not stand a chance, and the *semaine sanglante* that followed saw an estimated 10,000 Communards liquidated by government forces. The *fédérés* responded in kind with the execution of the archbishop of Paris, Georges Darboy, but such excesses only gave the provincial soldiers the excuse they needed to commit further atrocities against the Communards. "The breechloaders could no longer kill fast enough; the vanquished were shot down in hundreds by *mitrailleuse* fire," in Engels's dramatic account. "The 'Wall of the Fédérés' at the Père Lachaise cemetery, where the final mass murder was consummated, is still standing today, a mute but eloquent testimony to the frenzy of which the ruling class is capable as soon as the working-class dares to stand up for its rights."[14]

One of the consequences of this bloodbath was a rare falling out between Engels and his conservative mother, who naturally took the side of the government when it came to crushing the Commune and told him so. Engels took some time to respond: "If I have not written to you for so very long, it was because I wanted to answer your latest comments on my political activity in a way that would not give you offence." He then went on to accuse his mother of forgetting "the 40,000 men, women and children whom the Versailles troops massacred with machinery after people disarmed." Beyond Engels's exaggeration of the casualty figures, there was the old saw of his being led astray. Mrs. Engels clearly thought Marx himself responsible for the entire dreadful episode and was furious that he had dragged her innocent son into it. Engels, who always put friend before family, cleared Marx of any responsibility for the atrocities (if not the Commune itself): "If Marx were not here or did not even exist, nothing about the situation would have altered. Hence it is very unjust to blame him for this, and I cheerfully recall that a long time ago Marx's relations maintained that *I* had corrupted him."[15] By the end of the letter, though, Engels was back to his loving filial self, regaling Elise with tales of his Ramsgate holiday and trips to the Viennese beer hall in the Strand and thanking her for her ongoing efforts to unite him with his warring brothers. It was to be one of his final letters to his mother: she died without much warning in the autumn of 1873. Her death severed Engels's last truly affectionate connection to his family on the Continent.

Elise Engels had not been alone in blaming Karl Marx for the bloody events of 1871. Despite his lack of practical influence over the Communards and the relatively minor role played by the International in the struggle, Marx became irrevocably connected with the Commune in public opinion, thanks to his polemical defense of it, *The Civil War in France*. Widely translated and sold in multiple editions across the Continent, the pamphlet cemented the idea that the sinister, shady, elusive International was directing the worldwide working-class movement. "Little as we saw or heard openly of the influence of the 'International,' it was in fact the real motive force whose hidden hand guided, with a mysterious and dreaded power, the whole machine of the Revolution," judged the conservative *Fraser's Magazine*. The Catholic weekly the *Tablet* branded it "a society whose behests are obeyed by countless thousands from Moscow to Madrid, and in the New World as in the Old, whose disciples have already waged desperate war against one government, and whose proclamations pledge it to wage war against every government."[16] Needless to say, Marx was delighted by this belated celebrity. "I have the honour to be at this moment the most calumniated and the most menaced man in London," he wrote to his medical friend Ludwig Kugelmann. "That really does one good after a tedious twenty years' idyll in the backwoods."[17]

. . .

So what was the International, this terrifying subterranean force able to shake nations and tumble governments? Marx generally played down its conspiratorial aura, describing it as "nothing but the international bond between the most advanced working men in the various countries of the civilised world." Established in 1864 at St. Martin's Hall in central London, just after the Polish insurrection and amid a growing sense of international solidarity among the elite of the British working class, the International Working Men's Association was a predominantly European workers' movement, uniting Proudhonists, trade unionists, revolutionary Blanquists, utopian socialists, and a few Marxist adherents in the broader class struggle. In London, the body was initially closely associated with the exile circles around the Italian nationalist leader Giuseppe Mazzini as well as with workers in the London building trade. Marx had reluctantly gone along to the first meeting as an observer but ended the evening with a seat on the General Council and responsibility for composing the inaugural address. Engels was initially highly skeptical about the society, seeing it as yet another unwanted distraction from Marx's work on *Das Kapital*. He also thought that it would be highly susceptible to the factional infighting so endemic on the left. "I suspect that there will very soon be a split in this new association between those who are bourgeois in their thinking and those who are proletarian, the moment the issues become a little more specific," Engels predicted. And he was downright frosty about the suggestion that he should start up a chapter in Manchester: "It's quite out of the question."[18] Coordinating political activities with local working-class radicals would seriously imperil his position at Ermen & Engels, to say nothing of his standing with the Cheshire Hounds.

As the International grew in stature—with an estimated 800,000 regular members by the end of the 1860s and strategic alliances across a range of trade unions—Engels's hostility eased, not least because he had always believed passionately in the internationalism of the proletarian cause. "No working man in England—nor in France either, by-the-bye—ever treated me as a foreigner," he wrote to the working men of England in his 1845 introduction to *The Condition*. "With the greatest pleasure I observed you to be free from that blasting curse, national prejudice and national pride, which after all means nothing but *wholesale selfishness.*"[19] More importantly, Marx desperately needed some political assistance. Through the late 1860s, Engels's friend had fought an exhausting turf war against a powerful Proudhonist faction in an attempt to make Marxism the International's official creed. But now he was facing an altogether more tenacious and formidable opponent: Michael Bakunin.

If one had set out to design a figure specifically calculated to infuriate Marx and Engels, one could hardly have done better than Bakunin. Of high birth, raffishly charismatic, romantic, impetuous, and, worst of all, Russian, he was an intellectual heavyweight with sharp organizational abilities. Unsurprisingly, he has earned the affection of twentieth-century historians and intellectuals—from E. H. Carr to Isaiah Berlin to Tom Stoppard (who is notably admiring of him and fellow Russian exile Alexander Herzen in the *Coast of Utopia* trilogy)—all bewitched by the story of a life so rich in incident and adventure. Engels had last seen Bakunin in the lecture halls of 1840 Berlin, where both of them, along with the other Young Hegelians, had been hectoring poor old Schelling. Since then, Bakunin had participated in the 1848 uprising in Paris and in 1849 manned the barricades in Dresden alongside Richard Wagner as they joined the attempt to install a revolutionary government. Having failed to flee before the Saxon troops turned up, Bakunin was arrested, briefly jailed, and then handed over to the authorities in Austria, who wanted him for inciting the Czechs. The Austrians kept Bakunin for nine months, chained to the wall of Olmütz fortress, before eventually passing him on to the Russians. His next stop was St. Petersburg's notoriously barbaric Peter and Paul fortress, where his health deteriorated sharply. A change of tsar and entreaties from his well-connected family ultimately secured him exile for life in Siberia. But northern Siberia's sleepy officialdom was no match for Bakunin: by the spring of 1861 he escaped to the Amur River and thence, hopping from ship to ship, to Yokohama and San Francisco. Having relieved an English clergyman of $300, Bakunin found the journey across America to be no problem, and by December 1861 he was back in London, knocking on Herzen's door.[20]

Bakunin's extended incarceration and absence meant that he had avoided all the reactionary fervor of post-1848 politics and returned to political life with his revolutionary zeal undiminished. He was now more skeptical, however, of the nationalist bourgeois cast of the 1848–49 revolutions and, like many in communist circles, concluded that the next stage of the struggle would have to be international in character. He established a League of Peace and Freedom and an International Alliance of Socialist Democracy, but his mind's eye was always fixed on infiltrating the International Working Men's Association itself. If Bakunin had been nothing more than a magnetic personality, he could have been swiftly dispatched. What Marx and Engels found more threatening was the strength of his ideas. Bakunin's doctrine of anarchism was predicated on the notion of total freedom, of life, as the philosopher and historian Leszek Kolakowski puts it, as "an endless, indefatigable endeavour towards freedom for every individual, every community, and the whole human race."[21] In Bakunin's view Marx and Engels's communism presented the prospect of a state authoritarianism as suffocating and dictatorial as the existing bourgeois iniquities. "I am not a communist," he wrote, "because communism concentrates and swallows up in itself for the benefit of the State all the forces of society, because it inevitably leads to the concentration of property in the hands of the State, whereas I want the abolition of the State, the final eradication of the principle of authority and patronage proper to the State, which under the pretext of moralizing and civilizing men, has hitherto only enslaved, persecuted, exploited, and corrupted them."[22] His constituency was the industrial age's social residuum—the paupers, peasantry, and lumpenproletariat—who would never be served well by the centralized logic of Marxian socialism. Bakunin offered them a vision of a society organized into small autonomous communes, with absolute freedom among the members. As a doctrine, this meant a commitment to abolish immediately the authority of the capitalist state—in sharp contrast to Marx and Engels's idea that the state would dissolve of itself ("wither away") as a consequence of the social revolution and temporary "dictatorship of the proletariat."

For Marx and Engels, Bakunin was making the putschist mistake of

wanting political change before the material, socioeconomic preconditions were in place. Nevertheless, his promise of human freedom—
which, just to add to Engels's fury, also applied to the Pan-Slav
peoples—had its admirers. As his Alliance of Socialist Democracy picked
up followers in Switzerland, Spain, and Italy, Bakunin grandiosely proposed a merger with the far more powerful International. Engels, the
party organizer, instantly spotted the maneuver: "It is clear as daylight
that the International cannot get involved in this fraud. There would be
two General Councils and even two Congresses: this would be a state
within the state and right from the start, conflict would break out." But
he warned Marx to play his hand carefully, since "if you violently oppose
this Russian intrigue, you will unnecessarily arouse the very numerous—
particularly in Switzerland—political philistines among the journeymen, and harm the International. With a Russian . . . one must never
lose one's TEMPER." This was not to suggest that Engels was ever soft on
the man he called "that fat Bakunin." On the contrary. "If this damned
Russian really thinks of intriguing his way to the top of the workers'
movement," Engels resolved, "then the time has come to give him once
and for all what he deserves."[23]

Engels always liked to lead a hunt and from the moment of his election to the association's General Council, he propelled himself to the
forefront of the struggle against Bakuninist attempts to undermine the
International as a centralized policy-making organization. To the
military-minded Engels, a man whose sense of discipline crossed imper-
ceptibly from personal to party matters, the anarchists' ambition—to
run the International on antiauthoritarian lines as "a simple office for
correspondence and statistics"—threatened to undo the entire communist cause. Moreover, he regarded Bakunin's countervision as a direct
affront to Marx's authority and an alternative power center that had to
be eliminated. So from his elegant marble-and-pine study at No. 122,
with its handily placed mailbox just across the road, Engels orchestrated
every manner of procedural shenanigan against the anarchists. All the
tricks he had learned running the Paris Communist League were now deployed against the Bakuninist insurgency in Spain and Italy. In an essay
for the Italian paper *Almanacco Republicano* entitled "On Authority,"

which Lenin much admired, he confronted the anarchist farrago by reminding his readers of the principle that he and Marx had first set out in *The German Ideology*: class struggle was an arduous task requiring tight discipline and organization in the face of the ruling elite. And revolution was "certainly the most authoritarian thing there is; it is the act whereby one part of the population imposes its will upon the other part by means of rifles, bayonets and cannons—authoritarian means, if such there be at all."[24] To Paul Lafargue, who was serving his apprenticeship at the Spanish International in Madrid, Engels wrote, "I should very much like to know whether the good Bakunin would entrust his portly frame to a railway carriage if that railway were administered on the principle that no one need be at his post unless he chose to submit to the authority of the regulations. . . . Just try abolishing 'all authority, even by consent,' among sailors on board a ship!"[25] In the wake of the violent demise of the Paris Commune, which Engels ascribed to the absence of an organized workers' party, such anarchist self-indulgence was shortsighted and politically dangerous: "Just now, when we have to defend ourselves with all the means at our disposal, the proletariat is told to organize not in accordance with requirements of the struggle it is daily and hourly compelled to wage, but according to the vague notions of a future society entertained by some dreamers."[26]

The animosity came to a head at the 1872 Hague Congress, where Marx and Engels used foul means and fair to purge Bakunin and his Swiss followers from the organization. With the support of Paul Lafargue, Engels led the prosecution of Bakunin as both a terrorist provocateur, happy to use the services of Russian gangsters, and as a member of a wider political conspiracy "got up to hamper the proletarian movement." On the last day of the congress a vote was called. "Then I saw Engels," the German social democrat Theodor Cuno later recalled. "He was sitting to the left of the presiding officer, smoking, writing, and eagerly listening to the speakers. When I introduced myself to him he looked up from his paper, and seizing my hands he joyfully said: 'Everything goes well, we have a big majority.'"[27] By twenty-seven votes to seven, Bakunin was out. But Marx and Engels hardly felt victorious. Even before the vote, they had already stunned the congress by announcing that the International would move its General Council to New York City. Marx claimed that he was exhausted by the endless European politicking; Engels played up the prospect of a fresh start in a virgin political landscape full of proletarian promise. In truth, the move was an admission of unexpected political vulnerability in the face of Bakunin's faction: anarchism had made serious inroads into the International and the entire organization needed to be dissolved, they felt, and founded again from first principles. Marx and Engels had won the battle against Bakunin, but he had dealt their political operation a significant blow. The International never quite took root in the States and was dissolved four years later.

Fat Bakunin was not the only charismatic ideologue Marx and Engels had to face down: the exotic Ferdinand Lassalle proved another rival for the hearts and minds of the European workers' movement. The son of a self-made Jewish tailor and another product of Berlin's Young Hegelian circle, Lassalle was a philosopher and activist who had never quite got the romance of "Young Germany" out of his system. After the failure of '48, Lassalle was involved with various proletarian parties before establishing the General German Workers' Association in 1863. Never overburdened by crises of confidence, Lassalle seemed impervious to the allegations of misappropriated funds and dictatorial treatment of colleagues that followed him wherever he pitched his political tent. "It would be a pity about the fellow because of his great ability, but these goings-on are really too bad," Engels wrote to Marx in 1856 after the Düsseldorf communists complained about Lassalle's high-handed ways. "He was always a man one had to keep a devilish sharp eye on and as a real Jew from the Slav border was always ready to exploit anyone for his own private ends on party pretexts."[28] Marx was inclined to be more lenient since Lassalle was helping him to find a publisher for *Das Kapital*, but Engels fell out permanently with him over the 1859 Franco-Austrian war: whereas Engels placed the struggle against Bonaparte above all else, Lassalle feared an Austrian victory would only accelerate nationalistic reaction in Germany.

Lassalle did not remain long in Marx's good graces either. Marx had traveled to Prussia in 1861 in an attempt to reclaim his citizenship and, while awaiting the (negative) decision, enjoyed a high-society summer with Lassalle and his Berlin fast set. The next year, Lassalle returned the favor, staying with the Marxes in London for three long weeks and, in the process, sending their precarious family finances into free fall. The great philosopher was furious with this spendthrift popinjay, and the rift brought all their political differences to the fore. Lassalle's notion of a Malthusian-derived "iron law of wages" (which would naturally stay low as more and more working-class children entered the labor market) moved him to argue for a Proudhonian future of producer cooperatives, but set up by the state. Alongside this economic policy was a Chartist-like commitment to extending the suffrage, a necessary step toward crafting a modern *Volksstaat*. All of which, to Marx's mind, failed to appreciate the preeminent task: to abolish the existing capitalist order. Indeed, Lassalle retained a romantic, almost Hegelian belief in the state as the highest form of human organization and thus a potential agent of working-class emancipation. He even entered into secret talks with Chancellor Bismarck in the hope of crafting this ideal state on the back of a grand electoral pact—the working class and Junker aristocracy united against the exploitative bourgeoisie, whom he and Bismarck both despised. But before Lassalle could realize this political master plan, his Don Juan inclinations got the better of him: in 1864 he was fatally shot in the stomach by the enraged fiancé of a young girl he had been courting. Suddenly, Engels rather admired the man. "Whatever Lassalle may have been in other respects as a person, writer, scholar—he was, as a politician, undoubtedly one of the most significant men in Germany," Engels wrote on hearing of the death. "But what an extraordinary way to lose one's life. . . . Such a thing could only happen to Lassalle, with his strange and altogether unique mixture of frivolity and sentimentality, Jewishness and chivalresquerie."[29] But as soon as Engels was informed about Lassalle's secret alliance with Bismarck, it was straight back to the insults: "Baron Izzy," "Lazarus," "Smart Ephraim," or, in pointed reference to Lassalle's dark complexion, "the Jewish nigger."

Such ad hominem attacks on political opponents were stock in trade for Engels; physical deformities, sexual peccadilloes, and personal habits were all subject to merciless ridicule. Yet his particular focus on ethnicity—he complained about the number of Jews at the Schiller Institute in Manchester, was affectionately obsessed with Paul Lafargue's Creole heritage, and repeatedly used the term *nigger*, which was then already a prejudicial term—does give one pause. Like many others of his milieu, Engels certainly thought Western Europeans were more civilized, advanced, and cultured than Africans, Slavs, Arabs, and the slaves of the American South. Still, when it came to the raw politics of race, he was always on the right side: he supported the North against the South in the Civil War and, as we have seen, was appalled by the butchery unleashed on the Jamaican rebels by Governor Eyre during the 1865 Morant Bay rebellion. Despite his own cultural reflex toward anti-Semitism, he also consistently condemned Jewish persecution when it reemerged—among both socialists and conservatives—in late 1870s Germany. Indeed, he wrote an essay condemning anti-Semitism as backward and noxious, "nothing but the reaction of the medieval, decadent strata of society against modern society, only serv[ing] reactionary ends." Engels wanted the socialists to make the struggle against anti-Semitism their struggle and he outlined just how indebted the movement was to Jews, from Heine and Börne to Marx, Victor Adler, and the leading German social democrat Eduard Bernstein. And, like Marx, he believed that anti-Semitism would ultimately die out along with capitalism, even if he himself could never fully shake off his Prussian instincts.[30]

Whether it was due to his "Jewish cunning" or not, Lassalle's intellectual legacy certainly had a significant impact on German working-class politics. "Izzy has given the movement a Tory-Chartist character, which it will be difficult to get rid of," Engels regretfully noted after Lassalle's death.[31] This was especially dangerous given the direction the German state was heading: Bismarck, it seemed, had learned much from his old opponent Napoleon III and was now successfully imitating the Bonapartist template of populist authoritarianism. Managed elections and a strictly controlled political equilibrium cunningly allowed "the real governmental authority" to remain "in the hands of a special caste of army officers and state officials."[32] Bismarck's reverence for state absolutism was now camouflaged by supportive public opinion and an expanded suffrage—a trap that Lassalle and his followers seemed content to blunder straight into.

Thankfully, Marx and Engels had their own party to counter Lassalle's Bismarckian appeasement—or so they thought. Huge rail, road, and naval infrastructure projects, along with major advances in the chemical, metallurgic, and electrical industries, saw an unprecedented expansion of the urban working class during the second half of the nineteenth century. This was the age of the booming Ruhr valley, of factory production lines, vast foundries, cartels, and joint-stock companies backed by the big four banks—Deutsche, Dresdner, Darmstädter, and Disconto-Gesellschaft. With mass industrialization and urbanization came new support for radical politics in the overcrowded laborers' quarters of Berlin, Munich, Hamburg, and Frankfurt. In 1869, these constituencies gained a voice in the German Social Democratic Workers Party, founded in Eisenach by August Bebel and Wilhelm Liebknecht. With its hostility toward alliances with centrist middle-class parties, its suspicion of Prussian aggrandizement, and its more obviously Marxian approach to socialism, Marx and Engels were enormously proud of the Eisenach party, regarding it as the most authentic, practical realization of the International ideal. There was none of the sloth that undermined the English working-class movement, the confusion of Proudhonism among the French and Belgians, or the Bakuninist plague that infected Spain and Italy. Of course, the founding fathers were never slow to point out where the Eisenachers were going wrong and they tended to give Liebknecht a particularly hard time for the various compromises the management of a democratic party inevitably entailed. Their criticisms reached a crescendo in 1875 when, at a meeting in Gotha, Liebknecht took the Eisenachers into alliance with Lassalle's General German Workers' Association, uniting the two groups under the banner of the Socialist Workers Party of Germany (Sozialistische Arbeiterpartei Deutschlands, or SAPD).

In Regent's Park Road, Engels was incredulous. While Marx penned his withering *Critique of the Gotha Program*, highlighting all the Lassallean fallacies that the Eisenachers had fallen for, Engels castigated Bebel for dropping the commitment to trade unionism, accepting the flawed notion of an "iron law of wages," and subscribing to the utopian nonsense of eliminating social and political inequality. Engels, the Bohemian aficionado of the high life, was never a Leveler: "Living conditions will always evince a certain inequality which may be reduced to a minimum but never wholly eliminated. The living conditions of Alpine dwellers will always be different from those of the plainsmen. The concept of a socialist society as a realm of equality is a one-sided French concept." Liebknecht, with his wretched kowtowing to Lassallean doctrine, had shown signs of ideological freelancing and Engels pompously warned Bebel that "Marx and I could never recognise a new party set up on that basis and shall have to consider most seriously what attitude—public as well as private—we should adopt towards it. Remember that abroad we are held responsible for any and every statement and action of the German Social Democratic Workers Party." They directed most of their ire toward Liebknecht for his failure to consult them beforehand and his desperate "anxiety to achieve unity and pay *any* price for it."[33]

Bismarck was highly perturbed by this specter of organized, unified socialism, and two hapless attempts on the life of Emperor Wilhelm I provided just the excuse he needed to crack down on the movement. In 1878, he introduced the notorious, repressive *Sozialistengesetz*, prohibiting all organizations "that seek by means of Social Democratic, Socialistic, or Communistic activities to overthrow the existing political and social order." While individual social democrats were free to stand for election, the antisocialist law prohibited all assemblies and publications, outlawed trade unions, forced party members out of jobs, and declared the SAPD organization illegal. Inevitably, this torrent of state persecution served both to radicalize party members and to engender a highly effective underground organization. While Engels expressed deep sympathy for jailed activists and their families (whom he supported financially), he was delighted by the political consequences of this clampdown, which he hoped would move the SAPD leftward from the compromises involved in its formation. "Mr Bismarck who, for seven years, has been working for us as if he was in our pay, now appears incapable of moderating his offers to speed up the advent of socialism," he wrote to his Russian correspondent Pyotr Lavrov.[34] To Engels's mind, Bismarck had been forced into the *zugzwang* impasse, the situation in chess where any move only hastens the player's demise. "In Germany we have fortunately reached the stage when every action of our adversaries is advantageous to us," he told Bebel, "when all historical forces are playing into our hands, when nothing, absolutely nothing, can happen without our deriving advantage from it. . . . Bismarck is working for us like a real Trojan." The first results came at the October 1881 elections, when social democrats secured 312,000 votes in predominantly urban areas, translating into twelve Reichstag seats. "Never has a proletariat conducted itself so magnificently," declared Engels. "In Germany, after three years of unprecedented persecution and unrelenting pressure, during which any form of public organization and even communication was a sheer impossibility, our lads have returned, not only in all their former strength, but actually stronger than before."[35] Gratifyingly, the German working class had finally reclaimed the proletarian leadership from the French and English.

But even this stunning advance had its risks. Electoral success allowed political power to move upward from the militant grassroots to a parliamentary leadership often made up of members of the middle class and dangerously susceptible to reformist rather than radical ideas. Engels, who always contended "that the masses in Germany have been far better than their leaders," now combed every announcement from the Reichstag group for signs of weak-willed opportunism. Frequent, sometimes daily, bulletins issued from the Regent's Park Road presidium with detailed instructions about what political stance to take on any given controversy and how to vote on individual bills (from protective tariffs to the minutiae of the Schleswig-Holstein canal, which Engels decreed too shallow at nine meters). Such extreme micromanagement kept Engels alert to "the voices of the representatives of the petty bourgeoisie, terrified lest the proletariat, impelled by its revolutionary situation, should 'go too far.'" With half an eye to covering his own bourgeois

tracks, Engels was adamant that class struggle had to remain fundamental to the movement: "The emancipation of the working class must be
achieved by the working class itself."[36] And so he and Marx were greatly
relieved when, at a clandestine 1880 Congress of Social Democracy in
Wyden Castle in Switzerland, the SAPD retreated from its Reichstag re-
formism and recommitted itself to the revolutionary struggle "with all
means."

Engels spent a large part of the 1870s concerned with managing his own
means, the cash and stock capital he had taken out of Ermen & Engels
on retirement. No longer a cotton lord, he now assumed another role
from the repertoire of Marxism's stock villains: the rentier. As it hap-
pens, he had picked a highly propitious time. The British economy, mir-
roring Engels's move from north to south, was shifting its profit center
from the industrial north to the City of London, with its financial services sector. Economic historians have called the last third of the nineteenth century "the Great Depression," as wages stalled and prices fell.
But for those with a regular income, it was boom time. "We here are now
in the full swing of prosperity and thriving business," Engels wrote in
Der Volkstaat in 1871. "There is a surplus of capital on the market and it
is looking everywhere for a profitable home; bogus companies, set up for
the happiness of mankind and the enrichment of the entrepreneurs, are
shooting up out of the ground like mushrooms. Mines, asphalt quarries,
horse-drawn tramways for big cities, and iron works seem to be the most
favoured at the moment."[37] Engels was thriving in the London of Trollope's coruscating novel *The Way We Live Now*, a city of joint-stock capitalism and a roaring stock exchange, its cast of international financiers
perfectly summed up by Trollope's baroque crook Augustus Melmotte,
who "could make or mar any company by buying or selling stock, and
could make money dear or cheap as he pleased." It was the London of
innumerable black-coated clerks filling the countless offices of commerce,
banking, shipping, insurance, and real estate. In Marxian terms, the
British economy was on its way to a more concentrated form of monopoly capitalism. "'Floating'—transforming large private concerns into

limited companies—has been the order of the day for the last ten years and more," Engels reported in 1881. "From the large Manchester warehouses of the City to the ironworks and coalpits of Wales and the North and the factories of Lancashire, everything has been, or is being, floated."[38] And the surplus capital that resulted from this stock market flotation was soon at work across the globe. Imperial London became "the clearinghouse of the world," funding railways in Peru, trams in Lisbon, mining in New South Wales, and tea plantations in India. Between 1870 and 1914, the United Kingdom was responsible for 44 percent of foreign investment (compared with 19.9 percent by France and 12.8 percent by Germany), with an ever-increasing proportion of British funds heading to major infrastructure projects and extractive industries in the empire. "Britain was becoming a parasitic rather than a competitive economy," in the words of Eric Hobsbawm, "living off the remains of world monopoly, the underdeveloped world, her past accumulations of wealth and the advance of her rivals. . . . The prophets already—and not incorrectly—predicted the decline and fall of an economy symbolized now by the country house in the stockbrokers' belt of Surrey and Sussex and no longer by hard-faced men in smoke-filled provincial towns."[39]

Primrose Hill was some way from Surrey, but Engels was distinctly a part of this colonial-capitalist, stockbroking coterie. The contradictions had not ended with his last day at the mill. "I, too, have stocks and shares, buying and selling from time to time," Engels told Eduard Bernstein, entering the rather surreal debate as to whether *Der Sozial-demokrat*, the German socialists' paper in exile, should run a finance page. Engels, like Marx, preferred to peruse the *Economist*. "I am not so simple as to look to the socialist press for advice on these operations. Anyone who does so will burn his fingers, and serve him right!" Engels's own portfolio of shares was extensive and quite lucrative. His will revealed stock holdings worth £22,600 at his death (some $4 million in today's money), with shares in the London and Northern Railway Company, the South Metropolitan Gas Company, the Channel Tunnel Corporation Ltd., and even some imperial investments, notably the Foreign and Colonial Government Trust Company.[40]

Fortunately, investment in the stock exchange was deemed ideologically sound. "You are right in describing the outcry against the stock exchange as petit-bourgeois," Engels informed Bebel from on high. "The stock exchange simply adjusts the distribution of the surplus value already stolen from the workers." In fact, as the stock exchange tended to centralize and concentrate capital, it served an essentially revolutionary purpose, "so that even the most stupid can see where the present economy is taking them." One just had to look beyond its obvious rascality to realize that there was no shame in living indirectly on the exploitation of others: "One can perfectly well be at one and the same time a stock exchange man and a socialist and therefore detest and despise the class of stock exchange men." Of course, Engels was no stranger to a life of contradiction. "Would it ever occur to me to apologise for the fact that I myself was once a partner in a firm of manufacturers? There's a fine reception waiting for anyone who tries to throw that in my teeth!"[41]

As ever, the question was what one did with the profits after tax. "We poor *rentiers* are made to bleed," he once complained of the Treasury take, but Engels remained faultlessly generous to party causes and personal cases alike. In addition to subsidizing Marx to the tune of at least £350 per year, Engels paid for the education of the children of Eugene Dupont, a Manchester factory foreman he knew, covered the funeral expenses for various impoverished Soho socialists, and regularly supported party newspapers and émigré charities. Sadly, Engels's philanthropic spirit was regularly abused by those he loved best. His weak spot had always been the Marx daughters and their various renegade partners knew it all too well. By far the worst offender was Paul Lafargue, Laura Marx's husband—the doctor turned Proudhonist turned member of the International General Council. Having assisted Engels in the struggle against Bakuninism in Spain, Lafargue returned to London and, as future author of the tract *The Right to Be Lazy*, practiced what he preached. A halfhearted attempt to establish a photolithography workshop soon collapsed for lack of investors, and so Lafargue naturally turned to Uncle Engels. "I am ashamed of pestering you again when you have just advanced me several large amounts; but to settle my debts and be able to back my invention, it is imperative for me to have the sum of £60," he wrote peremptorily to Engels in June 1875. Luckily for him,

Engels admired Lafargue's intellect and advocacy skills and felt a growing affection for this willful, sensuous, cocky young man. In turn, Lafargue enjoyed the company of the more open-minded Engels as an
avuncular counterweight to his stern father-in-law. "To the great be-
header of champagne bottles, fathomless swallower of ale and other
adulterated trash, secretary to the Spaniards: Greetings and may the god
of good carousals watch over you," opened a typically bantering letter
from Lafargue, before going on to ask, "Does Mrs Burns take baths in the
'*baignoire*' I brought you from Bordeaux that you might extinguish
the fire residing in your bowels?"

More often than not, these letters would then end, "I shall need another £50 to pay my landlord." And so it went on with demands for rent,
taxes, utility expenses, and even underwear. "Your bank-note arrived
like manna in the midst of the desert," Lafargue wrote (sounding re-
markably like Karl Marx) in 1882 from Paris, where he had returned to
socialist politics. "Unfortunately we have not been able to make it last
forever; I would beg you to send me some money, as I need to buy some
underclothes for Laura." But he was certainly pushing his luck in 1888
when he asked Engels to send him a cheque for £15 "to fill the gap left by
the wine."[42] Yet Engels could rarely say no to the Marx daughters; he indulged their literary aspirations, underwrote their husbands, and even
supported Tussy's ill-fated adventures on the stage. "The girl showed a
great deal of self possession and looked quite charming," he reported
proudly to Marx. "If she really wants to make her mark in public she
must unquestionably strike out a line of her own, and she'll do that all
right."[43] What Engels really enjoyed doing with his money, however, was
paying for family holidays, with Lizzy, the Marx clan, and he heading
out to the English seaside. Renting a summer house stocked with plenty
of Pilsener was Engels's idea of heaven. "After being fortified by me at the
station with a glass of port," Engels wrote from the resort of Ramsgate to
the absent Marx in the summer of 1876, "she [Jenny Marx] and Lizzy are
loafing about on the sands and rejoicing at not having to write any
letters."[44]

The sea air was as much for medicinal purposes as for holiday relax-
ation. Lizzy had a frail constitution at the best of times, and by the late

1870s she was suffering badly from asthma, sciatica, and an aggressive tumor of the bladder. In the summer of 1878, Engels feared he wouldn't even be able to get her to the seaside. "Last week she scarcely ever left her bed. The thing is exceedingly grave and might turn out very badly," he wrote to their mutual friend Philipp Pauli.[45] During these darkening years of decline, Engels proved himself an attentive carer, seeing to Lizzy's modest needs and helping out with household chores. But he was fighting the inevitable, and by the evening of 11 September 1878, Lizzy was in her last hours. At which point, something unexpected and rather touching occurred: Engels the great materialist, atheist, and scourge of bourgeois family values rushed around the corner to St. Mark's Church to collect the Reverend W. B. Galloway. Although Lizzy had for years been acknowledged as "Mrs. Engels," her final wish was to have the fifteen-year relationship sanctified in the eyes of God before she met her maker. As she lay dying in her bed upstairs at Regent's Park Road, she and Engels were married by special license according to the rites of the Church of England. It was a very rare, loving moment as Engels placed Lizzy's desires before ideological purity. His dearly beloved wife died at 1:30 the following morning and was buried as "Lydia"—complete with a Celtic cross on the gravestone—at the Roman Catholic cemetery of St. Mary's in northwest London. Her death was altogether less sudden than Mary's collapse and Engels appeared far more stoical about the loss. And—perhaps because they had finally officially married or perhaps because his censorious mother was no longer around—he felt able to send out the official bereavement notice he had omitted after Mary's death: "I herewith notify my friends in Germany that in the course of last night death deprived me of my wife, *Lydia*, nee *Burns*."[46]

This time, in public at least, Marx behaved himself when it came to his friend's grief. But in private he snidely poked fun at Engels and his illiterate Irish love in a letter sent to Jenny just a couple of days after Lizzy's death:

When Tussy, Mrs Renshaw and Pumps ... were sorting out the dead woman's odds and ends, Mrs Renshaw [Lizzy and Engels's friend] found, amongst other things, a small packet of letters and made as if to hand them to Mr Chitty [Engels], who was present at the operation. "No," said he, "burn them! I need not see her letters. I know she was unable to deceive me." Could Figaro (I mean the real one of Beaumarchais) have *trouvé cela*? As Mrs Renshaw remarked later to Tussy: "Of course, as he had to write her letters, and to read to her the letters she received, he might feel quite sure that these letters contained no secrets for him—but they might do so, for her."[47]

The real object of Marx's mirth was Lizzy's niece Pumps. Mary Ellen Burns enters stage left into Engels's life like some bumbling jester ostensibly providing light relief but, in fact, a source of intense annoyance to all around. Everything Engels thought Hegel had proffered about history as tragedy and farce is embodied in the character of "the drunken enchanter," "the amiable tippler" Pumps. The eldest of ten poor children, she was originally taken on by Lizzy sometime during the mid-1860s to help with the household. A pretty, flirtatious, temperamental creature, she accompanied the household in the move south before being sent to Heidelberg in 1875 (at Engels's expense) to attend finishing school. But when a very much more self-aware Pumps returned to London in 1877, she refused to assist the ailing Lizzy in running the household and went sulking back to her parents in Manchester. The sweaty, smelly reality of work in her brother's fish shop soon led her to reexamine her choices, and she slinked back south in the spring of 1878.[48]

Lizzy's death gave Pumps the chance to seize control of Regent's Park Road. She "has already put on quite the air, not to say behaviour, of a *'princesse regnante,'* along with the five guinea mourning gown," Marx noted waspishly four days after Lizzy's demise. "This last, however, has only served to increase her ill-conceived 'glee.'"[49] Now firmly established as housekeeper, she was for Marx a perennially irksome presence. She did, though, provide him with a steady stream of gossip, since apparently few of the socialists passing through No. 122 could escape her buxom charms. "There is little going on in 'our circle,'" Marx wrote to his daughter Jenny Longuet in 1881. "Pumps still awaits 'news' from [Friedrich] Beust [of the Cologne Workers' Association]; has in the meanwhile thrown an eye upon [Karl] 'Kautsky' who, however, did not yet 'declare'; and she will always feel grateful to [Carl] Hirsch for having not only virtually 'declared', but, after a refusal, renewed his 'declaration,' just before his trip to Paris." Two months later, a new suitor was sniffing around. "Hartmann [a socialist émigré] has on Friday last left for New York and I am glad that he is out of harm's way," Marx updated Jenny. "But foolishly, a few days before his departure, he *asked the hand of Pumps from Engels*—and this was by writing, telling him at the same time that he believed he committed no mistake in doing so, *alias* [sic], he (Hartmann) believed in his (Hartmann's) acceptance on the part of Pumps—the which girl had indeed rather flirted with him, but only to stir Kautsky."[50]

For all the tiresome marriage proposals and histrionics, Pumps was a pretty young woman and her feminine attractions probably outweighed the nonsense that Engels otherwise had to put up with. She was also a living connection with the Burns sisters and his Manchester past. Unfortunately, Pumps was also a little too giving with her affection and allowed herself to be seduced by a London ne'er-do-well named Percy Rosher. Despite his much-vaunted ideological distaste for the bourgeois hypocrisy of marriage, Engels made Rosher do the decent thing and marry the girl, but over the coming years he was the one who had to foot the bill. Rosher, a failing chartered accountant, apparently shared the sentiments of the other hapless sons-in-law surrounding Marx and Engels—the conviction that he was owed a living by his elders. He took Pumps off Engels's hands in 1881, but the quarreling couple soon became regular Sunday guests, perennial holiday companions (which, at least, allowed a delighted Engels to play the role of grandfather to Pumps's growing brood), and frequent visitors to Regent's Park Road, often for weeks at a time. Still, Pumps's boisterous girlish behavior helped ease Engels out of his post-Lizzy depression. By the summer of 1879, he was back on form, suggestively asking Marx whether he thought it a good idea if they were "to shake-off the Eternal-Feminine for once and go at being BACHELORS somewhere or other for a week or two."[51]

Engels's return to health thrust him back into his position as communist strategist, uncovering the last redoubts of Bakuninist and Lassallean heresies and overseeing the activities of Liebknecht and Bebel. He also turned his mind to the prospects of revolution in Russia. From their pioneering days in 1840s Paris, Marx and Engels had regarded the proletarian revolution as contingent upon a certain level of industrial and economic progress bringing in its train class consciousness, class struggle, and all the other precursors of change. Markedly underdeveloped tsarist Russia—that reactionary, feudal autarky—hardly seemed a likely candidate. Yet ever the optimist, Engels in 1874 regarded a Russian revolution as "far closer than it would appear on the surface." A year later it was "in the offing," and by 1885 he was sure that it was "*bound* to break out some time or other; it *may* break out any day."[52]

The question that bedeviled Marx and Engels and the entire Russian Marxist movement was—what form the revolution would take. In the later decades of the nineteenth century there were two schools of thought on the subject. The first, under the Emancipation of Labor group headed up by Georgi Plekhanov, argued along orthodox lines that Russia would have to follow the Western European course of progressive industrialization, working-class immiseration, and the development of class consciousness before a proletarian revolution (which would, in the event, be assisted by the mass Russian peasantry) could occur. The second approach was adopted by the *narodniki*, or "populists," who, inspired by the writings of Nikolai Chernyshevski, suggested that Russia's unique heritage of primitive village communes known as *obschina* meant that the country would follow a different road to socialism. Rather than enduring the horrors of Western capitalist transition, it could—particularly if spurred on by some terrorist outrages—take an accelerated path to a communist future founded on its heritage of joint land ownership, communal relations of production, and basic agrarian socialism. Alexander Herzen and Peter Tkachov went so far as to suggest that the Russian peasants were, in fact, the chosen people of socialism, born communists, destined to take the mantle from the slothful Europeans.

Previously, Marx and Engels had been highly dismissive of rural forms of communal life. In their writings on India, Asia, and even Ireland, they had condemned the village commune as the backward adjunct of "oriental despotism" and an anachronistic drag on the global march toward socialism. In the 1870s, though, as the prospect of revolution in Western Europe receded and as both men became more and more interested in early human history (specifically the era of *gens*, tribes, and communal living they read about in American anthropologist Lewis Henry Morgan's influential study of 1877, *Ancient Society; or, Researches in the Lines of Human Progress from Savagery through Barbarism to Civilization*), they looked again at the political possibilities of primitive communism. Dropping his anti-Slav prejudice, Engels suddenly thought the Russian model should no longer be dismissed. "The possibility undeniably exists," he wrote in an 1875 essay, "of raising this form of society to a higher one without it being necessary for the Russian peasants to go through the intermediate stages of bourgeois small holdings." There was one condition: "This, however, can only happen if, before the complete break-up of communal ownership, a proletarian revolution is successfully carried out in Western Europe, creating for the Russian peasant the precondition requisite for such a transition."[53]

Marx and Engels further revised this sequence in their 1882 preface to the second Russian edition of *The Communist Manifesto*: "If the Russian Revolution becomes a signal for a proletarian revolution in the West, so that both complement each other, the present Russian common ownership of land may serve as the starting point for a communist development." Marx made the point again in an endlessly rewritten and ultimately unsent letter to the Russian socialist Vera Zasulich:

Theoretically speaking, then, the Russian "rural commune" can preserve itself by developing its basis, the common ownership of land, and by eliminating the principle of private property which it also implies; it can become a direct point of departure for the economic system towards which modern society tends; it can turn over a new leaf without beginning by committing suicide; it can gain possession of the fruits with which capitalist production has enriched mankind, without passing through the capitalist regime, a regime which, considered solely from the point of view of its possible duration, hardly counts in the life of society.[54]

Clearly, Marx no longer believed in the necessity of a uniform process of socioeconomic capitalist advance applicable to all nations. Engels, however, regretted this rethinking and, in one of the few examples of philosophical divergence between the two men, reverted to the original paradigm. Against his better judgment, he acknowledged, he had been attracted by the charisma of the *narodniki* and regarded tsarist Russia as such a reactionary despotism that even Blanquist terrorism might be justified to get the revolution going. But as the 1880s wore on, he became increasingly convinced that the now steadily industrializing Russian society was no different from England, Germany, or America and would have to undergo exactly the same process of economic development. "I am afraid we shall have to treat the [commune] as a dream of the past, and reckon, in future, with a capitalist Russia," he told Nikolai Danielson, the Russian translator of *Das Kapital*.[55] The Russian commune had existed for hundreds of years, was showing little sign of positive development, and, if anything, now acted as a "fetter" on the progress of the peasantry. What was more, he dismissed as "childish" the suggestion that the communist revolution might "spring not from the struggles of the West European proletariat but from the innermost interior of the Russian peasant." It was "an historical impossibility that a lower stage of economic development should solve the enigmas and conflicts which did not arise, and could not arise, until a far higher stage."[56]

To help the Russian Marxists understand their historical conundrum, he drew a parallel with the experience of the early utopian socialist Robert Owen. The workmen Owen employed in his factory at New Lanark in the 1820s had, like the Russian peasantry of the *obschina*, been "raised on the institutions and customs of a decaying communistic gentile society, the Celtic-Scottish clan," but they showed absolutely no understanding of socialist principles.[57] Russia would just have to accept that there was no shortcut to socialism via the commune and resign itself to the slow, painful march of history. In one of Engels's prescient predictions he forecast that, in Russia, "the process of replacing some

500,000 landowners and some 80 million peasants by a new class of bourgeois landed proprietors cannot be carried out but under fearful sufferings and convulsions. But history is about the most cruel of all goddesses, and she leads her triumphal car over heaps of corpses, not only in war, but also in 'peaceful' economic development."[58]

Neither Marx nor Engels lived long enough to witness Russia's savage convulsions of 1917 and beyond. As they entered their seventh decade, life's sorrows were accumulating for the old Londoners. By the summer of 1881, Jenny Marx was visibly weakening under the weight of cancer and on 2 December she succumbed. The last three weeks of her life were spent cruelly separated from her "wild black boar," her "wicked knave," her "Moor," as Marx's wracking bronchitis and pleurisy kept him confined. He couldn't even attend her funeral, held in an unconsecrated corner of Highgate cemetery in North London. It was left to Engels to give a generous eulogy, celebrating her "full conviction" in "atheist Materialism" and declaring that "we shall often miss her bold and prudent counsels, bold without brag, prudent without sacrifice of honour."[59]

Marx soon followed her to the grave. The second half of the 1870s had seen him increasingly disabled by a range of ailments, from headaches and carbuncles to insomnia, kidney and liver trouble, and, finally, an unshakable catarrh. These were certainly serious physical afflictions, but there might also have been a return of his psychosomatic condition. Marx never finished volumes 2 and 3 of *Das Kapital* and the less he wrote and the more distracted he became by other topics (such as the primitive Asian commune), the faster his body deteriorated. Whether the economics of *Das Kapital* no longer seemed credible or the political possibilities of communism realistic, Marx appeared to be stealthily retreating from his philosophical *grand projet*. He set out on numerous trips to Carlsbad to take the waters for his liver troubles and to the Isle of Wight for the mild, ion-rich sea air. After Jenny's death the search for a healthy resort became all the more urgent as a warm, dry climate was desperately needed to placate his bronchitis. In a sure sign of his illness, he was now for the first time finding Engels uncomfortable company. "Engels's excitement in fact has upset me," he wrote to his daughter Jenny Longuet. "I felt I could no longer stand it; hence my impatience to get from London away on any condition whatever!"[60] He trudged from Algiers to Monte Carlo to France to Switzerland, and at every location he brought the bad weather with him. The bronchitis became chronic. Then, in January 1883, came another blow: Jenny Longuet died from cancer of the bladder. Marx returned home.

In the miserable winter of early 1883, every afternoon saw Engels stroll the brief distance from Regent's Park Road to Maitland Park Road to visit his lifelong companion. At 2:30 p.m. on 14 March 1883, he "arrived to find the house in tears":

> It seemed that the end was near. I asked what had happened, tried to get to the bottom of the matter, to offer comfort. There had been only a slight haemorrhage but suddenly he had begun to sink rapidly. Our good old Lenchen, who had looked after him better than a mother cares for her child, went upstairs to him and then came down. He was half asleep, she said, I might come in. When we entered the room he lay there asleep, but never to wake again. His pulse and breathing had stopped. In those two minutes he had passed away, peacefully and without pain.[61]

Marx's death took away not just Engels's dearest friend but also Western philosophy's greatest intellectual partnership. "Yours is not an ordinary, or a family, loss," Engels's old Chartist ally Julian Harney wrote to him. "Your friendship and devotion, his affection and trust, made the fraternal connection of Karl Marx and Friedrich Engels something beyond anything I have known of other men. That there was between you a tie 'passing the love of woman,' is but the truth. I seek in vain in words to express my sense of your bereavement; and my profound sympathy for and with your sorrow."[62]

Shattered by the loss, Engels found solace in the thought that Marx's death, like his life, conveyed his greatness. In a letter to their mutual American friend Friedrich Sorge, he paid tribute to Marx's bravery: "Medical skill might have been able to give him a few more years of vegetative existence, the life of a helpless being, dying—to the triumph of the doctors' art—not suddenly, but inch by inch. But our Marx could never have borne that."[63] Only hours after he had seen his friend's final features "rigid in death," Engels looked to cement the magnitude of his genius. "We all of us are what we are because of him; and the movement is what it is today because of his theoretical and practical activities; but for him we should still be in a welter of confusion," he told Liebknecht, generous to the end.[64] In Marx's absence, the challenge now was to see the struggle through. "What else are we here for?" Having given so many years of his own life to their philosophical mission, Engels would not let Marx's ideas die with him.

9

MARX'S BULLDOG

"An immeasurable loss has been sustained both by the militant proletariat of Europe and America, and by historical science, in the death of
this man," was Engels's somber judgment on the morning of 17 March
1883, when Marx was laid to rest alongside his wife, Jenny, in Highgate's
steep eastern cemetery. Today, the Gothic catacombs and meandering
wooded paths of this sprawling "Victorian Valhalla" enjoy a steady traffic of tourists and ideologues drawn to Marx's 1950s shrine; the cemetery's edge has blossomed into a communist redoubt with Iraqi, South
African, and Jewish socialists all buried in the shadow of their first
prophet. In 1883, it was a much lonelier place, with only eleven mourners present. Tussy and Marx's sons-in-law Paul Lafargue and Charles
Longuet huddled by the graveside, along with scientists E. Ray Lan-
kester and Carl Schorlemmer and old communist hands Wilhelm Liebknecht and Friedrich Lessner. Telegrams came in from France, Spain,
and Russia, and wreaths from *Der Sozialdemokrat* and the Communist
Workers' Education Society. But it was Engels's short, secular eulogy
that dominated the proceedings.

Wasting little time on Marx's marriage and children or even their
own forty-year friendship, Engels moved quickly to codify exactly what

Marxism meant. It was a speech intended more for the European communist diaspora than for his fellow mourners, and sentiment had no place when it came to laying down an ideological legend. "Just as Darwin discovered the law of development of organic nature, so Marx discovered the law of development of human history. . . . But that is not all. Marx also discovered the special law of motion governing the present-day capitalist mode of production and the bourgeois society that this mode of production has created. . . . Such was the man of science," Engels declaimed. He would miss him terribly. "He died beloved, revered and mourned by millions of revolutionary fellow-workers—from the mines of Siberia to California, in all parts of Europe and America—and I make bold to say that though he may have had many opponents, he had hardly one personal enemy. His name will endure through the ages, and so also will his work!"[1]

This posthumous sanctification of Marx's legacy didn't end on the paths of Highgate cemetery. A few weeks later, Engels could be found denouncing in the most strident terms an Italian communist, Achille Loria, for daring to misinterpret Marx's work and traduce his reputation. "What you are not entitled to do, and what I shall never permit anyone to do, is slander the character of my departed friend," Engels declated before signing off to Loria "with all the sentiments you deserve."[2] "When Marx died nothing concerned him [Engels] so much as the defence of his memory," as the political theorist Harold Laski puts it. "Few men have ever been so eager to prove the greatness of a colleague at the expense of their own eminence."[3]

After Marx's death as during his life, Engels embraced the role of Marx's bulldog, determined at all costs to guard his friend's political heritage. And yet historians have often looked skeptically at Engels's efforts in the years following the funeral, with some claiming that he deliberately reworked the meaning of his collaborator's oeuvre. The graveside comparison with Darwin's evolutionary biology and Newton's laws of motion hints at the scientistic cast of Engels's mind and his desire to associate Marx's thought with the rigors of science. As a result, Engels has been accused of falsely remolding Marxism, of letting his own scientific enthusiasms drive out the humanistic impulse of the authentic, original Marx, replacing it, in his friend's absence, with a mechanistic politics devoid of the inspiring promise of socialism.

Partly as a consequence, Engels has been held responsible for the official ideology of Stalin's Soviet Union and the horrors of Marxism-Leninism. It is a convenient charge to make—helpfully exculpating Marx of the crimes perpetrated in Marxism's name—but one that misreads the nature of the Marx-Engels collaboration. It is true that Engels, one of the most voracious intellects of his day, was mesmerized by the scientific advances of the time and sought, alongside Marx, to position their socialism within this epoch of scientific change. With Marx's blessing, he helped to systematize his friend's ideological canon into a popular and coherent doctrine that would help shift European social democracy in a fundamentally Marxist direction. Marxism as a mass political movement begins not with *Das Kapital* or the ill-fated First International but with Engels's voluminous pamphlets and propaganda of the 1880s. Engels's great gift to his departed comrade was to transform Marxism into one of the most persuasive and influential political philosophies in human history—while remaining true to the ideology they had developed together.

"A great city, whose image dwells in the memory of man, is the type of some great idea," Benjamin Disraeli wrote in his 1844 novel *Coningsby*. "Rome represents Conquest; Faith hovers over the towers of Jerusalem; and Athens embodies the pre-eminent quality of the antique world—Art." But the world was changing, Disraeli thought, and a new civilization approaching. "What Art was to the ancient world, Science is to the modern; the distinctive faculty. In the minds of men the useful has succeeded to the beautiful. Instead of the city of the Violet Crown, a Lancashire village has expanded into a mighty region of factories and warehouses. Yet rightly understood, Manchester is as great a human exploit as Athens."[4]

If Engels's early years were spent in the emotional grip of the romantics, his middle age was given over to science, technology, and useful knowledge. There were few better places to pursue such studies than Manchester, where Disraeli's "distinctive faculty" of the modern age was in full flower. Northern Europe in the nineteenth century had witnessed a series of paradigm shifts in the natural and physical sciences. In chemistry, the French aristocrat Antoine-Laurent Lavoisier had opened up the field of quantitative chemistry, which Justus von Liebig then applied to the realm of organic compounds. In biology, the German botanist Matthias Schleiden had made a series of advances in cellular theory that his friend the physiologist Theodor Schwann extended to the animal world. In physics, William Robert Grove was carrying out pioneering work with the first fuel cell and anticipating the theory of the conservation of energy, while James Clerk Maxwell was taking Michael Faraday's work on electricity toward a unified theory of electromagnetism.

Manchester was the setting for much of this scientific revolution. It was the chemist John Dalton, a lecturer at Manchester New College and stalwart of the city's Literary and Philosophical Society (where many of his experiments were carried out), who developed Lavoisier's quantitative work into modern atomic theory, establishing the framework for the periodic table. He was a civic hero, and after his death in 1844 his body lay in state at the town hall as forty thousand Mancunians filed past in a single day to pay their respects. Dalton's pupil James Joule was just as remarkable. The wealthy scion of a brewing dynasty, Joule set himself to investigate the controversial question—which Grove had been struggling with—as to whether energy could be conserved. Through a series of painstaking experiments, using his family's beer-making technology, he demonstrated that the total amount of energy remains constant while being transferred from one source to another, in his case from the mechanical act of stirring into heat. William Thomson (the future Lord Kelvin) and the German scientists Hermann von Helmholtz and Rudolf Clausius used Joule's results to formulate the first two laws of thermodynamics, establishing principles of the conservation of energy and of the universe's ever-increasing entropy. Statues of Joule and Dalton, placed by Manchester's civic elders in the town hall's tessellated portico, made abundantly clear the city's great pride in and passion for scientific progress.

The democracy of science, its pursuit by ordinary technicians and businessmen, was an essential part of Manchester's self-image. In the city's Literary and Philosophical Society, Geological Society, and Natural History Society, science was revered as a purposefully meritocratic discipline in which Manchester's unfashionable provincials could flourish just as much as could the elites in London and Oxbridge. Indeed, more so: the city's combination of technology, industry, and commercial pragmatism endowed it with an intellectual advantage over the rarefied university towns. A rich exchange of scientific and technological expertise soon developed between the industrializing communities of northwest England and Rhenish Germany, with German chemists particularly in demand. Scientific debate and discovery were alive in the mills, workshops, and laboratories as well as in the city's athenaeums, lyceums, and debating societies. In her 1848 novel, *Mary Barton*, Elizabeth Gaskell enthusiastically describes how "in the neighbourhood of Oldham there are weavers, common hand-loom weavers, who throw the shuttle with unceasing sound, though Newton's 'Principia' lies open on the loom, to be snatched at in work hours, but revelled over in meal times, or at night." She goes on to extol Manchester's factory-hand botanists— "equally familiar with either the Linnaean or the Natural system"—and its amateur entomologists, "who may be seen with a rude-looking net, ready to catch any winged insect."[5] By the mid-1860s, this expanding scientific interest prompted the creation of "penny science lectures," with thousands of Manchester mechanics and artisans crammed into Hulme Town Hall or the Free Trade Hall to hear speakers like T. H. Huxley on "The Circulation of the Blood," W. B. Carpenter on "The Unconscious Action of the Brain," John Tyndall on "Crystalline Molecular Forces," and William Spottiswoode on "The Polarization of Light."

From his earliest days in Salford, where he had attended public experiments at the Owenite Hall of Science, Engels delighted in this scientifically minded milieu. "I must now go to the Schiller Institute to chair the *Comité*," he wrote to Marx in 1865. "By the by, one of the fellows there, a chemist, has recently explained Tyndall's experiment with sunlight to me. It is really capital."[6] His most obvious connection to the world of science was through his socialist friend Carl Schorlemmer, a

chemistry professor rechristened "Jollymeier" in the Marx-Engels vernacular, who tutored him in the fundamentals of chemistry and the
scientific method. Author of *The Rise and Development of Organic Chemistry* (1879), Schorlemmer was an expert on hydrocarbons and alcohol
compounds. He had worked for thirty years in the Owens College laboratories as private assistant to the scientist and politician Sir Henry Roscoe, who noted that Schorlemmer's knowledge "of both branches of
chemistry was wide and accurate, whilst his sustained power of work,
whether literary or experimental, was truly Teutonic."[7] Others within
Engels's scientific circle included the English geologist John Roche
Dakyns and another German chemist, Philipp Pauli, who worked for an
alkali company in St. Helens and later provided a home for Pumps during her time at finishing school in Rheinau. Science offered an intellectual balm to the boredom of Ermen & Engels office life, and Engels
eagerly immersed himself in the scientific controversies of the day. He
read the geologist Charles Lyell and evolutionary theorist T. H. Huxley
("both very interesting and pretty good"), Grove on physics, and August
Wilhelm von Hofmann on chemistry ("for all its faults, the latest chemical theory does represent a great advance on the old atomistic theory").
He also was an early supporter of the French practice of vivisection as a
means of understanding the "functions of certain nerves and the effects
of interfering with them."[8] Engels saw even the terminal ailments of his
friends as proper subjects for dispassionate analysis. "Anyone who has
but once examined the lung tissue under the microscope, realises how
great is the danger of a blood vessel being broken if the lung is purulent,"
he wrote to Friedrich Sorge of Marx's condition two days before his
friend died.[9] He would be equally clinical in a letter to Carl Schorlemmer's brother during Schorlemmer's final hours, noting that, "in the past
week or so he has been found beyond doubt to have developed a carcino-
genic tumour of the right lung extending pretty much over the whole of
the upper third of the organ."[10]

Like so many other Victorians, Engels was fascinated by Charles
Darwin's *On the Origin of Species* and the theory of evolution by natural
selection. "Darwin, by the way, whom I'm reading just now, is absolutely
splendid," Engels wrote to Marx in December 1859 just after the book's

publication. "Never before has so grandiose an attempt been made to demonstrate historical evolution in Nature, and certainly never to such good effect. One does, of course, have to put up with the crude English method."[11] Marx, who thought the work a telling reflection of mid-Victorian capitalist savagery, was particularly attentive to Darwin's notion of evolutionary progress based on conflict and struggle, needed no encouragement. "It is remarkable how Darwin rediscovers, among the beasts and plants, the society of England with its division of labour, competition, opening up of new markets, 'inventions,' and Malthusian 'struggle for existence,'" Marx wrote to Engels some years later while going over the works of Ricardo and Darwin in preparation for *Das Kapital*.[12] Indeed, Marx was so enamored of Darwin's work that he later sent an edition of *Das Kapital* to the great evolutionist at Downe House—where, sadly for Marx, its pages remained for the most part uncut. Darwin thought the Germanic notion of a connection "between Socialism and Evolution through the natural sciences" to be, quite simply, "a foolish idea."[13]

By the mid-1870s, Engels himself was having doubts about the school of "social Darwinism" that was forming around the philosopher Herbert Spencer. In contrast to Marx, he had become far more skeptical of attempts to translate evolutionary theory from the animal world to human society. Stretching back to *The Condition of the Working Class in England*, with its harrowing accounts of the bestiality of Manchester's proletariat, it had always been Engels's contention that capitalism's great crime was to reduce man to the state of animality. In human society he now argued, the outcome of the struggle for existence—as social Darwinists would have it—was not an *individual* "survival of the fittest" but rather the dominance of an entire class: "The producing class [the proletariat] takes over the management of production and distribution from the class that was hitherto entrusted with it [the bourgeoisie] but has now become incompetent to handle it, and there you have the socialist revolution."[14]

Engels's most significant scientific contribution, though, went beyond this vulgar take on Darwinist theory. Instead, it was rooted in an effort to connect the extraordinary scientific advances of the mid-nineteenth century—in atomic theory, cell biology, and physical energy—with the philosophy of the man who had first ushered Marx and Engels toward communist enlightenment.

In July 1858, a bored Engels had asked to borrow Marx's copy of Hegel's *Philosophy of Nature*. "I am presently doing a little physiology which I shall combine with comparative anatomy," he wrote of his extracurricular endeavors (in reply to which Marx inquired whether it was "on Mary you're studying physiology, or elsewhere?"). "Here one comes upon highly speculative things, all of which, however, have only recently been discovered; I am exceedingly curious to see whether the old man may not already have had some inkling of them," Engels continued. He was particularly keen to see whether anything in Hegel's philosophical writings had forecast the recent breakthroughs in physics and chemistry. For properly understood, Engels suggested, "the cell is Hegelian 'being in itself' and its development follows the Hegelian process step by step right up to the final emergence of the 'Idea'—i.e. the completed organism."[15] From his earliest days reading Hegel with a glass of punch in his Barmen bedroom, Engels had always admired the methodology of the dialectic, the critical process by which, through each progressive, contradictory stage of thought, Spirit was eventually realized. Previously, Marx and Engels had applied Hegel's dialectic to the realms of history, economics, and the state. In *The Poverty of Philosophy* (1847), Marx had criticized Proudhon for failing to understand that the roots of modern capitalism were embedded in preexisting economic systems—"that competition was engendered by feudal monopoly"—and used Hegel's method for revealing as much:

Thesis: Feudal monopoly, before competition.

Antithesis: Competition.

Synthesis: Modern monopoly, which is the negation of feudal monopoly in so far as it implies the system of competition, and the negation of competition insofar as it is monopoly.

Thus modern monopoly, bourgeois monopoly, is synthetic monopoly, the negation of the negation, the unity of opposites.[16]

Similarly, the dialectic was helpful when it came to explaining the historic transition from feudalism to the bourgeois age and thence to the proletarian revolution. Now Engels thought he had also discovered signs of the Hegelian method in the newly revealed processes of the natural and physical sciences. As a materialist and atheist, Engels took as his starting point the presence of matter, which existed independently of and prior to human consciousness. In contrast to the mechanical materialists of the eighteenth century, who held a static view of nature and humanity, Engels regarded matter as being in a constant Hegelian state of change and transformation. "Motion is the mode of existence of matter," he wrote in an essay on natural philosophy. "Never anywhere has there been matter without motion, nor can there be."[17] This was where the genius of Hegel's dialectical method came in, as its rhythms of contradiction and progress offered a perfect explanation for the transformations that the nineteenth-century scientific revolution was now revealing—energy from heat, man from ape, the division of cells. "The modern scientific theory of the interaction of natural forces (Grove's *Correlation of Forces*, which I think appeared in 1838) is, however, only another expression or rather the positive proof of Hegel's argument about cause, effect, interaction, force, etc.," he wrote in 1865 to the German philosopher Friedrich Lange, explicitly linking advances in physics to Hegel's philosophy.[18] Again and again Engels returned to "old man Hegel" as a prophet whose theories forecast the new terrain of evolutionary biology and atomic theory. "I am deeply immersed in the doctrine of essence," he noted to Marx in 1874 after reading some speeches by the physicist John Tyndall and Darwin popularizer T. H. Huxley. "This brought me back again . . . to the theme of dialectics," which Engels thought "goes much more nearly to the heart of the matter" than the empirically minded English scientific community could possibly appreciate.[19]

Clearly, there was a book in all this. "This morning in bed the following dialectical points about the natural sciences came into my head," Engels wrote to Marx in 1873 before expounding at length on Newtonian matter in motion, the mathematics of trajectories, and the chemical nature of animate and inanimate bodies.[20] A distracted Marx, far more concerned about the poor marital prospects of his daughters, failed to reply to most of the points. Undeterred, Engels plowed on, happy to use his Primrose Hill retirement to pursue fundamental scientific questions. "When I retired from business and transferred my home to London," he later reflected, "I went through as complete a 'moulting,' as [Justus von] Liebig calls it, in maths and the natural sciences, as was possible for me, and spent the best part of eight years on it."[21]

These investigations produced a jumbled mass of notes and short essays that became the *Dialectics of Nature*—though not until 1927, when the Marx-Engels Institute in Moscow published the collection for the first time. Eduard Bernstein, one of Engels's literary executors, had shown the manuscripts to Albert Einstein, who judged the science confused, especially the mathematics and physics, but the overall work of such historical note as to be worthy of a broader readership.[22] Composed between 1872 and 1883, the *Dialectics* is a magpie's melange of German, French, and English notations on the scientific and technological developments of the day. "Wenn Coulomb von particles of electricity spricht, which repel each other inversely as the square of the distance, so nimmt Thomson das ruhig hin als bewiesen," reads a typical sentence. Just as he had earlier attempted with military history, Engels sought to explain the scientific advances emerging out of industrial England, France, and Germany as responses to changing modes of production. His lifetime in the Barmen and Manchester cotton industries had thoroughly familiarized him with the interplay between economic necessity and technical breakthroughs in such fields as dyeing, weaving, metallurgy, and milling.

Engels's grander ambition was to explain the nineteenth century's seemingly disparate scientific discoveries as the logical, tangible fulfillment of Hegelian dialectics. Whereas Hegel's philosophy had been limited to the realm of Spirit, Engels's concern was to connect theory with practice (praxis) just as he and Marx had done earlier when they reinterpreted socioeconomic change in light of Hegelian thinking. "In nature, amid the welter of innumerable changes, the same dialectical laws of motion impose themselves as those which in history govern the apparent fortuitousness of events," Engels announced, linking Hegel's "cunning of reason" in history to the logic behind the seeming randomness of results in the laboratory.[23] The great merit of the Hegelian system was, Engels argued, that "for the first time the whole world, natural, historical, intellectual, is represented as a process—i.e., as in constant motion, change, transformation, development; and the attempt is made to trace out the internal connection that makes a continuous whole of all this movement and development."[24] By turning Hegel the right way up—by regarding ideas as the product of nature and history—one could show that the apparent confusion of the physical world was in fact governed by eminently explicable rules of nature: "If we turn the thing round, then everything becomes simple, and the dialectical laws that look so extremely mysterious in idealist philosophy at once become simple and clear as noonday."[25]

Leaning heavily on three areas of scientific inquiry—the conservation of energy, cellular structure, and Darwinian evolution—Engels followed Newton in proposing three laws of what would later become known as dialectical materialism.* The first law, "of the transformation of quantity into quality and vice versa" proposed that *qualitative* change in the natural world is the result of *quantitative* change of matter or motion following an accumulation of stresses. An increase in the number of atoms in a molecule would produce substantive, qualitative change (say, ozone instead of oxygen); an increase in temperature could transform H_2O from solid ice to liquid water to steam. The second law, "of the interpenetration of opposites," stated in faithful Hegelian fashion that "the two poles of antithesis, like positive and negative, are just as inseparable from each other as they are opposed, and despite all their opposition they mutually penetrate each other."[26] In other words, contradictions inherent within natural phenomena were the key to their development. This contention was buttressed by Engels's third and final dialectic, "the law of the negation of the negation," in which the internal contradictions of a phenomenon give rise to another system, an opposite, which is then

---

* Engels himself did not use the term *dialectical materialism*. Instead, in *Ludwig Feuerbach and the End of Classical German Philosophy*, he talks of the "materialist dialectic." Only in the twentieth century, thanks to the popularization of the term by Georgi Plekhanov, was dialectical materialism officially coined as the philosophy of Marxism. In this chapter, the term is employed slightly anachronistically but signifies what Engels meant by the "materialist dialectic."

itself negated as part of a teleological process leading to a higher plane of development. Using the same thesis-antithesis-synthesis format employed by Marx in *The Poverty of Philosophy*, Engels offered in *Dialectics of Nature* a totalizing vision of the natural and physical world, which he illustrated with a series of test cases: "Butterflies, for example, spring from the egg by a negation of the egg, pass through certain transformations until they reach sexual maturity, pair and are in turn negated, dying as soon as the pairing process has been completed and the female has laid its numerous eggs." Similarly, "the whole of geology is a series of negated negations, a series in which old rock formations are successively shattered and new ones deposited."[27]

In the shadow of Darwin, Engels put his dialectics to the test with a materialist account of man's early evolution. (This chapter, entitled "The Part Played by Labour in the Transition from Ape to Man," was regarded by the evolutionary biologist Stephen Jay Gould as one of the more impressive side alleys of Darwinian thought in the nineteenth century.)[28] As ever, where Hegelianism was concerned, Engels had his aim trained on the idealist tradition, which, in this case, meant the false doctrine by which homo sapiens were identified primarily in terms of their brain power. Matter, not mind, was still this Young Hegelian's mantra. Focusing on three essential features of human evolution—speech, a large brain, and upright posture—Engels sought to prove how "labour created man." When man came down from the trees and "adopted a more and more erect posture," according to Engels, he freed his hands for using tools. "Mastery over nature began with the development of the hand, with labour, and widened man's horizon at every advance." The demands of labor slowly brought communities together, nurtured systems of mutual support, and created the context in which speech and other intellectual acts could then occur. Whereas Darwin assumed the growth in brain size and intellect developed prior to walking upright and the use of tools, for Engels the material demands of labor came first, followed only later by speech. And with tools and then hunting instruments man was able to move "from an exclusively vegetable diet to the concomitant use of meat," which, in turn, led to the further nourishment and growth of brain capacity.[29]

In the midst of this intriguing if rambling essay, Engels observed that one of the basic differences between the animal world and human society was the latter's ability to manipulate the natural environment to its advantage.[30] By contrast, animals were limited to utilizing their accumulated sensory knowledge of the environment for safety and food. That said, the animal instinct was an impressive natural capacity that Engels had seen at work on numerous occasions from his Cheshire mount: "While fox-hunting in England one can daily observe how unerringly the fox makes use of its excellent knowledge of the locality in order to elude its pursuers, and how well it knows and turns to account all favourable features of the ground that cause the scent to be lost."[31] Yet another solid socialist reason for riding to hounds.

Engels's contribution to mathematical theory was less noteworthy. Always strong in arithmetic, he started to develop an interest in calculus, geometry, applied maths, and theoretical physics as early as the 1870s. Mathematics, like the sciences, had undergone a significant process of intellectual evolution during the nineteenth century, which both Marx and Engels followed closely. Karl Weierstrass had rethought the calculus; Richard Dedekind had developed a new understanding of algebraic integers; there were advances as well in differential equations and linear algebra. As with his researches into biology, physics, and chemistry, Engels thought a dialectical method and an appreciation of materialist fundamentals were essential to explaining all developments in the discipline. "It is not at all true that in pure mathematics the mind deals only with its own creations and imaginations," he confidently asserted. "The concepts of number and form have been derived from no source other than the world of reality."[32] To Engels's mind, there was nothing in math that was not already in nature; mathematics was simply a reflection and an explanation of the physical world. As a result, he attempted to crowbar all sorts of mathematical models into his system of dialectics. "Let us take an arbitrary algebraic magnitude, namely a," begins one passage in *Dialectics of Nature*. "Let us negate it, then we have $-a$ (minus a). Let us negate this negation by multiplying $-a$ by $-a$, then we have $+a$, that is the original positive magnitude, but to a higher degree, namely to the second power."[33] As the Trotskyist scholar Jean van Heijenoort points out, this is all horribly confused: to take just one example, "nega-tion" in Engels's usage can refer to any number of differing mathemati-cal operations.[34] Worse was to come as Engels, playing the reductive philistine, dismissed complex numbers and theoretical mathematics—those parts of theoretical science that went beyond a reflection of natural phenomena—as akin to quackery: "When one has once become accus-tomed to ascribe to the [square root of] −1 or to the fourth dimension some kind of reality outside of our own heads, it is not a matter of much importance if one goes a step further and also accepts the spirit world of the mediums."[35]

Despite the obvious limitations of Engels's scientific modeling, in the twentieth century it proved among his most durable—and damaging—legacies. For generations of communists, Engels's writings on the natu-ral and physical sciences offered a guide to academic research in and out of the laboratory. Eric Hobsbawm remembers scientists of the 1930s ear-nestly hoping their benchwork would fit within Engels's template.[36] In the Soviet Union and communist Eastern bloc, this aspiration became government policy: the official practice of science had to take place within the strict paradigm of dialectical materialism, while any research suspected of subjectivism or idealism was summarily dismissed as "bourgeois science." In a celebrated 1931 paper, for example, the Soviet physicist Boris Hessen reanalyzed Isaac Newton's work on gravitational attraction as the inevitable product of decaying feudalism and a rising mercantile capitalist society. Similarly, a 1972 biography of Engels pro-duced in the GDR could straight-facedly explain twentieth-century sci-entific advances entirely in light of the *Dialectics of Nature*: "The discoveries in the field of quantum theory [have] proved the dialectical thesis of the unity of the continuity and discontinuity of matter; in the field of physics, Einstein's theory of relativity concretized the philosoph-ical ideas of Engels about matter, motion, space, and time, and the the-ory of the elementary particles confirmed the views of Engels and Lenin on the inexhaustibility of atoms and electrons."[37]

Scientific research among British communists was also carried out against the backdrop of Engels's system. In 1940, an English edition of *Dialectics of Nature* was published with a foreword by the British

geneticist and communist J. B. S. Haldane helpfully explaining how dialectics "can be applied to problems of 'pure' science as well as to the
social relations of science."[38] The cult intensified after the war with the
establishment of the Engels Society by the philosopher Maurice Corn-
forth (author of *Dialectical Materialism: An Introductory Course*) and a
small band of Communist Party scientists. Intended to be open to "all
science workers who are concerned with approaching and developing the
problems of their science from the standpoint of Marxism-Leninism,"
the society aimed to combat reactionary tendencies in science, to counter the "misuse" of scientific knowledge by the West, to take a stand
"against very long-term objectives, divorced from contemporary problems of practice," and to oppose "agnosticism and impotence, which are
characteristic of decaying capitalism." It set up groups in London, Birmingham, Manchester, and Merseyside to discuss dialectical theory
along with chemistry, physics, psychology, and astronomy. A taste of the
society's debates is given by the 1950 edition of the *Transactions of the
Engels Society*, which includes a paper entitled "Against Idealist Cosmol-
ogy." The authors gleefully report how "modern bourgeois astronomy
finds itself in a condition of chronic ideological crisis" whereas Soviet
astronomy is in good health thanks to its being "firmly based on the
materialist conception of the infinity of the universe."

Even such enthusiasts as the Engels Society, though, recoiled from
the campaign of academic repression launched by "comrade-scientist"
Josef Stalin and his science adviser Trofim Lysenko. In his later years,
Engels had consistently warned of the dangers of reading Marx too rigidly, but now Marx's writings were summoned to justify the most terrible assaults on intellectual freedom. In philosophy, linguistics,
physiology, physics, and especially biology, Stalin demanded that scientific inquiry follow the "correct" party line. What this meant in the biological sciences was a total disavowal of genetics (a bourgeois invention
with obvious affinities to Nazi eugenics); in its place, Lysenko revived
the neo-Lamarckian ideas of the early-twentieth-century agriculturalist
Ivan Michurin, who believed in environmental determinism. At the
1948 congress of the All-Union Agricultural Academy, the genetic theories of Gregor Mendel and Thomas Hunt Morgan were denounced as

"unscientific" and "reactionary," and woe betide anyone who fell on the wrong side of this decree.[39] Mendel and Morgan's leading advocate, the geneticist Nikolai Vavilov, had already been killed in the labor camps and scientists after him heeded the warning. In the Engels Society archives, there is a terrifying example of frightened self-denunciation by a freethinking Soviet academic, Yuri Zhdanov, addressed to Comrade Stalin himself:

> In my contribution to discussion at the Lecturers Training College on the disputed question of Modern Darwinism, I undoubtedly committed a number of grave errors. . . . In this, the "university habit" of giving my point of view without reflection in various scientific discussions made its appearance. . . . I consider it my duty to assure you, Comrade Stalin, and through you to the C.C. of the C.P.S.U. (B), that I was and remain a convinced follower of Michurin. My faults result from my not having studied sufficiently the historical side of the problem, so as to organise a struggle for the defence of Michurinism. All this is the result of inexperience and lack of maturity. I will correct my faults by action.[40]

To their credit, the members of the Engels Society chose to criticize the Lysenko purges, making a principled plea for intellectual pluralism. In the process, they remained far truer to Engels's original beliefs about scientific debate and research than did the academic thugs of the Politburo.

Part of the reason the *Dialectics* was published only posthumously was that Engels interrupted his studies to indulge in his and Marx's favorite pastime: ideological knockabout. "It is all very well for you to talk," he wrote to Marx in 1876 with an air of mock-indignation. "You can lie warm in bed and study ground rent in general and Russian agrarian conditions in particular with nothing to disturb you—but I am to sit on the hard bench, swill cold wine, suddenly interrupt everything again and break a lance with the tedious Dühring."[41]

Eugen Dühring, the object of their ire, was a blind philosophy lecturer at the University of Berlin whose brand of socialism was proving increasingly popular on the political fringes of German social democracy. Among his early acolytes was the up-and-coming socialist theoretician Eduard Bernstein. Like Bakunin and Proudhon before him, Dühring criticized the centralism and economic determinism proffered by Marx and Engels and proposed instead a gradualist political program that would secure concrete material gains for the working class in the here and now. Dühring believed in "direct political force" and stressed the role of strikes, collective action, and even violence as the most efficacious means of achieving his ideal social system of *Wirtschaftscommunen*—autonomous communes of working people.[42] Dühring's street politics had an obvious appeal and numerous leading German socialists saw it as an attractive alternative to the arcane and seemingly unrealizable philosophies of Marx. All of which infuriated Engels. "Never before has anyone written such arrant rubbish," he wrote to Marx from his Ramsgate summer cottage in July 1876. "Windy platitudes—nothing more, interspersed with utter drivel, but the whole thing dressed up, not without skill, for a public with which the author is thoroughly familiar—a public that wants by means of beggar's soup and little effort to lay down the law about everything."[43] More worrisomely, Dühring was just as aggressive an ideological combatant as the old Londoners. He dismissed Marx as a "scientific figure of fun" but saved his real spleen for Engels, the "Siamese twin" who "had only to look into himself" to come up with his exploitative portrait of the manufacturer in *The Condition of the Working Class*. Dühring aimed directly for Engels's Achilles' heel: "Rich in capital but poor in insight about that capital, he is one of those who are—in accordance with a time-honored theory once established in Jerusalem—commonly compared to a rope or a camel that cannot pass through the eye of a needle."[44]

Encouraged by Wilhelm Liebknecht and putting aside some initial qualms about attacking a blind man ("the chap's colossal arrogance precludes my taking that into account"), Engels launched a sustained denunciation of Dühring and his works in the pages of *Vorwärts*, Germany's leading socialist newspaper.[45] Although Engels dismissed Dühring's arguments as no more than "mental incompetence due to megalomania," the text went beyond the usual Marx-Engels invective into a broader definition and defense "of the dialectical method and of the communist world outlook."[46] The philosophy of dialectical materialism that Engels had been developing in his *Dialectics* notebook was now refined, polished, and served up in book form as *Herr Eugen Dühring's Revolution in Science*—which would become more popularly known as *Anti-Dühring* (1878). All of Engels's skills as a propagandist and popularizer were on display as he countered the allure of Dühring with a lively and engaging explanation of the *science* of Marxism. For after his sustained immersion in math, biology, physics, and chemistry, Engels had begun to regard his and Marx's analysis as belonging to the same scientific template.

To help the readers of *Anti-Dühring* appreciate the context, Engels transported them back to the founding moment of Marxism in the 1840s: the move from Hegelian idealism to Marxist materialism via the philosophy of Feuerbach. Marx's genius, as Engels originally pointed out in an 1859 essay, was to replace Hegel's idealism with material realities. Where Hegel had charted the march of Spirit toward the Idea, Marx was concerned with questions of material circumstances. "Marx was and is the only one who could undertake the work of extracting from the Hegelian logic the kernel containing Hegel's real discoveries in this field, and of establishing the dialectical method, divested of its idealist wrappings, in the simple form in which it becomes the only correct mode of the development of thought."[47] As Marx himself put it in an 1873 afterword to *Das Kapital*, "The mystification which dialectic suffers in Hegel's hands by no means prevents him from being the first to present its general form of working in a comprehensive and conscious manner. With him it is standing on its head. It must be turned right side up again, if you would discover the rational kernel within the mystical shell."[48] After years of playing down its importance, Engels was now forthright about recording his and Marx's debt to the Hegelian tradition. "Marx and I were pretty well the only people to salvage conscious dialectics from German idealist philosophy for the materialist conception of nature and history," was how he inelegantly put it in the preface to *Anti-Dühring*.[49] The metaphysical clutter of idealist philosophy was stripped away to leave the pristine dialectical method ready to explain everything from science and history to modern class antagonism.

Engels's real success in *Anti-Dühring* was to apply the method of dialectical materialism, richly informed by his immersion in the natural sciences, to capitalism. His three laws—the struggle of opposites, the transformation of quantitative change into qualitative, and the negation of the negation—could now explain not only biology, chemistry, and evolution but existing tensions within bourgeois society. "Both the productive forces engendered by the modern capitalist mode of production and the system of distribution of goods established by it have come into crying contradiction with that mode of production itself," he proclaimed in full dialectical flow, "so much so that if the whole of modern society is not to perish, a revolution in the mode of production and distribution must take place, a revolution which will put an end to all class distinctions."[50] The opposites had to be opposed, the negation negated, and, just as the butterfly springs from the chrysalis, a new society would emerge from the inherent contradictions of the old. This critical tool for reading society's endlessly shifting contradictions and readiness for revolution was Marx's definitive contribution to Western thought.

For Engels, the point of philosophy was always to change the world, rather than just to interpret it. And the political implications of dialectical materialism were also spelled out in a section of *Anti-Dühring* that was eventually revised by Engels and published separately as *Socialism: Utopian and Scientific* (1880, 1882). The idea for this more focused primer in scientific socialism came from Marx's son-in-law Paul Lafargue, who, like Liebknecht in Germany, was having a difficult time in France establishing Marxism as the dominant socialist faith. The French communist movement was split between the so-called collectivists (centered on Lafargue and Jules Guesde) and the possibilists (led by Benoît Malon), who advocated a political agenda little different from the municipal socialism on the rise in various British cities. While Marx and Engels might have criticized some of Guesde's insurrectionary grandstanding and "revolutionary phrase-mongering"—inviting Marx's famous quip "All I know is that I am not a Marxist!"—they both supported the collectivists' philosophical stance: Marx helped to draft the preamble to their 1880 manifesto, while Engels's pamphlet was designed to endorse their ideological position.

The three chapters of *Socialism: Utopian and Scientific* distinguished the scientific rigor of Marxism from the lofty nostrums of the early utopian socialists (for whom the possibilists still had a soft spot). The early pages were taken up with a clinical dismemberment of the "pure phantasies" and utopian dreams of Saint-Simon, Robert Owen, and Charles Fourier. Yet the language was not nearly as harsh as it had been in the early 1840s. Instead, the mature Engels found much of worth in Fourier's critique of sexual relations in bourgeois society; he expressed admiration (as a former factory employer himself) for Owen's industrial paternalism; and he saluted Saint-Simon's analysis of the way that economic realities dictated political forms. Nonetheless, the utopians' core failure remained a misguided vision of socialism as a kind of eternal truth about the human condition that had simply to be discovered and then explained to the people for its demands to be implemented. By contrast, Engels presented socialism as a science that "had first to be placed upon a real basis" and then actively struggled for.[51] And it was Marx who provided that real, materialist basis with his explanation of capitalist production (through the theory of surplus value) and the realities of class struggle (through the materialist conception of history). While Marx's method exposed the true nature of class-based capitalist society, the genius of his dialectical system was to chart a future course.

After an accumulating series of stresses, Engels explained, quantitative change would become qualitative. Just as steam comes from water and butterflies from caterpillars, "the capitalist relation is not done away with. It is, rather, brought to a head."[52] Tensions inherent within capitalist society, the disjuncture between the economic base and the political superstructure, reach a tipping point. What then? In the ensuing workers' revolution, the proletariat seizes political power, Engels announced, and transforms the means of production into state property. "But, in doing this, it abolishes itself as proletariat, abolishes all class distinction and class antagonisms, abolishes also the State as State."[53] Here was the great political miracle of communism, as startling in its way as the conservation of energy or the biology of the cell: "State interference in social relations becomes, in one domain after another, superfluous, and then dies out of itself; the government of persons is replaced by the administration of things, and by the conduct of processes of production." Just as Saint-Simon first predicted, future socialist rule would dissolve traditional politics and become a question of rational technocratic management. Or, in the more obviously biological terminology of Engels, "The state is not abolished. It withers away."[54] At last exploitation is no more and the Darwinian struggle for survival is over as "anarchy in social production is replaced by systematic, definite organization." Under the leadership of the proletariat, humanity is finally liberated from its animal instincts: "It is the ascent of man from the kingdom of necessity to the kingdom of freedom."[55] This was the epic political end point for all Engels's lofty speculation on Hegelian idealism, atomic theory, Darwinian evolution, and the negation of the negation. Here was where Marx's dialectical materialism led: the proletariat revolution, emerging from the chrysalis of bourgeois society into the coming communist dawn.

Far in excess of *The Condition of the Working Class in England* or *The Peasant War in Germany* or even his military writings, *Socialism: Utopian and Scientific* was Engels's best seller. He proudly described it as making a "tremendous impression" in France. "Most people are too lazy to read stout tomes such as *Das Kapital* and hence a slim little pamphlet like this has a much more rapid effect," he explained to his American friend Friedrich Sorge.[56] Lafargue, who commissioned the work, was equally pleased to see it having "a decisive effect on the direction of the socialist movement in its beginnings."[57] Neither man exaggerated its impact. Combined with *Anti-Dühring*, Engels's *Socialism: Utopian and Scientific* was instrumental in shaping the direction of Continental communism: social democrats in France, Germany, Austria, Italy, and England finally had a comprehensible guide to Marxism. According to David Ryazanov, the first director of the Marx-Engels Institute, *Anti-Dühring* "was epoch-making in the history of Marxism. It was from this book that the younger generation which began its activity during the second half of the 1870s learned what was scientific socialism, what were its philosophic premises, what was its method. . . . For the dissemination of Marxism as a special method and a special system, no book, except *Capital* itself, has done as much as *Anti-Dühring*. All the young Marxists who entered the public arena in the early eighties were brought up on this book."[58] Together with August Bebel, Georgi Plekhanov, Victor Adler, and Eduard Bernstein (who recanted his Dühring affiliation and converted to Marxism after reading Engels's work), Karl Kautsky was part of the generation then entering the public arena who only came fully to understand scientific socialism under Engels's tutelage. "Judging by the influence that *Anti-Dühring* had upon me," Kautsky wrote toward the end of his life, "no other book can have contributed so much to the understanding of Marxism. Marx's *Capital* is the more powerful work, certainly. But it was only through *Anti-Dühring* that we learned to understand *Capital* and read it properly."[59]

Yet starting with the Marxist scholar György Lukács and continuing with Jean-Paul Sartre and Louis Althusser, another current of thought has held that what Engels codified in the 1880s was never really Marxism. It was *his* materialism, *his* dialectics, *his* scientism, and *his* false conjunction of Marx with Hegel. "The misunderstanding that arises from Engels's account of dialectics can in the main be put down to the fact that Engels—following Hegel's mistaken lead—extended the method to apply also to nature," Lukács writes. "However, the crucial determinants of dialectics—the interaction of subject and object, the unity of theory and practice, the historical change in the reality underlying the categories as the root cause of changes in thought, etc.—are absent from our knowledge of nature."[60] Marxism as it appeared in *Anti-Dühring* and *Socialism: Utopian and Scientific* was thus an "Engelsian inversion," or "Engelsian fallacy," that grossly misinterpreted Marx's thinking. In the harsh strictures of Norman Levine, "The first deviant from Marxism was Engels. And thus it was Engelism which laid the basis for the future dogmatism, the future materialistic idealism of Stalin."[61] As for evidence, these "true Marxists" point to a series of silences in the Marx-Engels correspondence that suggest that Marx never approved of Engels's later writings and sought subtly to distance himself without hurting his friend's feelings.

Whatever revisions Marxism experienced in the twentieth century, however, it is a misreading of the Marx-Engels relationship to suggest either that Engels knowingly corrupted Marxian theory or that Marx had such a fragile friendship with him that he (Karl Marx!) could not bear to express disagreement. There is no evidence that Marx was ashamed of or concerned about the nature of Engels's popularization of Marxism. Indeed, he was the prime mover behind *Anti-Dühring*, had the entire manuscript read to him, contributed a small section on economics, and recommended the book in 1878 as "very important for a true appreciation of German Socialism."[62] Like Engels, Marx had been energized by the scientific progress of the day. "Especially on the field of natural science," as Wilhelm Liebknecht recalled,

> —including physics and chemistry—and of history Marx closely followed every new appearance, every progress; and Moleschott, Liebig, Huxley—whose "Popular Lectures" we attended conscientiously—were names mentioned in our circle as often as Ricardo, Adam Smith, McCulloch and the Scotch and Irish economists. And when Darwin drew the consequences of his investigations and presented them to the public we spoke for months of nothing else but Darwin and the revolutionizing power of his scientific conquests.[63]

Marx himself had also been drawn back in the 1870s to the work of Hegel and was the first to claim that dialectical laws applied to both nature and society. Whatever one thinks of *Anti-Dühring*'s grand theoretical system, there is no denying that it was the expression of authentic, mature Marxist opinion. For the previous thirty years, Engels had devoted himself to explaining and popularizing the work of his "first fiddle," and there seems little reason why in the 1870s he would have suddenly started, under Marx's watch, to invert, falsify, or deviate from his leader's position.[64] In the ensuing decades, as we shall see, others reinterpreted Engels's interpretation, but that is something for which he is not intellectually culpable.

After Marx's death, Engels had to break off his scientific work to take on the Herculean task of ordering his friend's literary estate. "Quotations from sources in no kind of order, piles of them jumbled together, collected simply with a view to future selection. Besides that there is the handwriting which certainly cannot be deciphered by anyone but me, and then only with difficulty," he wrote despairingly to August Bebel after wading through the Maitland Park archives.[65] Knowing his life-long devotion to Marx and inevitable loneliness without him, Bebel, Kautsky, and Liebknecht all urged Engels to leave London after Marx's funeral and join them on the Continent. Engels, who had grown affectionately accustomed to England's low-barometer life, refused point-blank. "I shall not go to any country from which one can be expelled. But that is something one can only be safe from in England and America," he told his young disciples. "Only here does one have the peace one needs if one is to go on with one's theoretical work."[66] Primrose Hill had evolved into the organizational hub of global communism, and Engels was determined to hold on to "the many threads from all over the world which spontaneously converged on Marx's study."[67]

Besides taking care of the international Marxist movement, Engels now also had to play paterfamilias to the Marx clan. Happily, that meant taking on as housekeeper the Marx family retainer, Helene Demuth, or "Nim," at 122 Regent's Park Road (where the two of them nostalgically sifted through Marx's correspondence and enjoyed a midmorning tipple), and, unhappily, dealing with the two grieving, warring Marx daughters. "I requested you, the other day, to inform me (which, as you had made a public declaration, I had a right to do) whether Mohr had told *you* that he wished Tussy to be his literary executrix," wrote an angry Laura Lafargue from Paris to Engels in June 1883, fearful that she was being carved out of Marx's intellectual inheritance.[68] Laura had assumed that she, rather than Samuel Moore, would be translating *Das Kapital* and was furious that Engels and Tussy, in London, were unilaterally commandeering her father's legacy. "You know very well there is on my part no other desire but to consider your wishes as much as possible and in every respect," Engels wrote back soothingly. "What we all of us are desirous of seeing carried out, is a befitting monument to the memory of Mohr, the first portion of which will and must be the publication of his posthumous works."[69]

That was no simple matter. "Had I known," Engels lamented to Bebel, "I should have pestered him day and night until it was all finished and printed."[70] To his horror and indignation, what Engels discovered when he entered Marx's study and started leafing through his papers was that the much-anticipated volume 2 of *Das Kapital* had succumbed to Marx's usual procrastination, his weakness for pursuing tangential topics, and his gluttonous habit of gathering ever more evidence. Whether deliberately or not, Marx had scuttled his masterwork: "Had it not been for the mass of American and Russian material (there are over two cubic metres of books of Russian statistics alone), Volume II would have long since been printed. These detailed studies held him up for years."[71] So in addition to overseeing translations of Marx's work into English, Italian, Danish, and French ("Try to be more faithful to the original," Engels berated Lafargue, who was struggling with *The Poverty of Philosophy*. "Marx isn't a man with whom one can afford to take liberties"), Engels also set about supervising the publication of volumes 2 and 3 of *Das Kapital*.[72]

In his study at Regent's Park Road, from the summer of 1883 to the spring of 1885, he worked feverishly to decipher and collate the myriad revisions, statistical charts, discontinued lines of thought, and incomprehensible jottings that would become the first German edition of *Das Kapital*, volume 2, *The Process of Circulation of Capital*. It was an arduous, frustrating task, and yet Engels reveled in the sensation that "I can truly say that while I work at this book, I am living in communion with him [Marx]."[73] Enjoyable as it was to be conversing with his old comrade, the line-by-line editing of Marx's impenetrable, cramped handwriting was endangering Engels's health. The manuscripts, according to Edward Aveling, were in a terrible state: "They contain abbreviations which have to be guessed at, crossings-out and innumerable corrections which have to be deciphered; it is as difficult to read as a Greek palimpsest with ligatures."[74] By the mid-1880s, Engels's eyes were weakening and he began suffering from conjunctivitis and myopia. To ease the strain, Engels was forced to initiate a new generation—"two competent gentlemen," Karl Kautsky and Eduard Bernstein—into the hieroglyphic mysteries of Marx's handwriting and finally to employ a German socialist typesetter, Oskar Eisengarten, to take dictation. But even with this help, the final checking of Marx's manuscript was still up to Engels. By 1887, he developed chronic ophthalmia, which severely restricted his ability to read with anything other than natural light. Thankfully, after much trial and error the scientifically minded Engels found a remedy. "Last year and up till August I used cocaine and, as this grew less effective (on account of habituation), went on to $ZnCl_2$, which works very well," he informed his physician friend Ludwig Kugelmann.[75] But when it came to his aging body, his real worry was a doctor's warning that "I'm unlikely to be able to mount a horse again—hence unfit for active service, dammit!"[76]

True to his conscientious nature, Engels released volume 2 of *Das Kapital* in May 1885, barely two years after Marx's death. Its publication allowed Engels to continue the battle against the usual range of bourgeois critics—notably the German economist Johann Karl Rodbertus, who had accused Marx of plagiarism—and once again position Marxism and the theory of surplus value as part of the nineteenth century's scientific paradigm shift. "Marx stands in the same relation to his predecessors in the theory of surplus value as Lavoisier stood to Priestley and Scheele," Engels declared in his introduction, using one of his favorite chemistry analogies. "The existence of that part of the value of products which we now call surplus value had been ascertained long before Marx. . . . But they [the previous economists] did not get any further. . . . Marx saw that this was a case neither of dephlogisticated air nor of fire-air, but of oxygen."[77] What volume 2 didn't address were the questions that Engels had first asked in 1867 and that Marx had promised to answer at a later stage: whether constant capital (machinery) was able to generate profits through surplus value and, given the different ratios of variable to constant capital (of labor to machinery) at work in any factory, how profit rates could be determined across different capitals. In other words, in Meghnad Desai's formulation, "was (non-labour) capital relevant to profitability or not?"[78] Instead of providing a solution, Engels weakly threw the issue back at Marx's critics: "If they can show how an equal average rate of profit can and must come about, not only without a violation of the law of value, but rather on the very basis of it, we are willing to discuss the matter further with them."[79]

Even with the publication in 1894 of the third and final volume of *Das Kapital, The Process of Capitalist Production as a Whole*, the

problems remained unresolved. Engels was not overly exercised. He regarded the last volume of Marx's masterwork as even more influential
and significant than the first. "Our theory is thereby provided for the
first time with an unassailable basis while we ourselves are enabled to
hold our own successfully on all fronts," he wrote bullishly to August
Bebel. "As soon as this [volume] appears, the philistines in the party will
again be dealt a blow that will give them something to think about."[80]
The manuscript had been in even worse shape than the previous volumes ("The section on Banks and Credit offers considerable difficulties"), a dizzying jumble of notes, drafts, paraphrasing, and equations.
But there was one aspect that came as a relief in Marx's absence: Engels
at last had the freedom to mold the text as he saw fit, filleting the illustrations and eliminating the literary carbuncles. "As this crowning volume is such a splendid and totally unanswerable work," he told Nikolai
Danielson, the Russian translator of *Das Kapital*, "I consider myself
bound to bring it out in a shape in which the whole line of argument
stands forth clearly and in bold relief."[81]

The publication in 1993 of Marx's original volume 3 manuscript reveals just how liberal this editorial initiative was. In order to get the "line
of argument" clear, Engels integrated footnotes into the text, amalgamated sections, added subdivisions, and inserted his own thoughts. He
also changed Marx's intent on some occasions, most obviously in the
much-debated part 3, "The Law of the Tendency of the Rate of Profit to
Fall," in which Marx outlined how profits tend to decline under capitalism as labor-saving technology progressively reduces the scope for extracting surplus value from living labor. Marx connected this falling
profitability to the vulnerability of capitalism itself.[82] But whereas Marx's
original manuscript referred to the "shaking" of capitalist production,
Engels spoke more definitively of the "collapse" of capitalism. A small
change, but one with far-reaching consequences for twentieth-century
Marxists who repeatedly looked for a systemic "crisis" or "breakdown"
of capitalism to usher in the communist dawn. Just momentarily, Marx's
bulldog appeared to have slipped the leash, but it was all for the greater
good of the cause. "Engels wanted to be not just editor, but curator of

Marx's legacy and editor all in one," as one recent scholar puts it. "Engels produced a readable version of Marx's manuscript for the users for whom it was meant, a group that ranged from theoretically aware workers to philologically interested academics."[83] With the publication of volume 3, he felt at last the job was done, Marx's memory honored. "I am glad your long voyage with Marx's *Capital* is nearly ended," Engels's old Chartist friend Julian Harney wrote to him in 1893. "Never, I think, at least in modern times, has any man found so faithful, so devoted a friend and champion, as Marx has found in you."[84]

Engels's fragile health had not been the only obstacle to the speedy publication of Marx's papers. The irritating presence of Pumps's slow-witted and increasingly deaf husband, Percy Rosher, was another drain on Engels's energy, emotions, and bank balance. To no one's surprise, Rosher was not proving a great success as a chartered accountant. So as Engels wrestled with dialectical materialism, new editions of *Das Kapital,* and the competing factions of international socialism, he also had to deal with the Roshers' family finances. By December 1888, Engels was warning the other habitual sponger on his books, Paul Lafargue, that in light of Percy's affairs "going rather badly" it could shape up to be a tight financial year. The following autumn saw the hapless Percy "completely smashed up," and it was left to Engels to negotiate on Percy's behalf with his brother and father to avoid an outright bankruptcy. "However it may end," Engels sagely predicted, "it's sure to cost me a lot of money."[85] And so it did, as Pumps and Percy never ceased touching kind Uncle Engels for cash—much to the annoyance of the Lafargues. "I am sorry to come pestering you just when you have so many worries and troubles over Percy's affairs, but I am compelled to do so, for we have exhausted our means," Paul Lafargue wrote to Engels in November 1889 as he saw worrying signs of Engels's resources being diverted.[86]

Over the next five years, Engels, the most revered communist strategist and theoretician in the world, was dragged ever deeper into the tragicomic world of the Roshers and their various schemes for making money—from the "Rainbow Engineering Company" to the "Rosher System for Swimming Baths." The worst of it was having to deal with Percy's father and employer, Charles Rosher, whose demands for loans and "investments" in various business projects were couched in a series of brazen letters. "No one with whom he [Percy] is connected has a deeper sense of your kindness and generosity to Percy—than I have," began one ludicrous correspondence. "Personally I have to be very careful . . . to make ends meet. . . . I venture to say that Percy with his allowance from you, plus salary is [having] more income than I am." Charles Rosher went on to intimate in very clear language that he would pay Percy a salary only if Engels agreed to bankroll the company. "So far as I have had opportunity of judging it will be a long time before he will be worth much in my business," Charles shamelessly concluded, summing up his son's singularly unimpressive abilities.[87] And when Engels declined to provide Rosher with yet more money, Percy was duly sacked.

It was no better with Percy's brother Howard, for whom Percy then went to work in a builders' and gardeners' materials company on the Isle of Wight. By the early 1890s, demands for loans, cash injections, and commercial advice arrived with seemingly every post. "My dear Mr Engels," went a familiar request from Howard Rosher, "I much regret having to ask if you could kindly oblige us again with an exchange cheque."[88] Engels knew his good nature was being abused, but he stoically put up with it so that he could enjoy the memory of the Burnses, the beery company of Pumps, and seaside holidays outings with her and her children. "He *does* love the tipsy Pumps," Tussy explained to her sister. "He rages against Pumps—and loves her."[89] But in 1894 his patience finally snapped after Percy quit his job, "spent a lot of money (not his own)," gave Engels's name in surety for a loan, and turned up destitute on Engels's doorstep at Primrose Hill. "After all I have done for them, I am not going to quietly submit to such treatment, and did not receive them very heartily," he told Laura Lafargue. "What Percy is going to do and how this is to end, is more than I know."[90] And that, thankfully, is the last we hear of Percy Rosher.[91]

• • •

Amid the piles of letters, jottings, and unfinished essays that Engels brought over from Marx's study at Maitland Park Road was a set of notes that particularly sparked his interest: an inspiring collection of thoughts on the nature of prehistoric society. In the early 1880s, Marx had drawn up a detailed synopsis of Lewis Henry Morgan's *Ancient Society; or, Researches in the Lines of Human Progress from Savagery through Barbarism to Civilization* (1877). A hybrid of Darwinism and materialism, Morgan's book sought to trace the evolution of human social organization from its primitive state to modernity. Relying primarily on a study of the Iroquois confederacy of tribes in northern New York State, Morgan charted the impact of technological development and changing conceptions of property rights on tribal and family structure. Progress from savagery to civilization, he argued, meant the inexorable move from consanguineous tribes to a patriarchal, "monogamian" (or nuclear) family household.

As Marx's extensive *Ethnological Notebooks* attest, this was a topic of wide-ranging dialogue between him and Engels, who had by then added anthropology to his list of scientific enthusiasms. In the mid-1860s, the two had disagreed over the significance of Pierre Trémaux's *Origin and Transformation of Man and Other Beings*, with its clumsy causational theory about the function of geology and soil in the formation of racial characteristics. In early 1882, as Marx was fighting off his chest infection on the Isle of Wight, Engels again wrote to him with an anthropological note, "in order finally to get clear about the parallel between the Germans of Tacitus and the American Redskins."[92] He had just read Hubert Howe Bancroft's *Native Races of the Pacific States of North America* (1875), which raised his materialist hackles by stressing the role of blood bonds over the means of production in shaping early American communities.

But the origins of the family and societal forms were most especially on Engels's mind in the early 1880s, following the publication of August Bebel's *Women and Socialism* (1879), republished in 1883 as *Woman in the Past, Present, and Future*. Bebel delved deep into early human history to argue that "from the beginning of time oppression has been the common lot of the woman and the labouring man." Before the development of the family, Bebel suggested, women were already "the property of the horde or tribe, without the right of choice or refusal."[93] It was a theme pursued by Karl Kautsky in a series of articles on primitive sexual relations, "The Origin of Marriage and the Family" (1882–83), that spurred Engels's thinking on the connections between early land ownership patterns and marriage systems.[94] In contrast to Bebel and Kautsky, Engels thought primitive human societies were based not on patriarchy but rather on a system of communal sexual relationships. The common ownership of partners and land rights generally went together. "Just as it may confidently be asserted that wherever—e.g. with the *Hutz-wang* [the ancient German tradition of fences being removed from individual plots for the period between harvest and sowing to allow communal pasture]—the land periodically reverts to common ownership there will once have been complete common ownership of land," Engels suggested in a letter to Kautsky, "so too, I believe, one may confidently conclude that there has been community of wives wherever women—symbolically or in reality—periodically revert to concubinage." What was more, "the argument that community of sexes is dependent on repression is itself false and a modern distortion arising out of the idea that common ownership in the sexual sphere was only of women by men and at the latter's pleasure. This is totally foreign to the primitive state. Common ownership in this sphere was available to both sexes."[95]

Engels's discovery of Marx's notes on Morgan convinced him of the need to write something in order to ward off further ideological deviation. When Bernstein stayed at Regent's Park Road in early 1884, Engels read to him, "night after night, until the small hours of the morning, passages from Marx's manuscripts, and the synopsis of his future book in which he connected Marx's extracts with the American writer Lewis Morgan's *Ancient Society*."[96] Engels hoped the project would be the "fulfilment of a behest": to connect Morgan's researches with Marx's materialist reading of history and, in the process, extend some of his own biological insights from the world of butterflies and insects to womanhood and gender relations. Somewhat unexpectedly, the womanizing Engels ended up authoring the foundation text of socialist feminism.

The Origin of the Family, Private Property, and the State, in Light of the Researches by Lewis H. Morgan (1884) began with what Engels clearly regarded as a progressive feminist principle: "According to the materialistic conception, the determining factor in history is, in the final instance, the production and reproduction of immediate life."[97] At a stroke, he placed female production of human life on the same theoretical plane as the production of the means of existence—which, in the communist canon, was the highest virtue. His next move, in Hegelian fashion, was to historicize the family form by showing its fluid nature over the preceding epochs and to point to its future incarnation under communist governance. "The family [says Morgan] represents an active principle. It is never stationary, but advances from a lower to a higher form as society advances from a lower to a higher condition."[98] Just as the proletariat had to understand that capitalism was a transitory state, so women could hope that current gender inequalities were a passing phase.

Engels began by unpicking the materialist foundations of Morgan's chronology: the progression from a tribal system of shared partners ("unrestricted sexual freedom prevailed, . . . every woman belonging equally to every man and every man to every woman") to the modern form of the "pairing family" was intimately connected to the advances in the mode of production. The family was simply another component of the superstructure as molded by the economic base. Morgan had rediscovered, according to Engels, "the materialistic conception of history discovered by Marx forty years ago. . . . The lower the development of labor and the more limited the amount of its products, and consequently, the more limited also the wealth of the society, the more the social order is found to be dominated by kinship groups."[99] As such, the modern family, with all its failings—its patriarchy, hypocrisy, frustration, and subterfuge—was the product of private property.

What made Engels's interpretation especially noteworthy was that he looked at family life from women's perspective and was particularly sensitive to the history of female diminishment as society moved from matrilineal to patrilineal kinship patterns. "The more the old traditional sexual relations lost their naïve, primeval character, as a result of the development of the economic conditions of life," he wrote, "the more degrading and oppressive they must have appeared to the women."[100]

For, as Morgan had outlined, the early consanguineous system of group marriage and polygamy was far more egalitarian and autonomous than modern philistine prejudice, with its "brothel-tainted imagination," might suggest: "Woman occupied not only a free but also a highly respected position among all savages and all barbarians of the lower and middle stages and partly even of the upper stage."[101] Engels's analysis exposed sexism as a historical and sociological construct. Whereas August Bebel had argued that "from the beginning of time" oppression had been the common lot of the woman—and, indeed, that private property and the division of labor *followed* from man's egoistical "possession" of woman—Engels ascertained that male supremacy was a relatively recent phenomenon closely bound up with the development of a competitive private-property economy. "One of the most absurd notions taken over from eighteenth-century enlightenment is that in the beginning of society woman was the slave of man," he wrote in a direct challenge to Bebel. "Among all savages and all barbarians of the lower and middle stages, and to a certain extent of the upper stage also, the position of women is not only free, but honourable."[102]

The fall from grace came with the introduction of individual and family property rights (as distinct from broader clan or tribe rights) and, accompanying it, the practice of inheritance through the male line. Individual ownership and private property signaled "the world historic defeat of the female sex." As the husband seized the reins, the woman became "degraded, enthralled, . . . the slave of the man's lust, a mere instrument for breeding children."[103] Gender relations became another element of the social divide: women now joined the ranks of those oppressed by the capitalist mode of production. "The first class opposition that appears in history coincides with the development of the antagonism between man and woman in monogamous marriage, and the first class oppression coincides with that of the female sex by the male," Engels declared.[104] In the family, the husband was the bourgeois and the wife the proletarian, with predictably brutal outcomes.

It was the high-bourgeois mid-Victorian family that Engels had particularly in mind—the veneer of pious virtue behind which festered oppression, prostitution, and abuse. Indeed, Marx and Engels had long trained their critical eye on the hypocrisy of middle-class domesticity. "On what foundation is the present family, the bourgeois family, based?" they had first asked in *The Communist Manifesto*. "On capital, on private gain. In its completely developed form, this family exists only among the bourgeoisie. But this state of things finds its complement in the practical absence of the family among the proletarians, and in public prostitution."[105] In *The Origin*, Engels returned to the theme. "This Protestant monogamy leads merely, if we take the average of the best cases, to a wedded life of leaden boredom, which is described as domestic bliss," he wrote with the authority of one who had lived for two decades among the dissenting elites of northern England. "The wife differs from the ordinary courtesan only in that she does not hire out her body, like a wage worker, on a piecework, but sells it into slavery once and for all."[106] The inevitable accompaniments of monogamy—in dialectical terms, the inherent contradictions in the form—were prostitution and hetaerism. For whereas in primitive communities sexual license was unashamedly enjoyed by both genders, in the private-property family "the right of conjugal infidelity" is solely the prerogative of the male. Sex love, as Engels clumsily put it, was possible only among the proletariat, which lacks both private property and bourgeois social norms. Accordingly, Engels romantically if mistakenly maintained, proletarian marriages did not suffer the abusive practices of their bourgeois counterparts.

Having set out the transience of various family forms through history, Engels now advocated a further revolution in sexual relations. It was a theme he had first touched upon in *The Condition of the Working Class in England*, when he charted the effects of female employment in Manchester's mills and factories on the family unit. The new industrial reality of working women and unemployed men had served only to desexualize both parties: "The wife supports the family, the husband sits at home, tends the children, sweeps the room and cooks." Engels reported a friend's experience of visiting a former workmate in St. Helen's, Lancashire, who "sat and mended his wife's stocking with his bodkin": " 'No, I know this is not my work, but my poor missus is i' th' factory . . . so I have to do everything for her what I can, for I have no work, nor had any for more nor three years, and I shall never have any more work while I live'; and then he wept a big tear."[107] Yet the conclusion that the precocious twenty-four-year-old Engels had drawn from this was not that women should be prevented from working (indeed, industrialization promised them a new era of liberation free from domestic servitude) but rather that "if the reign of the wife over the husband, as inevitably brought about by the factory system, is inhuman, the pristine rule of the husband over the wife must have been inhuman too."[108] The domestic upset produced by mass female employment graphically exposed the essential inequality of the modern family. Industrialization had ripped away the veneer of "natural" patriarchy, and Engels optimistically believed that with the spread of female wage earners "no basis for any kind of male supremacy is left in the proletarian household, except, perhaps, for something of the brutality toward women that has spread since the introduction of monogamy."[109]

It might well seem that capitalism and its demands for female labor offered the surest route to sexual equality, but the iniquities of modern family life could be fully solved only by the transition to communism. Once inherited wealth was turned back into a shared pool of social property, the narrow economic foundations of the "pairing" family would disintegrate. As Engels put it in a letter in 1885, "True equality between men and women can, or so I am convinced, become a reality only when the exploitation of both by capital has been abolished, and private work in the home been transformed into a public industry."[110] Women could emerge from under patriarchal rule once the family ceased to exist as an economic unit, private housekeeping became a socialized event, and—most radically of all—"the care and upbringing of children becomes a public affair."[111] Private property, wealth, and even children all had to be passed to the wider community as shared goods. With almost Fourierist verve, Engels then laid out the utopian promise offered by this sexual revolution: women marrying for love rather than money (which would lead to "a gradual rise of more unrestrained sexual intercourse" and, with it, "a laxer public opinion regarding virginal honour and female shame"), wives no longer having to tolerate their husband's infidelities for fear of losing their property, and marriages built on mutual affection and respect, sparing couples "the useless mire of divorce proceedings." If not quite Fourier's free-love phalanstery, this was not very far off.

Still, there were some sexual topics that could bring out Engels's Calvinist upbringing in full force. One freedom that Engels was not willing to sanction was homosexuality. In 1869, Karl Marx had sent him a copy of the *Argonauticus*, a book by the German lawyer Karl Ulrich, who argued that same-sex desire was inborn, proposed that masculinity and femininity should be regarded as a continuum, and coined the term *Urning* to describe homosexual and lesbian attraction. Engels was appalled by such "unnatural revelations." "The paederasts are beginning to count themselves, and discover that they are a power in the state," he wrote to Marx in a hyperbolic homophobic rant. "*Guerre aux cons, paix aus trous de cul* ['War on the cunts, peace to the arse-holes'] will now be the slogan. It is a bit of luck that we, personally, are too old to have to fear that, when this party wins, we shall have to pay physical tribute to the victors. . . . Just wait until the new North German Penal Code recognizes the *droits du cul*. . . . Then things will go badly enough for poor frontside people like us, with our childish penchant for females."[112] By way of contrast, the English socialist Edward Carpenter took Engels's critique of the bourgeois family to a different conclusion, arguing for the virtue of nonprocreative sex and, with it, the cultural and legal acceptance of homosexuality as part of a broader process of socialist emancipation.[113] Carpenter's ideal vision of "comradeship" offered an altogether different socialism from Engels's utopia of free love and communal child rearing.

Never as influential as his writings on dialectical materialism, Engels's theories of the family nonetheless proved a significant contribution to socialist thought in the twentieth century, shaping schooling and child-rearing policies in the Soviet Union. More startling was the success of *The Origin* among an entire generation of Marxist feminists in the West. The feminist activist Kate Millett writes in her 1970 book, *Sexual Politics*, that Engels's treatment of marriage and the family as historical institutions "subject to the same processes of evolution as other social phenomena . . . laid the sacred open to serious criticism, analysis, even to possible drastic reorganization. The radical outcome of Engels's analysis is that the family, as that term is presently understood, must go."[114] Similarly, Shulamith Firestone's *Dialectic of Sex: A Case for Feminist Revolution* (1970) draws on Engels's writings to make the case for postpatriarchal communal living. What many feminists admired about Engels's approach was his treatment of gender differences as economically produced rather than biologically determined: patriarchy was another function of bourgeois class society, and both needed to be undone.[115]

More recently, Engels's work has been criticized, principally by anthropologists, for its failure to acknowledge male domination in primitive societies and for the implicit assumptions that litter his text about the division of labor between men and women being innate rather than socially constructed. In addition, a new wave of feminists has taken Engels to task for failing to appreciate female sexual desires as distinct from the reproductive process, for depicting women as naturally yearning for permanent marriage, and, more significantly, for not attending "seriously to questions of sexuality, ideology, domesticity or the division of labour and power between women and men generally."[116] These objections notwithstanding, it is surely remarkable that Engels—the great lothario, devotee of Parisian grisettes, and rough seducer of Mrs. Moses Hess—had become passionately committed to feminist ideas. He even endorsed plans in the German Reichstag for outlawing prostitution, while warning of the repercussions on sex workers if the experience of England's Contagious Diseases Act was anything to go by. "It is my belief that, in dealing with this matter, we should above all consider the interests of the girls themselves as victims of the present social order, and protect them as far as possible from ending up in the gutter," the reformed john told August Bebel.[117]

In truth, though Engels had frequented boudoirs and brothels in his raffish youth, for much of his adulthood he lived according to his beliefs. Contradictions of Hegelian proportions may have tormented his professional existence, but when it came to his personal affairs Engels refused to submit to bourgeois norms. It was only on Lizzy's deathbed that he finally wed his partner to soothe her religious qualms. Cynics might say that this had more to do with inheritance rights and shares in Ermen & Engels, but there is no evidence that his reluctance was anything but a principled objection to what he regarded as the hypocrisy of marriage. Engels was also acutely aware of the fragile position of women within bourgeois society—an appreciation of which led him to make sure Percy Rosher married Pumps after their liaison—and their isolation in the aftermath of a relationship's collapse. When in October 1888 Karl Kautsky announced he was leaving his wife, Louise, for a young woman he had met in Salzsburg, Engels upbraided him for having dealt "the most terrible blow a woman can possibly receive." At great length, he spelled out the consequences of divorce in contemporary society: while no social stigma attached to the husband, "the wife loses her status altogether; she has got to begin all over again and do so under more difficult circumstances." Engels urged Kautsky to reflect very carefully on the matter and then, if there was no other option, proceed "only in the most considerate manner possible."[118]

Such admirable examples of Engels's empathy for the situation of women are all, alas, overshadowed by his less sympathetic response to the women's movement of the day. He had been attracted to Mary and then Lizzy Burns partly for their earthy, illiterate ways, which he contrasted favorably with the "priggishness and sophistry of the 'heddicated' and 'sensitive' daughters of the bourgeoisie." In fact, purposeful, intelligent women who were neither pretty nor named Marx were frequently the subject of misogynistic abuse by Engels. There are numerous comments in Engels's letters showing his abhorrence for "affected, 'eddicated' Berlin ladies."[119] He particularly disliked middle-aged female intellectuals, so the secularist, feminist theosophist Annie Besant was "Mother Besant," the journalist and war correspondent Emily Crawford "Mother Crawford," the activist and sexual-health campaigner Gertrud Guillaume-Schack "Mother Schack." He was highly dismissive of the campaign for female suffrage ("these little madams, who clamour for women's rights") and regarded the cause as a distraction behind which class rule would flourish.[120] "Those Englishwomen who championed a women's formal right to allow themselves to be as thoroughly exploited by capitalists as men are have, for the most part, a direct or indirect interest in the capitalist exploitation of both sexes," he wrote to Mother Schack, explaining that he was focused more on the coming generation than on formal equality among the existing one.[121] Yet when, in 1876, a female candidate bounced up the steps of No. 122 Regent's Park Road seeking Engels's vote for the London school board elections (which women were eligible to stand for following the 1870 Education Act), he couldn't help but give her all his seven votes. "As a result, she had more votes than any of the other seven candidates for election. Incidentally, the ladies who sit on school boards here are notable for the fact that they do very little talking and a great deal of working—as much on average as three men."[122]

After five years of arduous hand-to-hand combat with Marx's manuscripts, with his eyes fading and his rheumatic legs going, Engels finally rewarded himself with a holiday. Even into his old age, he enjoyed the prospect of travel; indeed, new people, ideas, and places were the secret to Engels's energy. In 1888 the United States of America promised all three. What was more, an American edition of *The Condition of the Working Class in England* had appeared in 1886 and, after suffering decades of egregious exploitation, the American working class seemed to be evolving toward class consciousness. "At this very moment I am receiving the American papers with accounts of the great strike of 12,000 Pennsylvanian coal-miners in the Connellsville district," Engels wrote in the appendix to the American edition of *The Condition*, "and I seem but to read my own description of the North of England colliers' strike of 1844."[123]

Mark Twain famously christened this period the Gilded Age, an epoch of robber barons and an urban proletariat, of vast wealth and stunning inequality. The industrial might of the Vanderbilts, Morgans, Dukes, and Carnegies (who would become champions of Herbert Spencer's social Darwinism) existed alongside workplace unrest and the first stirrings of socialism. In 1886, the year of the "great upheaval," over 700,000 workers went on strike or faced employer lock-outs, as disputes over wage cuts, mechanization, and de-skilling intensified.[124] In Chicago, some 90,000 workers marched through the streets in the first May Day rally brought together by the Federation of Organized Trades and Labor

Unions (soon renamed the American Federation of Labor)—a show of strength that turned to tragedy three days later with the Haymarket Square massacre, in which police opened fire on demonstrators after an anarchist bomb was thrown. In contrast to the quiescence of Britain's working class, the "American vigor" of the U.S. labor movement was highly encouraging to Engels: "The last Bourgeois Paradise on earth is fast changing into a Purgatory, and can only be prevented from becoming, like Europe, an Inferno by the go-ahead pace at which the development of the newly fledged proletariat of America will take place," he wrote to his U.S. translator, Florence Kelley Wischnewetzky. "I only wish Marx could have lived to see it!"[125]

There were, of course, some problems with the U.S. situation—not least an unfortunate lack of ideological rigor. "Theoretical ignorance is an attribute of all young nations," Engels placidly observed. But with youth also came a welcome absence of the cultural and intellectual preconceptions that made European socialism so sclerotic. America was notable for its "purely bourgeois institutions unleavened by feudal remnants or monarchical traditions, and without a permanent and hereditary proletariat."[126] As such, it offered a clean slate, an open space in which bourgeois hegemony could quickly be followed by a proletarian revolution. On this "more favoured soil," the organized working class had managed to achieve in months the sort of political and electoral advances their European counterparts took years to accomplish. Frustratingly, such progress risked being undone by the all too familiar split within the progressive movement. After the May Day riots, the Federation of Organized Trades and Labor Unions retreated to "business" unionism, that is, to narrowly guarding the interests of its members rather than opposing the capitalist order. Those workers who were more politically active were divided between a Socialist Labor Party, controlled for the most part by German émigrés, and the Noble and Holy Order of the Knights of Labor, a guildlike fraternal order founded in 1869 by Philadelphia garment workers and open to all "producers" (except bartenders and lawyers). At an earlier period in his life, Engels would have dismissed the Knights—with their plans for cooperatives and working-class mutuals—as dreamy, Proudhonist, and petit bourgeois.

Now, however, the politically astute Communist elder thought them "the unavoidable starting point" for U.S. proletarian politics. By contrast, the Socialist Labor Party, though highly orthodox in its Marxian philosophy, displayed the classic faults of an overintellectualized émigré circle: too much idealist philosophy and not enough practical politics.

Engels was eager to see it all for himself, so on 8 August 1888 he set out for New York. Accompanying him aboard the *City of Berlin* were Carl Schorlemmer, Eleanor Marx, and her lover, Edward Aveling. Tussy recalled the sixty-eight-year-old Engels as in high spirits aboard the steamer, "always ready in any weather to go for a walk on deck and have a glass of lager. It seemed to be one of his unshakeable principles never to go round an obstacle but always to jump or climb over it."[127] Yet when they reached America, Engels had no desire to address socialist congresses, rally the proletarian troops, tour Pittsburgh railroads, or visit Pennsylvania steel mills. Instead, in an echo of his 1849 walking tour, Engels opted to act the tourist, traveling incognito on a monthlong journey from New York to Boston, on to Niagara Falls, and then to Canada and Lake Ontario.

Engels's journal of the trip sounds the familiar European refrain about the speed and bustle of U.S. life—"An American cannot bear the idea of anyone walking in front of him in the street, he must push and brush past him"—but also displays his surprise at the aesthetics of late-nineteenth-century America. "Don't you believe that America is a new country—it is the most old-fashioned place in the world," he reported back to Laura Lafargue.[128] The cabs and carriages they endured along the eastern seaboard could have come from the seventeenth century, while the decor of the houses and hotel rooms they stayed in were remarkable for their faux Old World vogue: "everywhere, the chairs, tables and cupboards mostly look like the heirlooms of past generations."[129]

The people were a different matter. Whether because of his own background in trade or because he had spent so much of his life in thrusting, bartering, entrepreneurial Manchester, Engels could not help but admire the unapologetic vitality and social mobility of the U.S. immigrant ethos. And no one embodied this aspiration more than his nephew, Pumps's brother Willie Burns, starting out on a new life in Boston after emigrating from Lancashire. In contrast to the hopeless Percy, Burns was "a wonderful fellow, bright, energetic and with his heart and soul in the movement. He is doing well, works for the Boston & Providence Railroad (now the Old Colony), gets $12 a week, has a nice wife (whom he brought with him from Manchester) and three children." In the land of the free, unencumbered by class prejudice and feudal remnants, "nothing would induce him to return to England; he's just the lad for a country like America."[130]

For Engels the urbanist, the high point of his tour was not "very pretty" Cambridge, Massachusetts, or "beautiful, elegant" Concord (where he enjoyed a prison visit) but the "grandest site for the capital of Capitalist Production you can see"—New York City. Like many Marxists after him, Engels found in America the ne plus ultra of the late capitalist form. While Max Horkheimer, Theodor Adorno, and Herbert Marcuse would discover it along the freeways of Los Angeles and on the campuses of Southern California, in the 1880s it was the East Coast that seemed to point to capitalism's future.[131] "We got into New York after dark and I thought I got into a chapter of Dante's *Inferno*," Engels began his account to Laura Lafargue somewhat predictably, before describing his wonderment at the "elevated railways thundering over your head, tram-cars by the hundred with rattling bells, awful noises on all sides." In 1840s Manchester, it was the mills, factories, and Oxford Road slums that expressed the capitalist urban essence; in 1880s New York, it was the manipulated mass culture and the technological spectacle of the modern city. Manhattan was, in the later idiom of Walter Benjamin, a dream world of high-bourgeois consumer commodification. "Naked electric arc-lights over every ship," Engels noted, "not to light you but to attract you as an advertisement, and consequently blinding you and confusing everything before you." New York was, in short, "a town worthy to be inhabited by the most vile-looking crowd in the world, they all look like discharged croupiers from Monte Carlo."[132]

Despite these revealingly English reservations about the vulgarity of New Yorkers, Engels enormously enjoyed his trip across the Atlantic. The clean air, the go-ahead Yankees, the first-rate food, and the widespread availability of German beer convinced him he would return.

"The voyage has done me a tremendous amount of good," he wrote to his brother Hermann on the steamer back, enjoying its supply of Californian Riesling. "I feel at least five years younger, all my little infirmities have faded into the background, even my eyes have improved."[133] He came back to London physically invigorated and politically exhilarated about the prospects of proletarian revolution. Back with Nim in Regent's Park Road, he was now ready to put aside the science and philosophy of the last decade, to embrace again the dirty business of politics and make Marx's ideas matter on the street. In the 1890s, the septuagenarian Engels returned full time to the workers' struggle—which, to his great joy, had finally reached the British proletariat. Some fifty years after crossing the Channel to sniff out the scent of revolution, he sensed that England was at last ready to rise.

FIRST FIDDLE AT LAST

"On 4th May, 1890, the English proletariat, rousing itself from forty years of hibernation, rejoined the movement of its class."[1] On London's inaugural May Day march—an event later to be subsumed into the Soviet calendar of military parades and Red Square hardware—the capital witnessed a bravura display of socialist prowess, with workers and activists gathering at dawn along the Victoria Embankment. Leading the procession were the dock laborers and gasworkers of the East End, followed by the ranks of the Women's Trade Union League, the Bloomsbury Socialist Society, the North Camberwell Progressive Club, the East Finsbury Radical Club, the West Newington Reform Club, and a myriad of trade unions. Accompanying them on their procession to Marble Arch through the heart of commercial London were councillors, parliamentarians, school board members, and such stars of the socialist firmament as playwright George Bernard Shaw, the Socialist MP Robert Cunninghame Graham, the gasworkers' leader Will Thorne, a young George Lansbury, and Engels himself. For a brief, delirious day the center of empire was under the sway of the radical left.

By the time the procession entered Hyde Park—the once fashionable parade ground of London high society, transformed during the nineteenth century into the "Park of the People"—it had swelled to over

200,000, with radical banners and placards dotting the horizon. "I was on platform 4 (a heavy goods wagon)," Engels recalled, "and could only see part—a fifth, say, or an eighth—of the crowd, but it was one vast sea of faces, as far as the eye could reach." Inevitably, there were personal rivalries, factional disputes, and the usual lack of fraternal feeling within the socialist hierarchy. But for Engels the rally heralded the reemergence of the English working classes, who, after the collapse of the mid-Victorian boom, had finally shed their liberal confusion and rediscovered their Chartist, socialist inheritance. "What wouldn't I give for Marx to have witnessed this awakening, he who, on this self-same English soil, was alive to the minutest symptom!" he wrote wistfully to August Bebel. For the first time in almost half a century, Engels heard the voice of the British proletariat ring out, and it did him a power of good. "I carried my head a couple of inches higher as I climbed down from the old goods wagon."[2]

Just as remarkable as the crowds was Engels's presence at Hyde Park. The steely operator who had functioned so long in the shadow of Marx, who had kept a low public profile since 1840s Paris, was reemerging in his own right. "Only now did he, who so far, to use his own words, had been second fiddle, show all he was capable of," recalled Wilhelm Liebknecht. As an adviser, exhorter, and mentor in the struggles of the international working-class movement, "he showed that he could play first fiddle too." "At every difficulty that we who work in the vineyard of our master, the people, come across, we go to Engels," wrote his devoted Tussy in 1890. "And never do we appeal to him in vain. The work this single man has done in recent years would have been too much for a dozen ordinary men."[3] As May Days were commemorated across the Continent and Marxism was adopted as the official ideology of an ever-greater number of socialist parties—from Austria to Spain, Russia to America, and now, gratifyingly, England—Engels's decrees (typically prefaced by the lament "if only Marx were alive today") acquired more and more weight. The grand lama of Regent's Park Road spent his final years energetically grappling with the intellectual and organizational issues confronting socialism, from the continued vitality of capitalism to the political challenge of welfarist social democracy to the suffrage strategy of mass workers' parties. In the face of rapidly shifting political terrain, Engels revealed himself a surprisingly supple tactician, rarely ashamed to rethink his approach or to question sacred tenets.

From the practical to the philosophical, in his ebbing days the General always stood ready to assist the cause. His unrelenting love of life was accompanied by a conviction that history was on his side, that the forward march of socialism was more realizable than ever before. He was determined to last just a few years longer, to "take a peek into the new century" and witness the Marxist triumph he had made his life's work.

"We are all socialists now," was the insouciant response of liberal statesman Sir William Harcourt to the changing political weather of late 1880s Britain. The once unshakable ideological tenets of the mid-Victorian era—individualism, laissez-faire, self-help, evangelical certitude—were starting to crumble in the face of a growing desire for ameliorative state action. In Birmingham, Glasgow, and London, local councils were experimenting with radical programs of municipal socialism involving the extension of city government into the provision of utilities, transport, and even leisure; in Oxford, the English idealist philosopher T. H. Green was reviving Hegel to offer a new philosophy of progressive state intervention laying the intellectual foundations of new liberalism; Henry George's seminal text, *Progress and Poverty* (1879), with its powerful demand for land reform, was making waves across England and Ireland; and in Bloomsbury drawing rooms, Sheffield halls of science, and East End radical clubs, socialist ideas of equality and class consciousness were being debated with enthusiasm for the first time in forty years. From Engels's viewpoint, these stirrings in the nation that had given birth to the Industrial Revolution and nurtured the first proletariat were long overdue.

Ten years earlier, at the start of the 1880s, he had optimistically thought socialism was on the verge of revival and agreed to contribute a series of articles to the trade unionist paper the *Labour Standard*. Through the summer of 1881, Engels slogged away, encouraging the trade unions to mobilize their members, drop their parochial, guildlike mentality, and confront the exploitative capitalist class. "There are plenty of symptoms that the working class of this country is awakening to the consciousness that it has for some time been moving in the wrong groove," he wrote, urging the union barons to forgo demands for higher wages and shorter hours and concentrate on "the wages systems itself."[4] But it did no good. "I do not see any progress," he complained in a resignation letter to the paper's editor, George Shipton, in August 1881.[5] To Engels's frustration, the engrained pusillanimity of the English proletariat was proving more intractable than ever. "For five whole months I tried, through *The Labour Standard*, for which I wrote leading articles, to pick up the threads of the old Chartist movement and disseminate our ideas so as to see whether this might evoke some response," he explained to his '48 comrade Johann Philipp Becker. The result? "Absolutely nothing."[6] The unfortunate truth, Engels concluded, was that so long as the English working class continued to share in the fruits of the British Empire's industrial monopoly there was no hope of socialism. They were getting rich off colonial hegemony and, seeing little reason to upset such a profitable arrangement, had auctioned themselves off to the Liberal Party. Only the demise of Britain's commercial advantage in the face of American competition and a sustained period of impoverishment could possibly spur the workers to action. "On no account whatever allow yourself to be bamboozled into believing that a real proletarian movement is afoot here," Engels complained to Bebel in 1883. "Participation in the domination of the world market was and is the economic basis of the English workers' political nullity."[7]

To Engels's great amazement—and disappointment—the revival of English socialism, when it happened, was not the result of a grand socioeconomic climacteric. On the contrary, it was highly intellectual, even spiritual, in origin and led by annoyingly middle-class thinkers. "Needless to say that today there is indeed 'Socialism again in England,' and plenty of it," Engels wrote in 1892 in a new introduction to *The Condition of the Working Class in England*. "Socialism of all shades; Socialism conscious and unconscious, Socialism prosaic and poetic, Socialism of the working class and of the middle class, for, verily, that abomination of abominations, Socialism, has not only become respectable, but has actually donned evening dress and lounges lazily on drawing-room *causeuses*."[8] Henry Hyndman's account of a day of socialist action makes it clear that such criticisms were cringingly correct: "It was a curious scene, Morris in his soft hat and blue suit, Champion, Frost and Joynes in the morning garments of the well-to-do, several working-men comrades, and I myself wearing the frock-coat in which Shaw said I was born, with a tall hat and good gloves, all earnestly engaged in selling a penny Socialist paper during the busiest time of the day in London's busiest thoroughfare."[9] The pioneers of 1890s English socialism were a class apart from those they hoped to emancipate. There was the Christian, or "sacramental," socialist grouping around Stewart Headlam's Guild of St. Matthew; Edward Carpenter's Millthorpe commune of New Lifers, manly comradeship, and Eastern mysticism; Thomas Davidson's vaguely Owenite Fellowship of the New Life (which would, in turn, sprout the Fabian Society); and an eclectic range of other societies, from the East End–based Labor Emancipation League to the Land Reform Union to the National Secular Society. What drew all these Bohemian radicals and angst-ridden bourgeois toward socialism, according to the Fabian grande dame Beatrice Webb, was "a consciousness of sin, . . . a growing uneasiness, amounting to conviction, that the industrial organisation, which had yielded rent, interest, and profits on a stupendous scale, had failed to provide a decent livelihood and tolerable conditions for a majority of the inhabitants of Great Britain."[10] For numerous other English socialists, it was a spiritual conveyor belt from Nonconformity to secularism and then to a religion of humanity built upon an ethical notion of socialism and fellowship. Few had read *Das Kapital*, their political connections with Continental communism were minimal, and their grasp of dialectical materialism was abysmal. Just one among the English socialists could honestly count himself a convinced Marxist—the tall-hatted and good-gloved Hyndman, founder of the most influential socialist sect in 1880s London, the Social Democratic Federation (SDF). There was only one problem: Engels couldn't stand him.

Henry Mayers Hyndman, the son of a West India merchant, had trained for the bar, tried his hand at journalism, and, in the end, married well. His epiphany came in 1880, when he read *Das Kapital* in French and introduced himself to Karl Marx, "the Aristotle of the nineteenth century." He quickly became a persistent and, in Engels's view, tiresome presence at Maitland Park. Hyndman always claimed it was his intimate friendship with Marx that antagonized the resentful Engels, driving him "to break down what he thought might be a rival influence to his own." As was so often the case with the upper reaches of socialist politics, much came down to personalities. Hyndman dismissed the Marx-Engels relationship as built on the financial dependence of the former on the latter, with the "exacting, suspicious, jealous" Engels demanding (in Hyndman's well-turned play on *Das Kapital*) "the exchange value of his ready cash" in friendship. "Mrs Marx could not bear to think of it," Hyndman wrote in his autobiography. "She spoke of him [Engels] to my wife more than once as Karl Marx's 'evil genius' and wished that she could relieve her husband from any dependence upon this able and loyal but scarcely sympathetic coadjutor."[11] And Hyndman didn't reserve these views for posterity. He repeatedly used his SDF paper, *Justice*, to attack Engels and his "Marxist clique" for failing to support him, the SDF, and a unified socialist party in Britain. "Engels has a perfect genius for overthrowing good understanding and for setting men by the ears," he railed. "If there were nobody else to intrigue and plot against, he would intrigue and plot against himself."[12]

While Engels did have a proprietary attitude toward his friendships, his dislike of Hyndman had more substantial roots. Both he and Marx were infuriated by Hyndman's shameless plagiarism of *Das Kapital* for his communist credo, *England for All* (1881). More than that, Engels thought that behind Hyndman's socialist veneer lurked an old-fashioned Tory whose instinct was to play upon the jingoist and populist sentiments that were never far beneath the surface of English working-class politics. "Hyndman is shrewd and a good business man, but superficial and STOCK-JOHN-BULL," Engels confided to Kautsky. "Moreover his ambition far outruns his talents and achievements."[13] Never entirely at ease with the masses, Hyndman ran the SDF with a combination of imperiousness and rigid Marxist orthodoxy. Indeed, the strictures he imposed were too much even for Engels. "The SDF is in fact a sect pure and simple," the suddenly pluralist Engels told Kautsky. "It has ossified Marxism into a hard and fast dogma" and was in danger of repelling prospective supporters.[14] Worst of all was Hyndman's demagogic vanity, which Engels thought dangerously on display when Hyndman, John Burns, and their wealthy backer H. H. Champion led a rally in February 1886 through Pall Mall and Piccadilly that sparked an afternoon of rioting by eight thousand unemployed East Enders happy to tear up the West End for the day. "What has been achieved is to equate socialism with looting in the minds of the bourgeois public and, while this may not have made matters much worse, it has certainly got us no further," was Engels's sour judgement of "Bloody Monday."[15] Everything pointed to the fundamental problem with the SDF and its executive of socialist charlatans: they were "determined to conjure up overnight a movement which, here as elsewhere, necessarily calls for years of work."[16] No one in Britain seemed capable of the kind of steady organizational and ideological slog that Liebknecht and Kautsky were undertaking in Germany and Lafargue and Guesde were pursuing in France.

So Engels was delighted when, in 1884, Edward Aveling and William Morris split from the SDF to establish a rival Socialist League. He instantly summoned them to Regent's Park Road for a quick primer on party management, discipline, and propaganda. This tutorial resulted in the creation of Morris's elegant journal, *Commonweal*, and the establishment of a network of Socialist League branches that siphoned off disgruntled SDF members. The relationship between Morris and Engels, however, was never going to be easy. The aesthetically minded Morris rarely disguised his lack of interest in the rational, technical precepts of scientific socialism. "To speak frankly, I do not know what Marx's Theory of Value is, and I'm damned if I want to know," he explained to one public meeting. "It is enough political economy for me to know that the idle rich class is rich and the working-class is poor, and that the rich are rich because they rob the poor."[17] His utopian tract *News from Nowhere* advocated a return to the preindustrial past, complete with medieval garb and craft guilds; London would be rid of industry altogether and the houses of Parliament turned into a dung heap. Morris's vision was diametrically opposed to Engels's belief that the communist future depended upon the kind of technological advances and widespread prosperity produced by the Industrial Revolution. Unsurprisingly, Engels was initially wont to dismiss Morris as "a very rich but politically inept art lover." Their friendship warmed briefly after the split from the SDF and the discovery of a shared interest in Old Norse mythology, but as soon as Morris started to flirt with anarchism, Engels excommunicated him as "a sentimental dreamer pure and simple." Engels feared it would take an exhaustive course of biweekly seminars to teach Morris about socialism, "but who has the time to do it, and if you drop him for a month, he is sure to lose himself again. And is he worth all that trouble even if one had the time?"[18]

At least Morris, in his misguided way, was pulling in the right direction, with its emphasis on the value of labor and the alienating effects of capitalism—unlike the Fabians. George Bernard Shaw, Sidney Webb, Sydney Olivier, Annie Besant, Frank Podmore, and the rest of this group committed two cardinal crimes in Engels's eyes: they dared to criticize Marx's economics and they were suspiciously "eddicated," middle-class types—"a dilettante lot of egregiously conceited mutual admirers who soar above such ignorant people as Marx," as he petulantly put it to Laura Lafargue.[19] Engels was willing to give the Fabian Society some credit for its reorientation of the London County Council in a more socialist direction—with its municipalization of essential services, public works policy, and attack upon the commercial City interests—but he regarded it in the main as an unhelpful wing of the welfarist Liberal Party, whose gradualist strategy of political permeation was an exercise in class futility. While these objections all had an element of truth, such high-handed dismissiveness, along with the contempt meted out to Hyndman and Morris, would have been more credible if Engels had had his own candidate—someone of skill and industry, with a popular following—ready to lead the socialist movement. He did not. Instead, out of a misplaced sense of loyalty to the Marx clan, Engels decided to promote for leadership one of the most reviled and distrusted characters in British socialism.

• • •

"I must give you some other news. . . . You must have known, I fancy, for some time that I am very fond of Edward Aveling—and he says he is fond of me—so we are going to 'set up' together. . . . I need not say that this resolution has been an easy one for me to arrive at. But I think it is for the best. . . . Do not misjudge us—He is very good—and you must not think too badly of either of us. Engels, as always, is all that is good." Such was the roundabout way in which Tussy informed her sister Laura of her "marriage" to Edward Bibbins Aveling in 1884. The fourth son of a Congregationalist minister, Aveling had enjoyed a stellar career as a scientist, with a fellowship at University College London and a lecture-ship in comparative anatomy, until his vocal secularism cost him his tenure. In the early 1880s, he relaunched himself as "the people's Dar-win," using the public platform of the National Secular Society, an advo-cacy group to bring a broad, mostly working-class audience to atheism and Darwinian thought. He transcribed his lectures and courses into a series of popular, easily understandable penny tracts such as *The Stu-dent's Darwin* and *Darwin Made Easy*.[20] Aveling's subsequent journey toward Marxism began in 1884 after his growing involvement with Lon-don school board politics brought him in contact with Hyndman and the SDF, and he quickly revealed himself to be a gifted, intelligent, in-dustrious, and conscientious servant to the socialist cause. Unfortu-nately, he was also a dissolute wretch. Hyndman thought him "a man of very bad character," Kautsky "an evil creature," and even the normally generous Bernstein "a despicable rogue."[21] For George Bernard Shaw, Aveling was "one of the several models who sat unconsciously for Dube-dat," the unattractive antihero for his play *The Doctor's Dilemma*. Ave-ling, he recalled, was "morbidly scrupulous as to his religious and political convictions and would have gone to the gallows sooner than recant a syllable of them. But he had absolutely no conscience about money and women."[22] This was obvious in Aveling's relations with Tussy, with whom he eloped in 1884 despite still being legally wed to an Isabel Campbell Frank, daughter of a highly prosperous poulterer, whom he never offi-cially divorced. For Engels, such bourgeois foibles were of little concern. "The fact is that Aveling has a lawful wife whom he cannot get rid of *de jure* although he has for years been rid of her *de facto*," he briskly

explained to the skeptical Eduard Bernstein, after having blessed the
union and given the happy couple £50 for a honeymoon in the Peak District.[23] But Aveling did not have nearly so kind a heart as Engels. In succeeding years, he would torment Tussy with serial infidelities, humiliate
her (after Campbell Frank's death in 1892) with a *de jure* marriage to an
actress, and ultimately play a role in her suicide. That said, there was
some good in Aveling: in the early years, he encouraged Tussy in her political activism, supported her writing, and gave her a degree of emotional fulfillment she had been lacking since the death of her father.

From the start, both Tussy and Engels had to put up with Aveling's
accumulating debts and embarrassing financial irregularities. Soon after Aveling left the National Secular Society, his old boss, Charles Brad-
laugh, accused him of misappropriating the society's funds. While the
allegation could be put down to political rivalry, the next set of charges
was altogether more damaging. "Aveling's Unpaid Labour: The Socialists
Are Disgusted and Say So about His Exorbitant Bill," was the *New York
Herald* headline following the Socialist Labor Party's investigation of
nearly $1,600 in expenses that Aveling and Tussy had run up during
their 1886 U.S. speaking tour (equivalent to roughly $35,000 in today's
money). "The enterprising socialist lecturers went to study poverty at a
first class hotel in Baltimore, and patronized the wine cellar so liberally
that their bill for two days amounted to $42," the paper noted in a well-
sourced demolition job.[24] The nub of the case was that Aveling had tried
to sneak in the charges for Tussy's trip when the American socialists had
agreed to pay only for his own expenses. In fact, the allegations and media leaks (which the British press gleefully recycled) were mainly driven
by deeper ideological differences within the U.S. socialist movement,
with the Aveling scandal just a surface manifestation. Engels was having
none of it. In a sharp letter to his American translator and a prominent
SLP functionary, Florence Kelley Wischnewetzky, he grimly declared,
"Woe be to the man who, being of bourgeois origin or superior education, goes into the movement and is rash enough to enter into money
relations with the working-class element." He then laid out a line of reasoning that he would maintain over the coming years: "I have inherited
from Marx the obligation to stand by his children as he would have done

himself, and to see, so far as lies in my power, that they are not wronged."[25] Aveling was now a protected member of the family firm, so he was repeatedly shielded from criticism by a grievously indulgent Engels. When money went missing or a check bounced or a contract was reneged on (as was invariably the case), Engels would airily dismiss the dereliction as "the slapdash literary Bohemian in Aveling."[26] Marx would most likely have cut Aveling loose as an embarrassment to the cause, but Engels stuck with him out of clan loyalty and a secret admiration for his rakish, arrogant demeanor. He described him affectionately to his American friend Friedrich Sorge as a "very talented and serviceable sort of chap and thoroughly honest, but gushing as a flapper, with a perpetual itch to do something silly. Well, I can still recall the time when I was much the same kind of idiot."[27]

Above all, Engels endorsed Aveling's ideological outlook and political strategy. Although Aveling did a poor job of helping Sam Moore with the translation of *Das Kapital*, Engels respected him as an effective and appropriately scientific popularizer of Marxism for the English market. To Aveling's mind, Marx and Darwin shared not only physical and moral attributes—"The physical presence of each was commanding. . . . In moral character the two men were alike. . . . The nature of each was beautiful, kindling affection in, and giving affection to, all that was worthy"—but also methodology. "That which Darwin did for Biology, Marx has done for Economics. Each of them by long and patient observation, experiment, recordal, reflection, arrived at an immense generalisation, a generalisation the likes of which their particular branch of science had never seen." In language that Engels could only have approved, Aveling outlined in *The Student's Marx* (1891) the scientific nature of Marx's breakthrough: "Electricity now has its ohms, its farads, its amperes; chemistry had its periodic law; the physiologists are reducing the bodily functions to equations; and the fact that Marx could express many of his generalisations in Political Economy in mathematical terms is so much evidence that he had carried that science further than his predecessors."[28]

And there was more to Aveling than just talk. Using his background in the street propaganda of the National Secular Society—with its

open-air meetings and earnest lectures in workingmen's clubs—he got ·
to work with Tussy, trying to build up an independent, properly proletarian workers' party in the godless slums of "outcast London." East of
Aldgate Pump, a long way from Primrose Hill, in the alleys and rookeries of Whitechapel, Bethnal Green, Mile End, and Hoxton, lay the hidden poverty of Victorian London: a landscape peopled in the popular
imagination by a residuum of Jews, dockers, Negresses, and "rough" ne'er-
do-wells whose threat was symbolized by the unnatural crimes of Jack
the Ripper. Here was the dark source of London's immorality, drunkenness, and depravity, a eugenic bog rising up from the Hackney marshes,
best sealed off from the rest of the capital and forgotten. But to Tussy, the
poverty of these cold, hungry streets was replete with political promise.
That promise came nearer on 13 November, when the hunger-stricken
East End once again marched on the plutocratic West End. London's
metropolitan commissioner, Sir Charles Warren, promptly unleashed
his troops on the hundred thousand demonstrators, with William Morris, Annie Besant, John Burns, Edward Carpenter, Tussy, and Aveling
among them. Tussy turned up at Regent's Park Road afterwards, as Engels relayed it to Paul Lafargue, "her coat in tatters, her hat crushed and
torn by a blow from a staff, having been arrested by bobbies but released
on the orders of an inspector." Although Engels had some tactical criticisms of confronting mounted police in Trafalgar Square ("being the
place most favourable to the government . . . with barracks close by and
with St James's Park—in which to muster reserves of troops—a stone's
throw away from the field of battle"), the unwarranted violence of this
"Bloody Sunday" dramatically energized the East End, where for months
the socialists had been fruitlessly preaching in radical clubs and pubs.[29]

What kept the political momentum going was the unexpected, long
overdue, but very welcome intervention of organized labor. In the spring
of 1889, Will Thorne, a socialist stoker at the Beckton gasworks, started
to unite his fellow workers into a National Union of Gasworkers and
General Labourers in an attempt to improve the site's appalling terms
and conditions. Using a constitution drawn up with the help of Tussy
and Aveling, the union signed up some twenty thousand members
within four months and Thorne secured a cut in the basic working day

from twelve hours to eight. In the tightly knit communities of working-class East London, there was a long tradition of gasworkers doubling as dock laborers, and Thorne's success in winning concessions from the gasworks increased the pressure on the reactionary dock corporations. In the 1890s, ten miles of docklands—from West India Docks to St. Katherine's Dock to Millwall Dock to Victoria Dock—stretched along the wide eastern estuary of the Thames, with nearly thirty thousand men employed in the vast complex of warehouses, wharves, basins, and jetties that made London the "emporium of the world." Conditions there were among the most brutal in Britain, as the great London chronicler Henry Mayhew discovered one October morning: "The scuffling and scrambling, and stretching forth of countless hands high in the air, to catch the eye of him whose voice may give them work. . . . It is a sight to sadden the most callous, to see *thousands* of men struggling for only one day's hire, the scuffle being made the fiercer by the knowledge that hundreds out of the number there assembled must be left to idle the day out in want."[30] Ben Tillett, the secretary of the small Tea Operatives' Union, soon found himself besieged by men insisting he follow Thorne's lead and confront the dock owners. But his demands for an increase in wages from four pence to six pence an hour, with eight pence for overtime and a minimum employment period of half a day, were rejected out of hand by the dock bosses. They remained confident that the East End's vast reserve army of labor would always undermine worker solidarity. Together with the socialist activists Tom Mann and John Burns (and supported by Aveling and Tussy in the background), Tillett proved them wrong, founding the Dock, Wharf, Riverside and General Labourers' Union of Great Britain and Ireland in 1889. The dock laborers' leaders then mounted a disciplined monthlong strike of almost sixty thousand men and launched a powerful public relations offensive that included open-air meetings in Tower Hill, dignified marches through the City of London, and a well-run relief fund. Whether it was this specter of politicized labor, or the calming intervention of Cardinal Henry Edward Manning, or the arrival of £30,000 in strike support funds from the Australian dockers, in the end the wharf bosses yielded to Burns's demand for "the full round orb of the docker's tanner."

Reading the reports of the strike in the London papers, Engels was ecstatic. "The dock strike has been won. It's the greatest event to have taken place in England since the last Reform Bills and marks the beginning of a complete revolution in the East End," he wrote to Karl Kautsky in September 1889.[31] "Hitherto the East End had been in a state of poverty-stricken stagnation, its hallmark being the apathy of men whose spirit had been broken by hunger, and who had abandoned all hope. . . . Then, last year, there came the victorious strike of the [Bryant & May] match-girls. And now, this gigantic strike of the most demoralized elements of the lot, the dock labourers," he told Bernstein.[32] What was so encouraging about the dock laborers' protest, he explained in the *Labour Leader*, was that even the lumpen proletariat now appeared ready to rise: "If Marx had lived to witness this! If these poor down-trodden men, the dregs of the proletariat, these odds and ends of all trades, fighting every morning at the dock gates for an engagement, if they can combine, and terrify by their resolution the mighty Dock Companies, truly then we need not despair of any section of the working class."[33] The dock laborers' and gasworkers' trade unions were symbolic of a tectonic shift in labor politics: the challenge by a new generation of trade unions, with their belief in class solidarity and socialist ideology, to the guildlike conservatism of the old craft unions. "These new trade unions of unskilled men and women are totally different from the old organizations of the working-class aristocracy and cannot fall into the same conservative ways," Engels told Laura, recounting with almost paternal pride Tussy's heroic role in radicalizing the East End.[34] These, then, were Engels's people—not the SDF demagogues or the Fabian beard strokers but the East End activists, trade unionists, and socialists. It was they, he hoped, who would lead a British socialist workers' party along the German model. As a public signal of approbation, Engels invited the trade union leaders into his home at Regent's Park Road. "Of the English, William Thorne was the most welcome visitor of those outside the family circle," remembered Edward Aveling. "For him Engels had the very greatest admiration, respect, and affection; of his character, and his value to the movement, the very highest opinion."[35] Engels also compared John Burns favorably to Oliver Cromwell. The union leaders, in turn, honored him, the grand old man of European socialism, with pride of place on their May Day platform.

In the event, leadership of the British labor movement fell not to Aveling, Thorne, or Burns but to the prickly, teetotaling Nonconformist ex-miner Keir Hardie. Explicitly opposed to "the State Socialists of the German type," Hardie promoted a socialism that was, in the words of his biographer, Kenneth O. Morgan, a "fundamentally ethical vision of justice and equality" owing more to the Puritan "good old cause" than to Marxian communism. His vehicle was the Independent Labour Party, which emerged from the Trade Unions Congress in the early 1890s and had much more of a generally liberal feel to it than any specifically socialist intent. Nonetheless, it seemed the only credible national political grouping dedicated to workers' interests, and Engels gave it the benefit of the doubt. "Since the *bulk* of its members are undoubtedly first class, since its centre of gravity lies in the provinces rather than in that hive of intrigue, London, and its programme is substantially the same as our own, Aveling did right in joining it and in accepting a position on the Executive," Engels told Sorge in January 1893.[36] But within a matter of weeks, as a result of some mischievous disinformation from Aveling, Engels had turned against Hardie, accusing him of demagogic ambitions, collaboration with the Tories, and financial irregularities. By January 1895, Engels had grown altogether impatient of the ILP and was dismissing Hardie as "a cunning, crafty Scot, a Pecksniff and arch-intriguer, but too cunning, perhaps, and too vain."[37] Hardie himself was oblivious to this withdrawal of favor; after Engels's death, he wrote warmly of his Regent's Park Road chats and remained adamant that both Engels and Marx would have endorsed the political development of the ILP.[38] The truth is that, by this time, Engels was out of touch with much that was going on in British socialism, largely as a result of his continuing dependence on Aveling. It is difficult to overemphasize the widespread distrust, even loathing, that so many in the British socialist camp felt toward Aveling, whom they regarded as a man on the make and whose highly immoral personal comportment, they felt, was damaging to their political cause and offensive to their working-class Puritan morality. Resentful of Engels's attempts to "foist" Aveling "as a leader upon the English Socialist and Labour movement," activists started to shun Regent's Park Road, and Engels's personal influence over the political direction and ideology of English socialism markedly diminished.[39] "Why was there no Marxism in Great Britain?" has been a long-standing academic conundrum and, if by no means the determining reason, Engels's misguided allegiance to Aveling certainly contributed to the lack of a unified Marxist party.[40] It was a rare political misjudgment, driven by an abiding sense of loyalty to the Marx clan.

The Continental socialist movement posed a different set of problems for Engels. "I have to follow the movement in 5 large and a lot of small European countries and the U.S. America," he grumbled to Laura Lafargue in 1894. "For that purpose I receive 3 German, 2 English, 1 Italian dailies and from January 1 the Vienna daily, 7 in all. Of weeklies I receive 2 from Germany, 7 Austria, 1 France, 3 America (2 English, 1 German), 2 Italian, and 1 each in Polish, Bulgarian, Spanish and Bohemian, 3 of which in languages I am still gradually acquiring."[41] In addition, there was a bottomless postbag of international correspondence and "calls from the most varied sorts of people." Well into the 1890s, Regent's Park Road remained the center of international socialism, host to a growing number of exiles, Russian disciples, and, even in 1893, an Anglo-Franco-German socialist summit attended by August Bebel, Paul Lafargue, and John Burns. The Primrose Hill comings and goings had intensified in mid-1888, when the entire editorial team of *Der Sozialdemokrat*—Eduard Bernstein, Julius Motteller, Leonard Tauscher, and Hermann Schlüter—moved from Zurich to London and settled on the other side of the tracks in Kentish Town and Tufnell Park. Naturally, every Sunday they trekked across North London to join Engels's table for an afternoon of Pilsener, political gossip, and scientific socialism. Presiding over it all was Marx's old housemaid, Nim, who ordered Engels's life with loving firmness, hiring and firing staff, sitting at the head of the Sunday table, and providing Engels with the domestic freedom to pursue his political and philosophical projects. A lovely insight into Engels's world at the end of the 1880s is offered by his account of New Year's Eve 1888. "We got into it in a very queer way," he recounted to Laura Lafargue:

> We went as usual to Pumps' in a cab, the fog was thickening. . . . After a full hour's drive in the dark and cold we arrived at Pumps' where we found Sam Moore, Tussy and the Schluters (Edward never turned up) and also Tauscher. . . . Well, it got blacker and blacker, and when the New Year came, the air was as thick as pea-soup. No chance of getting away; our cabman, ordered for one o'clock, never arrived, and so the whole lot had to stop where they were. So we went on drinking, singing, card-playing and laughing till half-past five, when Sam and Tussy were escorted by Percy to the station and caught the first train; about 7 the others left, and it cleared up a little; Nim slept with Pumps, Schorlemmer and I in the spare bed, Percy in the nursery (it was after seven when we went to sleep) and got up again at about 12 or 1 to return to Pilsener etc. . . . The others drank coffee about half past four, but I stuck to claret till seven.[42]

The happy cohabitation of Engels and Nim—with its nostalgic mix of Marx memories, midmorning sharpeners, and shared weakness for party gossip—came to an abrupt end in 1890 when Nim collapsed with a suspected uterine tumor. As he did for Lizzy, Engels cared for the dying Helene Demuth with extraordinary tenderness. "My good, dear, loyal Lenchen fell peacefully asleep yesterday afternoon after a short and for the most part painless illness," Engels wrote sadly to Sorge on 5 November 1890. "We had spent seven happy years together in this house. We were the only two left of the old guard of the days before 1848. Now here I am, once again on my own."[43] He followed this letter with a note to Nim's nephew Adolf Riefer, one of her few known relatives, announcing the plans for her estate. For there still remained one living, breathing lie—Nim and Marx's illegitimate son, Freddy Demuth—that the discreet, loyal Engels had to tidy up. "The deceased made a will in which she named as her sole heir Frederick Lewis, the son of a deceased friend," Engels wrote, "whom she had adopted when he was still quite small and whom she gradually brought up to be a good and industrious mechanic." Dissembling still further, Engels explained to Riefer how Freddy, "out of gratitude and with her permission," had decided to assume the name Demuth and, as such, was named in the will.[44] Thus was one of the last pieces of subterfuge on Engels's part enacted—another posthumous protection of Marx's reputation. The ill-treated Freddy Demuth, of 25 Gransden Avenue, Hackney, East London, rightly received Helene's entire estate, valued at £40. To the disinherited Riefer, this act of generosity to the adult son of an old friend he had never heard of must have seemed a little odd.

After burying Helene alongside Karl and Jenny Marx at the family plot in Highgate, Engels sank into a deep depression. Her death deprived him of another intimate connection to the Marxes as well as of the kind of doting, jokey female company he relished. It was in this disheartened state that Engels replied to a condolence telegram from Louise Kautsky, Karl Kautsky's former wife, whom he had defended so chivalrously during her divorce. "What I have been through these many days, how terribly bleak and desolate life has seemed and still seems to me, I need not tell you," he wrote. "And then came the question—what now? Whereupon, my dear Louise, an image, alive and comforting, appeared before my eyes, to remain there night and day, and that image was you."[45] Engels's unexpected solution to his lonely state was for Louise, a struggling Viennese midwife, to take up Nim's former position in Regent's Park Road. There would, of course, be no "manual services," just a supervisory role of the household staff and total freedom to pursue other interests.

Louise jumped at the chance to move to London, and the delighted Engels soon had a new woman in his life. With her, as he put it, "a little sunshine has returned." In Engels's final years, the two of them enjoyed a highly productive, supportive, and affectionate relationship, with the younger Louise acting—far more than Nim had—as a secretarial assistant, taking care of correspondence, organizing papers, monitoring the international press, and even proofreading Engels's articles. Engels's letters to his global circle of correspondents became inundated with mentions of her; soon she started adding her own notes to the letters and signing off as "The Witch." Did Engels take more than just a professional interest in the witty, pretty thirty-year-old Louise? Most probably, but as he wrote to August Bebel, "the difference in our ages precludes marital no less than extra-marital relations, so that nothing remains but that self-same housewifeliness."[46] Over time, these sentiments developed into paternal affection, as Engels grew to regard Louise "as I do Pumps, Tussy or Laura, just as though she were my own child."[47]

There was one sour note in this harmonious scene: Pumps was far from happy with Louise's arrival. Whereas she had coexisted easily enough with the unthreatening Nim, playing the flirty girl to Nim's staid matron, she rightly sensed that the entrance of stylish, attractive Louise into Regent's Park Road would undermine her lucrative relationship with Engels. Ever her father's daughter, Tussy Marx watched the unfolding family drama with unrestrained glee. "Finally Louise arrived," she reported back to Laura. "Meantime the General had screwed his courage to the sticking point and Pumps had been informed that on my (!!) invitation Louise was coming over, and must be properly treated." But the threats didn't work. Pumps repeatedly humiliated Louise until it all came to a head: "On the General's [seventieth] birthday Pumps getting more drunk than usual confided to Louise that she 'knew she had to behave to her, or she'd get cut out of the Will!' "[48] Engels had to give Pumps a proper talking to—"my lecture and a few hints"—so she clearly understood "that her position in my house depends very much upon her own behaviour."[49] Revealing something of her true mettle, Louise held her nerve against the shameless niece, and Pumps was forced to accept that the days of her Primrose Hill primacy were firmly over.

In comparison to such high-strung domestic diplomacy, dealing with the factional infighting of European socialism was relatively straightforward. Most of Engels's time in 1888–89 was taken up with preparations for the Paris congress scheduled for July 1889, the hundredth anniversary of the storming of the Bastille. The problem was that two competing congresses were being planned by the two main factions: the International Workers' Congress, organized by the renegade French possibilists in conjunction with the SDF and various English trade unions, and the official Marxist International Socialist Labor Congress, coordinated by Lafargue, Guesde, and their French Workers' Party. Engels's task was to ensure the latter eclipsed the former by securing the involvement of the German and Austrian Marxist parties, which had a rather thorny relationship with Lafargue and the French socialists. In the early months of 1889, an increasingly ill-tempered correspondence bounced back and forth from Primrose Hill to Berlin, Vienna, and Paris. "One thing I do know," Engels exploded to Wilhelm Liebknecht after ending up at one sulky impasse too many, "you can arrange the next congress yourselves; I shall wash my hands of it."[50] Yet the reality was that Engels was the only figure capable of bringing the European communist parties together; he alone, as acting "first fiddle," enjoyed the stature and authority to unify the inherently factious movement. In the event, the congress just about worked, with nearly four hundred delegates representing the worker and socialist parties of twenty nations converging on the French capital. "You can congratulate yourself on having saved the congress," Lafargue wrote to Engels, who had personally declined to join the throng. "But for you and Bernstein, the Germans would have left us and deserted to the Possibilists."[51] Held in the shadow of the "hideous" Eiffel Tower and amid the vulgar commercial-imperial bustle of the 1889 World's Fair, the congress witnessed the launch of what became the Second Socialist International. "The capitalists have invited the rich and powerful to the *Exposition universelle* to observe and admire the product of the toil of workers forced to live in poverty in the midst of the greatest wealth human society has ever produced," Paul Lafargue proclaimed in language redolent of his late father-in-law. "We, socialists, have invited the producers to join us in Paris on 14 July. Our aim is the emancipation of the workers, the abolition of wage-labour and the creation of a society in which all women and men irrespective of sex or nationality will enjoy the wealth produced by the work of all workers."[52] Despite the often reformist and compromising tone prevalent in some of the debates, Engels was delighted with the outcome. "Our Congress is in session and proving a brilliant success," he reported to Sorge.[53] After the unimpressive decline of the First International, Engels felt that events in Paris showed the global socialist struggle gaining a far more secure footing. There was an end to anarchist influence, a welcome settlement between socialist theory and workers' activism, and clear policy commitments on political engagement, sexual equality, trade union rights, and the establishment of May Day as International Labor Day.

While Paris might have been the venue for the founding of the Second International, the intellectual and organizational energy behind late-nineteenth-century socialism came from Berlin and Vienna. To Bismarck's disbelief, his antisocialist laws had served only to swell the left-wing ranks of what in 1890 became the Sozialdemokratische Partei Deutschlands (SPD). Alarmed, the German chancellor changed tack, seeking to neutralize the socialist challenge through a program of progressive welfare reforms. But despite the introduction of health insurance, accident insurance, and old age and disability pensions, the SPD vote jumped from 7.5 percent in 1878 to 19.7 percent in 1890. "Since last Thursday evening when the telegrams announcing victory came raining in here thick and fast, we are in a constant intoxication of triumph," Engels wrote to Laura Lafargue after the socialists won an astonishing million and a half votes, translating to thirty-five deputies in the Reichstag. "The old stability is gone forever."[54]

With an expanded franchise, the prospect of real political power was now in the offing, and Engels felt it more important than ever that the SPD adopt a correct ideological line purged of any remaining Lassallean traits—most notably, the illogical belief in an "iron law of wages" and the conviction that proletarian emancipation depended upon the beneficence of the state. In the wake of the SPD's electoral triumph, a congress was set for Erfurt in October 1891, and in the run up to it Engels deployed all his political cunning to ensure Marx's posthumous control over the direction of German socialism. He mischievously reprinted Marx's "Marginal Notes" on the reviled 1875 Gotha program, with its sharp critique of Liebknecht and Bebel's surrender to Lassallean influence, and reissued Marx's *Civil War in France*, with its defense of the Commune's dictatorship of the proletariat. Engels then heavily edited the first draft of the Erfurt social democratic program, urging the SPD not to walk away from a confrontation with the feudal German state and restating his conviction about the necessity for a democratic way station to communism. "If one thing is certain," he emphasized, "it is that our party and the working class can only come to power under the form of a democratic republic."[55]

As it turned out, Engels's fears of ideological backsliding were unwarranted. Although Erfurt adopted a series of highly reformist policies (universal suffrage, free schooling, a progressive income tax, medical care, and legal aid), to the European socialist movement as a whole the SPD congress signaled the ideological triumph of Marxism with a philosophical program echoing *Das Kapital*. "We have had the satisfaction of seeing Marx's critique win all along the line," Engels wrote to Sorge with the intense personal satisfaction of having honored Marx's legacy in the country of his birth. "Even the last traces of Lassalleanism have been eliminated."[56] After Erfurt and the SPD's official conversion, Marxism took control of the Second International. As Leszek Kolakowski put it, Marxism was no longer "the religion of an isolated sect but the ideology of a powerful political movement."[57]

The SPD's commitment to suffrage, municipal socialism, even the proportional representation voting system highlighted a broader shift in the political climate that, as Engels clearly understood, required adjustments of theory as well. The hero of the '48 revolution, the stalwart who had wanted to deliver the socialist revolution by bloody force, now tailored his political strategy to an age of mass democracy. As Europe's economies moved from the Industrial Revolution to monopoly capitalism—with its underpinnings of state cartels, colonial exploitation, and high finance—capitalism emerged as something far sturdier than previously imagined. If the capitalist system was not likely to be brought to a juddering halt by an immediate economic crisis, then the way to proletarian triumph had to involve the sort of democratic party politics that Marx and Engels had first supported in 1848. The difference in 1891 was that Engels thought democratic socialist parties could now move straight to power via the ballot box, without having to endure the interlude of bourgeois rule that had seemed necessary in the reactionary, feudal days of 1848.[58] There was the real possibility, Engels concluded, of a direct transition to socialism under a proletarian government voted into power by the newly enfranchised working class—as the SPD seemed on track to be in Germany. Given the growing working-class vote, he noted, "the possibility of our coming to power is merely a calculation of probability in accordance with mathematical laws."[59] The prospect of ultimate, peaceable socialist triumph delighted Engels. "This very lack of undue haste, this measured but nonetheless inexorable advance, has about it something tremendously impressive which cannot but arouse in the rulers the same sense of dread as was experienced by the prisoners of the state inquisition in that room in Venice where the walls moved inwards an inch each day," he mused to August Bebel's wife, Julie.[60]

Democracy, of course, was slower and less romantic than revolution, but Engels had come to regard universal suffrage as a respectable weapon in the socialist armory. Like a democratic ingenue, Engels hailed the wonder of elections for allowing socialists to reveal their strength every three years, enabling the party leadership to stay in touch with the workers, and offering a platform for socialist advocacy in Parliament, perhaps even the opportunity to rule. Never afraid to adopt a new political strategy in the face of changing circumstances, Engels, who once caricatured himself readying a guillotine, announced that "the time of surprise attacks, of revolutions carried through by small conscious minorities at the head of the masses lacking consciousness is past."[61] What was more, thanks to the overwhelming force that state armies could mobilize, "the era of barricades and street fighting has gone for good."[62] Contrary to Lenin's later assertions, Engels was no vanguardist. He even opposed plans for a much-debated general strike in response to the potential outbreak of a European war as unnecessarily provocative to bourgeois authorities itching to impose a military clampdown. "We, the 'revolutionaries,' the 'overthrowers'—we are thriving far better on legal methods than on illegal methods and overthrow. The parties of order, as they call themselves, are perishing under the legal conditions created by themselves."[63]

In coming to terms with the new electoral landscape thrown up by expanding suffrage, Engels reached for an unexpected analogy. In the early 1880s, his voracious reading had alighted on the history of the early Christian church in the late Roman Empire. Drawing on his Young Hegelian heritage of biblical criticism, he had penned a small article on the book of Revelation and, in the process, recounted "how Christianity got hold of the masses, exactly as modern socialism does."[64] We hear no more in this vein until a decade later, when Engels was struck again by the similarity between the inexorable march of socialism across Europe and the unstoppable spread of Christianity within the Empire. The aggressive atheist and teenage baiter of the Christian Graeber brothers was, in his old age, altogether more willing to give some credence to at least the social gospel of Jesus. "The history of early Christianity has notable points of resemblance with the modern working-class movement," Engels wrote in a historical essay on the early church. "Like the latter, Christianity was originally a movement of oppressed people; it first appeared as the religion of slaves and freedmen, of poor people deprived of all rights, of peoples subjugated or dispersed by Rome." And even if the one promised salvation in the afterlife and the other social transformation here on earth, they shared an unquenchable eagerness for struggle and a bloody heritage of martyrdom: "Both are persecuted and subjected to harassment. . . . And in spite of all persecution, nay, even spurred on by it, they forge victoriously, irresistibly ahead."[65]

In contrast to the Christians, Marx and Engels were never inclined to turn the other cheek. For all Engels's talk of an end to the barricades and the futility of armed insurrection, he adamantly refused "to subscribe heart and soul to absolute legality" and was always careful to defend the socialist's moral right to force. Legality was a political tactic relevant for the SPD in the current German political climate rather than any kind of ethical absolute. "I preach those tactics only for the Germany of today and even then with many reservations," he explained in a letter to Paul Lafargue after some within the SPD hierarchy misinterpreted Engels's views as a blanket commitment to peaceable means. "For France, Belgium, Italy, Austria, such tactics could not be followed as a whole and for Germany, they could become inapplicable tomorrow."[66] To Engels's frustration, these caveats were overlooked; thanks to the ensuing revisionism of Eduard Bernstein, in future years he would also be blamed not

only for the militant excesses of Marxist-Leninism but for SPD reform-
ism and its commitment to political gradualism. Engels was never, ever
a Fabian: if a mass workers' party, elected into office, was the swiftest
way to socialism, then so be it. Otherwise, the retired Cheshire hunts-
man was still raring to join the cavalry charge.

As Second International socialism surged across the European continent, Engels wanted to witness it firsthand. His opportunity was an International Workers' Congress set for Zurich in August 1893 and he
excitedly set off to it with Louise. Meeting the new generation of socialist
leaders face to face—Filipo Turati from Italy, Pavel Axelrod from Russia,
Stanislaw Mendelson from Poland—and seeing once again old friends
such as August Bebel and Victor Adler, Engels declared himself highly
impressed with the commitment of the activists. But what really took his
breath away was the beauty of the female delegates. "The women were
splendidly represented," he reported back to Laura Lafargue. "Besides
Louise, Austria sent little [Adelheid] Dworzak, a charming little girl in
every respect; I fell quite in love with her. . . . These Viennese are born
Parisians, but the Parisians of fifty years ago. Regular grisettes. Then the
Russian women, there were four or five with wonderfully beautiful shining eyes."[67] He found the details of the Zurich debates deeply tedious
and, excusing himself from the complicated motions, sped off to the
canton of Graubunden to visit his brother Hermann. Engels had parted
ways with Hermann, the former commander of counterrevolutionary
forces in 1848, in the wake of the failed uprising. But in recent years the
brothers' relationship had warmed and the two elderly men now ex-
changed frequent letters sharing news about their illnesses, tax rates,
and even their lustful thoughts.

On 12 August, Engels returned to Zurich to give the closing speech at
the congress. "We wanted to close the meeting: the last votes were taken
in feverish haste," recalled the young Belgian socialist party leader Emile
Vandervelde of the last day. "One name was on every lip. Friedrich Engels entered the hall: among storms of cheering he came to the platform."[68]
This was surely Engels's moment, stepping out from the shadow of Marx

and imprinting his own legacy on the socialist movement that he had done so much to found, nurture, and support. But even then he would not take the credit. "I could not but experience deep emotion at the unexpectedly splendid reception which you have given me, accepting it not for myself personally but as a collaborator of the great man whose portrait hangs up there," he told the four hundred delegates, pointing upward to a picture of Marx. Some fifty years since he and Marx first began publishing their tracts in the *Deutsch-Französische Jahrbücher*, "socialism has developed from small sects to a mighty party which makes the whole official world quail. Marx is dead, but were he still alive there would be not one man in Europe or America who could look back with such justified pride over his life's work." He then made a principled plea for freedom of debate within the movement, "in order not to become a sect," before leaving the hall to huge acclamation and a boisterous rendition of the *Marseillaise*.[69]

After Zurich, Engels continued his tour of the Continent, which quickly turned into something of a victory lap. In Vienna—where "the women especially are charming and enthusiastic"—he addressed rapturous crowds of six thousand. "When you have heard for years nothing but bickering and squabbles from France, from Italy, from America, and then go amongst these people . . . and see the unity of purpose, the splendid organization, the enthusiasm . . . you cannot help being carried away and saying: this is the centre of gravity of the working-class movement," he reflected to Laura.[70] His journey culminated in Berlin, the place of his officer training and the city that he and Marx had once reviled above all others. He was welcomed back by the socialist newspaper *Vorwärts*: "When Friedrich Engels, with his 73 years, today looks out on the capital city of the Reich, it may give him a joyful and elevating feeling that out of the calcified and pedantic royal residence of the king of Prussia of the year 1842 has developed the powerful proletarian native city which today greets him as—*Social Democratic Berlin*."[71] Some three thousand socialists packed into Concordia Hall to hear Liebknecht recount Engels's history of service and sacrifice to the party. "You know that I am not an orator or a parliamentarian; I work in a different field, chiefly in the study and with the pen," Engels modestly replied before revealing his delight at the transformation of Berlin from Junker playpen to socialist powerhouse.[72] He went on to pay tribute to the discipline and the electoral success of the SPD, which he felt sure, given steady industrialization and proletarianization, was set to enjoy further triumphs. The Continental excursion, with its vast crowds, glowing newspaper coverage, and motivated activists, had convinced Engels that the suffrage strategy was correct: the workers' vote was growing with irreversible vigor, allowing the socialists to make an ever-greater series of political demands until they either achieved electoral success or engineered a necessary confrontation with the bourgeois state. All they had to do was keep their nerve, avoid unnecessary provocation, and stay the course.

There was one pitfall that had to be avoided. "I would consider a European war to be a disaster; this time it would prove frightfully serious and inflame chauvinism everywhere for years to come, since all peoples would be fighting for their own existence," Engels had written to Bebel in 1882. "Such a war would, I believe, retard the revolution by ten years, at the end of which, however, the upheaval would doubtless be all the more drastic."[73] This fear of the antirevolutionary effects of a European conflagration marked another reversal of thinking. Until the early 1870s, both Marx and Engels were adamant that war would naturally advance the socialist cause, since it would eliminate the great reactionary obstacle of tsarist Russia. Just as the French wars of the 1790s intensified revolutionary sentiment, the communists assumed a Continental conflict would unite and radicalize the European working class. But after Bismarck's annexation of Alsace-Lorraine and the growing nationalist antagonism between France and Germany, Engels thought that war might in fact divert the workers' movements into an unedifying upsurge of nationalism. "It is precisely because everything's going so marvelously," he wrote to Bebel, "that I wouldn't exactly wish for a world war."[74] Even if a workers' revolution rose from the ashes of a world war, the transformation of European armies into industrialized killing machines meant that this route to communism would entail a very high body count. "Eight to ten million soldiers will strangle one another, and in the process will eat all Europe more bare than any swarm of locusts," he wrote presciently in 1887. "The devastation of the Thirty Years War, compressed into three or four years and extended over the whole continent: famine, pestilence, general barbarization of armies and peoples alike through extreme want."[75]

The way to avoid war and salvage the prospect of a less violent revolution, Engels believed, was to transfer the party's electoral strategy to the military sphere. In the wake of SPD success in the 1877 Reichstag elections, Engels reflected on the fact that "at least half if not more of these men of 25 (the minimum age) who voted for us spent two to three years in uniform and they know perfectly well how to handle a needle gun and a rifled cannon."[76] As socialism attracted increasing popular support, it was essential that its philosophy make its way into the barracks and battalions of the Prussian regiments, where soldiers would then begin to question the orders of their reactionary, bellicose commanders. "When every able-bodied man serves in the army, this army increasingly reflects popular feelings and ideas, and this army, the great means of repression, is becoming less secure day by day: already the heads of all the big states foresee with terror the day when soldiers under arms will refuse to butcher their fathers and brothers."[77] Engels, the once steadfast skeptic of the militia system, now urged mass conscription as an even more effective democratic tool than the franchise. The unstoppable mathematics of socialist advance would draw the army in its wake, and once the armed forces turned socialist, the sort of jingoistic wars urged by the leaders of France, Russia, and Germany would prove impossible. At the same time, the troops' traditional counterrevolutionary function—so bloodily on display in the Paris Commune— would be neutralized. "I have more than once heard him say," the SDF activist Ernest Belfort Bax recalled, "that as soon as one-third of the German army actually in service could be relied on by the Party leaders, revolutionary action ought to be taken."[78]

This, then, was Engels at seventy-three: advancing the Marxist cause, inspiring the faithful, delivering the latest volumes of *Das Kapital*, providing analyses of Sino-Russian relations, the German peasant question, the Russian *obschina* (an urgent issue in light of the 1891–92 famine), the

ILP, and the SPD. He remained the same restless, inquisitive, productive, and passionate architect of scientific socialism who first emerged in
the 1840s. He took care to avoid both dogma and platitude, to make sure
that his political interventions were neither overly prescriptive nor un-
helpfully vague. As always, he did not hesitate to tell his socialist colleagues, in the bluntest language, where they went wrong. His health
remained good and he continued to celebrate his birthdays in characteristically robust style. "We kept it up till half past three in the morning,"
Engels boasted of his seventieth birthday to Laura Lafargue, "and drank,
besides claret, 16 bottles of champagne—the morning we had had 12
dozen oysters. So you see I did my best to show that I was still alive and
kicking."[79] One visitor to Regent's Park Road in 1891 described meeting
"a tall, bearded, vigorous, bright-eyed and genial septuagenarian" who
proved "a generous and delightful host."[80] Tussy called him "the youn-
gest man I know. As far as I can remember he has not grown any older in
the last 20 years."[81] He continued to take his daily walks on Hampstead
Heath ("London's Chimborazo"), but he was beginning to suffer recurring groin trouble from a foxhunting fall years before. His ever more
aggressive bouts of bronchitis, stomachaches, and rheumatism of the
legs forced him to give up smoking and reduce his Pilsener intake. Yet
what most seemed to worry him was the specter of "encroaching bald-
ness."

At home, with Pumps banished to the Isle of Wight, Louise Kautsky
was in charge of the domestic routine. "You know the General is always
under the thumb of the 'lady of the house,'" Tussy wrote to Laura.
"When Pumps was with him, lo, she was good in his sight; now Pumps
is dethroned and Louise is the queen who can do no wrong." Tussy was
less amused by Louise's introduction of a foreign body into Engels's
household: her new husband, Ludwig Freyberger, an Austrian physician
and member of the National Liberal Club. Tussy thought him an anti-
Semite of dubious political leanings and felt that he was transforming
122 Regent's Park Road from a laughter-filled socialist redoubt to an
uneasy Viennese ménage à trois. "I would not trust a fly to his tender
mercies," she wrote angrily to Laura in March 1894 with a litany of complaints about Freyberger's various manipulations. "He is an adventurer

pure and simple, and I am heartily sorry for Louise."[82] She was even more upset when, in autumn 1894, the Freybergers persuaded the seventy-four-year-old Engels to move out of his home.

After the birth of their child, Ludwig and Louise had decided that No. 122 was too cramped for their familial needs. So for another £25 in yearly rent, the quartet marched five hundred paces down the road to No. 41. On the face of it, Engels didn't seem to mind this change of residence. "Downstairs we have our communal living-rooms, on the first floor my study and bedroom, on the second Louise, her husband, the baby daughter," Engels described the layout for Sorge. "On the third floor the two housemaids, lumber-room and visitor's room. My study is at the front, has three windows and is so big that I can accommodate nearly all my books in it and yet, despite its size, very nice and easy to heat. In short, we are a lot better off."[83] Engels, who doted on all of Pumps's, Laura's, and Jenny's children like a grandfather, had no problem sharing the house with an infant. He remained devoted to Louise and even appreciated Freyberger's "draconian medical supervision" of his various physical ailments. But for the fragile, emotional Tussy, who was contending with her own domestic crises, it seemed the General had been taken from her: she now depicted him as a feeble old man held against his will by the evil Freybergers. "I don't think the poor old General even fully realizes what he is made to do, he has come to the condition where he is a mere child in the hands of the monstrous pair," she complained to Laura. "If you knew how they bully and frighten him by constantly reminding him he is too old for this and too old for that . . . and saw how utterly depressed, and lonely, and miserable he is."[84] Tussy was particularly concerned that her father's manuscripts were at risk of falling into the Freybergers' hands, although Engels had repeatedly affirmed that upon his death all of Marx's papers would be handed straight over to her.

Tussy also accused Louise of spreading rumors about her and Aveling and generally interfering in the London Marxist circle, and this strife must have been a source of anguish to Engels. In Tussy's defense, it does seem that the Freybergers were highly controlling, even regulating the access that Engels's Sunday afternoon crowd had to him. They also evidently had half an eye on their landlord's estate. But given that both the Lafargues and the Avelings had over the previous years ignored numerous heartfelt invitations from the lonely Engels to join him for Christmas or for the summer, Tussy's fury was clearly not driven only by her concern for Engels himself. Her exaggerated accounts of Engels's loneliness and her intense anxiety about the Marx manuscripts (which led to a blazing row between Engels and the Avelings over Christmas 1894) may well have been displacements for her much deeper fear of losing "Uncle Angel" altogether—and, with him, that deep, abiding connection to her late, adored Mohr. Perhaps Tussy had sensed what Dr. Freyberger had so far missed: Engels was dying.

Friedrich Engels had begun his remarkable life in the heart of Germany's Industrial Revolution, among the yarn bleacheries and textile works of the Wupper valley; he concluded it amid the Victorian elegance of Eastbourne, the Duke of Devonshire's fastidiously English seaside retreat. By the 1880s, this gentlemanly resort had become Engels's favorite holiday spot. He liked to take a well-situated house along Cavendish Place and host Nim, Schorlemmer, or Pumps and her brood, as well as Laura or Tussy if he was lucky. And there sat Engels, the lover of good things and happy times, Pumps's children crawling around his knees, an open bottle of Pilsener close at hand, and the usual letter in progress—content even in the face of the August mist and rain. In the summer of 1894, he appears to have suffered a small stroke while on holiday and began to fear he might not make that longed-for peek into the new century. "Between ourselves, my 75th year doesn't hold out quite so much promise as previous ones," he wrote mordantly to Sorge.[85] By the following spring, an unwelcome complication had arisen. "Sometime ago I got a swelling on the right side of the neck, which after some time resolved itself into a bunch of deep-seated glands infiltrated by some cause or other," he wrote to Laura in the matter-of-fact tone he liked to adopt on medical issues. "The pains arose from direct pressure of that lump on the nerve and will of course only give way when that pressure disappears."[86] To aid the healing process, Engels departed for Eastbourne earlier than normal, in June 1895. He planned to work there on a new edition of his *Peasant War in Germany* and to tidy up some of Kautsky's forthcoming *History of Socialism*.

What Engels the keen physiologist didn't realize was that he was already suffering from an aggressive cancer of the esophagus and larynx, which Freyberger had detected in early March 1895 and had discussed with the Austrian doctor and socialist Victor Adler. They thought it best to keep their patient in the dark, and the ensuing weeks saw a heartrending correspondence as Engels latched on to every suggestion of returning health. "Thank you for your letter—there is some improvement but, in accordance with the principles of dialectics, the positive and the negative aspects are both showing a cumulative tendency," he joked in a suitably scientistic vein to Bernstein in early July 1895. "I am stronger, eat more and with a better appetite and look very well, or so I am told; thus my general condition has improved." He was already having trouble swallowing, but on the other hand, "I have found out several weak sides of my capricious appetite and take *lait de poule* [egg nog] with brandy, custards with stewed fruits, oysters up to nine a day etc."[87] By the 21 July, however, his condition had become extremely grave. Sam Moore, Engels's old friend from his Manchester days, met Ludwig Freyberger off the train from Eastbourne and reported back to Tussy: "I am sorry to say that his report is anything but cheering; he says that the disease has attained such a hold that, considering the General's age, his state is precarious. Apart from the diseased glands of the neck there is danger either from weakness of the heart or from pneumonia—and in either of these two cases the end would be sudden."[88] With his health rapidly deteriorating, Engels was moved from Eastbourne back to London. "Tomorrow we return," he wrote to Laura, who was waiting for him at Regent's Park Road, in his last known letter. "There seems to be at last a crisis approaching in my potato field on my neck, so that the swellings may be opened and relief secured. At last! So there is hope of this long lane coming to a turning." He then went on to ridicule both the SDF and the ILP for their poor showing in the recent general election and signed off in vintage Engels fashion: "Here's your good health in a bumper of *lait de poule* fortified by a dose of *cognac vieux*."[89]

Despite the bonhomie and bluster, Engels knew the end was near and took care to add a late codicil to his will. As could be expected, both documents were businesslike, pragmatic, and extraordinarily generous to the loving clique who surrounded him. Engels's estate was to be divided into eight parts, with three parts going to Laura Lafargue, three parts to Tussy, and the remaining two parts to Louise Freyberger. With the estate valued at £20,378 after death duties (around $4 million in today's money), this worked out to a very sizable £5,000 each for Tussy and Laura (after a third of their settlement was allocated to a trust fund for the children of their sister, Jenny Marx Longuet) and almost £5,100 for Louise.[90] Tussy, Laura, and Jenny's children were also to receive any continuing royalties from the sales of *Das Kapital*. Pumps was left a lump sum of £2,230 (with which she emigrated to the United States), Ludwig Freyberger received £210 for medical assistance, and Louise was given the rights to the lease on Regent's Park Road as well as the household effects. All loans to Pumps and Percy, Laura and Paul Lafargue, and Edward Aveling were forgiven. Most important of all, Engels acceded to the wishes of the Marx daughters in regard to their father's papers: not only were all his manuscripts and family correspondence to be given to Tussy as Marx's literary executor, he now commanded that *all* letters to Marx that he was in possession of were to be handed over to her. His own letters from known correspondents were to be returned to them, with the rest passed on to his literary executors, August Bebel and Eduard Bernstein. In addition, he allocated a further £1,000 to Bebel and Paul Singer as a fund for helping SPD candidates in elections. His brother Hermann was handed back an oil painting of their father.

The reading of the will was not long in coming. By early August, the General could take nourishment only in fluid form, was drifting in and out of consciousness, and had lost his power of speech. Bebel visited him and found he could still "make bad jokes on his writing board."[91] He could also chalk out, in these dying days, the identity of Freddy Demuth's true father to a distraught Tussy and so exculpate himself from that particular misdemeanor. Soon after 10:00 p.m. on 5 August, Louise Freyberger briefly left his side to change clothes. When she came back, "all was over."[92] "So he was laid low," Wilhelm Liebknecht lamented.

That titanic mind who together with Marx laid the foundations of scientific socialism and taught the tactics of socialism, who at the early age of 24 wrote the classical work *Condition of the Working Class*, the co-author of the *Communist Manifesto*, Karl Marx's alter ego who helped him to call to life the International Working Men's Association, the author of *Anti-Dühring*, that encyclopaedia of science of crystal transparency accessible to anybody who can think, the author of *The Origin of the Family* and so many other works, essays and newspaper articles, the friend, the adviser, the leader and the fighter—he was dead.[93]

The funeral was not as Engels would have wished. Although the plan had been for an intimate private gathering of mourners to witness the cremation, word got out and nearly eighty people crammed into the rooms of the Necropolis Company at the Westminster Bridge Road station of the London and South Western Railway. In addition to the Avelings, Lafargues, Roshers, Longuet children, and Freybergers and some Engels cousins, the SPD's Liebknecht, Singer, Kautsky, Lessner, and Bernstein, August Bebel for the Austrian party, Vera Zasulich for the Russians, and Will Thorne from the Socialist League attended. There were wreaths from the Belgian, Italian, Dutch, Bulgarian, and French Socialist parties, and speeches from, among others, Engels's nephew Gustav Schlechtendahl and Samuel Moore. After some secular valedictions, the train bearing Engels's body eased out of London, heading along a single track to the Woking crematorium.

"To the west of Eastbourne the cliffs along the coast gradually rise until they form the great chalky headland of Beachy Head, nearly six hundred feet in height. Overgrown with grass on the top, it slopes gently at first, and then suddenly falls steeply to the water, while down below it exhibits all manner of recesses and outlying masses." It was to this quintessentially English setting, "on a very rough day in autumn," that Eduard Bernstein recalled traveling together with Tussy, Aveling, and Friedrich Lessner. These four rough-hewn socialists—an incongruous quartet in genteel Eastbourne—hired a small boat and started to row steadily out into the English Channel. "About five or six miles off Beachy Head" they turned to face the dramatic shoreline of the South Downs and then, following the clear dictates of his will, cast the urn and ashes of Friedrich Engels into the sea. In death as in life there was nothing to detract from the glory of Marx: no Highgate headstone or family tomb, no public memorial for the man of such fascinating contradictions and limitless sacrifice. After his brief years as first fiddle, Engels returned to the orchestra.[94]

EPILOGUE

Let us return to the city of Engels on the banks of the Volga River. Given its everyday grim modernity, it is easy to forget this city's remarkable origins in the mid-eighteenth-century reign of Catherine the Great. As the European-born empress of Russia, Catherine II had been determined to inject some Western culture into Russia's bloodstream, raise the country's economic productivity, and populate the lawless Volga region with dependable, industrious settlers. This meant enticing thousands of German farmers, laborers, and tradesmen to leave their Hessian towns and villages for the fertile plains of southern Russia. Over the course of the 1760s, some thirty thousand Germans were induced to choose a new life in colonies stretching over two hundred miles up and down the Volga valley.[1] Among the most popular destinations was the region around Saratov, where the soil was known to be especially fecund, and the small settlement of Pokrovskaia, on the other side of the river, which grew as a lucrative trading and storage hub on the salt transportation routes. Over generations, the Volga Germans transformed their lands into some of the most prosperous and peaceable enclaves in the Russian empire. In 1914, the unincorporated settlement was officially christened Pokrovsk in honor of the Holy Blessed Virgin (after *pokrov*, a protective shroud or veil), and after the 1917 Russian Revolution it joined

Saratov as a patriotic member of the Autonomous Soviet Socialist Republic of Volga Germans.

In 1931 the name was changed again, this time under less consensual circumstances. The Soviet regime had not been gentle to the Volga republic. During the early 1920s, in the aftermath of the Russian civil war, the region had suffered a devastating famine, with grass, roots, bark, hides, and straw all becoming staple ingredients in the once well-fed district. Rocketing mortality rates and mass emigration reduced the population by nearly one-third. Then, just as the soil started to recover and harvests revive, the 1927 Congress of the Communist Party set out a new draconian peasant policy. To secure the industrial transformation of the Soviet economy, General Secretary Joseph Stalin demanded the transfer of food supplies into the cities, an end to rural grain hoarding, and the mass collectivization of agriculture. To deliver this agroindustrial revolution, Stalin unleashed an unrelenting war against the kulaks—those rural smallholders eking out an existence a little above the average, with perhaps half a dozen acres of land and some livestock and hired labor. "We have gone from a policy of *restricting* the exploiting proclivities of the kulaks to the policy of *eliminating* the kulaks as a class," Stalin boasted in a 1929 speech to agricultural students.[2] The smallholders were subject to punitive taxation and demands for grain "contributions," and their land was forcibly reallocated. Later came the nighttime knocks of the secret police as the gulags started to fill up. By 1930, nearly 80 percent of the private holdings in the Volga region had been forcibly integrated into local collectives, and almost 500,000 colonists from the Volga, Caucasus, and south Russia were deported.

The antikulak terror destroyed millions of lives, but Stalin's Five-Year Plan also brought about clear economic gains. Saratov and Pokvrosk underwent rapid industrialization: in short order, there appeared railway repair depots, brickworks, bread-baking plants, and glue factories, along with the beginnings of an aircraft assembly plant. Shock brigades at the bone-processing plants and Stakhanovite workers at the railway junctions pledged themselves to struggle ever harder to meet Moscow's "productional-financial plan." And it was to celebrate precisely such progress, as well as to commemorate the Volga's proud Germanic heritage, that the presidium of the central executive committee of the USSR decided in October 1931 to rename Pokrovsk in honor of Engels, Prussia's second-greatest socialist. (The nearby town of Ekaterinenstadt had already rebranded itself as Marksstadt.) The name Pokrovsk, according to one official statement, "was yellowed and dried out like her mother—the 'Virgin Mary.'" In this scientific Soviet era, it was an embarrassing hangover from feudal and superstitious times, recalling "the atrocious period of tsarist rule, which used national religion as a smokescreen for the egregious enslavement of the working masses."[3]

The renaming also offered a chance for emphasizing the connections between the great work of the Soviet Union and Marxism's lead apostle. For were not Stalin's farsighted policies—crushing the kulaks, Mensheviks, and "bourgeois nationalists"; collectivizing the farms; rationalizing production; taking "giant steps" toward a modern industrial future—being dutifully carried out in the name of Friedrich Engels? The Soviet propaganda machine had no doubt. Engels was a name, one Volga newspaper asserted, "worthy of what we have accomplished and will accomplish in the socialist reformation of agriculture based upon consolidated collectivization and the liquidation of kulakism as a class."[4] "The city of Engels, the center of the first national republic of consolidated collectivization, the center that with its industrial development has become the forge of mighty national proletarian cadres," as a different editorial had it, "will take its place among the proletarian centers of the country of socialist development worthy of the name of Karl Marx's fellow combatant and friend."[5]

This prestigious name did not come without responsibilities. "It demands of us the tireless fulfillment of all of the tasks we face in building the socialist system. Our Volga-German Komsomol [party youth organization] must meet them by carrying out a veritable assault to fulfill and overfulfill the grain supply, . . . to solve the socialist stock-breeding problem, . . . to tirelessly liquidate illiteracy in time for the anniversary of the October Revolution." Only such selfless industry could properly honor the inspirational life of the town's new patron saint. For "Marx's victory was only possible thanks to Engels's great willingness to sacrifice himself. . . . He stuck to 'damned commerce' in order to earn enough to allow Marx to dedicate himself to his great life's work uninterrupted." The residents of Engels would all strive to follow the lofty example. "To work, Komsomol! Show that we are worthy of transferring the name of this revolutionary, who accomplished so astoundingly much for the international proletariat, to the center of our Volga-German Republic! Once upon a time, there was Pokrovsk—watch out: here's Engels!"[6]

But ten years later, as Hitler launched Operation Barbarossa with an audacious invasion of Russia in June 1941 and Stalin confronted the specter of total war with Nazi Germany, such ideological devotion secured no clemency. On 28 August 1941, the Soviet presidium issued a decree, "Pertaining to the Resettlement of the Germans in the Volga District." "According to trustworthy information received by the military authorities," the edict began ominously,

> there are, among the German population living in the Volga area, thousands and tens of thousands of diversionists and spies who, on a signal being given from Germany, are to carry out sabotage in the area inhabited by the Germans of the Volga. . . . None of the Germans of the Volga area have reported to the Soviet authorities the existence of such a large number of diversionists and spies among the Volga Germans; consequently the German population of the Volga area conceals enemies of the Soviet people and of Soviet authority in its midst.

In textbook Soviet logic, the edict declared that since they had failed to offer up the presumed Nazi traitors in their midst, all were guilty and all had to suffer. "In case of diversionary acts which would be carried out by German diversionists and spies in the Volga province upon a signal from Germany, the Soviet government, in accordance with wartime laws, will be compelled to take punitive measures against the entire German population of the Volga province."[7] As the Wehrmacht scythed its way through Ukraine, the Crimea, and southern Russia, Stalin ordered the region's loyal, industrious Volga Germans rounded up en masse. After surviving the horrors of collectivization, the Great Famine, and the Great Terror, the Volga settlers were now subject to wholesale removal. The autonomous province was officially erased from Soviet geography, its citizens joining Stalin's growing list of undesirables—rightists, Trotskyists, saboteurs, wreckers, collaborators, and "fifth columnists" rounded up in the dead of night by the secret service and dispersed to the eastern edges of Siberia. And just as the protection of the Holy Blessed Virgin had failed to save the inhabitants of Pokrovsk from previous Soviet cruelties, so now the communist halo of Engels offered no cover to the town's inhabitants. In their tens of thousands, the Volga Germans became another statistical testament to the industrial inhumanity of Stalin's state.

Any biography of Marx's General must surely ask whether Engels the man was in some way responsible for the fate of Engels the city. Did his philosophy, as the Volga propaganda sheets claimed, help to shape the contours of Stalin's Soviet Union? For ideological opponents of Marx and Engels, the usual method of invalidating their philosophy has long been the rush to the gulag: a quick reference to force as the midwife of every old society pregnant with a new one, and the reader is on his way to the Krasnoyarsk camps. "In his own idiosyncratic ways, indeed, he [Lenin] could not have been more loyal to the doctrines and doings of Marx and Engels," as a recent history of communism by Robert Service puts it. "The co-founders of Marxism had approved of violent revolution, dictatorship and terror. . . . Many assumptions of Leninism sprang directly from the Marxism of the mid-nineteenth century."[8] What is more, many of the political leaders of the Soviet Union and the Eastern bloc, as well as the anti-imperial communist movements, came to their Marxism specifically through the works of Engels. His writings—*Anti-Dühring*, the abridged *Socialism: Utopian and Scientific, Ludwig Feuerbach and the End of Classical German Philosophy*—provided an easily accessible conduit to the complexities behind *Das Kapital*. And nowhere were they read more diligently than in Russia.

As we have seen, Marx and Engels were always circumspect about the prospect of a proletarian revolution's taking place in Russia. Endless tergiversations about the role of the *obschina*, concerns over the oriental predilection for despotism, and debates about the speed of industrialization and the role of the peasantry led Marx to conclude that there could be a Russian transition to socialism only if it coincided with a complementary proletarian revolution in the advanced West. Engels would not even admit to that much: in his final years he remained adamant that the still feudal tsarist state would have to pass through all the intermediate stages of mass industrialization, working-class immiseration, and bourgeois rule before any revolution would be in the offing.

But history arrived early for Russia, and in 1917 Lenin's Bolsheviks successfully diverted a popular revolution into their extraordinary ideological experiment. The first chair of the Council of the People's Commissars certainly knew his Marx, but he often seemed to prefer his Engels. Indeed, Lenin thought it "impossible to understand Marxism and to propound it fully without taking into account the entire work of Engels."[9] Lenin's earliest and arguably most influential instructor in the Marxist doctrine was the exiled Russian leader of the Emancipation of Labor group, Georgi Plekhanov. From his Geneva outpost, Plekhanov had turned time and again to Engels for philosophical and strategic advice about the most efficacious way of implementing Marxism in Russia. "First of all, please spare me 'mentor'—my name is simply Engels," the Grand Lama replied to one particularly effusive Plekhanov inquiry.[10]

What Plekhanov took from his reading of Engels was a belief in Marxism as a complete theoretical system capable of explaining history, natural science, economics, and, most importantly of all, political action. Plekhanov was the first to describe the philosophy of Marxism as "dialectical materialism," by which he meant a rigorous worldview based on Marx and Engels's application of Hegelian dialectics. With its step-by-step account of contradictions, qualitative and quantitative change, and the negation of the negation, dialectical materialism seemed to provide a clear political map for Russia's revolutionaries. However, Plekhanov always retained an intellectual's purity: he never swayed from Engels's conviction that socialism—in Russia and elsewhere—could not be imposed overnight but had to follow a period of bourgeois-democratic rule and sustained industrial growth. Convinced that the contradictions of capitalist society were the necessary preconditions for a communist transformation, Plekhanov was deeply hostile to the kind of top-down socialist revolution led by a vanguard elite that Lenin advocated. The result of such a putsch in Russian society, he feared, would be "a political abortion after the manner of the ancient Chinese or Persian empires—a renewal of Tsarist despotism on a communist basis."[11]

While Lenin ignored such reservations, he certainly held fast to Plekhanov's version of Engels's version of Marx. In this philosophical variant of the telephone game, Engels's Marxism—with all its provisional humility and capacity for revision—metamorphosed into a dogma. "Dialectics IS the theory of knowledge of (Hegel and) Marxism," Lenin bluntly declared.[12] For him, Marxism was a complete body of theory akin to "a single piece of steel [from which] you cannot eliminate even one basic premise, one essential part, without departing from objective truth, without falling a prey to bourgeois-reactionary falsehood."[13] The unalterable natural laws of the dialectic explained the inevitable scientific ascent of socialism. Once in power—and rightly understood—they offered a complete program for communist governance. "This insistence on the integrality of Marxism was inherited from Plekhanov by Lenin, and became part of the ideology of the Soviet state," in the judgment of Leszek Kolakowski.[14] The dialectic also gave Lenin a profound intellectual self-confidence and allowed for an awesome degree of ideological rigor. In an overheated passage from *The Teaching of Karl Marx*, Lenin favorably compared the inspiring mystery of dialectical materialism to Darwinian evolution:

A development that repeats, as it were, the stages already passed, but repeats them in a different way, on a higher plane ("the negation of negation"); a development, so to speak, in spirals, not in a straight line; a development in leaps and bounds, catastrophes, revolutions; "intervals of gradualness"; transformation of quantity into quality, inner impulses for development, imparted by the contradiction, the conflict of different forces and tendencies reacting on a given body or inside a given phenomenon or within a given society; interdependence, and the closest, indissoluble connection between all sides of every phenomenon (history disclosing ever-new sides); a connection that provides the one world-process of motion proceeding according to law—such are some

of the features of dialectics as a doctrine of evolution more full of meaning than the current one.[15]

Stalin took the practical implementation of dialectical materialism to
even greater heights. The more violently the Soviet regime appeared to
depart from Marx and Engels's principles—the end to alienation, the
withering away of the state, the global call of communism—the more
fulsome its official rhetoric became in its claims to orthodoxy. "Marxism
is not only the theory of socialism; it is an integral world outlook, a
philosophical system, from which Marx's proletarian socialism logically
follows," Stalin declared. "This philosophical system is called dialectical materialism."[16] He went on to outline precisely what he meant in a
personal contribution to one of the most important publications in official Soviet literature, the *Short Course: History of the Communist Party
of the Soviet Union (Bolsheviks)* (1938). Stalin's chapter, "Dialectical and
Historical Materialism," which set out the Marxist fundamentals of the
Soviet system, opened with the rigid authority of a commissar's edict:
"Dialectical materialism is the world outlook of the Marxist-Leninist
Party." Citing various scientific transformations lifted straight from Engels's *Dialectics of Nature*—water to steam, oxygen to ozone—Stalin explained how these sharp shifts in form confirmed Engels's assertion that
nature was a connected and integrated whole, that it was in a state of
continuous movement with change occurring rapidly and abruptly, and
that driving its development were the internal contradictions inherent
to all natural phenomena. With much greater precision than either Engels or Lenin, Stalin spelled out the political ramifications of dialectical
materialism in a direct challenge to any reformist or social democratic
interpretations. "If the passing of slow quantitative changes into rapid
and abrupt changes is a law of development," he reasoned, "then it is
clear that revolutions made by oppressed classes are a quite natural and
inevitable phenomenon. Hence the transition from capitalism to socialism and the liberation of the working class from the yoke of capitalism
cannot be effected by slow changes, by reforms, but only by a qualitative
change of the capitalist system, by revolution."[17]

Making a play for total ideological legitimacy, Stalin tied the actions of the Soviet state inextricably to the scientific principles of Marxism-Leninism: "The bond between science and practical activity, between theory and practice, their unity, should be the guiding star of the party of the proletariat."[18] And since the Communist Party, which to all intents and purposes meant the will of Stalin, necessarily embodied the true interests of the proletariat, every policy it pursued logically enjoyed the ideological imprimatur of Marxist sanctity. Cornelius Castoriadis explains the Soviet rationale best: "If there is a true theory of history, if there is a rationality at work in things, then it is clear that the direction this development takes should be left to the specialists of this theory, to the technicians of this rationality. The Party's absolute power has a philosophical status. . . . If this conception is true, this power *must* be absolute."[19] In the Soviet system what the party decreed instantly became scientific truth.

Against a backdrop of terror and total control, the Stalinist state transformed the nuances and complexities of Marxist philosophy into a rigid orthodoxy that infected almost every element of Russia's cultural, scientific, political, and private life.[20] While Engels had compared socialism to the early Christian church, in the USSR it was akin to the worst form of heresy-hunting medieval Catholicism with its totalizing liturgies, undeviating rituals, and a panoply of communist saints. There were no doubts; the faith provided the way, the truth, the life, and a complete scheme of social salvation. Stalin's *Short Course* was its sacred text, an indisputable explication of Marxism-Leninism that stipulated the correct party line on all matters of socialist thought. "It was published and taught everywhere without ceasing," Kolakowski recalls. "In the upper forms of secondary schools, in all places of higher learning, party courses etc., wherever anything was taught, the *Short Course* was the Soviet citizen's main intellectual pabulum."[21]

As the Soviet Union's geopolitical sphere of influence extended, so the *Short Course* made its way around the world in tens of millions of copies with smart covers and high-quality Moscow print. The effect was to make dialectical materialism one of the most influential philosophies of the twentieth century, memorized and recited in communist circles from Phnom Penh to Paris to North London, where a young historian-to-be named Raphael Samuel welcomed its icy certainties. "As a science of society, it offered itself as an all-embracing determinism, in which accidents were revealed as necessities, and causes inexorably followed by effects," he later wrote in a memoir of his upbringing in the London milieu of the Communist Party of Great Britain. "As a mode of reasoning, it provided us with *a priori* understandings and universal rules—laws of thought which were both a guide to action and a source of prophetical authority." But the point of Marxist philosophy still remained to change the world. "Stalin's dictum: 'Theory without Practice is Barren; Practice without Theory is Blind,' became as familiar to generations of Communists as Engels's boiling kettle [exemplifying the shift from water to steam as a quantitative to qualitative shift] was in classes on dialectics."[22] Stalin's *Short Course* quoted extensively from *Anti-Dühring*; Plekahnov and Lenin often turned more readily to Engels's writings than to Marx's; and it was dialectical materialism—far more than the theory of surplus value—that provided the driving philosophy for the Soviet-directed global communist movement. "It is the *Dialectics of Nature* which has become the constantly quoted authoritative source for the exposition of the dialectic in Soviet Marxism," reported Herbert Marcuse in the 1950s.[23]

So to repeat: was Engels responsible for the terrible misdeeds carried out under the banner of Marxism-Leninism? Even in our modern age of historical apologies, the answer has to be no. In no intelligible sense can Engels or Marx bear culpability for the crimes of historical actors carried out generations later, even if the policies were offered up in their honor. Just as Adam Smith is not to blame for the inequalities of the free market West, nor Martin Luther for the nature of modern Protestant evangelicalism, nor the Prophet Muhammad for the atrocities of Osama bin Laden, so the millions of souls dispatched by Stalinism (or by Mao's China, Pol Pot's Cambodia, and Mengistu's Ethiopia) did not go to their graves on account of two nineteenth-century London philosophers.

This is not just because of the simple anachronism of the charge. Engels was highly skeptical of vanguard-led, top-down revolutions like those with which communist parties seized power in the twentieth century. He always believed in a workers' party led by the working class itself (rather than by intellectuals and professional revolutionaries), and he remained adamant that the proletariat would arrive at socialism through the contradictions of the capitalist system and the development of political self-consciousness rather than by having it imposed upon them by a self-selecting communist leadership. "The Social Democratic Federation over here and your German-American Socialists share the distinction of being the only parties that have contrived to reduce Marx's theory of development to a rigid orthodoxy which the working man is not expected to arrive at by virtue of his own class consciousness; rather it is to be promptly and without preparation rammed down his throat as an article of faith," he complained pointedly to Adolph Sorge in May 1894.[24] The emancipation of the masses could never be the product of an external agent, a political deus ex machina, even if it came in the form of V. I. Lenin. Moreover, as his support for the German SPD suggests, Engels was inclined toward the end of his life to advocate the peaceable, democratic road to socialism, acting through the ballot box rather than the barricades (while always retaining the moral right to insurgency). In the specific Russian context, it is most likely that Plekhanov's post-1917 "Menshevik" demands for a period of bourgeois rule and capitalist development before any effective transition to a socialist state would have been more in tune with Engels's thinking than the Bolshevik will to power.

Despite the easy caricature by anticommunists and Marx apologists alike, Engels was never the narrow-minded, mechanistic architect of dialectical materialism exalted by twentieth-century Soviet ideology. A broad philosophical chasm lies between "Engelsism" and Stalinism, between an open, critical, and humane vision of scientific socialism and a scientistic socialism devoid of any ethical precepts. As philosopher John O'Neill argues, Engels's socialism has no necessary connection with twentieth-century state Marxism, since the link depends on Engels's adhering to a dogmatic conception of science committed to "methodological certainty" and "doctrinal orthodoxy"—both of which Engels rejected when it came to scientific inquiry and historical materialism.[25] The closed logic of Stalin's *Short Course* would have been anathema to the perpetually inquisitive Engels: behind his soldierly demeanor, the

General was interested in challenging ideas, following new trends, and often rethinking his own positions. "So-called 'socialist society' is not, in my view, to be regarded as something that remains crystallized for all time, but rather as being in process of constant change and transformation like all other social conditions," he wrote in 1890. "I see absolutely no difficulty in carrying out this revolution over a period, i.e. gradually."[26] In many ways Engels's thinking was far more heuristic and less rigid than Marx's. In *Anti-Dühring*, he concluded that the most valuable result of his scientific investigations was to "make us extremely distrustful of our present knowledge, in as much as in all probability we are just about at the beginning of human history."[27] And he adopted something of a proto-Popperian stance on questions of scientific fallibility: "The knowledge which has an unconditional claim to truth is realized in a series of relative errors; neither the one nor the other can be fully realized except through the unending duration of human existence."[28] When it came to historical materialism, he similarly pleaded with one correspondent not to "take every word I have said above for gospel" and told another that "our view of history is first and foremost a guide to study, not a tool for constructing objects after the Hegelian model."[29] This is not the language of a closed, totalizing political philosopher yearning to construct a new Leviathan. What is more, Engels directly and repeatedly criticized those Marxist parties—like Hyndman's SDF, the young, militant so-called *Jungen* faction of the SPD, or the German Socialist Labor Party in the United States—that attempted to seal off Marxism from further debate, "turning our theory into the rigid dogma of an orthodox sect."[30]

To some extent, the difference between Engels and his acolytes in the Soviet Union and elsewhere can be attributed to their respective starting points. Engels and Marx came to a scientific appreciation of their political philosophy during the 1860s and 1870s as they tried to redefine historical materialism in light of Darwinism and other advances in the natural and physical sciences. Much of their intellectual framework, stretching back to their earliest readings of Hegel, was already fully formed by the time they sought to connect their ideas with the emergent scientific vogue. By contrast, the next generation of socialists came to their Marxism along a very different ideological trajectory: in the words of Kautsky, "they had started from Hegel, I started from Darwin." Kautsky, along with Bernstein, Adler, Aveling, Plekhanov, Lenin, and the political leadership of the Second International—whose ideological awakening began with an immersion in the works of Charles Darwin, Herbert Spencer, and the positivist Auguste Comte—read Marx and Engels from a perspective that already encompassed evolutionary theory.[31] The Italian communist Enrico Ferri's *Socialism and Positive Science* (1894), Ludwig Woltmann's *Darwinian Theory and Socialism* (1899), Karl Kautsky's highly influential *Ethics and Historical Materialism* (1906), and the extract above from Lenin (who thought "the idea of development, of evolution, has almost completely penetrated social consciousness") were just a few of the contributions to a burgeoning communist literature that assumed a link between Darwinism and Marxism. These works provided the indispensable intellectual bridge from late-nineteenth-century Marxism to the dialectical materialism of Soviet orthodoxy. Obviously, Engels cannot be held responsible for what a later generation nurtured on a different set of philosophical and scientific premises read into his work.

A few months before the end of his life, Engels told the German political economist Werner Sombart in very clear terms how "Marx's whole way of thinking is not so much a doctrine as a method. It provides, not so much ready-made dogmas, as aids to further investigation and the method for such investigation."[32] Engels, like Marx, only rarely thought himself a Marxist in a narrow, partisan sense. Instead, he approached Marxism as an altogether grander truth that did not require the kind of protective genuflection that some party adherents were already beginning to practice.

Just as importantly, the essential characteristics of Engels the man—which surface only fitfully in his texts—were sharply at odds with the brazen inhumanity of Marxism-Leninism. He was more than just good to his dogs. For all his scientific enthusiasms, belief in rational progress, and fervor for technological advance, Engels retained elements of both the utopian socialist tradition (against which he had so self-consciously defined his and Marx's approach) and the Protestant eschatological inheritance he had abjured as a teenager. His telos was a dialectical culmination of the global class struggle: the withering away of the state, the liberation of mankind, and a workers' paradise of human fulfillment and sexual possibility—in sum, the leap from the kingdom of necessity to the kingdom of freedom. Neither a Leveler nor a statist, this great lover of the good life, passionate advocate of individuality, and enthusiastic believer in literature, culture, art, and music as an open forum could never have acceded to the Soviet communism of the twentieth century, all the Stalinist claims of his paternity notwithstanding.

Nor could he have accepted our current situation. If we can now strip away the accretions of twentieth-century Marxism-Leninism, the "dictatorial deviation" that so poisoned the well of social justice, and return to the authentic Engels of nineteenth-century Europe, a very different and strikingly contemporary voice reemerges. From his aerie in the Manchester cotton industry, Engels understood as few other socialists did the true face of rampant capitalism. And as our post-1989 liberal utopia of free trade and democracy totters under the dual strains of religious orthodoxy and free market fundamentalism, his critique resonates down the ages. The cozy collusion of government and capital, the corporate hunger for cheap labor and low skills, the restructuring of family life around the proclivities of the market, and even the design of our cities as dictated by the demands of capital—all of these were foreseen and dissected by Engels a century ago. And the recent events in the world's stock markets and banking sector have brought Engels's critique into even sharper focus.

Engels's relentless denunciation of the devastating processes of capitalism is particularly apposite when it comes to the unregulated global market. "The cheap prices of its commodities are the heavy artillery with which it batters down all Chinese walls," explained *The Communist Manifesto*. "It compels all nations, on pain of extinction, to adopt the bourgeois mode of production; it compels them to introduce what it calls civilization into their midst, i.e., to become bourgeois themselves." While Marx and Engels would have regarded today's opposition to globalization per se as being illogical, Engels's critique of the human costs of capitalism is most relevant in the countries at the sharp end of the world economy—notably the emerging markets of Brazil, Russia, India, and China. For here all the horrors of unregulated industrialization— capitalism transforming social relations, destroying old customs and habits, turning villages into cities, and workshops into factories—display the same savagery previously on show in nineteenth-century Europe. With China now claiming the mantle of "workshop of the world," the pollution, ill health, political resistance, and social unrest prevalent in the special economic zones of Guangdong Province and Shanghai appear eerily reminiscent of Engels's accounts of Manchester and Glasgow. Compare and contrast, as the scholar Ching Kwan Lee does, Engels's description of employment conditions in an 1840s cotton mill—

> In the cotton and flax spinning mills there are many rooms in which the air is filled with fluff and dust. . . . The operative of course has no choice in the matter. . . . The usual consequences of inhaling factory dust are the spitting of blood, heavy, noisy breathing, pains in the chest, coughing and sleeplessness. . . . Accidents occur to operatives who work in rooms crammed full of machinery. . . . The most common injury is the loss of a joint of the finger. . . . In Manchester one sees not only numerous cripples, but also plenty of workers who have lost the whole or part of an arm, leg or foot.

—with the testimony of a Chinese migrant worker in Shenzhen in 2000:

> There is no fixed work schedule. A twelve-hour workday is minimum. With rush orders, we have to work continuously for thirty hours or more. Day and night . . . the longest shift we had worked non-stop lasted for forty hours. . . . It's very exhausting because we have to stand all the time, to straighten the denim cloth by pulling. Our legs are always hurting. There is no place to sit on the shop floor. The machines do not stop during our lunch breaks. Three workers in a group will just take turns eating, one at a time. . . . The shop floor is filled with thick dust. Our

bodies become black working day and night indoors. When I get off from work and spit, it's all black.[33]

No matter how much the Communist Party of China might want to claim Engels's imprimatur, the unleavened exploitation produced by its policies clearly never was Engels's notion of the ideal society. From his teenage years as a manufacturer's heir amid the riches and poverty, the misery and degradation of the Barmen bleacheries, he was convinced that there was a more dignified place for humanity in the modern age. For him and Marx, the welcome abundance offered by capitalism deserved to be distributed through a more equitable system. For millions of people around the world that hope still holds. There is little doubt that today, some two decades after the fall of the Berlin Wall and the global collapse of state communism, Friedrich Engels, that Victorian embodiment of self-sacrifice and self-contradiction, would once more be predicting the negation of the negation and the fulfillment of his good friend Karl Marx's promise.

NOTES

PREFACE

1. *Reminiscences of Marx and Engels* (Moscow, 1958), p. 185.
2. *Frederick Engels: A Biography* (Dresden, 1972), p. 9.
3. Paul Lewis, "Marx's Stock Resurges on a 150-Year Tip," *New York Times*, 27 June 1998.
4. *Times* (London), 20 October 2008.
5. Meghnad Desai, *Marx's Revenge: The Resurgence of Capitalism and the Death of Statist Socialism* (London, 2002).
6. *Marx-Engels Collected Works* (New York, 1975–2005), vol. 6, pp. 486–87 [henceforth *MECW*].
7. "Marx after Communism," *Economist*, 21 December 2002.
8. Francis Wheen, *Karl Marx* (London, 1999).
9. See Gustav Mayer, *Friedrich Engels: Eine Biographie* (The Hague, 1934) and *Friedrich Engels* (London, 1936); Grace Carlton, *Friedrich Engels: The Shadow Prophet* (London, 1965); *Frederick Engels: A Biography*; W. O. Henderson, *The Life of Friedrich Engels* (London, 1976); David McLellan, *Engels* (Sussex, 1977); Terrell Carver, *Engels* (Oxford, 1981) and *Friedrich Engels: His Life and Thought* (London, 1991); J. D. Hunley, *The Life and Thought of Friedrich Engels* (London, 1991).
10. E. P. Thompson, *The Poverty of Theory and Other Essays* (London, 1978), p. 261.
11. Richard N. Hunt, *The Political Ideas of Marx and Engels* (Pittsburgh, 1974), p. 93.

12. Norman Levine, "Marxism and Engelsism," *Journal of the History of the Behavioural Sciences* 11, no. 3 (1973): 239.
13. *MECW*, vol. 26, p. 382.
14. Tony Judt, *Reappraisals* (London, 2008), p. 125.
15. *MECW*, vol. 26, p. 387.

1: SIEGFRIED IN ZION

1. *MECW*, vol. 2, pp. 578–79.
2. *Reminiscences of Marx and Engels* (Moscow, 1958), p. 183.
3. Quoted in Michael Knieriem, ed., *Die Herkunft des Friedrich Engels: Briefe aus der Verwandtschaft* (Trier, 1991), pp. 39–40.
4. See *Frederick Engels: A Biography* (Dresden, 1972), p. 16.
5. T. C. Banfield, *Industry of the Rhine* (1846; rpt. New York, 1969), pp. 122–23.
6. *MECW*, vol. 2, p. 8.
7. Banfield, *Industry of the Rhine*, p. 142.
8. Christopher Clark, *Iron Kingdom* (London, 2006), p. 125.
9. *Die Herkunft des Friedrich Engels*, pp. 555, 600.
10. Hughes Oliphant Old, *The Reading and Preaching of the Scriptures in the Worship of the Christian Church* (Cambridge, 1998), vol. 5, p. 104.
11. *MECW*, vol. 2, p. 555.
12. *Die Herkunft des Friedrich Engels*, p. 21.
13. See Gustav Mayer, *Friedrich Engels: Eine Biographie* (The Hague, 1934), vol. 1, p. 7.
14. Quoted in Manfred Kliem, ed., *Friedrich Engels: Dokumente seines Lebens* (Leipzig, 1977), p. 37.
15. *MECW*, vol. 44, p. 394.
16. *MECW*, vol. 2, p. 14.
17. *Die Herkunft des Friedrich Engels*, p. 463.
18. See James J. Sheehan, *German History, 1770–1866* (Oxford, 1989).
19. *Die Herkunft des Friedrich Engels*, pp. 463, 464, 470.
20. *MECW*, vol. 6, p. 259.
21. *MECW*, vol. 2, p. 553.
22. *MECW*, vol. 38, p. 30.
23. *MECW*, vol. 2, p. 582.
24. *MECW*, vol. 2, pp. 20, 585. See also Volkmar Wittmütz, "Friedrich Engels in der Barmer Stadtschule, 1829–1834," *Nachrichten aus dem Engels-Haus* 3 (1980).
25. Hugh Trevor-Roper, *The Romantic Movement and the Study of History* (London, 1969), p. 2.
26. See Celia Applegate, "Culture and the Arts," in Jonathan Sperber, ed., *Germany, 1800–1870* (Oxford, 2004).
27. Madame de Staël, *Germany* (London, 1813), p. 8.

28. Sheehan, *German History, 1770–1866*.

29. Jack Zipes, *The Brothers Grimm* (London, 2002), p. 26.

30. See Christopher Clark, *Iron Kingdom*.

31. *MECW*, vol. 2, p. 33.

32. *MECW*, vol. 2, p. 95.

33. *MECW*, vol. 2, p. 585.

34. *MECW*, vol. 2, p. 399.

35. Quoted in *Reminiscences of Marx and Engels*, p. 193.

36. *MECW*, vol. 2, p. 117.

37. *MECW*, vol. 2, pp. 499, 503.

38. *MECW*, vol. 2, p. 528.

39. Quoted in *Reminiscences of Marx and Engels*, pp. 192, 174.

40. Ibid., p. 94.

41. *MECW*, vol. 2, p. 511.

42. *MECW*, vol. 2, p. 530.

43. Quoted in Sheehan, *German History, 1770–1866*, p. 573.

44. *MECW*, vol. 2, p. 421.

45. Friedrich Engels, *The Condition of the Working Class in England* (Harmondsworth, 1987), p. 245.

46. See Richard Holmes, *Shelley: The Pursuit* (London, 1987).

47. See James M. Brophy, "The Public Sphere," in Sperber, ed., *Germany, 1800–1870*.

48. *MECW*, vol. 2, p. 558.

49. Quoted in Paul Foot, *Red Shelley* (London, 1984), p. 228. Eleanor Marx, together with her lover Edward Aveling, would later take up the Shelley baton in their joint work, *Shelley and Socialism* (1888).

50. Heinrich Heine, *Sämtliche Werke* (Hamburg, 1867), vol. 12, p. 83.

51. *MECW*, vol. 2, p. 422.

52. Mayer, *Eine Biographie*, vol. 1, p. 17.

53. *MECW*, vol. 2, p. 392.

54. *MECW*, vol. 2, p. 135.

55. See Sheehan, *German History, 1770–1866*, pp. 646–47.

56. *MECW*, vol. 2, p. 9.

57. *MECW*, vol. 24, p. 114.

58. *Frederick Engels: A Biography*, p. 30.

59. *MECW*, vol. 2, p. 25.

60. *MECW*, vol. 2, p. 426.

61. *MECW*, vol. 2, p. 454.

62. Quoted in David McLellan, *The Young Hegelians and Karl Marx* (London, 1969), p. 3.

63. *MECW*, vol. 2, pp. 426, 454, 461–62.

64. *MECW*, vol. 2, p. 471.

65. *MECW*, vol. 2, p. 528.
66. *MECW*, vol. 2, p. 486.
67. See William J. Brazill, *The Young Hegelians* (London, 1970).
68. *MECW*, vol. 16, p. 474.
69. *MECW*, vol. 2, p. 489.
70. See Gareth Stedman Jones, "Engels and the History of Marxism," in Eric Hobsbawm, ed., *The History of Marxism* (Brighton, 1982), vol. 1, p. 301.
71. *MECW*, vol. 2, pp. 99, 169.

2: THE DRAGON'S SEED

1. *MECW*, vol. 2, p. 181.
2. E. H. Carr, *Michael Bakunin* (London, 1975), p. 95; Alastair Hannay, *Kierkegaard: A Biography* (Cambridge, 2001), pp. 162–63.
3. *MECW*, vol. 2, p. 187.
4. *MECW*, vol. 26, p. 123.
5. In 1963, the barracks were renamed the Friedrich Engels barracks, home to the "Wachregiment Friedrich Engels" of the National People's Army of the GDR.
6. See Anthony Read and David Fisher, *Berlin* (London, 1994); Robert J. Hellman, *Berlin: The Red Room and White Beer* (Washington, 1990); Alexandra Richie, *Faust's Metropolis* (London, 1999).
7. Heinrich Heine, *Sämtliche Werke* (Hamburg, 1867), vol. 1, p. 240.
8. *MECW*, vol. 3, p. 515.
9. *MECW*, vol. 26, p. 357.
10. Quoted in Peter Singer, *Hegel* (Oxford, 1983), p. 32.
11. Leszek Kolakowski, *Main Currents of Marxism* (London, 2005), p. 61.
12. John Edward Toews, *Hegelianism* (Cambridge, 1980), p. 60.
13. Christopher Clark, *Iron Kingdom* (London, 2006), p. 434.
14. *MECW*, vol. 26, p. 363.
15. *MECW*, vol. 6, pp. 162–63.
16. *MECW*, vol. 6, pp. 359–60.
17. *MECW*, vol. 2, p. 197.
18. *MECW*, vol. 26, p. 364.
19. Quoted in David McLellan, *The Young Hegelians and Karl Marx* (London, 1969), p. 88; William J. Brazill, *The Young Hegelians* (London, 1970), p. 146; *MECW*, vol. 3, pp. 462, 3.
20. Ludwig Feuerbach, *Provisional Theses for the Reformation of Philosophy*, quoted in Lawrence S. Stepelevich, ed., *The Young Hegelians* (Cambridge, 1983), p. 156.
21. Ibid., p. 167.
22. *MECW*, vol. 2, p. 537.
23. *MECW*, vol. 2, p. 550.
24. *MECW*, vol. 48, pp. 393–94.

25. See Brazill, *The Young Hegelians*; Hellman, *Berlin*.
26. Stephan Born, *Erinnerungen eines Achtundvierzigers* (Leipzig, 1898), pp. 26–27.
27. See Engels's essay "Alexander Jung, 'Lectures on Modern German Literature,'" in the *Rheinische Zeitung*, 7 July 1842, for evidence of his clear break with Young Germany.
28. For those who are unfamiliar:

> I'm very well acquainted, too, with matters mathematical
> I understand equations, both the simple and quadratical
> About binomial theorem I'm teeming with a lot o' news
> With many cheerful facts about the square of the hypotenuse
>
> I'm very good at integral and differential calculus
> I know the scientific names of beings animalculous
> In short, in matters vegetable, animal, and mineral
> I am the very model of a modern Major-General.

29. *MECW*, vol. 2, pp. 321, 322, 335, 336.
30. Much of the following account of Marx's early life is drawn from David McLellan, *Karl Marx: His Life and Thought* (London, 1983), pp. 1–104; Francis Wheen, *Karl Marx* (London, 1999), pp. 7–59; and Eric Hobsbawm's essay in the *Dictionary of National Biography*.
31. Stephan Born, *Erinnerungen eines Achtundvierzigers*, p. 68.
32. "Ink in His Blood," *Times Literary Supplement*, 23 March 2007, p. 14.
33. *MECW*, vol. 50, p. 503.
34. Marx-Engels Papers, M4 (M2/1), International Institute of Social History, Amsterdam.
35. *MECW*, vol. 2, p. 586.
36. See Eric Hobsbawm, "Marx, Engels, and Pre-Marxian Socialism" in Eric Hobsbawm, ed., *The History of Marxism* (Brighton, 1982), vol. 1. Or, as Kolakowski puts it, "At the time when Marx came into the field as a theoretician of the proletariat revolution, socialist ideas already had a long life behind them" (Kolakowski, *Main Currents of Marxism*, p. 150).
37. A further word about socialists and communists. In the 1830s and 1840s, the French followers of Saint-Simon and Charles Fourier were widely known as socialists. By contrast, the Parisian secret societies organized around the ideas of Étienne Cabet and Louis-Auguste Blanqui, who looked back to the French Revolution for inspiration, were described as communists. During the early to mid-1840s, Marx and Engels followed contemporary practice in using the terms *communist* and *socialist* without clear demarcations. In the words of Raymond Williams, "until c.1850 the word [*socialist*] was too new and too general to have any predominant use." As we shall see, Marx and Engels's

political alliance with the militant working-class Communist League and their belief in a more "proletarian" form of socialism led them in the later 1840s to describe themselves specifically, for a number of years, as communists (as in *The Communist Manifesto*) to differentiate themselves from the more middle-class, utopian socialism of Fourier, Saint-Simon, and Robert Owen. By the latter half of the nineteenth century, as communism often came in the popular mind to be associated with insurrection (notably in the aftermath of the 1871 Paris Commune) and Michael Bakunin's philosophy of anarchism gained traction, Marx and Engels were inclined to describe themselves as "socialists"—or even "scientific socialists," in contrast to the utopian socialist tradition. The use of *communist* fully reemerges only from 1918, with the renaming of the Russian Social-Democratic Labor Party as the All-Russian Communist Party (Bolsheviks) following the Russian Revolution of 1917 and its clear differentiation from European social democracy. For a good account, see Raymond Williams, *Keywords: A Vocabulary of Culture and Society* (London, 1988).

38. For a good example of this tradition, see Tony Benn, *Arguments for Socialism* (London, 1979), pp. 21–44.

39. Henri de Saint-Simon, *Letters from an Inhabitant of Geneva*, in Ghita Ionescu, ed., *The Political Thought of Saint-Simon* (Oxford, 1976), p. 78.

40. Ibid., p. 10.

41. Quoted in F. A. Hayek, *The Counter-Revolution of Science* (Glencoe, 1952), p. 121.

42. Saint-Simon, *The New Christianity*, in Ionescu, *The Political Thought of Saint-Simon*, p. 210.

43. *Oeuvres complètes de Charles Fourier* (Paris, 1966–68), vol. 6, p. 397, quoted in Jonathan Beecher and Richard Bienvenu, eds., *The Utopian Vision of Charles Fourier* (London, 1975), p. 119.

44. See Gareth Stedman Jones, "Introduction," in Charles Fourier, *The Theory of the Four Movements* (Cambridge, 1996).

45. Quoted in Beecher and Bienvenu, *Fourier*, pp. 116–17.

46. Frank Manuel implies that the frigid banality of Fourier's own life inspired some of his loftier visions: "Fourier the bachelor lived alone in a garret and ate *table d'hôte* in the poorer Lyons restaurants, disliked children and spiders, loved flowers and cats.... From all accounts he was a queer duck.... One sometimes wonders whether this inventor of the system of passionate attraction ever experienced one" (*The Prophets of Paris* [Cambridge, 1962], p. 198).

47. *MECW*, vol. 24, p. 290.

48. *MECW*, vol. 4, p. 643; vol. 24, p. 290. Engels's view of the utopian socialists waxed and waned over the years. By 1875, he was notably more generous about their contribution to communism and suggested that "German theoretical socialism will never forget that it rests on the shoulders of Saint-Simon,

Fourier and Owen—three men who, in spite of all their fantastic notions and all their utopianism, stand among the most eminent thinkers of all time and whose genius anticipated innumerable things the correctness of which is now being scientifically proved by us" (*MECW*, vol. 23, pp. 630–31).

49. Isaiah Berlin, "The Life and Opinions of Moses Hess," in *Against the Current* (London, 1997), p. 214.

50. Moses Hess, *Rom und Jerusalem* (Leipzig, 1899), p. 16.

51. Quoted in Shlomo Avineri, *Moses Hess* (London, 1985), p. 11.

52. Berlin, *Against the Current*, p. 219.

53. See André Liebich, ed., *Selected Writings of August Cieszkowski* (Cambridge, 1979).

54. Quoted in McLellan, *The Young Hegelians and Karl Marx*, p. 10.

55. "Über die sozialistische Bewegung in Deutschland," in Moses Hess, *Philosophische und sozialistische Schriften, 1837–1850*, ed. Auguste Cornu and Wolfgang Mönke (Liechtenstein, 1980), p. 293.

56. See Gareth Stedman Jones, "Introduction," *The Communist Manifesto* (Harmondsworth, 2002).

57. Quoted in Avineri, *Moses Hess*, p. 61.

58. Ibid., p. 84.

59. *MECW*, vol. 3, p. 406.

60. "Die Europäische Triarchie," in Hess, *Philosophische und sozialistische Schriften*, p. 117.

61. Moses Hess, *Briefwechsel* (Amsterdam, 1959), p. 103.

3: MANCHESTER IN BLACK AND WHITE

1. *Manchester Guardian*, 27 August 1842.

2. *Manchester Times*, 7 July 1842.

3. Friedrich Engels, *The Condition of the Working Class in England* (Harmondsworth, 1987), p. 239.

4. See Alan Kidd, *Manchester* (Keele, 1996).

5. *The Life of Thomas Cooper, Written by Himself* (London, 1873), p. 207.

6. Engels, *Condition of the Working Class*, pp. 82, 156.

7. *MECW*, vol. 3, p. 392.

8. *MECW*, vol. 26, p. 317.

9. *Reasoner*, vol. 5 (1850), p. 92.

10. See Kidd, *Manchester*; W. D. Rubinstein, "The Victorian Middle Classes: Wealth, Occupation, and Geography," *Economic History Review* 30, no. 4 (1977).

11. Alexis de Tocqueville, *Journeys to England and Ireland* (1835; rpt. London, 1958), pp. 94, 107.

12. Quoted in L. D. Bradshaw, *Visitors to Manchester* (Manchester, 1987), p. 25.

13. Léon Faucher, *Manchester in 1844* (Manchester, 1844), p. 16.

14. Thomas Carlyle, "Chartism," *Selected Writings* (Harmondsworth, 1986), p. 211.

15. Robert Southey, *Letters from England by Don Manuel Alvarez Espriella* (London, 1808), p. 83.

16. Quoted in Bradshaw, *Visitors to Manchester*, p. 54.

17. Hippolyte Taine, *Notes on England* (1872; rpt. London, 1957), p. 219.

18. J. P. Kay, *The Moral and Physical Condition of the Working Classes Employed in the Cotton Manufacture in Manchester* (1832; rpt. Manchester, 1969), p. 8.

19. Edwin Chadwick, *Report on the Sanitary Conditions of the Labouring Population of Great Britain* (Edinburgh, 1965), p. 78.

20. Ibid., p. 111.

21. Wilmot Henry Jones [Geoffrey Gimcrack], *Gimcrackiana; or, Fugitive Pieces on Manchester Men and Manners* (Manchester, 1833), pp. 156–57.

22. *Manchester Guardian*, 6 May 1857.

23. Quoted in Bradshaw, *Visitors to Manchester*, p. 28.

24. R. Parkinson, *On the Present Condition of the Labouring Poor in Manchester* (Manchester, 1841), p. 85.

25. Faucher, *Manchester in 1844*, p. 69.

26. Benjamin Disraeli, *Sybil; or, The Two Nations* (London, 1981), p. 66.

27. *MECW*, vol. 2, p. 370.

28. Engels, *Condition of the Working Class*, p. 68.

29. *MECW*, vol. 2, pp. 370, 373, 378.

30. Engels, *Condition of the Working Class*, p. 182.

31. F. R. Johnston, *Eccles* (Eccles, 1967), p. 88.

32. On Ermen & Engels, see J. B. Smethhurst, "Ermen and Engels," *Marx Memorial Library Quarterly Bulletin*, 41 (1967); Roy Whitfield, *Frederick Engels in Manchester: The Search for a Shadow* (Salford, 1988); W. O. Henderson, *The Life of Friedrich Engels* (London, 1976).

33. *MECW*, vol. 38, p. 20. The factory referred to in this letter is actually the Engelskirchen one. The sentiment remains the same.

34. Engels, *Condition of the Working Class*, p. 27.

35. *MECW*, vol. 4, p. 226.

36. Faucher, *Manchester in 1844*, p. 25.

37. Engels, *Condition of the Working Class*, p. 245.

38. *MECW*, vol. 3, pp. 387, 380.

39. *MECW*, vol. 3, pp. 380, 387, 388.

40. *MECW*, vol. 25, pp. 346–47.

41. John Watts, *The Facts and Fictions of Political Economists* (Manchester, 1842), pp. 28, 35, 36, 13.

42. *Manchester Guardian*, 26 September 1838.

43. Engels, *Condition of the Working Class*, p. 241; *MECW*, vol. 2, p. 375.

44. See G. D. H. Cole, "George Julian Harney," *Chartist Portraits* (London, 1941).

45. *Reminiscences of Marx and Engels* (Moscow, 1958), p. 192.

46. F. G. Black and R. M. Black, eds., *The Harney Papers* (Assen, 1969), p. 260.

47. Engels, *Condition of the Working Class*, p. 160.

48. James Leach, *Stubborn Facts from the Factories by a Manchester Operative* (London, 1844), p. 40.

49. *MECW*, vol. 6, p. 486.

50. Engels, *Condition of the Working Class*, p. 242; *MECW*, vol. 3, p. 450.

51. Thomas Carlyle, "Signs of the Times," *Selected Writings*, p. 77.

52. Thomas Carlyle, *Past and Present* (1843; rpt. New York, 1965), p. 148.

53. *MECW*, vol. 3, p. 463.

54. *MECW*, vol. 10, p. 302.

55. Engels, *Condition of the Working Class*, p. 276.

56. George Weerth, *Sämtliche Werke* (Berlin, 1956–57), vol. 5, pp. 111, 128. This is, perhaps, a little unfair. The more civic-minded J. B. Priestley would later describe prewar Bradford as "at once one of the most provincial and yet one of the most cosmopolitan of English provincial cities," celebrated for its foreign residents. "I can remember when one of the best-known clubs in Bradford was the *Schiller-verein*. And in those days a Londoner was a stranger sight than a German. . . . A dash of the Rhine and the Oder found its way into our grim runnel—'t' mucky beck.' " See Priestley, *English Journey* (1933; London, 1993), pp. 123–24.

57. Eleanor Marx-Aveling to Karl Kautsky, 15 March 1898, Karl Kautsky Papers, International Institute of Social History, Amsterdam, DXVI, p. 489.

58. See Whitfield, *Engels in Manchester*, p. 70.

59. Edmund Wilson, *To the Finland Station* (London, 1991), p. 159. W. O. Henderson concurs. He describes Mary as "an Irish millhand who lived in Ancoats at 18 Cotton Street, off George Leigh Street, in the factory district." See Henderson, *Marx and Engels and the English Workers* (London, 1989), p. 45.

60. Max Beer, *Fifty Years of International Socialism* (London, 1935), p. 77.

61. Heinrich Gemkow, "Fünf Frauen an Engels' Seite," *Beiträge zur Geschichte der Arbeiterbewegung* 37, no. 4 (1995): 48.

62. Engels, *Condition of the Working Class*, p. 182.

63. Edmund Frow and Ruth Frow, *The New Moral World: Robert Owen and Owenism in Manchester and Salford* (Salford, 1986).

64. Weerth, *Sämtliche Werke*, vol. 1, p. 208.

65. Engels, *Condition of the Working Class*, p. 170.

66. Whitfield, *Engels in Manchester*, p. 21.

67. Engels, *Condition of the Working Class*, p. 30.

68. *MECW*, vol. 3, pp. 418, 423, 441.

69. *MECW*, vol. 3, p. 440.

70. *MECW*, vol. 3, p. 399.

71. *MECW*, vol. 4, p. 32.

72. *MECW*, vol. 4, pp. 431, 424. See also Gregory Claeys, "Engels' *Outlines of a Critique of Political Economy* (1843) and the Origins of the Marxist Critique of Capitalism," *History of Political Economy* 16, no. 2 (1984).

73. Many of the ideas in Engels's "Outlines" would reappear in Marx's *Economic and Philosophical Manuscripts*, where, along with Hess, it is described as "the only *original* German work of any interest in this field." See Karl Marx, *Early Writings* (Harmondsworth, 1992), p. 281. Crucially, Marx then extended the notion of alienation to the activity of labor itself.

74. Karl Marx to Friedrich Engels, 9 April 1863, *MECW*, vol. 41, p. 466.

75. *MECW*, vol. 38, p. 10.

76. Engels, *Condition of the Working Class*, p. 31.

77. *Reminiscences of Marx and Engels*, p. 137.

78. *MECW*, vol. 38, p. 13.

79. Engels, *Condition of the Working Class*, p. 31.

80. *MECW*, vol. 38, pp. 10–11.

81. Engels, *Condition of the Working Class*, p. 30.

82. Ibid., pp. 89, 92.

83. Ibid., p. 98.

84. *MECW*, vol. 3, p. 390.

85. Engels, *Condition of the Working Class*, p. 125.

86. Ibid., pp. 193–94.

87. Ibid., p. 184.

88. Ibid., pp. 31, 174, 216, 69.

89. Ibid., p. 275.

90. Ibid., p. 86.

91. Ibid., p. 87.

92. *MECW*, vol. 23, p. 365.

93. Steven Marcus, *Engels, Manchester, and the Working Class* (London, 1974), p. 145.

94. Simon Gunn, *The Public Culture of the Victorian Middle Class* (Manchester, 2000), p. 36. See also Marc Eli Blanchard, *In Search of the City* (Stanford, 1985), p. 21.

95. *Guardian*, 4 February 2006. See also Asa Briggs's comment that "if Engels had lived not in Manchester but in Birmingham his conception of 'class' and his theories of the role of class history might have been very different" (Briggs, *Victorian Cities* [London, 1990], p. 116). By contrast, W. O. Henderson describes Engels's motives as follows: "He was a young man in a bad temper who vented his spleen in a passionate denunciation of the factory system. . . . The unrestrained violence of his language and his complete failure to understand any point of view different from his own . . . may be explained by the fact . . . Engels was suffering from an overwhelming sense of frustration." See Henderson and W. H. Chaloner, eds., *The Condition of the Working Class in England* (London, 1958), p. xxx.

96. Engels, *Condition of the Working Class*, p. 61.

97. Ibid., pp. 143–44. For Lenin, the book's signal achievement was that it revealed that the proletariat was not just "a suffering class" but that "in fact, the disgraceful economic condition of the proletariat was driving it irresistibly forward and compelling it to fight for its ultimate emancipation." See *Reminiscences of Marx and Engels*, pp. 61–62.

98. Engels, *Condition of the Working Class*, p. 52.

99. Gareth Stedman Jones, "The First Industrial City? Engels' Account of Manchester in 1844," unpublished paper, p. 7. See also Stedman Jones, "Engels and the Industrial Revolution," in Douglas Moggach, ed., *The New Hegelians: Politics and Philosophy in the Hegelian School* (Cambridge, 2006).

100. Engels, *Condition of the Working Class*, p. 100.

101. Tocqueville, *Journeys to England and Ireland*, p. 108.

102. *MECW*, vol. 23, p. 324.

103. Engels, *Condition of the Working Class*, p. 64.

104. Ibid., p. 243.

105. Ibid., p. 291.

106. *MECW*, vol. 23, p. 347.

107. Friedrich Engels, *Anti-Dühring* (Peking, 1976), pp. 385–86.

108. *MECW*, vol. 23, p. 389.

109. *Der Bund der Kommunisten*, documents and materials, vol. 1 (Berlin, DDR), p. 343, quoted in Michael Knieriem, ed., *Über Friedrich Engels: Privates, Öffentliches und Amtliches Aussagen und Zeugnisse von Zeitgenossen* (Wuppertal, 1986), p. 27.

110. Quoted in Jürgen Kuczynski, *Die Geschichte der Lage der Arbeiter unter dem Kapitalismus* (Berlin, 1960), vol. 8, pp. 168–69.

111. Karl Marx, *Capital* (Harmondsworth, 1990), vol. 1, p. 349.

112. For a proper appreciation of the work's significance, see S. H. Rigby, *Engels and the Formation of Marxism* (Manchester, 1992), p. 63.

4: "A LITTLE PATIENCE AND SOME TERRORISM"

1. Honoré de Balzac, *Old Goriot* (1834; rpt. Harmondsworth, 1951), pp. 304, 37–38). Engels, like Marx, was a great fan of Balzac, preferring him even over Zola. "*La Comédie humaine* gives us a most wonderfully realistic history of French 'Society,' especially of *le monde parisien*, describing, chronicle-fashion, almost year by year from 1816 to 1848 the progressive inroads of the rising bourgeoisie upon the society of nobles, that reconstituted itself after 1815 and set up again, as far as it could, the standard of *la vieille politesse française*. He describes how the last remnants of this, to him, model society gradually succumbed before the intrusion of the vulgar monied upstart, or were corrupted by him," Engels wrote to his correspondent Margaret Harkness in 1888 (*MECW*, vol. 48, p. 168).

2. Quoted in David McLellan, *Karl Marx: His Life and Thought* (London, 1983), p. 57.
3. Quoted in David McLellan, ed., *Karl Marx: Interviews and Recollections* (London, 1981), p. 8.
4. Quoted in Shlomo Avineri, *The Social and Political Thought of Karl Marx* (Cambridge, 1968), pp. 140–41.
5. Isaiah Berlin, *Karl Marx: His Life and Environment* (Oxford, 1978), p. 60.
6. Karl Marx, "Paris Manuscripts," *The Early Texts* (Oxford, 1971), p. 148.
7. *MECW*, vol. 26, p. 317.
8. Quoted in *Reminiscences of Marx and Engels* (Moscow, 1958), p. 64.
9. Gustav Mayer, *Friedrich Engels: Eine Biographie* (The Hague, 1934), vol. 1, p. 175.
10. Quoted in *Reminiscences of Marx and Engels*, p. 92.
11. Ibid., p. 91.
12. *MECW*, vol. 26, p. 382.
13. *MECW*, vol. 47, p. 202.
14. *MECW*, vol. 46, p. 147.
15. *MECW*, vol. 29, p. 264; vol. 26, p. 382.
16. *MECW*, vol. 5, pp. 36–37.
17. *MECW*, vol. 4, p. 241.
18. *MECW*, vol. 4, p. 7.
19. *MECW*, vol. 4, pp. 7, 93.
20. *MECW*, vol. 38, p. 6.
21. *MECW*, vol. 38, pp. 18, 28, 17–18, 25.
22. *MECW*, vol. 38, pp. 29, 3.
23. *MECW*, vol. 38, pp. 3, 4.
24. *MECW*, vol. 4, pp. 230–31.
25. *MECW*, vol. 38, p. 4.
26. *MECW*, vol. 38, p. 232.
27. *MECW*, vol. 38, p. 23.
28. Quoted in Gustav Mayer, *Eine Biographie*, pp. 215–17.
29. *MECW*, vol. 4, p. 243.
30. *MECW*, vol. 4, p. 252.
31. *MECW*, vol. 4, p. 255.
32. *MECW*, vol. 4, p. 263.
33. *MECW*, vol. 38, p. 572.
34. Heidelberg University Library, manuscript 2560 (Cod. Heid. 378 XXX), quoted in Michael Knieriem, ed., *Über Friedrich Engels: Privates, Öffentliches und Amtliches Aussagen und Zeugnisse von Zeitgenosen* (Wuppertal, 1986), p. 8.
35. *MECW*, vol. 38, p. 39.
36. Quoted in *Reminiscences of Marx and Engels*, p. 194.
37. *MECW*, vol. 38, pp. 29, 33.

38. *MECW*, vol. 43, p. 518.

39. *Guardian*, 4 February 2006.

40. F. G. Black and R. M. Black, eds., *The Harney Papers* (Assen, 1969), p. 239.

41. Quoted in E. H. Carr, *Michael Bakunin* (London, 1975), p. 146.

42. Stephan Born, *Erinnerungen eines Achtundvierzigers* (Leipzig, 1898), p. 74.

43. Max Beer, *Fifty Years of International Socialism* (London, 1935), p. 78.

44. Born, *Erinnerungen*, p. 73.

45. Eleanor Marx-Aveling to Karl Kautsky, 15 March 1898, Karl Kautsky Papers, International Institute of Social History, Amsterdam, DXVI, p. 489.

46. Max Stirner, *The Ego and Its Own* (Cambridge, 1995), p. 323. See also Lawrence S. Stepelevich, "The Revival of Max Stirner," *Journal of the History of Ideas* 35, no. 2 (1974).

47. *MECW*, vol. 38, p. 12.

48. *MECW*, vol. 5, pp. 36–37.

49. *MECW*, vol. 6, p. 166.

50. *MECW*, vol. 5, p. 90.

51. Quoted in *The Writings of the Young Marx*, trans. and ed. Lloyd D. Easton and Kurt H. Guddat (Garden City, 1967), p. 431.

52. *MECW*, vol. 5, p. 47.

53. *MECW*, vol. 26, pp. 313–14.

54. *MECW*, vol. 6, p. 5.

55. Born, *Erinnerungen*, p. 72.

56. *MECW*, vol. 6, p. 79.

57. *MECW*, vol. 6, p. 56.

58. *MECW*, vol. 6, p. 529.

59. *MECW*, vol. 26, p. 320.

60. Quoted in *Reminiscences of Marx and Engels*, p. 270.

61. *MECW*, vol. 26, p. 318.

62. *MECW*, vol. 26, p. 319.

63. *MECW*, vol. 38, pp. 39–40.

64. P. J. Proudhon, *Confessions d'un révolutionnaire* (Paris, 1849), quoted in Francis Wheen, *Karl Marx* (London, 1999), p. 107.

65. *MECW*, vol. 6, p. 512.

66. Born, *Erinnerungen*, p. 47.

67. Eugène Sue, *The Mysteries of Paris* (Cambridgeshire, 1989), p. 9.

68. Quoted in Colin Jones, *Paris* (London, 2004), p. 349.

69. See David H. Pinkney, *Decisive Years in France, 1840–1847* (Princeton, 1986); Philip Mansel, *Paris Between Empires* (London, 2001).

70. *MECW*, vol. 38, pp. 80–83.

71. *MECW*, vol. 38, p. 91.

72. *MECW*, vol. 38, p. 16.

73. *MECW*, vol. 38, p. 16.

74. Born, *Erinnerungen*, pp. 51–52.

75. *MECW*, vol. 5, p. 559.

76. *MECW*, vol. 38, p. 115.

77. Isaiah Berlin, *Against the Current* (London, 1997), p. 219.

78. *MECW*, vol. 38, pp. 56, 65, 108, 153.

79. Eleanor Marx-Aveling to Karl Kautsky, 15 March 1898. To add to the confusion, Stephan Born writes of Engels having to leave Paris after chivalrously intervening with a French count who had dumped his mistress without providing for her. The count then contacted some amenable government ministers, who had Engels deported. See Born, *Erinnerungen*, p. 71.

80. Born, *Erinnerungen*, p. 49.

81. *MECW*, vol. 6, p. 98.

82. *MECW*, vol. 6, p. 98.

83. *MECW*, vol. 6, p. 102.

84. *MECW*, vol. 38, p. 139.

85. *MECW*, vol. 6, pp. 345, 348, 351, 354.

86. Quoted in *Reminiscences of Marx and Engels*, p. 153.

87. *MECW*, vol. 26, p. 322.

88. Wilhelm Liebknecht, *Karl Marx: Biographical Memoirs* (London, 1975), p. 26.

89. For an analysis of the textual and intellectual interstices between *The Condition of the Working Class* and *The Communist Manifesto*, see Terrell Carver, *Friedrich Engels: His Life and Thought* (London, 1991).

90. *MECW*, vol. 6, p. 487.

91. *MECW*, vol. 6, p. 558.

5: THE INFINITELY RICH '48 HARVEST

1. *MECW*, vol. 6, p. 559.

2. *MECW*, vol. 6, p. 647.

3. *MECW*, vol. 38, p. 169.

4. *MECW*, vol. 38, pp. 159–60.

5. See Christopher Clark, *Iron Kingdom* (London, 2006); James J. Sheehan, *German History, 1770–1866* (Oxford, 1989), p. 658.

6. See David E. Barclay, "Political Trends and Movements, 1830–50," in Jonathan Sperber, ed., *Germany, 1800–1870* (Oxford, 2004).

7. *MECW*, vol. 26, p. 123.

8. Quoted in P. H. Noyes, *Organization and Revolution: Working-Class Associations in the German Revolution of 1848–49* (Princeton, 1966), pp. 286–87.

9. See Jonathan Sperber, *Rhineland Radicals* (Princeton, 1991).

10. See Oscar J. Hammen, *The Red '48ers* (New York, 1969).

11. *MECW*, vol. 26, p. 122.

12. *MECW*, vol. 38, pp. 171, 173.

13. *MECW*, vol. 26, p. 123.

14. *MECW*, vol. 11, p. 40.
15. See Philip Mansel, *Paris Between Empires* (London, 2001); Hammen, *The Red '48ers*.
16. *MECW*, vol. 7, pp. 124, 130, 128.
17. *MECW*, vol. 7, pp. 131–32.
18. *MECW*, vol. 7, p. 587.
19. *MECW*, vol. 38, p. 541.
20. *MECW*, vol. 7, p. 460.
21. *Neue Rheinische Zeitung*, 7 November 1848, quoted in David McLellan, *Karl Marx: His Life and Thought* (London, 1983), p. 189.
22. *MECW*, vol. 7, p. 514.
23. *MECW*, vol. 7, pp. 518, 519.
24. *MECW*, vol. 7, pp. 526–29.
25. See Istvan Deak, *The Lawful Revolution: Louis Kossuth and the Hungarians* (New York, 1979); Ian Cummins, *Marx, Engels, and National Movements* (London, 1980).
26. *MECW*, vol. 7, p. 423.
27. Quoted in Roman Rosdolsky, *Engels and the "Nonhistoric" Peoples: The National Question in the Revolution of 1848* (Glasgow, 1986), p. 135.
28. *MECW*, vol. 8, p. 234.
29. *MECW*, vol. 8, p. 366.
30. *MECW*, vol. 46, pp. 206–07.
31. *MECW*, vol. 8, p. 238.
32. *MECW*, vol. 26, p. 128.
33. *MECW*, vol. 8, p. 439.
34. *MECW*, vol. 9, p. 171.
35. Sheehan, *German History*, p. 691.
36. Ibid., p. 399.
37. Ibid., p. 447.
38. See Sperber, *Rhineland Radicals*.
39. C. H. A. Pagenstecher, *Lebenserinnerungen von Dr. Med. C. H. Alexander Pagenstecher* (Leipzig, 1913), vol. 3, p. 63.
40. *MECW*, vol. 9, p. 448.
41. *MECW*, vol. 10, pp. 602–03.
42. Pagenstecher, *Lebenserinnerungen*, p. 66.
43. Carl Hecker, *Der Aufstand in Elberfeld im Mai 1849 und mein Verhaltniss zu Demselben* (Elberfeld, 1849), p. 38.
44. *Elberfelder Zeitung*, 3 June 1849.
45. The story originates from a very brief account in the Wuppertal archives by the Barmen manufacturer's son Ernst von Eynern, "Friedrich von Eynern: Ein bergisches Lebensbild," *Zeitschrift des Bergischen Geschichtsvereins* 35 (1900–01): 1–103.

46. Pagenstecher, *Lebenserinnerungen*, p. 66.

47. H. J. M. Körner, *Lebenskämpfe in der Alten und Neues Welt* (Zurich, 1866), vol. 2, p. 137.

48. *MECW*, vol. 9, p. 448.

49. *MECW*, vol. 9, p. 449.

50. Quoted in Manfred Kliem, *Friedrich Engels: Dokumente seines Lebens* (Leipzig, 1977), p. 280.

51. *MECW*, vol. 10, p. 172.

52. *MECW*, vol. 10, pp. 193, 202.

53. *MECW*, vol. 38, p. 204.

54. *MECW*, vol. 38, p. 203.

55. *MECW*, vol. 10, p. 211.

56. *MECW*, vol. 10, p. 224.

57. *MECW*, vol. 38, p. 203.

58. See Martin Berger, *Engels, Armies, and Revolution* (Hamden, 1977), p. 37.

59. *MECW*, vol. 10, p. 237.

60. *MECW*, vol. 38, p. 203.

61. *MECW*, vol. 38, p. 207.

62. *MECW*, vol. 10, pp. 150–51.

63. *MECW*, vol. 38, p. 213.

6: MANCHESTER IN SHADES OF GRAY

1. *MECW*, vol. 40, p. 236.

2. *MECW*, vol. 38, p. 250.

3. *MECW*, vol. 42, p. 172.

4. Alexander Herzen, *My Past and Thoughts* (London, 1968), vol. 3, p. 1045.

5. Ibid., vol. 10, p. 381.

6. Ibid., vol. 38, p. 222.

7. Ibid., vol. 24, p. 12.

8. Ibid., vol. 10, p. 24.

9. Ibid., vol. 10, p. 283.

10. Ibid., vol. 38, p. 289.

11. Jenny Marx, "A Short Sketch of an Eventful Life," in Robert Payne, ed., *The Unknown Karl Marx* (London, 1972), p. 125.

12. Letter from Jenny Marx to Joseph Weydemeyer, 20 May 1850, quoted in Francis Wheen, *Karl Marx* (London, 2000), p. 158.

13. *MECW*, vol. 38, p. 241.

14. Quoted in W. O. Henderson, *Marx and Engels and the English Workers* (London, 1989), p. 20.

15. Quoted in Gustav Mayer, *Friedrich Engels* (London, 1936), p. 130.

16. *MECW*, vol. 38, p. 379.

17. A. J. P. Taylor, "Manchester," *Encounter* 8, no. 3 (1957): 9.

18. *Manchester Guardian*, 11 October 1851.

19. *MECW*, vol. 38, p. 255.

20. *MECW*, vol. 38, p. 281.

21. Thomas Cooper, *The Life of Thomas Cooper, Written by Himself* (London, 1873), p. 393.

22. *MECW*, vol. 40, p. 344.

23. *MECW*, vol. 38, p. 264.

24. *MECW*, vol. 41, p. 465.

25. Manfred Kliem, ed., *Friedrich Engels: Dokumente Seines Lebens* (Leipzig, 1977), p. 114.

26. *MECW*, vol. 38, p. 250.

27. *MECW*, vol. 38, p. 302.

28. Quoted in Gustav Mayer, *Friedrich Engels: Eine Biographie* (The Hague, 1934), vol. 2, p. 12.

29. *MECW*, vol. 38, p. 379.

30. *MECW*, vol. 38, pp. 383, 401.

31. *MECW*, vol. 42, p. 88.

32. Ernst von Eynern, "Friedrich von Eynern: Ein bergisches Lebensbild," *Zeitschrift des Bergischen Geschichtsvereins* 35 (1900–01): 1–103.

33. *MECW*, vol. 42, pp. 192, 195.

34. Quoted in J. B. Smethhurst, "Ermen and Engels," *Marx Memorial Library Quarterly Bulletin* 41 (Jan–March 1967): 10.

35. *Frederick Engels: A Biography* (Dresden, 1972), p. 332.

36. *MECW*, vol. 42, p. 172.

37. *MECW*, vol. 41, p. 332.

38. *MECW*, vol. 39, p. 581.

39. David McLellan, *Karl Marx: A Biography* (London, 1995), p. 264.

40. *MECW*, vol. 42, p. 172.

41. Marx, "Short Sketch," pp. 130–31.

42. *MECW*, vol. 39, p. 590.

43. Wheen, *Karl Marx*, p. 84.

44. *Reminiscences of Marx and Engels* (Moscow, 1958), p. 185.

45. *MECW*, vol. 38, pp. 321, 395, 451.

46. *MECW*, vol. 39, p. 58.

47. *MECW*, vol. 41, pp. 74, 197, 203, 230.

48. *MECW*, vol. 41, p. 141.

49. *MECW*, vol. 41, p. 423.

50. R. Arthur Arnold, *The History of the Cotton Famine* (London, 1864), p. 113.

51. Quoted in W. O. Henderson, *The Lancashire Cotton Famine* (Manchester, 1969), p. 107.

52. See John Watts, *The Facts of the Cotton Famine* (London, 1866).

53. *MECW*, vol. 38, p. 409.

54. *MECW*, vol. 38, p. 419.

55. Quoted in McLellan, *Karl Marx: A Biography*, p. 284.

56. *MECW*, vol. 39, p. 391.

57. *MECW*, vol. 39, p. 164.

58. *MECW*, vol. 39, p. 212; vol. 40, pp. 451–52.

59. *MECW*, vol. 38, p. 494.

60. *MECW*, vol. 41, p. 14.

61. *MECW*, vol. 40, pp. 256, 283.

62. *MECW*, vol. 41, p. 351.

63. *MECW*, vol. 43, p. 160.

64. *MECW*, vol. 42, p. 390.

65. *MECW*, vol. 41, pp. 394, 411, 414.

66. Marx, "Short Sketch," p. 126.

67. For a fuller account of this story and the historiographic debates surrounding it, see McLellan, *Karl Marx: A Biography*, pp. 264–74; Wheen, *Karl Marx*, pp. 170–75; Terrell Carver, *Friedrich Engels: His Life and Thought* (London, 1991), pp. 166–69; Yvonne Kapp, *Eleanor Marx: The Crowded Years* (London, 1976), pp. 430–40; Kapp, "Frederick Demuth: New Evidence from Old Sources," *Socialist History* 6 (1994).

68. See Kliem, *Friedrich Engels: Dokumente Seines Lebens*, p. 488.

69. See Roy Whitfield, *Frederick Engels in Manchester: The Search for a Shadow* (Salford, 1988).

70. *MECW*, vol. 39, p. 443.

71. In the archives of the Working Class Movement Library, Salford, is a 1970 letter from John Millar, city planning officer, in response to Ruth Frow's request for a plaque to be placed on the house. In light of the demolition, he felt there would be "little point." See "Engels in M/CR" box.

72. *MECW*, vol. 41, pp. 344, 427.

73. *MECW*, vol. 24, p. 170.

74. *MECW*, vol. 27, p. 305. For a full life of Schorlemmer, see Karl Heinig, *Carl Schorlemmer: Chemiker und Kommunist Ersten Ranges* (Leipzig, 1974).

75. See W. O. Henderson, "Friends in Exile," *The Life of Friedrich Engels* (London, 1976).

76. *MECW*, vol. 40, p. 490.

77. See Ralph Greaves, *Foxhunting in Cheshire* (Kent, 1964); Gordon Fergusson, *The Green Collars* (London, 1993).

78. Marx-Engels Archives, R49, International Institute of Social History, Amsterdam.

79. *MECW*, vol. 40, p. 97.

80. *Reminiscences of Marx and Engels*, p. 88.

81. *MECW*, vol. 14, p. 422.

82. *Reminiscences of Marx and Engels*, p. 88.

83. *MECW*, vol. 40, pp. 264–65.

84. *MECW*, vol. 40, p. 131.

85. See Alan Kidd, *Manchester* (Keele, 1996).

86. *MECW*, vol. 19, p. 360.

87. Marx-Engels Archives, M17, International Institute of Social History, Amsterdam.

88. See *Sphinx*, 1 May 1869.

89. *MECW*, vol. 39, p. 479.

90. *MECW*, vol. 39, p. 249. There is an irony in Engels's embrace of Manchester's civil society. According to the critical theorist Jürgen Habermas, the voluntary societies of the nineteenth-century European city provided the "theatrical scaffolding" for what he terms "the bourgeois drama." Through the social leadership of clubs such as the Albert, the Brazenose, and the Schiller Anstalt, the middle classes established a cultural hegemony within the public sphere of the urban world that both codified interclass relations and underpinned the mid-Victorian stability Engels so abhorred. The myriad middle-class civil associations that honeycombed Manchester helped to construct, in the words of historian Martin Hewitt, a "moral imperialism" that subtly but effectively kept the working classes in their place. Collectively, they constituted a strategy of social control and cultural deproletarianization: instead of realizing class consciousness and seeing the bourgeoisie as their class enemy, the working class started to ape the middle-class ethic of rational recreation and useful knowledge. Bourgeois notions of leisure and sociability—in concert halls, gentlemen's clubs, charities, and educational institutes—subtly helped to unpick the radical ambition of the Manchester proletariat. Whether Engels realized it or not, he was a willing participant in the cultural hegemony transforming Manchester from the crucible of physical-force Chartism to the scene of placid Hallé soirees.

91. *MECW*, vol. 40, pp. 82, 104, 105.

92. *MECW*, vol. 40, pp. 131, 149.

93. *MECW*, vol. 40, p. 151.

94. *MECW*, vol. 42, pp. 231, 225.

95. *MECW*, vol. 40, p. 202.

96. *MECW*, vol. 47, p. 229.

97. *MECW*, vol. 41, p. 138.

98. *MECW*, vol. 41, pp. 260, 267, 266.

7: AN END TO HUCKSTERING

1. *MECW*, vol. 24, p. 192.

2. *MECW*, vol. 29, p. 263.

3. *MECW*, vol. 11, p. 103. It might also be worth noting that Marx's celebrated introduction to *The Eighteenth Brumaire*—"Hegel remarks somewhere that all

great, world-historical facts and personages occur, as it were, twice. He has forgotten to add: the first time as tragedy, the second as farce"—was most likely inspired by a letter Marx received from Engels in December 1851 as he was composing the work. "But, after what we saw yesterday, there can be no counting on the *peuple*, and it really seems as though old Hegel, in the guise of the World Spirit, were directing history from the grave and, with the greatest conscientiousness, causing everything to be re-enacted twice over, once as grand tragedy and the second time as rotten farce," was Engels's response to Bonaparte's coup. See *MECW*, vol. 38, p. 505.

4. *MECW*, vol. 50, p. 266.
5. *MECW*, vol. 49, pp. 34–36.
6. *MECW*, vol. 21, p. 94.
7. *MECW*, vol. 10, p. 399.
8. *MECW*, vol. 10, p. 412.
9. *MECW*, vol. 10, p. 422.
10. *MECW*, vol. 10, p. 469.
11. *MECW*, vol. 38, p. 370.
12. *MECW*, vol. 38, p. 332.
13. *MECW*, vol. 39, pp. 423–25, 434–36.
14. *MECW*, vol. 13, p. 524.
15. *MECW*, vol. 40, p. 400.
16. *MECW*, vol. 41, p. 280.
17. See W. H. Chaloner and W. O. Henderson, eds., *Engels as Military Critic* (Manchester, 1959).
18. *MECW*, vol. 11, p. 204.
19. *MECW*, vol. 17, p. 437.
20. *MECW*, vol. 18, p. 540.
21. *MECW*, vol. 42, p. 399.
22. See Stephen Bull, *"Volunteer!" The Lancashire Rifle Volunteers, 1859–1885* (Lancashire, 1993).
23. For a good example of a different contemporary approach to the volunteer corps, see *The Sack; or, Volunteers' Testimonial to the Militia* (London, 1862).
24. *MECW*, vol. 44, pp. 7, 17, 32.
25. *MECW*, vol. 11, pp. 85–86.
26. *MECW*, vol. 25, pp. 154–55.
27. Friedrich Engels, *Anti-Dühring* (Peking, 1976), p. 221.
28. *MECW*, vol. 14, p. 416.
29. *MECW*, vol. 14, p. 545.
30. *MECW*, vol. 6, p. 472.
31. Karl Marx and Friedrich Engels, *On Colonialism* (Moscow, 1968), pp. 81–82.
32. *MECW*, vol. 39, p. 82.

33. Marx and Engels, *On Colonialism*, 1968, p. 152.
34. *MECW*, vol. 24, p. 11.
35. *MECW*, vol. 42, p. 205; vol. 47, p. 192.
36. *MECW*, vol. 18, p. 67.
37. *MECW*, vol. 46, p. 322.
38. See D. A. Farnie, *The English Cotton Industry and the World Market, 1815–1896* (Oxford, 1979), p. 105.
39. *MECW*, vol. 46, p. 322.
40. *MECW*, vol. 41, pp. 441–47.
41. Karl Kautsky Papers, International Institute of Social History, Amsterdam, DXVI, p. 489.
42. *MECW*, vol. 49, p. 378.
43. Yvonne Kapp, *Eleanor Marx: Family Life* (London, 1972), p. 107.
44. *MECW*, vol. 43, p. 311.
45. Quoted in *The Daughters of Karl Marx: Family Correspondence, 1866–1898* (London, 1982), p. 51.
46. *MECW*, vol. 43, p. 541.
47. *MECW*, vol. 43, p. 311.
48. Karl Marx and Friedrich Engels, *On Ireland* (London, 1971), p. 14. Extracts from Engels's "Unpublished History of Ireland" were later serialized by the *Irish Democrat* newspaper. See *Irish Democrat*, new series, nos. 71 and 72 (Nov.–Dec. 1950).
49. *MECW*, vol. 40, p. 49–50.
50. *MECW*, vol. 40, p. 49.
51. *MECW*, vol. 43, pp. 473–74.
52. Roy Foster, *Modern Ireland* (London, 1989), p. 391.
53. *Reminiscences of Marx and Engels* (Moscow, 1958), p. 88.
54. Max Beer, *Fifty Years of International Socialism* (London, 1935), p. 78.
55. *MECW*, vol. 42, p. 474.
56. *MECW*, vol. 42, p. 483.
57. *MECW*, vol. 43, p. 163.
58. *MECW*, vol. 42, p. 178.
59. *MECW*, vol. 42, p. 371.
60. *MECW*, vol. 42, p. 406.
61. *MECW*, vol. 43, p. 160; vol. 42, p. 381.
62. Robert Skidelsky, "What's Left of Marx?" *New York Review of Books*, 16 November 2000.
63. Karl Marx, *Capital* (Harmondsworth, 1990), p. 799.
64. *MECW*, vol. 42, pp. 363, 451, 467–68.
65. *MECW*, vol. 42, p. 426.
66. *MECW*, vol. 20, pp. 208, 227, 224, 231.
67. *MECW*, vol. 38, pp. 170, 187, 194.

68. *MECW*, vol. 43, p. 299.

69. *MECW*, vol. 43, pp. 302–03.

70. *MECW*, vol. 43, p. 252.

8: THE GRAND LAMA OF THE REGENT'S PARK ROAD

1. *MECW*, vol. 47, p. 355.

2. *Reminiscences of Marx and Engels* (Moscow, 1958), pp. 310–11.

3. *MECW*, vol. 43, p. 561; vol. 44, p. 142.

4. See Angus Webster, *The Regent's Park and Primrose Hill* (London, 1911); Friends of Chalk Farm Library, *Primrose Hill Remembered* (London, 2001).

5. Eduard Bernstein, *My Years of Exile: Reminiscences of a Socialist* (London, 1921), p. 153.

6. *Reminiscences of Marx and Engels*, p. 186.

7. Ibid., pp. 335, 316.

8. Bernstein, *My Years of Exile*, p. 197.

9. Marx-Engels Archives, M33, International Institute for Social History, Amsterdam.

10. *MECW*, vol. 47, p. 5.

11. *MECW*, vol. 44, pp. 47, 66, 120.

12. *MECW*, vol. 44, p. 131.

13. See Robert Tombs, *The Paris Commune* (London, 1999).

14. *MECW*, vol. 27, p. 186.

15. *MECW*, vol. 44, pp. 228–29.

16. Quoted in Francis Wheen, *Karl Marx* (London, 2000), p. 333.

17. *MECW*, vol. 44, p. 157.

18. *MECW*, vol. 42, pp. 20, 157.

19. Friedrich Engels, *The Condition of the Working Class in England* (Harmondsworth, 1987), p. 28.

20. See Edmund Wilson, *To the Finland Station* (London, 1991), pp. 264–68.

21. Leszek Kolakowski, *Main Currents of Marxism* (London, 2005), p. 205.

22. Quoted in E. H. Carr, *Michael Bakunin* (London, 1975), p. 341.

23. *MECW*, vol. 43, pp. 191, 193, 336.

24. *MECW*, vol. 23, p. 425.

25. *MECW*, vol. 44, pp. 295, 286.

26. *MECW*, vol. 23, p. 66.

27. *Reminiscences of Marx and Engels*, p. 209.

28. *MECW*, vol. 40, p. 27.

29. *MECW*, vol. 41, p. 558.

30. *MECW*, vol. 27, p. 51. See also Mario Kessler, "Engels' Position on Anti-Semitism in the Context of Contemporary Socialist Discussions," *Science & Society* 62, no. 1 (1998).

31. *MECW*, vol. 42, p. 88.

32. *MECW*, vol. 23, p. 363.

33. *MECW*, vol. 45, pp. 64, 94.

34. *MECW*, vol. 45, p. 317.

35. *MECW*, vol. 46, pp. 10, 152.

36. *MECW*, vol. 24, pp. 267, 269.

37. *MECW*, vol. 23, p. 34.

38. *MECW*, vol. 24, p. 417.

39. Eric Hobsbawm, *Industry and Empire* (London, 1990), pp. 192–93.

40. "Engels, Frederick," IR 59/166, National Archives, Kew.

41. *MECW*, vol. 46, pp. 434, 435, 448–49.

42. *Friedrich Engels–Paul and Laura Lafargue Correspondence* (London, 1959–63), vol. 1, pp. 21, 51, 54, 110; vol. 2, p. 91.

43. *MECW*, vol. 46, p. 104.

44. *MECW*, vol. 45, p. 139.

45. *MECW*, vol. 45, p. 315.

46. *MECW*, vol. 24, p. 567.

47. *MECW*, vol. 45, p. 324.

48. See Hermann Gemkow, "Fünf Frauen an Engels' Seite," *Beiträge zur Geschichte der Arbeiterbewegung* 37, no. 4 (1995); Yvonne Kapp, *Eleanor Marx: Family Life* (London, 1972).

49. *MECW*, vol. 45, p. 321.

50. *MECW*, vol. 46, pp. 89–90, 95.

51. *MECW*, vol. 45, p. 379.

52. *MECW*, vol. 24, pp. 11, 43; vol. 47, p. 280.

53. *MECW*, vol. 24, p. 48.

54. *MECW*, vol. 24, p. 354.

55. *MECW*, vol. 49, p. 384.

56. *MECW*, vol. 27, pp. 422, 426.

57. *MECW*, vol. 27, p. 426.

58. *MECW*, vol. 50, p. 112.

59. *MECW*, vol. 24, p. 420.

60. *MECW*, vol. 46, p. 224.

61. *MECW*, vol. 46, p. 462.

62. F. G. Black and R. M. Black, eds., *The Harney Papers* (Assen, 1969), p. 296.

63. *MECW*, vol. 46, p. 462.

64. *MECW*, vol. 46, p. 458.

9: MARX'S BULLDOG

1. *MECW*, vol. 24, pp. 467, 468.

2. *MECW*, vol. 47, p. 25.

3. *Manchester Guardian*, 4 August 1945.

4. Benjamin Disraeli, *Coningsby* (London, 1963), p. 127.

5. Elizabeth Gaskell, *Mary Barton* (1848; rpt. Harmondsworth, 1996), p. 39. For a broader explication of Manchester scientific culture, see Robert H. Kargon, *Science in Victorian Manchester* (Manchester, 1977); Arnold Thackray, "Natural Knowledge in Cultural Context: The Manchester Model," *American Historical Review* 69 (1974).

6. *MECW*, vol. 42, p. 117.

7. Henry E. Roscoe, *The Life and Experiences of Sir Henry Enfield Roscoe Written by Himself* (London, 1906), p. 107.

8. *MECW*, vol. 41, p. 465; vol. 42, pp. 383, 323.

9. *MECW*, vol. 46, p. 461.

10. *MECW*, vol. 49, p. 433.

11. *MECW*, vol. 40, p. 551.

12. *MECW*, vol. 41, p. 381.

13. Quoted in David Stack, *The First Darwinian Left* (Cheltenham, 2003), p. 2.

14. *MECW*, vol. 45, p. 108.

15. *MECW*, vol. 40, p. 326.

16. *MECW*, vol. 6, p. 195.

17. Friedrich Engels, *Anti-Dühring* (Peking, 1976), p. 74.

18. *MECW*, vol. 42, p. 138.

19. *MECW*, vol. 45, p. 123.

20. *MECW*, vol. 44, p. 500.

21. Engels, *Anti-Dühring*, p. 11.

22. See *Philosophical Quarterly* 2, no. 6 (1952): 89.

23. Engels, *Anti-Dühring*, p. 12.

24. *MECW*, vol. 24, p. 302.

25. *MECW*, vol. 25, p. 356.

26. *MECW*, vol. 24, pp. 300–01.

27. Engels, *Anti-Dühring*, p. 173.

28. See Stephen Jay Gould, *Ever Since Darwin* (London, 1978), pp. 210–11.

29. *MECW*, vol. 25, pp. 452–65.

30. Peter Singer takes issue with Engels's animal-human distinction, based around control of the natural environment, by pointing to the example of ants that grow and eat specialized fungi that would not have existed without their activity. See Peter Singer, *A Darwinian Left* (London, 1999), pp. 21–24.

31. *MECW*, vol. 25, p. 460.

32. Engels, *Anti-Dühring*, p. 47.

33. *MECW*, vol. 25, p. 127.

34. Jean van Heijenoort, "Friedrich Engels and Mathematics," *Selected Essays* (Naples, 1985), pp. 123–51.

35. *MECW*, vol. 25, p. 354.

36. Private conversation, November 2007. One obvious British example of this phenomenon would be the pioneering X-ray crystallographer J. D. Bernal

(1901–71), who thought that "in its endeavor, science is communism." See Helena Sheehan, *Marxism and the Philosophy of Science: A Critical History* (Atlantic Heights, 1993).

37. *Frederick Engels: A Biography* (Dresden, 1972), p. 414. For an up-to-date defense of Engels's insights into modern scientific practice and theory, see Paul McGarr, "Engels and Natural Science," *International Socialism* 65, no. 2 (1994). Also at http://www.marxists.de/science/mcgareng/index.htm.

38. J. B. S. Haldane, Preface, in Frederick Engels, *Dialectics of Nature* (London, 1940), p. vii.

39. See Peter Pringle, *The Murder of Nikolai Vavilov: The Story of Stalin's Persecution of One of the Great Scientists of the Twentieth Century* (New York, 2008).

40. See "Report on Engels Society–June 1949"; "Transactions of the Physics Group"; "Transaction of the Engels Society, no. 4, Spring 1950"; "To the Central Committee of the CPSU (B), to Comrade Stalin. Youri Zhdanov," CP/CENT/CULT/5/9, Archives of the People's History Museum, Manchester.

41. *MECW*, vol. 45, p. 122.

42. See Richard Adamiak, "Marx, Engels, and Dühring," *Journal of the History of Ideas* 35, no. 1 (1974).

43. *MECW*, vol. 45, p. 131.

44. Eugen Dühring, *Kritische Geschichte der Nationalokonomie und des Socialismus* (Leipzig, 1879), p. 547.

45. *MECW*, vol. 45, p. 175.

46. Engels, *Anti-Dühring*, p. 422.

47. *MECW*, vol. 16, p. 474.

48. *MECW*, vol. 35, p. 19.

49. Engels, "Preface to Second Edition" (1885), *Anti-Dühring*, p. 11.

50. Engels, *Anti-Dühring*, p. 201.

51. *MECW*, vol. 24, p. 297.

52. *MECW*, vol. 24, p. 319.

53. *MECW*, vol. 24, p. 320.

54. *MECW*, vol. 24, p. 321.

55. *MECW*, vol. 24, p. 323.

56. *MECW*, vol. 46, pp. 300, 369.

57. *Friedrich Engels–Paul and Laura Lafargue Correspondence* (London, 1959–63), vol. 3, p. 335.

58. David Ryazonov, *Marx and Engels* (London, 1927), p. 210.

59. *F. Engels' Briefwechsel mit K. Kautsky* (Vienna, 1955), p. 4.

60. Georg Lukács, *History and Class Consciousness* (London, 1971), p. 24.

61. Norman Levine, "Marxism and Engelsism," *Journal of the History of the Behavioural Sciences* 11, no. 3 (1973): 239. See also Terrell Carver, *Marx and Engels: The Intellectual Relationship* (Brighton, 1983), for a more refined advocacy of the same case.

62. *MECW*, vol. 45, p. 334.

63. Wilhelm Liebknecht, *Karl Marx: Biographical Memoirs* (1896; rpt. London, 1975), pp. 91–92.

64. By far the most cogent and detailed explanation of this approach remains S. H. Rigby, *Engels and the Formation of Marxism* (Manchester, 1992).

65. *MECW*, vol. 47, p. 53.

66. *MECW*, vol. 47, p. 16.

67. *MECW*, vol. 47, p. 17.

68. *Engels–Lafargue Correspondence*, vol. 1, p. 142.

69. *MECW*, vol. 47, p. 41.

70. *MECW*, vol. 47, p. 53.

71. *MECW*, vol. 47, p. 43.

72. *MECW*, vol. 47, p. 117.

73. *MECW*, vol. 47, p. 265.

74. *MECW*, vol. 48, p. 521.

75. *MECW*, vol. 27, p. 428.

76. *MECW*, vol. 47, p. 301.

77. *MECW*, vol. 36, p. 20.

78. Meghnad Desai, *Marx's Revenge* (London, 2002), p. 60.

79. Ibid., p. 23.

80. *MECW*, vol. 47, p. 271.

81. *MECW*, vol. 48, p. 347.

82. See Desai, *Marx's Revenge*, pp. 74–83.

83. Carl-Erich Vollgraf and Jürgen Jungnickel, "Marx in Marx's Words?" *International Journal of Political Economy* 32 (2002): 67.

84. F. G. Black and R. M. Black, eds., *The Harney Papers* (Assen, 1969), p. 351.

85. *MECW*, vol. 48, p. 398.

86. *Engels–Lafargue Correspondence*, vol. 3, p. 344.

87. Marx-Engels Papers, L5461, International Institute of Social History, Amsterdam.

88. Ibid., L5473.

89. Quoted in *The Daughters of Karl Marx: Family Correspondence, 1866–1898* (London, 1982), p. 230.

90. *MECW*, vol. 50, p. 331.

91. There is, in truth, one final, glorious twist: Percy Rosher persuaded Engels to take out a life insurance policy for him (so as to secure the future of Pumps's children). With no sense of irony, following Engels's death Percy threatened to sue the Engels estate for £87 in unpaid prospective contributions.

92. *MECW*, vol. 46, p. 395.

93. August Bebel, *Woman in the Past, Present, and Future* (London, 1988), pp. 7, 9.

94. See Karl Kautsky, *Die Entstehung der Ehe und Familie* (Stuttgart, 1882).

95. *MECW*, vol. 46, pp. 438, 452.

96. Eduard Bernstein, *My Years of Exile: Reminiscences of a Socialist* (London, 1921), p. 168.

97. *MECW*, vol. 26, p. 132.

98. Friedrich Engels, *The Origin of the Family, Private Property, and the State* (Harmondsworth, 1986), p. 60.

99. Ibid., pp. 35–36.

100. Ibid., p. 162.

101. Ibid., p. 158.

102. Ibid., p. 79.

103. Ibid., p. 165.

104. Ibid., p. 173.

105. Karl Marx and Friedrich Engels, *The Communist Manifesto* (Harmondsworth, 2002), p. 239.

106. Ibid., p. 179.

107. Friedrich Engels, *The Condition of the Working Class in England* (Harmondsworth, 1987), p. 167.

108. Ibid., p. 168.

109. Ibid., p. 103.

110. *MECW*, vol. 47, p. 312.

111. *MECW*, vol. 26, p. 183.

112. *MECW*, vol. 43, p. 296.

113. See Sheila Rowbotham, *Edward Carpenter: A Life of Liberty and Love* (London, 2008).

114. Kate Millett, *Sexual Politics* (London, 1970), p. 120.

115. See Lise Vogel, "Engels's *Origin*: Legacy, Burden, and Vision," in Christopher J. Arthur, ed., *Engels Today* (London, 1996).

116. Michelle Barrett, "Introduction," in Engels, *Origin of the Family*, p. 28. See also Josette Trat, "Engels and the Emancipation of Women," *Science and Society* 62, no. 1 (1998); Nanneke Redclift, "Rights in Women: Kinship, Culture, and Materialism," in *Engels Revisited: New Feminist Essays* (London, 1987), ed. Janet Sayers, Mary Evans, and Nanneke Redclift; Terrell Carver, "Engels's Feminism," *History of Political Thought* 6, no. 3 (1985).

117. *MECW*, vol. 50, p. 67.

118. *MECW*, vol. 48, pp. 224, 232.

119. See, for example, *MECW*, vol. 47, p. 355.

120. *MECW*, vol. 48, p. 253.

121. *MECW*, vol. 47, p. 312.

122. *MECW*, vol. 45, p. 197.

123. *MECW*, vol. 26, p. 402.

124. See Eric Arnesen, "American Workers and the Labor Movement in the Late Nineteenth Century," in *The Gilded Age: Perspectives on the Origins of Modern America*, ed. Charles W. Calhoun, (Wilmington, 1996).

125. *MECW*, vol. 47, p. 452.

126. Ibid.

127. *Reminiscences of Marx and Engels* (Moscow, 1968), p. 187.

128. *MECW*, vol. 48, p. 210.

129. *MECW*, vol. 26, p. 585.

130. *MECW*, vol. 48, p. 207.

131. See Mike Davis, *City of Quartz* (London, 2006), pp. 46–54. Indeed, Jean Baudrillard's description of Los Angeles, quoted by Davis, is an almost exact update of Engels's encounter with New York: "There is nothing to match flying over Los Angeles by night. Only Hieronymous Bosch's Hell can match the inferno effect."

132. *MECW*, vol. 48, p. 211.

133. *MECW*, vol. 48, p. 219.

10: FIRST FIDDLE AT LAST

1. *MECW*, vol. 27, p. 61.

2. *MECW*, vol. 48, pp. 493–95.

3. *Reminiscences of Marx and Engels* (Moscow, 1958), pp. 147, 187.

4. *MECW*, vol. 24, p. 387.

5. *MECW*, vol. 46, p. 123.

6. *MECW*, vol. 46, p. 197.

7. *MECW*, vol. 47, p. 55.

8. Friedrich Engels, *The Condition of the Working Class in England* (Harmondsworth, 1987), p. 45.

9. Quoted in Philip Henderson, *William Morris* (London, 1973), p. 308.

10. Beatrice Webb, *My Apprenticeship* (London, 1926), p. 180.

11. Henry Hyndman, *The Record of an Adventurous Life* (1911; rpt. London, 1984), p. 279.

12. "A Disruptive Personality," *Justice*, 21 February 1891.

13. *MECW*, vol. 47, p. 155.

14. *MECW*, vol. 49, p. 494.

15. *MECW*, vol. 47, p. 427.

16. *MECW*, vol. 47, p. 408.

17. Quoted in J. B. Glasier, *William Morris and the Early Days of the Socialist Movement* (London, 1921), p. 32.

18. *MECW*, vol. 47, pp. 155, 471, 484.

19. *MECW*, vol. 48, p. 108.

20. See Suzanne Paylor, "Edward B. Aveling: The People's Darwin," *Endeavour* 29, no. 2 (2005).

21. Quoted in W. O. Henderson, *The Life of Friedrich Engels* (London, 1976), pp. 685–86.

22. Quoted in Yvonne Kapp, *Eleanor Marx: Family Life* (London, 1972), p. 271.
23. *MECW*, vol. 47, p. 177.
24. Quoted in Yvonne Kapp, *Eleanor Marx: The Crowded Years* (London, 1976), pp. 171–73.
25. *MECW*, vol. 48, pp. 16–17.
26. *MECW*, vol. 49, p. 87.
27. *MECW*, vol. 48, p. 91.
28. Edward Aveling, *The Student's Marx* (London, 1907), pp. viii, ix, xi.
29. *MECW*, vol. 48, p. 113.
30. Henry Mayhew, *The* Morning Chronicle *Survey of Labour and the Poor: The Metropolitan Districts* (1849–50; rpt. London, 1980), vol. 1, pp. 71–72.
31. *MECW*, vol. 48, p. 377.
32. *MECW*, vol. 48, p. 364.
33. *MECW*, vol. 26, p. 545.
34. *MECW*, vol. 48, p. 389.
35. *Reminiscences of Marx and Engels*, p. 313.
36. *MECW*, vol. 50, p. 82.
37. *MECW*, vol. 50, p. 434.
38. See *Labour Leader*, 24 December 1898.
39. See Ernest Belfort Bax, *Reminiscences and Reflections of a Mid and Late Victorian* (London, 1918), p. 54.
40. For the classic exposition of this question, see Ross McKibben, *The Ideologies of Class* (Oxford, 1994).
41. *MECW*, vol. 50, p. 386.
42. *MECW*, vol. 49, p. 243.
43. *MECW*, vol. 49, p. 67.
44. *MECW*, vol. 49, p. 70.
45. *MECW*, vol. 49, p. 68.
46. *MECW*, vol. 49, p. 346.
47. *MECW*, vol. 49, p. 416.
48. *The Daughters of Karl Marx: Family Correspondence, 1866–1898* (London, 1982), pp. 223–24.
49. *MECW*, vol. 49, p. 76.
50. *MECW*, vol. 48, p. 290.
51. *Friedrich Engels–Paul and Laura Lafargue Correspondence* (London, 1959–63), vol. 2, p. 220.
52. *MECW*, vol. 48, p. 319.
53. *MECW*, vol. 48, p. 352.
54. *MECW*, vol. 48, p. 454.
55. *MECW*, vol. 27, p. 227.
56. *MECW*, vol. 49, p. 265.

57. Leszek Kolakowski, *Main Currents of Marxism* (London, 2005), pp. 355–56.

58. See Eric Hobsbawm, "Marx, Engels, and Politics," *The History of Marxism* (Brighton, 1982), vol. 1.

59. Ibid., p. 265.

60. *MECW*, vol. 48, p. 36.

61. *MECW*, vol. 27, p. 520.

62. *MECW*, vol. 50, p. 21.

63. *MECW*, vol. 27, p. 522.

64. *MECW*, vol. 26, p. 112.

65. *MECW*, vol. 27, p. 447. Of course, in the twentieth century, the notion of communism as a secular faith was a familiar and recurring trope. "If despair and loneliness were the main motives for conversion to Communism, they were greatly strengthened by the Christian conscience," Richard Crossman wrote in his introduction to Arthur Koestler's *The God That Failed*. "The emotional appeal of Communism lay precisely in the sacrifices—both material and spiritual—which it demanded of the convert. . . . The attraction of Communism was that it offered nothing and demanded everything, including the surrender of spiritual freedom." A former true believer, the historian Raphael Samuel, sums it up thus: "As a theory of struggle, Communism rested on a promise of redemption. Socialism was a sublime essence, a state of moral perfection, a transcendent object and end. It represented the highest form of human development, a culmination of morality, a consummation of progress, a discovery of the greatness of man." See Arthur Koestler et al., *The God That Failed* (London, 1965), pp. 5–6; Raphael Samuel, *The Lost World of British Communism* (London, 2007), p. 51.

66. *MECW*, vol. 50, p. 490.

67. *MECW*, vol. 50, pp. 182–83.

68. Quoted in Gustav Mayer, *Friedrich Engels: Eine Biographie* (The Hague, 1934), vol. 2, pp. 529–30.

69. *MECW*, vol. 27, p. 404.

70. *MECW*, vol. 50, pp. 187, 190.

71. Quoted in *Frederick Engels: A Biography* (Dresden, 1972), p. 547.

72. *MECW*, vol. 50, p. 409.

73. *MECW*, vol. 46, p. 514.

74. *MECW*, vol. 47, p. 489.

75. *MECW*, vol. 26, p. 451.

76. *MECW*, vol. 24, p. 173.

77. *MECW*, vol. 27, p. 177.

78. *Reminiscences of Marx and Engels*, p. 307.

79. *MECW*, vol. 49, p. 76.

80. William Stephen Saunders, *Early Socialist Days* (London, 1927), pp. 80–81.

81. *Reminiscences of Marx and Engels*, p. 187.

82. *Daughters of Karl Marx*, pp. 247, 251.

83. *MECW*, vol. 50, p. 355.

84. *Daughters of Karl Marx*, pp. 253, 255.

85. *MECW*, vol. 50, p. 377.

86. *MECW*, vol. 50, p. 507.

87. *MECW*, vol. 50, pp. 517, 525.

88. *MECW*, vol. 50, p. 535.

89. *MECW*, vol. 50, p. 526.

90. Engels also left £227 worth of "wine and other liquors" in his cellar. In addition, his wine merchants, Twigg & Brett, had 142 dozen wines in their cellars as the property of Friedrich Engels. These included 77 dozen bottles of claret, 48 dozen bottles of port, and 13 dozen bottles of champagne.

91. Quoted in *Frederick Engels: A Biography*, p. 579.

92. See Kapp, *The Crowded Years*, pp. 597–99.

93. *Reminiscences of Marx and Engels*, p. 147.

94. Eduard Bernstein, *My Years of Exile: Reminiscences of a Socialist* (London, 1921), p. 192.

EPILOGUE

1. See Fred C. Koch, *The Volga Germans* (University Park, 1977).

2. "Address to the Conference of Marxist Students of the Agrarian Question," in Joseph Stalin, *Leninism* (Moscow, 1940), p. 323.

3. "Engels," *Nachrichten des Gebietskomitees der KP(B)SU und des Zentralkomitees der ASRR der Wolgadeutschen*, 21 October 1931.

4. "Engels' zum Gruss," *Rote Jugend: Organ des GK des LKJVSU der ASRRdWD*, 24 October 1931.

5. "Zur Umbenennung der Stadt Prokrovsk in Engels," *Nachrichten des Gebietskomitees der KP(B)SU und des Zentralkomitees der ASRR der Wolgadeutschen*, 21 October 1931.

6. "Engels' zum Gruss."

7. Quoted in Koch, *Volga Germans*, p. 284.

8. Robert Service, *Comrades* (London, 2007), pp. 52–53.

9. V. I. Lenin, *Collected Works*, vol. 21, p. 91.

10. *MECW*, vol. 50, p. 303.

11. Quoted in Leszek Kolakowski, *Main Currents of Marxism* (London, 2005), p. 625.

12. Lenin, *Collected Works*, vol. 38, p. 362.

13. Lenin, *Collected Works*, vol. 14, p. 326.

14. Kolakowski, *Main Currents of Marxism*, p. 629.

15. Lenin, *Collected Works*, vol. 21, p. 54.

16. Joseph Stalin, *Anarchism or Socialism?* (Moscow, 1950), p. 13.

17. Joseph Stalin, *Dialectical and Historical Materialism* (Moscow, 1939), p. 12.

18. Ibid., p. 18.

19. Cornelius Castoriadis, *The Imaginary Institution of Society* (Cambridge, 1987), p. 59.

20. See Orlando Figes, *The Whisperers: Private Life in Stalin's Russia* (London, 2007), pp. 155–56.

21. Kolakowski, *Main Currents of Marxism*, p. 862.

22. Raphael Samuel, *The Lost World of British Communism* (London, 2007), pp. 49, 94.

23. Herbert Marcuse, *Soviet Marxism: A Critical Analysis* (London, 1958), p. 144.

24. *MECW*, vol. 50, p. 301.

25. See John O'Neill, "Engels without Dogmatism," in Christopher J. Arthur, ed., *Engels Today* (London, 1996).

26. *MECW*, vol. 49, p. 18.

27. *MECW*, vol. 25, p. 80.

28. Friedrich Engels, *Anti-Dühring* (Peking, 1976), p. 108.

29. *MECW*, vol. 50, p. 267; vol. 49, p. 8.

30. *MECW*, vol. 50, p. 356.

31. As David Stack comments, "The socialism and socialist movement that arose in the next half-century were forged and matured in an era when Darwinism was an established part of the 'mental furniture.'" See Stack, *The First Darwinian Left* (Cheltenham, 2003), p. 2. See also Gareth Stedman Jones, "Engels and the History of Marxism," in Eric Hobsbawm, ed., *The History of Marxism* (Brighton, 1982), vol. 1.

32. *MECW*, vol. 50, p. 461.

33. Ching Kwan Lee, *Against the Law: Labor Protests in China's Rustbelt and Sunbelt* (Berkeley, 2007), p. 235.

BIBLIOGRAPHY

PRIMARY SOURCES

Arnold, R. Arthur. *The History of the Cotton Famine* (London, 1864).

Aveling, Edward. *The Student's Marx* (London, 1907).

Balzac, Honoré de. *Old Goriot* (Harmondsworth, 1951).

Banfield, T. C. *Industry of the Rhine* (New York, 1969).

Bax, Ernest Belfort. *Reminiscences and Reflexions of a Mid and Late Victorian* (London, 1918).

Bebel, August. *Woman in the Past, Present, and Future* (London, 1988).

Beer, Max. *Fifty Years of International Socialism* (London, 1935).

Bernstein, Eduard. *My Years of Exile: Reminiscences of a Socialist* (London, 1921).

Black, F. G., and R. M. Black, eds., *The Harney Papers* (Assen, 1969).

Born, Stephan. *Erinnerungen eines Achtundvierziger* (Leipzig, 1898).

Burke, Edmund. *Reflections on the Revolution in France* (Harmondsworth, 1986).

Carlyle, Thomas. *Past and Present* (New York, 1965).

———. *Selected Writings* (Harmondsworth, 1986).

Chadwick, Edwin. *Report on the Sanitary Conditions of the Labouring Population of Great Britain* (Edinburgh, 1965).

Chaloner, W. H., and W. O. Henderson, eds. *Engels as Military Critic* (Manchester, 1959).

Cooper, Thomas. *The Life of Thomas Cooper, Written by Himself* (London, 1873).

The Daughters of Karl Marx: Family Correspondence, 1866–1898 (London, 1982).

Disraeli, Benjamin. *Coningsby* (London, 1963).

———. *Sybil; or, The Nations* (London, 1981).

Dronke, Ernst. *Berlin* (Frankfurt, 1846).

Dühring, Eugen. *Kritische Geschichte der Nationalokonomie und des Socialismus* (Leipzig, 1879).

Engels, Frederick. *Dialectics of Nature* (London, 1940).

———. *Anti-Dühring* (Peking, 1976).

———. *The Condition of the Working Class in England* (Harmondsworth, 1987).

———. *The Origin of the Family, Private Property, and the State* (Harmondsworth, 1986).

Faucher, Léon. *Manchester in 1844* (Manchester, 1844).

Fourier, Charles. *The Theory of the Four Movements* (Cambridge, 1996).

F. Engels' Briefwechsel mit K. Kautsky (Vienna, 1955).

Friedrich Engels–Paul and Laura Lafargue Correspondence (Moscow, 1959–63).

Gaskell, Elizabeth. *Mary Barton* (Harmondsworth, 1996).

Hecker, Carl. *Der Aufstand in Elberfeld im Mai 1849 und mein Verhaltniss zu Demselben* (Elberfeld, 1849).

Hegel, Georg Wilhelm Friedrich. *Philosophy of Right* (Oxford, 1942).

Heine, Heinrich. *Sämtliche Werke* (Hamburg, 1867).

Henderson, W. O., and W. H. Chaloner, eds. *The Condition of the Working Class in England*. By Friedrich Engels (London, 1958).

Herzen, Alexander. *My Past and Thoughts* (London, 1968).

Hess, Moses, *Rom und Jerusalem* (Leipzig, 1899).

———. *Briefwechsel* (Amsterdam, 1959).

———. *Philosophische und sozialistische Schriften, 1837–1850*. Ed. Auguste Cornu and Wolfgang Mönke (Liechtenstein, 1980).

Hyndman, Henry. *The Record of an Adventurous Life* (1911; rpt. London, 1984).

Jones, Wilmot Henry [Geoffrey Gimcrack]. *Gimcrackiana; or, Fugitive Pieces on Manchester Men and Manners* (Manchester, 1833).

Kautsky, Karl. *Die Entstehung der Ehe und Familie* (Stuttgart, 1882).

Kay, James Phillips. *The Moral and Physical Condition of the Working Classes Employed in the Cotton Manufacture in Manchester* (Manchester, 1969).

Kliem, Manfred, ed. *Friedrich Engels: Dokumente seines Lebens* (Leipzig, 1977).

Knieriem, Michael, ed. *Die Herkunft des Friedrich Engels: Briefe aus der Verwandtschaft, 1791–1847* (Trier, 1991).

Körner, H. J. M. *Lebenskämpfe in der Alten und Neues Welt* (Zurich, 1866).

Leach, James. *Stubborn Facts from the Factories by a Manchester Operative* (London, 1844).

Lenin, Vladimir Ilyich. *Collected Works* (London, 1908–).

Liebich, André, ed. *Selected Writings of August Cieszkowski* (Cambridge, 1979).

Liebknecht, Wilhelm. *Karl Marx: Biographical Memoirs* (London, 1975).

Marx, Karl. *The Early Texts* (Oxford, 1971).

———. *Capital* (Harmondsworth, 1990).

———. *Early Writings* (Harmondsworth, 1992).

Marx, Karl, and Friedrich Engels. *Werke* (Berlin, 1964–68).

————. *On Colonialism* (Moscow, 1968).

————. *On Ireland* (London, 1971).

————. *The Communist Manifesto* (Harmondsworth, 2002).

Marx-Engels Collected Works [MECW], 50 vols. (Progress Publishers, Moscow, in conjunction with International Publishers, New York, and Lawrence & Wishart, London, 1975–2005).

Mayhew, Henry. *The* Morning Chronicle *Survey of Labour and the Poor: The Metropolitan Districts* (1849–50; rpt. London, 1980).

Müller, Max. *My Autobiography: A Fragment* (New York, 1991).

Pagenstecher, C. H. A. *Lebenserinnerungen von Dr. Med. C. H. Alexander Pagenstecher* (Leipzig, 1913).

Parkinson, Richard. *On the Present Condition of the Labouring Poor in Manchester* (Manchester, 1841).

Reminiscences of Marx and Engels (Moscow, 1958).

Roscoe, Henry E. *The Life and Experiences of Sir Henry Enfield Roscoe* (London, 1906).

The Sack; or, Volunteers' Testimonial to the Militia (London, 1862).

Saunders, William Stephen. *Early Socialist Days* (London, 1927).

Southey, Robert. *Letters from England by Don Manuel Alvarez Espriella* (London, 1808).

Staël, Madame de. *Germany* (London, 1813).

Stalin, Joseph. *Dialectical and Historical Materialism* (Moscow, 1939).

————. *Leninism* (Moscow, 1940).

————. *Anarchism or Socialism?* (Moscow, 1950).

Stirner, Max. *The Ego and Its Own* (Cambridge, 1995).

Sue, Eugène. *The Mysteries of Paris* (Cambridgeshire, 1989).

Taine, Hipployte. *Notes on England* (London, 1957).

Tocqueville, Alexis de. *Journeys to England and Ireland* (London, 1958).

Watts, John. *The Facts and Fictions of Political Economists* (Manchester, 1842).

————. *The Facts of the Cotton Famine* (London, 1866).

Webb, Beatrice. *My Apprenticeship* (London, 1926).

Weerth, Georg. *Sämtliche Werke* (1956–57).

The Writings of the Young Marx. Trans. and ed. Lloyd D. Easton and Kurt H. Guddat (Garden City, 1967).

ARCHIVES

Engels-Haus, Wuppertal

International Institute of Social History, Amsterdam

Marx Memorial Library, London

National Archives, Kew

People's History Museum, Manchester

State Archives of the Russian Federation, Moscow

Working Class Movement Library, Salford
State Archives, Wuppertal

SECONDARY SOURCES

Attali, Jacques. *Karl Marx, ou l'esprit du monde* (Paris, 2005).

Avineri, Shlomo. *The Social and Political Thought of Karl Marx* (Cambridge, 1968).

———. *Moses Hess* (London, 1985).

Arthur, Christopher J. *Engels Today* (London, 1996).

Ball, Terence, and James Farr. *After Marx* (Cambridge, 1984).

Barrett, Michelle. "Introduction," *The Origin of the Family, Private Property, and the State* by Friedrich Engels (Harmondsworth, 1986).

Beecher, Jonathan, and Richard Bienvenu. *The Utopian Vision of Charles Fourier* (London, 1975).

Beiser, Frederick C. *The Cambridge Companion to Hegel* (Cambridge, 1993).

Benn, Tony. *Arguments for Socialism* (London, 1979).

Berger, Martin. *Engels, Armies, and Revolution* (Hamden, 1977).

Berger, Stefan. *Social Democracy and the Working Class in Nineteenth and Twentieth Century Germany* (Harlow, 2000).

Berlin, Isaiah, *Karl Marx: His Life and Environment* (Oxford, 1978).

———. *Against the Current* (London, 1997).

Bigler, Robert M. *The Politics of German Protestantism* (Berkeley, 1972).

Blackbourn, David. *The Fontana History of Germany* (London, 1997).

Blanchard, Marc Eli. *In Search of the City* (Stanford, 1985).

Blyth, H. E. *Through the Eye of a Needle* (Manchester, 1947).

Bradshaw, L. D. *Visitors to Manchester* (Manchester, 1987).

Brazill, William J. *The Young Hegelians* (London, 1970).

Briggs, Asa. *Chartist Studies* (London, 1959).

———. *Victorian Cities* (London, 1990).

Bull, Stephen. *"Volunteer!" The Lancashire Rifle Volunteers, 1859–1885* (Lancashire, 1993).

Calhoun, Charles W., ed. *The Gilded Age: Perspectives on the Origins of Modern America* (Wilmington, 1996).

Carlton, Grace. *Friedrich Engels: The Shadow Prophet* (London, 1965).

Carr, E. H. *Michael Bakunin* (London, 1975).

Carver, Terrell. *Engels* (Oxford, 1981).

———. *Marx and Engels: The Intellectual Relationship* (Brighton, 1983).

———. *Friedrich Engels: His Life and Thought* (London, 1991).

———. *The Cambridge Companion to Marx* (Cambridge, 1991).

Castoriadis, Cornelius. *The Imaginary Institution of Society* (Cambridge, 1987).

Claeys, Gregory. *Citizens and Saints* (Cambridge, 1989).

Clark, Christopher. *Iron Kingdom: The Rise and Downfall of Prussia* (London, 2006).

Cole, George Douglas Howard. *Chartist Portraits* (London, 1941).

Cummins, Ian. *Marx, Engels, and National Movements* (London, 1980).

Davis, Mike. *City of Quartz* (London, 2006).

———. *Planet of Slums* (London, 2006).

Deak, Istvan. *The Lawful Revolution: Louis Kossuth and the Hungarians* (New York, 1979).

Desai, Meghnad. *Marx's Revenge: The Resurgence of Capitalism and the Death of Statist Socialism* (London, 2002).

Evans, Richard, and Pogge von Strandmann, eds. *The Revolutions in Europe, 1848–1849* (Oxford, 2000).

Farnie, Douglas. *The English Cotton Industry and the World Market, 1815–1896* (Oxford, 1979).

Fergusson, Gordon. *The Green Collars: The Tarporley Hunt Club and Cheshire Hunting History* (London, 1993).

Figes, Orlando. *The Whisperers: Private Life in Stalin's Russia* (London, 2007).

Foot, Paul. *Red Shelley* (London, 1984).

Fortescue, William. *France and 1848* (Oxford, 2005).

Foster, Roy. *Modern Ireland* (London, 1989).

Friends of Chalk Farm Library. *Primrose Hill Remembered* (London, 2001).

Frow, Edmund, and Ruth Frow. *Frederick Engels in Manchester* (Salford, 1986).

Frow, Edmund, and Ruth Frow. *The New Moral World: Robert Owen and Owenism in Manchester and Salford* (Salford, 1986).

Gallie, W. B. *Philosophers of Peace and War* (Cambridge, 1978).

Gemkow, Heinrich, et al. *Frederick Engels: A Biography* (Dresden, 1972).

Glasier, John B. *William Morris and the Early Days of the Socialist Movement* (London, 1921).

Gould, Stephen Jay. *Ever Since Darwin* (London, 1978).

Greaves, Ralph. *Foxhunting in Cheshire* (Kent, 1964).

Gunn, Simon. *The Public Culture of the Victorian Middle Class* (Manchester, 2000).

Hahn, Hans Joachim. *The 1848 Revolutions in German-Speaking Europe* (London, 2001).

Hammen, Oscar J. *The Red '48ers* (New York, 1969).

Hannay, Alastair. *Kierkegaard: A Biography* (Cambridge, 2001).

Hayek, F. A. *The Counter-Revolution of Science* (Glencoe, 1952).

Hellman, Robert. *Berlin: The Red Room and White Beer* (Washington, 1990).

Heijenoort, Jean van. *Selected Essays* (Naples, 1985).

Heinig, Karl. *Carl Schorlemmer: Chemiker und Kommunist Ersten Ranges* (Leipzig, 1974).

Henderson, Philip. *William Morris: His Life, Work, and Friends* (London, 1973).

Henderson, W. O. *Engels as Military Critic* (Manchester, 1959).

———. *The Lancashire Cotton Famine* (Manchester, 1969).

————. *The Life of Friedrich Engels* (London, 1976).

————. *Marx and Engels and the English Workers* (London, 1989).

Hirsch, Helmut. *Friedrich Engels in Selbstzeugnissen und Bilddokumenten* (Hamburg, 1968).

Hobsbawm, Eric. *Industry and Empire* (London, 1990).

————, ed. *The History of Marxism* (Brighton, 1982).

Holmes, Richard. *Shelley: The Pursuit* (London, 1987).

Howe, Anthony. *The Cotton Masters* (Oxford, 1984).

Hunley, James D. *The Life and Thought of Friedrich Engels* (London, 1991).

Hunt, Richard N. *The Political Ideas of Marx and Engels* (Pittsburgh, 1974).

Hunt, Tristram. *Building Jerusalem: The Rise and Fall of the Victorian City* (London, 2004).

Ionescu, Ghita, ed. *The Political Thought of Saint-Simon* (Oxford, 1976).

Ivanon, N. N. *Frederick Engels: His Life and Work* (Moscow, 1987).

Jenkins, Mick. *Frederick Engels in Manchester* (1951).

Johnston, Francis. *Eccles* (Eccles, 1967).

Jones, Colin. *Paris: Biography of a City* (London, 2004).

Judt, Tony. *Reappraisals: Reflections on the Forgotten Twentieth Century* (London, 2008).

Kapp, Yvonne. *Eleanor Marx.* Vol. 1: *Family Life* (London, 1972).

————. *Eleanor Marx.* Vol. 2: *The Crowded Years* (London, 1976).

Kargon, Robert. *Science in Victorian Manchester* (Manchester, 1977).

Katznelson, Ira. *Marxism and the City* (Oxford, 1992).

Kidd, Alan. *Manchester* (Keele, 1996).

Kiernan, Victor. *Marxism and Imperialism* (London, 1974).

Knieriem, Michael, ed. *Über Friedrich Engels: Privates, Öffentliches und Amtliches Aussagen und Zeugnisse von Zeitgenossen* (Wuppertal, 1986).

Koch, Fred C. *The Volga Germans* (University Park, 1977).

Koestler, Arthur, et al. *The God That Failed* (London, 1965).

Kolakowski, Leszek. *Main Currents of Marxism* (London, 2005).

Krieger, Leonard, ed. *The German Revolutions* (Chicago, 1967).

Kuczynski, Jurgen. *Die Geschichte der Lage der Arbeiter unter dem Kapitalismus* (Berlin, 1960).

Kupisch, Karl. *Vom Pietismus zum Kommunismus: Historische Gestalten, Szenen und Probleme* (Berlin, 1953).

Lee, Ching Kwan. *Against the Law: Labor Protests in China's Rustbelt and Sunbelt* (Berkeley, 2007).

Levin, Michael. *Marx, Engels, and Liberal Democracy* (London, 1989).

Lukás, Georg. *History and Class Consciousness* (London, 1971).

Mann, Gottfried. *The History of Germany since 1789* (London, 1996).

Mansel, Philip. *Paris Between Empires* (London, 2001).

Manuel, Frank. *The Prophets of Paris* (Cambridge, 1962).

Marcus, Steven. *Engels, Manchester, and the Working Class* (London, 1974).

Marcuse, Herbert. *Soviet Marxism: A Critical Analysis* (London, 1958).

Mayer, Gustav. *Friedrich Engels: Eine Biographie* (The Hague, 1934).

———. *Friedrich Engels* (London, 1936).

McKibben, Ross. *The Ideologies of Class* (Oxford, 1994).

McLellan, David. *The Young Hegelians and Karl Marx* (London, 1969).

———. *Engels* (Sussex, 1977).

———. *Karl Marx: His Life and Thought* (London, 1983).

———. *Karl Marx: A Biography* (London, 1995).

———, ed. *Karl Marx: Interviews and Recollections* (London, 1981).

Miller, Susanne, and Heinrich Potthoff. *A History of German Social Democracy* (New York, 1986).

Millett, Kate. *Sexual Politics* (London, 1970).

Moggach, Douglas, ed. *The New Hegelians: Politics and Philosophy in the Hegelian School* (Cambridge, 2006).

Nova, Fritz. *Friedrich Engels: His Contribution to Political Theory* (London, 1968).

Noyes, P. H. *Organization and Revolution: Working-Class Associations in the German Revolution of 1848–49* (Princeton, 1966).

Old, Hughes Oliphant. *The Reading and Preaching of the Scriptures in the Worship of the Christian Church* (Cambridge, 1998).

Olsen, Donald J. *The Growth of Victorian London* (London, 1976).

Payne, Robert, ed. *The Unknown Karl Marx* (London, 1972).

Pelling, Henry. *Origins of the Labour Party* (Oxford, 1965).

Perkin, Harold. *Origins of Modern English Society* (London, 1991).

Pickering, Paul. *Chartism and the Chartists in Manchester and Salford* (London, 1995).

Pinkney, David. *Decisive Years in France, 1840–1847* (Princeton, 1986).

Prawer, Siegbert. *Karl Marx and World Literature* (Oxford, 1978).

Pringle, Peter. *The Murder of Nikolai Vavilov: The Story of Stalin's Persecution of One of the Great Scientists of the Twentieth Century* (New York, 2008).

Read, Anthony, and David Fisher. *Berlin* (London, 1994).

Richie, Alexandra. *Faust's Metropolis* (London, 1999).

Rigby, S. H. *Engels and the Formation of Marxism* (Manchester, 1992).

Rosdolsky, Roman. *Engels and the "Nonhistoric" Peoples: The National Question in the Revolution of 1848* (Glasgow, 1986).

Rowbotham, Sheila. *Edward Carpenter: A Life of Liberty and Love* (London, 2008).

Ryazanov, David. *Marx and Engels* (London, 1927).

Samuel, Raphael. *The Lost World of British Communism* (London, 2007).

Sassoon, Donald. *One Hundred Years of Socialism* (London, 1996).

Sayers, Janet, Mary Evans, and Nanneke Redclift. *Engels Revisited: New Feminist Essays* (London, 1987).

Service, Robert. *Comrades: A World History of Communism* (London, 2007).

Sheehan, Helena. *Marxism and the Philosophy of Science: A Critical History* (Atlantic Highlands, 1993).

Sheehan, James. *German History, 1770–1866* (Oxford, 1989).

Singer, Peter. *Hegel* (Oxford, 1983).

———. *A Darwinian Left* (London, 1999).

Sperber, Jonathan. *Rhineland Radicals* (Princeton, 1991).

———, ed. *Germany, 1800–1870* (Oxford, 2004).

Stack, David. *The First Darwinian Left* (Cheltenham, 2003).

Steger, Manfred, and Terrell Carver, eds. *Engels after Marx* (Manchester, 1999).

Stepelevich, Lawrence, ed. *The Young Hegelians* (Cambridge, 1983).

Stedman Jones, Gareth. "Introduction." *The Communist Manifesto* (Harmondsworth, 2002).

Stokes, John, ed. *Eleanor Marx: Life, Work, Contacts* (Aldershot, 2000).

Taylor, Ronald. *Berlin and Its Culture* (London, 1997).

Thompson, Edward. *William Morris* (London, 1977).

———. *The Poverty of Theory and Other Essays* (London, 1978).

Toews, Jonathan. *Hegelianism: The Path toward Dialectical Humanism, 1805–1841* (Cambridge, 1980).

Tombs, Robert. *The Paris Commune* (London, 1999).

Trachtenberg, Alan. *The Incorporation of America* (New York, 1982).

Trevor-Roper, Hugh. *The Romantic Movement and the Study of History* (London, 1969).

Ullrich, Horst. *Der Junge Engels* (Berlin, 1961).

Webster, Angus. *The Regent's Park and Primrose Hill* (London, 1911).

Wheen, Francis. *Karl Marx* (London, 2000).

Whitfield, Roy. *Frederick Engels in Manchester: The Search for a Shadow* (Salford, 1988).

Williams, Raymond. *Keywords: A Vocabulary of Culture and Society* (London, 1998).

Wilson, Edmund. *To the Finland Station* (London, 1991).

Zipes, Jack. *The Brothers Grimm* (London, 2002).

ARTICLES

Adamiak, Richard. "Marx, Engels, and Dühring." *Journal of the History of Ideas* 35, no. 1 (1974).

Cadogan, Peter. "Harney and Engels." *International Review of Social History* 10 (1965).

Carver, Terrell. "Engel's Feminism." *History of Political Thought* 6, no. 3 (1985).

Claeys, Gregory. "Engels' *Outlines of a Critique of Political Economy* (1843) and the Origins of the Marxist Critique of Capitalism." *History of Political Economy* 16, no. 2 (1984).

——. "The Political Ideas of the Young Engels, 1842–1845." *History of Political Thought* 6, no. 3 (1985).

Cohen-Almagor, Raphael. "Foundations of Violence, Terror, and War in the Writings of Marx, Engels, and Lenin." *Terrorism and Political Violence* 3, no. 2 (1991).

Gemkow, Heinrich. "Fünf Frauen an Engels' Seite." *Beiträge zur Geschichte der Arbeiterbewegung* 37, no. 4 (1995).

Kapp, Yvonne. "Frederick Demuth: New Evidence from Old Sources." *Socialist History* 6 (1994).

Kessler, Mario. "Engels' Position on Anti-Semitism in the Context of Contemporary Socialist Discussions." *Science & Society* 62, no. 1 (1998).

Kitchen, Martin. "Friedrich Engels' Theory of War." *Military Affairs* 41, no. 1 (1977).

Krishnamurthy, A. "'More Than Abstract Knowledge': Friedrich Engels in Industrial Manchester." *Victorian Literature and Culture* 28, no. 2 (2000).

Levine, Norman. "Marxism and Engelsism." *Journal of the History of the Behavioural Sciences*, 11, no. 3 (1973).

——. "The Engelsian Inversion." *Studies in Soviet Thought* 25 (1983).

McGarr, Paul. "Engels and Natural Science." *International Socialism* 65, no. 2 (1994).

Neimanis, George. "Militia vs. the Standing Army in the History of Economic Thought from Adam Smith to Friedrich Engels." *Military Affairs* 44, no. 1 (1980).

O'Boyle, L. "The Problem of an Excess of Educated Men in Western Europe, 1800–1850." *Journal of Modern History* 42, no. 4 (1970).

Paul, Diane. "'In the Interests of Civilization': Marxist Views of Race and Culture in the Nineteenth Century." *Journal of the History of Ideas* 42, no. 1 (1981).

Paylor, Suzanne. "Edward B. Aveling: The People's Darwin." *Endeavour* 29, no. 2 (2005).

Rubinstein, William. "The Victorian Middle Classes: Wealth, Occupation, and Geography," *Economic History Review* 30, no. 4 (1977).

Skidelsky, Robert. "What's Left of Marx?" *New York Review of Books*, 16 November 2000.

Smethhurst, J. B. "Ermen and Engels." *Marx Memorial Library Quarterly Bulletin* 41 (Jan.–March 1967).

Stedman Jones, Gareth. "Engels and the End of Classical German Philosophy." *New Left Review* 79 (1973).

——. "The Limitation of Proletarian Theory in England before 1850." *History Workshop* 5 (1978).

Stepelevich, Lawrence. "The Revival of Max Stirner." *Journal of the History of Ideas* 35, no. 2 (1974).

Taylor, A. J. P. "Manchester." *Encounter* 8, no. 3 (1957).

Thackray, Arnold. "Natural Knowledge in Cultural Context: The Manchester Model." *American Historical Review* 69 (1974).

Trat, Josette. "Engels and the Emancipation of Women." *Science and Society* 62, no. 1 (1998).

Vollgraf, Carl-Erich, and Jürgen Jungnickel. "Marx in Marx's Words?" *International Journal of Political Economy* 32 (2002).

Wittmütz, Volkmar. "Friedrich Engels in der Barmer Stadtschule, 1829–1834." *Nachrichten aus dem Engels-Haus* 3 (1980).

ACKNOWLEDGMENTS

For their generous assistance with the research, writing, and production of this book, the author would like to thank Alice Austin, Sara Bershtel, Phillip Birch, Georgina Capel, Michael V. Carlisle, Barney Cokeliss, Bela Cunha, Andrew and Theresa Curtis, Dermot Daly and the Cheshire Hunt, Virginia Davis and the Department of History, Queen Mary, University of London, Thomas Dixon, Orlando Figes, Giles Foden, Tom Graves, Michael Herbert, Eric Hobsbawm, Julian and Marylla Hunt, Stephen Kingston, Nick Mansfield, Ed Miliband, Seumas Milne, Liudmila Novikova, Alastair Owens, Stuart Proffitt, Caroline Read, Stephen Rigby, Donald Sassoon, Sophie Schlondorff, Roslyn Schloss, Bill Smyth, Gareth Stedman Jones, Juliet Thornback, Grigory Tovbis, Benjamin and Yulia Wegg-Prosser, Francis Wheen, Bee Wilson, Michael Yehuda. In addition, the staff of the British Library; Engels-Haus, Wuppertal; the International Institute of Social History, Amsterdam; the London Library; the Marx Memorial Library, London; the People's History Museum, Manchester; the Working Class Movement Library, Salford.

INDEX

Wagner, Richard, 169, 251

warfare, Engels on, 7, 8, 9, 216–22, 343–44

Watts, John, 89, 97, 185, 196
The Facts and Fictions of Political Economists, 89

Webb, Beatrice, 321

Webb, Sidney, 324

Weerth, George, 94, 123, 125, 161, 203
"Mary," 95

Weierstrass, Karl, 286

Weitling, Wilhelm, 71, 131–35, 137

Weydemeyer, Joseph, 216

Wheen, Francis, 5, 116

Whitfield, Roy, 201

Wilhelm I, emperor of Germany, 259

Willich, August von, 174, 175, 181, 193

Wilson, Edmund, 116

Wolff, Wilhelm, 141, 161, 202–3, 234

Woltmann, Ludwig, 364

Workers' Association, 155–56

working class, 35–38, 121
American, 312–15
Chartist movement, 7, 76, 89–92, 102, 110, 184, 185, 186, 318
Cologne, 155–58
communism and, 128–35, 142–47, 181

conditions and wages, 76, 80–81, 85, 101–6

dissent, 75–77, 84, 90, 120–21, 148–77, 184

1848 revolutions, 148–77

1890s socialist movement, 317–32, 335–44

feminism, 304–12

labor movement, 7, 109, 319, 328–32

Manchester, 73–74, 75–112, 184–85, 190

Owenites, 85–90, 110, 270

Paris, 115, 135, 136–37, 150–54

Plug Plot riots, 75–77, 90

post-1848 revolution, 181–87, 257–61

World War II, 3, 355

Wuppertal, Germany, 3, 12–17, 33, 36–37, 79, 120–23, 157, 169–70, 347
industrialization, 12–14, 36–38
Pietism, 15–17, 38, 39

Young Germany, 29–32, 34–38, 39, 43, 56, 255

Young Hegelians, 51–56, 61, 63, 71–74, 83, 97, 100, 108, 112, 115, 127, 251, 255, 285

Zimmerman, Wilhelm, 214

Zukunft, Die, 237

ABOUT THE AUTHOR

Tristram Hunt is a lecturer in history at the University of London. The author of *Building Jerusalem: The Rise and Fall of the Victorian City*, he writes political and cultural commentary for *The Guardian*, *The Times*, and the *London Review of Books*, among other publications.